M. STANTON
EVANS

M. STANTON
EVANS

CONSERVATIVE WIT,
APOSTLE OF FREEDOM

STEVEN F. HAYWARD

Encounter
BOOKS

New York • London

First American edition published in 2022 by Encounter Books, an activity of Encounter for Culture and Education, Inc., a nonprofit, tax-exempt corporation. Encounter Books website address: www.encounterbooks.com

Manufactured in the United States and printed on acid-free paper. The paper used in this publication meets the minimum requirements of ANSI/NISO Z39.48–1992 (R 1997) (*Permanence of Paper*).

FIRST AMERICAN EDITION

LIBRARY OF CONGRESS CATALOGING-IN-PUBLICATION DATA

Names: Hayward, Steven F., author.
Title: M. Stanton Evans: Conservative Wit, Apostle of Freedom Steven F. Hayward. Description: New York: Encounter Books, 2022. Includes bibliographical references and index.
Identifiers: LCCN 2021033848 (print) | LCCN 2021033849 (ebook) ISBN 9781641771764 (hardcover) | ISBN 9781641771771 (ebook)
Subjects: LCSH: Evans, M. Stanton (Medford Stanton), 1934-2015. Conservatives—United States—Biography. | Journalists—United States—Biography. | Conservatism—United States—History—20th century. Conservatism—United States—History—21st century.
Classification: LCC JC573.2.U6 H3925 2022 (print) | LCC JC573.2.U6 (ebook) | DDC 320.52092 [B]—dc23
LC record available at https://lccn.loc.gov/2021033848
LC ebook record available at https://lccn.loc.gov/2021033849

To the National Journalism Center, its staff, supporters, and hundreds of alumni—we are all Stan's children.

TABLE OF CONTENTS

Introduction: M. Stanton Evans
Conservative Wit, Apostle of Freedom   1

   1. Early Life and Education   23

   2. The Making of a Young Journalist   43

   3. At the Indianapolis News   59

   4. From Journalist to Activist   83

   5. From Sharon to San Francisco   103

   6. Regrouping: *One Step Back, Two Steps Forward*   127

   7. Nixon's Not the One: *The Manhattan Twelve*   151

   8. The Watergate Conundrum   179

   9. Preparing the Reagan Revolution   197

  10. "A Big Ball of Confusion and Misinformation":
      Modern Journalism and How to Fix It   225

  11. Front Row Seat for the Reagan Revolution   261

  12. A Literary Legacy   299

Epilogue   339

Appendix 1: A Sampler of Stan Evans's Greatest Quips   351

Appendix 2: Evans's Six Rules for Political Combat   355

Acknowledgments   357

Notes   359

Index   375

M. STANTON EVANS
Conservative Wit, Apostle of Freedom

"Stan always played the long game. He wasn't interested in quick whimsical ideas that came and went. He was more interested in changing the culture, changing people's ideas. But he knew that was a long-term undertaking and he was willing to do it."

—Alfred Regnery

A few days into the new year in January 1981, I loaded up my compact car with a few books, an electric typewriter, my Gerald Ford–era three-piece suit, two sport coats, and whatever remaining presentable clothing I owned and struck out from my family home in suburban Los Angeles for Washington, DC. I was taking up as an intern for M. Stanton Evans at his recently established National Journalism Center. Although the formal program only lasted twelve weeks, it turned out to be a decisive, life-altering journey.

The context of that moment helps in appreciating fully the intellectual and political portrait that follows. I had graduated from college the previous spring and spent the summer backpacking around Europe and the fall lounging around my parents' spacious house like Benjamin Braddock in *The Graduate* (which was actually set in my hometown in the novel) looking for a job in a tough market for recent graduates. I didn't turn up much beyond a couple of sketchy entry-level sales prospects. I really wanted to be a writer or journalist but had no idea how to go about starting such a career.

So my eyes perked up when I spotted a small classified ad in *National Review* about internships at the National Journalism Center (hereafter NJC). Twelve weeks, lodging, and $100 a week! Interest became excitement when I focused on the fact that M. Stanton Evans was the impresario of NJC. I was familiar with Evans's writing through his syndicated column that amazingly appeared in the *Los Angeles Times* (I was such a nerd as a teen that I read the *Times* op-ed page before the sports page every morning), but I was also familiar with him from his articles in *Human Events* and *National Review* as I subscribed to both. The most distinct impression, however, came from hearing his brief radio commentaries for CBS News's "Spectrum" series, which I'd heard as a teen when driving around with my father, who listened exclusively to news radio. More than once I recall reaching a destination but remaining in the car to hear the end of Stan's commentary. Along with the cogency and seriousness of his commentaries, what most struck me about Evans was his deep baritone voice. His best friend and fellow journalist, Ralph Bennett of *Reader's Digest*, ably described Evans as having "an enviably sonorous voice, with a finely civilized gravel to it. There was a whisper of Texas, Tennessee, and tobacco. It has that flat timbre of the Midwest, and a hint of Mississippi in the exit when he was relaxed and talking about basketball or rock and roll."

The opening weeks of 1981 coincided with the arrival of Ronald Reagan to begin the Reagan Revolution. Anyone who came of age in the late 1970s, when the conservative intellectual movement was alive with fertile creativity and new expression, couldn't help but sense the building critical mass that culminated in Reagan's landslide election. To paraphrase Wordsworth, "Bliss it was in that dawn to be alive / But to be a *young conservative* was very heaven." The more so in the company of similarly situated young conservatives starting out in the world—fellow NJC interns in my class included John Fund, Martin Morse Wooster, and John Barnes—under the tutelage of one of the key figures in the conservative movement.

The first thing you learned about Stan Evans upon meeting him was his genuine warmth and casual friendliness. There was nothing standoffish or elitist about this highly accomplished, Phi Beta Kappa, Yale-educated man. In fact "elitist" is the last adjective you'd ever attach to Stan Evans. In those days he seldom wore a conventional business suit or necktie, though he did own a tie that played the University of Indiana fight song. Stan preferred more casual attire, especially turtlenecks, going directly against the competitive sartorial conventions of Washington, which has the strictest dress code this side of Starfleet Academy. Daniel Oliver called Evans "everyman's Bill Buckley." One of his most famous quotes was his summary of how his thinking was the same as the farmers' you'd find in Seymour, Indiana. (See Chapter 3.)

If you only knew Stan Evans through his newspaper columns, radio commentaries, or books, you had no idea how darn funny he was. Had he not been a serious man, he could have had a career as a stand-up comic. He fully internalized Churchill's axiom that "a joke is a very serious thing." As with brand-name comics taking the stage, you smiled and suppressed a laugh before he began speaking. "M. Stanton Evans had only to stand before a microphone to bring smiles to an expectant conservative audience," Lee Edwards recalls. The libertarian legal scholar Roger Pilon said, "Whoever said conservatives were no fun didn't know Stan."

His writing style was workmanlike and direct and seldom included a hint of his sardonic wit. Partly this owes to his philosophy of journalism, which emphasized facts, objectivity, and direct-to-the-point declarative reporting over the idiosyncratic stylings of William F. Buckley Jr. or George Will. His fellow *National Review* contributor William F. Rickenbacker described Evans's style as "textbook English, unadorned, framed square, and double-joisted to carry a load of fact and logic." *National Review*'s Linda Bridges relates that Evans told her that "as a matter of principle, the author should stay out of the way, present the facts and analysis, but save any embellishments for another time." He did, however, deliver a pithy phrase from time to time, such as his description of *The New Yorker* that holds up perfectly for today's populist moment: "No other journal so elegantly combines the comforts of privilege with the glamor of dissent—that admixture of chic and iconoclasm which in our society marks the received, the anointed, and the superbly upper-middle-class."[1]

His plain style reflected a part of his character, which emphasized a distinct separation of his social life from his professional life—more on both of these aspects in due course. His comedic talents came out in person; as with many successful stand-up comedians, his wit came to life more by his superb timing as much as by the logic of the joke. His perfect timing, along with the character of his voice that Ralph Bennett described, provided him the ability to be sarcastic without sounding sarcastic. "Snark" is not a term you would ever apply to Stan. Many times I've heard someone try to retell one of Evans's original jokes only to fall flat for lack of his inimitable pacing and subtle inflection. (A link to online audio recordings is available in Appendix 1.) His wit was legendary among conservatives, and he was everyone's favorite to be master of ceremonies at any significant public gathering.

His humor specialized in turning liberal clichés and sentiments on their head and coming up with a mordant irony that exposed the superficiality of conventional political views. "I've discovered there is no absurdity that you can invent that a liberal will not state seriously," he explained. Among his most famous jibes was "I didn't approve of what Joe McCarthy was trying to do, but I admired his methods." That's the kind of line that does the work of ten op-ed articles explaining the insincerity and weakness of liberal professions of anti-Communism. Likewise, another bon mot derived from a favorite liberal editorial trope of the 1960s: "Any country that can land a man on the moon, can abolish the income tax." Or: "We need to repeal Obamacare, so we can find out what's not in it." Everyone has their list of favorites. Mine is: "Conservatives had to overcome the Goldwater defeat without grief counselors." (See Appendix I for a collection of his greatest hits.)

Evans relished how liberals were often taken in by his jokes. "It always surprised me—though not Stan—that liberals carried on saying these things when he had so thoroughly sent them up," John O'Sullivan wrote. I witnessed firsthand a scene of liberals appalled that anyone could find mirth in such irresponsible irony. "I wasn't for Nixon until after Watergate," he told an earnest academic audience at Princeton in 2006. "After wage and price controls, Watergate was a breath of fresh air. In fact, I called over to Pat Buchanan at the White House and told him, 'If only I had known you guys were doing all this *neat stuff*...'" There were some audible gasps among many of the stone-faced Princetonians at Evans's bad taste. Leftist historian Rick Perlstein was on the panel, took the riff literally, and said, "You've made my point" about the supposed amorality of conservatives. Cliff Kincaid, one of Evans's many students who took their own place in the conservative firmament, said, "Stan Evans showed that we can laugh at the ridiculousness of the liberals while taking seriously the threat they pose to the American way of life." Ralph Bennett observed, "He would leave you half-laughing and half-puzzled at odd moments."

But his targets weren't strictly political; they also included icons of pop culture and the entertainment world, from Elton John to Beavis and Butthead. "You would think the fellow named Butthead would be the most stupid of the two, but that's not so. It's Beavis." He even dilated on mosh pit etiquette. He loved to pick on the political pretensions of celebrities. "I hear Katy Perry says health care should be free. Well I think Katy Perry concerts should be free. Her concert tickets are really expensive!" One of his axioms was "Whenever there is a pressing public policy issue, I want to know what celebrities think. It is important for our lawmakers to hear from Bono." (Evans must surely be grinning in the afterlife over this CNN headline from September 20, 2021, by Fareed Zakaria: "I Wanted to Understand Europe's Populism. So I Talked to Bono.") Lady Gaga proved an irresistible target, prompting an observation that requires his slow-drawl delivery to appreciate fully:

I see that Lady Gaga showed up for the MTV Music Awards fully accessorized...*in meat.* A meat hat, a meat purse, a meat dress. I think there are two possible explanations. Perhaps she was trying to make a profound statement, about how God had given man dominion over the created order, and therefore has control over the lower animals to use as he saw fit. Or, [pause for effect]...maybe she was trying to call attention to herself, I don't know.

His wit was only the beginning of the personal exuberance unseen in his writing. He was an anti-elitist in "lifestyle"—a term he lampooned—with genuine fondness for junk food, convenience store chili dogs, Coors beer, and Big Gulps from 7-Eleven (a genuine innovation of Western Civilization, he said, combining drinking and weight training and then doubling as an ash tray when you finished them). He is said to have once sent back a White

Castle hamburger because "it wasn't greasy enough." He wasn't much for haute cuisine. "When I go to a French restaurant," he liked to say in a dead serious tone, "I want *French* fries, mister!" Allan Ryskind recalls Evans horrifying his dinner partners one night at a fancy restaurant when the waiter delivered his steak with a side of Bearnaise sauce, to which Evans offered the mock protest, "You're not going to ruin this perfectly good steak with that stuff are you?" His dessert preference on such occasions ran to red Jell-O, pronounced with great emphasis on each word (Red. Jell-O.). Needless to say he loved to watch sports, especially Indiana University basketball and the Los Angeles Dodgers (though he preferred the old Brooklyn Dodgers, like all true conservatives). Of the Dodgers, he wrote in a rare column about sports in 1963 that "the saga of the Dodgers [is] a romance of human tenacity in the face of long odds and perennial battering."[2]

He liked to pronounce "Chablis" the way it is spelled (sha-*bliss*) as well as the *t* in "gourmet" and declared he preferred wine that came in a box. He celebrated cigarette smoking without apology or bashfulness. "If there was something wrong with smoking," he said, "surely someone would say something about it." Or alternatively, "Tobacco is just the sort of green leafy vegetable the USDA suggests I have at least five servings a day…" Stan displayed a THANK YOU FOR SMOKING sign in his office, and Mal Kline, one of his NJC editors, relates a story of being on a smoke break with Stan one evening outside at a conference in North Carolina:

> Two teenage boys walked up and one of them said, "Hey, Mister, could I bum a cigarette?" Stan paused and looked him over in a lofty, faux-censorious grown-up sort of way, and then said, "Why yes. Here you go." The boy and his friend, grinning sheepishly, both took a cigarette from his box. He then said, "Care for a light?" They nodded. He elegantly pulled out his lighter, and as he lit

their cigarettes, he told them with great gravity, so as to impress the thought upon them: "SUPPORT SENATOR HELMS."

There was virtually no liberal piety or conventional sentiment that was off limits. To a homeless person who once asked Evans for money, Evans readily assented with the admonition: "Only if you're going to buy alcohol; I wouldn't want you to use it to buy food."

His other great cultural fixation was classic rock and roll, with Elvis Presley being his favorite. Perhaps it is not a coincidence, given his work on Soviet espionage in the U.S., that his favorite Elvis tune was "Suspicious Minds." His command of rock and roll was encyclopedic. He was known to hear a popular old tune come on in a bar or restaurant, and Stan not only could name the artist, title, and year but also name the B-side of the single. His command of rock music often extended to backhanded dismissals of current pop stars, such as the time he started a barroom debate on who was the most annoying Spice Girl. He was not indiscriminate in his taste for popular music. He once came back to the office following a visit to the dentist, saying, "The dentist was playing Boz Scaggs so I concentrated hard on the pain in my mouth so that I could block out the music." About The Doors hit "Light My Fire," Stan asked: "What do you mean there's no time to wallow in the mire? There's always time to wallow in the mire. Hey, you make time to wallow in the mire." About Elton John, he said, "When he first burst on the music scene, I said, 'He's good, but he'll never play Westminster Abbey.' If that can happen, anything can happen. Just like the fall of Communism."

If he heard of a bar that hosted rock and roll trivia contests when he was out on the road somewhere, you could be certain he'd head there and stay till the early hours of the morning, usually winning top prize. He once guessed the name of a tune on just three notes and was more than once disqualified from bar trivia contests because he won so regularly. Such ventures often included a turn on the dance floor, and it can be reported that Stan really did dance like no one was watching. According to Mal Kline, he once won a twist contest at a bar in Chicago at 3:00 a.m. He displayed his prize, a bottle of Thunderbird wine, on a shelf in his office for years.

If he wasn't quite a wild and crazy guy worthy of *Saturday Night Live*, he was nonetheless often the life of any gathering when he arrived. Jim Gaston of Franciscan University recalled a board dinner for the Intercollegiate Studies Institute (Evans was a long-time member of the ISI board) at a fancy restaurant in Washington, which included Heritage Foundation president Ed Feulner, several U.S. Senators, and some major ISI donors—about thirty people in all: "It was a very staid dinner—until Stan showed up. He arrived about a half hour late, with his tie undone, his coat over his shoulder, smoking a butt. The minute he came in the door everyone's demeanor changed. About 10 minutes later, after Stan started telling some jokes and funny stories, people were literally crying with laughter."

The converse side of his great wit was his personal warmth and generosity. His long-time aide de camp and self-described flak-catcher, Fred Mann, said that he only saw Evans lose his temper and be angry with anyone on one occasion, when an NJC intern for some inexplicable reason took it upon himself to cut down a tree outside the housing complex where interns lived. Dressing down the offending intern, Mann said, was one of the few times Evans raised his voice in Mann's presence. He was otherwise very lenient to the point of indulgence with interns. He gave one intern two days off to attend a Madonna concert and another a day off to watch the NBA draft in person at the Capital Center arena.

The present writer was surely not the first to wonder how and why Stan came to own a three-legged dog named Zip. Zip was almost always at his side in the office in the early 1980s and was the NJC mascot. The origin of Zip owed to a great charitable act. Ralph Bennett recounted the story:

> One evening [Stan's assistant] Mary Jo Buckland went to her horse stable in Falls Church, and found beside her stable, a quaking, brown, mixed-breed puppy with a badly mangled front leg. Some kids nearby had apparently dropped it from a nearby balcony, and in a remorseful moment of befuddlement, left it at Mary Jo's stable door. The pup was clearly suffering. Mary Jo called Stan: 'What should I do Stan?' He immediately told her, 'Put it in a box and wait for me.' They would have to find a veterinarian. There must be one open at night for emergencies. In those pre-internet days, they consulted phone books. They spent hours trying to find a veterinarian. As busy as Stan was, this dog should not have to suffer. They finally found an all-night veterinary hospital somewhere out in Maryland, and expensive surgery saved the puppy's life. Eventually the mangled leg had to be removed. Stan paid for everything. And adopted the dog. Thus came into being Zip, the wonder dog. Stan, ever conscious of Zip's feelings, would introduce him as 'more or less your average three-legged dog.'

In some ways "your average three-legged dog," as Evans described Zip, was the perfect pet companion for his relaxed demeanor. Evans never seemed to be in a hurry to get anywhere or do anything, and a three-legged dog would never pester him for long walks or to play fetch. A mugger once accosted Stan while he was out walking Zip late one night. Stan deflected the demand for his money with, "Money? I'm so poor I can't even afford a four-legged dog!" The young mugger thought better of the matter and retreated into the night. Never the healthiest dog, Evans couldn't bear to put Zip down as the dog's mobility reached its inevitable end. Mal Kline remembers: "Stan would carry her, and she was not a small dog, down three flights of stairs from his apartment, then lay her gently on the mattress he had placed for her in the back of the van. At the other end of the trip, he would carry her up two flights of stairs to his office, where he placed her on a bed he had made for her." Zip died of natural causes, and Evans buried Zip in his backyard at his country home in rural Virginia, telling Bennett: "He had 12 great years. And those were *dog* years."

But to celebrate Evans chiefly for his wit and personal warmth is to miss the central fact of his life and his larger legacy for his successors: he was *the perfect conservative.* This bold assertion is grounded in the fact that he combined four distinct aspects of his professional life in a way seldom found in any other modern conservative thinker.

First, he was a journalist of the first rank, with significant accomplishments as a news reporter, opinion journalist and columnist, and later as a writer of serious histories, especially his revisionist second look at the McCarthy era, *Blacklisted by History.* What made his journalism distinctive was his disposition to ask counterintuitive questions, to entertain the contrarian perspective, to probe for inconsistencies and telling hypocrisies, and above all not to accept liberal orthodoxy no matter how unanimously propounded by the high and mighty. No less an authority than Ronald Reagan, in one of his radio commentaries in the late 1970s, referred to Stan as "a very fine journalist." (President Reagan telephoned Stan on at least three occasions to praise something Stan had written.) He was one of the rare writers who was both literate and numerate, conversant with physics as well as with metaphysics. He was undaunted by the arcana of the federal budget, penetrating the fog of fiscal flimflam to expose out-of-control government spending. He wrote with authority about Supreme Court opinions, especially the bad ones. He could match the deep wonkery of any think tank analyst, in particular about health care, energy policy, transit subsidies, and regulation in general. Above all, he never met a tax increase he liked.

Beyond his example, there were his concrete steps to expand the ranks of conservative journalists. Today if you throw a rock out a window in Washington, there's a high chance you'll hit a conservative writer or online media outlet, but in Evans's heyday conservative journalists and columnists were scarce, and the number of serious conservative media outlets could be counted on the fingers of one hand. One aspect of Evans's larger story is the loneliness of a conservative journalist in the 1950s and 1960s. Consider the scene in those days: there was no Heritage Foundation, no Cato Institute, no Media Research Center, no *Washington Times*, and the American Enterprise Institute was a tiny and largely unheard-from entity. David Franke, one of Stan's early proteges in the late 1950s at *Human Events*, recalled that "in 1957 there may have been 30 people in Washington who self-identified as conservatives, and we all knew each other. *Human Events* was Ground Zero in Washington conservative circles, and Stan Evans was our gatekeeper to that tiny but exciting world." The number of self-consciously conservative reporters and editors in that era was very small (which is one reason why both Henry Luce at *Time* and William F. Buckley at *National Review* hired so many ex-Communists) and willy-nilly formed a tiny community of renegade writers who regarded themselves as such. Stan grew close especially with columnists Ralph de Toledano, Ralph Bennett of *Reader's Digest*, Don Lambro of The Associated Press, and, following his move to the right, Robert Novak. (Some of Evans's columns in the 1960s refer to Novak as a "liberal journalist.") In later years, after Hillary Clinton's infamous remark about "the vast right-wing conspiracy," Evans joked accurately that "when I was starting out, it was only half-vast."

After Evans became managing editor of *Human Events* in the late 1950s, Stan made it a practice to teach the fine points of journalism to the students and recent graduates the publication started to recruit even though Evans was just a few years older at that time. Bill Schulz, who became the Washington editor of *Reader's Digest*, got his start right out of college under Stan at *Human Events*. Schulz recalled in 1981: "I first read Hayek, heard Von Mises, worked with Stan Evans."[3] This disposition led to his founding of the National Journalism Center in 1977, which quickly became one of the key components in creating the thriving conservative media ecosystem we have today. More than 1,500 young aspiring journalists passed through the NJC program before Stan handed it off to the Young America's Foundation in 2002. He also taught journalism for decades at Troy University in Alabama.

Second, he was a political activist involved with the founding and nurturing of numerous conservative activist groups and closely involved behind the scenes of several important political campaigns. As we shall see, he was a key figure in the transition of postwar conservatism from being merely an intellectual movement to a political movement that aimed to win. He was present at the founding of the Young Americans for Freedom in 1960 and later served at a crucial time as chairman of the American Conservative Union at a key point in the 1970s. In fact, it was under Stan's ACU leadership that the Conservative Political Action Conference—nowadays known by the shorter CPAC—was founded, in 1974. A fierce critic of Richard Nixon, he was instrumental in fomenting a conservative rebellion against President Nixon in 1971 and galvanizing the insurgent primary challenger from Ohio Congressman John Ashbrook in 1972. "There are only two things I don't like about the Nixon Administration," he said at the time. "Its domestic policy, and its foreign policy."

Modesty, one of the core traits of Stan's character, precluded him from claiming any credit for advancing Ronald Reagan's presidential prospects, yet he was central to what in hindsight was a key moment in Reagan's presidential prospects: the late turnaround in the North Carolina primary in 1976. But for Reagan's come-from-behind surprise victory there, his presidential prospects would have ended once and for all. Jameson Campaigne Jr. commented, "Without Stan Evans, it is quite likely there would have been no Ronald Reagan in 1980."

In recent years Grover Norquist's Wednesday Group, where a broad coalition of conservative activist groups assemble every week to exchange information and form action plans on pending issues, has become prominent in media accounts of the right, but Stan Evans had the forerunner in a biweekly luncheon he hosted from the mid-1970s known as The Monday Club. It was attended chiefly by Capitol Hill staff, conservative activists, and think tank staff. Like the Wednesday Group (which Norquist started in 1993 initially to fight Hillarycare), Stan's Monday Club featured a guest speaker (occasionally even a Democrat!) and an open mic session when everyone could share news and ask for help on immediate issues or events like pending legislation in Congress. As always, the Monday Club was a forum for Stan to try out his latest witticisms against the left. He once described the Monday Club as "a body of men united around the principle that ketchup is a vegetable."

Third, his most unappreciated role is that of a first-rank thinker and theorist, a trait made most evident above all in a book that deserves to be considered a classic, *The Theme Is Freedom*. William F. Buckley Jr. gave up on writing a large synoptic statement of conservative political philosophy, finding the effort so discouraging that he took up writing novels instead. Stan faced no such difficulty, though it took him a long time to compose his treatise. William Campbell, professor of English literature at Louisiana State University and long-time secretary of the Philadelphia Society, expresses a widespread opinion: "He was the one man whom I thought was always right on every issue." Nor was Campbell alone in this sentiment. William Rusher told Neal Freeman: "If anybody ever wants to know what ol' Rusher would have thought about something, and Rusher's not around, ask Evans."

Yet for some reason, his thoughtful and timeless work on conservatism is seldom if ever included in any of the many anthologies of modern conservative thought. This is a woeful oversight. (An important exception is his early essay "The Conservative Case for Freedom," which Frank Meyer included in his 1964 edited volume, *What Is Conservatism?*) He was never out of his depth on just about any issue you can name. Legal scholar Michael Greve recalls Stan talking with him about his (Greve's) very dense and challenging book *The Upside-Down Constitution* and telling Greve, "I've read your book; explain to me how we can persuade our friends that *Erie* is the key and it's wrong." (*Erie Railroad v. Tompkins* is a 1938 Supreme Court case obscure to everyone except constitutional law specialists.) It's a good bet that legal journalist Linda Greenhouse has never heard of *Erie*, but Stan knew it cold.

One of the perennial pursuits of conservative intellectuals is harmonizing the disparate strands of conservative thought, especially the tension between liberty and order that has long been a point of theoretical and practical contention between Friedmanite libertarians and Burkean traditional conservatives. Frank Meyer is the best-known advocate for a broad reconciliation among discordant factions that became known as fusionism. Stan disliked "fusionism" as a term and pointedly didn't use it, but he deserves consideration for offering the most successful synthesis of the conflicting strains of conservatism in *The Theme Is Freedom*. His main reservation with the self-conscious idea of fusionism is that he thought there was not an essential conflict between so-called traditionalism and libertarianism. Unlike Russell Kirk, who assailed libertarians and libertarianism in strident terms (calling them "chirping sectaries" in one infamous essay), Stan regarded the two main strains as reciprocal, each requiring the other for liberty and limited government to thrive. The "theoretical confusion" that saw them in opposition was "unfortunate." In his 1964 essay for Meyer's book, he wrote: "An attack on traditional values, in the libertarian fashion, will not check the growth of state power but contribute to its increase. An assault on individual freedom, in the authoritarian manner, will not restore us to virtue, because virtue cannot be legislated. Freedom and virtue have declined together and must rise together. They are not opposites; they are not even, in the American context, separate matters to be dealt with independently. They are complementarities which flourish or wither in a direct and dependable ratio."[4]

To give one hint of what we shall see in due course, Evans studied with and derived his grasp of free market economics from Ludwig von Mises (among others) but also wrote of the centrality of the Bible as a source for a principled understanding of freedom. And aside from his formal thinking, Stan also lived by a variation of the Eleventh Commandment: "Thou shalt not speak ill of a fellow conservative." He had criticisms of other conservatives from time to time, but he usually offered them privately and with latent generosity. For example, he complained privately that George Will was "always giving conservative reasons to do liberal things," though his disagreements with Will did once spill out into a shouting match at a campus event in 1972 (most likely over Will's hostility to then-conservative hero Vice

President Spiro Agnew). In a rare departure from public criticism of another conservative, Evans did write a harsh review of Will's 1983 book, *Statecraft as Soulcraft*, but given that Will later repudiated the book himself, one would have to count this as another vindication for Evans. About Will's fondness for baseball as a metaphor for any number of more profound matters, Evans said, "I have always thought baseball is a metaphor for softball."

Fourth, as we shall see in the course of this narrative, Evans was ahead of his time in perceiving decades before many other conservatives the essence of large issues that dominate our current moment, such as the extraconstitutional nature of the administrative state, the class interest of the people who ran our elite institutions and the increasingly adversarial culture of those institutions both public and private, and the relentless conformity of our campuses. While much of Stan's body of work, such as about the Soviet Union and the arms race, are nowadays artifacts of a historical age that has passed, much of his other work could be reprinted today with only changes to the date and names, and it would be just as fresh and relevant as when it first appeared.

Many young conservatives coming of age today are well schooled in the canon of key conservative thinkers such as Friedrich Hayek, Milton Friedman, Russell Kirk, and William F. Buckley to go along with their enthusiasm for current thought leaders and intellectual combatants such as Ben Shapiro, Jonah Goldberg, and Jordan Peterson. Yet Stan Evans is not well-known among the rising conservative generation. This is partly attributable to his modesty previously mentioned. If ever the sign on Reagan's desk—"There's no limit to what you can accomplish if you don't care who gets the credit"—applied to anyone, it would be Stan Evans. "There was not a shred of pretension about Stan," Ralph Bennett said at a memorial gathering for Evans. "His Phi Beta Kappa key—did anyone ever see it?" His self-effacement extended to never claiming credit or boasting of his principal authorship of one of the founding documents of the modern conservative movement, the Sharon Statement that launched Young Americans for Freedom in 1960 (see Chapter 5). Even when Stan referenced the Sharon Statement in later books, lectures, or articles, he never once even hinted at his authorship. If asked, he'd no doubt say that the ideas weren't his but are the deep inheritance of civilization and as such there's no reason for him to claim credit merely for restating them.

Perhaps so, but this modesty is an injustice since Stan did so much in the earliest innings of the postwar conservative movement to plant conservatism on college campuses and assist in the formation and growth of conservative campus activism and then political organization on the national level at the American Conservative Union and other organizations. You could say that he was a turning point before there was Turning Point USA. Though he may seem a relic of a bygone era of the Old Right on the surface, very distant from the sensibilities ascendant in the age of Trumpian populism when the right is rethinking many old orthodoxies about political economy, in fact a lot of Evans's old and seemingly dated work actually foreshadows the roots of many of today's leading controversies. For example, his very first book in 1961, *Revolt on the Campus*, describes the origin of what today we call "political correctness" and "cancel culture" at colleges and universities. As we shall see, he was also early to the problem of what today we call the "administrative state" or the "deep state," the extraconstitutional rule of bureaucratic "experts." He was alert to the problem of personnel in Republican administrations and how "going native" from the blandishments of the bureaucracy sapped the courage of Republican presidential initiatives. As far back as the Nixon years, Evans asked, "Why is it that when one of us gets into a position of power in Washington, he's no longer one of us?" (Evans may also be the original author of the remark that "Too many conservatives go to Washington intending to drain the swamp, only to discover that Washington is a hot tub.") And while Evans's fierce anti-Communism made him a full-fledged Cold Warrior, deep down he quietly shared an Old Right inclination toward anti-interventionism abroad.

Another aspect of his personal modesty and lack of pretension deserves notice. His unassuming bearing concealed his ambition, which no doubt filled his soul, without which his relentless output cannot be explained. Yet he engaged in very little visible self-promotion throughout his career. He didn't need to. His rise and early preeminence in the conservative movement is attributable to his talent, productivity, personality, and ideological clarity. It is evident from his immense output that he must have been writing almost constantly, and when he wasn't writing, he was reading *everything*. There was hardly a current book or major government study that he hadn't read and mastered.

And about his personality: Beneath his legendary humor, impressive erudition, and controlled prose, there was an intensity behind his grasp of the crisis of our age. For several reasons it lay concealed. Unlike, for example, Whittaker Chambers, Evans never exhibited a countenance of pessimism, despair, or sadness even though he often thought the nation's leadership class was taking us to the brink of ruin. He was a happy warrior par excellence.

His personal modesty was connected to the kind of humility that is a hallmark of Christian faith, which was another important aspect of Stan's life that is not evident on the surface. "Anyone who knows me knows that I am not a particularly pious person, and I don't consider myself to be particularly good Christian," he once told a radio interviewer. But, he added, "I'm a believing Christian." He was never publicly identified with the religious right—his affinity for the devil's rock-n-roll might have disqualified him—but he stoutly supported the essential position of the religious right on issues such abortion, school prayer, and secularism in general from his earliest moments. As we shall see, his belief in the Bible as the key pillar of individual liberty and limited government became central to his mature thought as laid out in his most complete statement of his philosophy, *The Theme Is Freedom* (1995). One of his early mentors, Frank Chodorov, likely inspired some of his early interest in his synthesis of Jerusalem and Athens (though Stan was actually more attached to Rome than to Athens), but his grasp of Christian theology was also perhaps a congenital inheritance from his grandfather, a Methodist minister. Somewhere in his private faith, the Christian teaching of hope no doubt resided.

The combination of his personal and intellectual virtues made him a universally trusted figure, the consensus choice at key moments for important duties, from drafting the Sharon Statement at the launch of the Young Americans for Freedom in 1960 to crafting the Manhattan 12 declaration of conservative opposition to President Nixon in 1971. Neal Freeman, the Washington editor of *National Review* in the 1970s, remarked that "Stan was always the person in the room you turned to for wisdom and for any public statement that needed to be written."

One reason Evans was the trusted person for such prominent assignments was his exacting judgment and uncompromising standards. Evans didn't accept conservative rhetoric from Republicans at face value. Unlike Charlie Brown when facing Lucy's football, he was seldom taken by surprise when Republicans compromised too easily once in office. In many cases he suspected such Republicans were closet liberals. Most of the time he thought they were merely weak-minded. He had unerring radar for detecting aspiring Republicans who would turn into unreliable toadies of establishment liberalism. He never liked Nixon after 1960, and during his years at the *Indianapolis News* he was an early and vocal skeptic of a rising local Republican star named Richard Lugar. His favorite politicians were those few who seriously opposed government spending and had a voting record to match up with their words.

Finally, Stan should also be credited with discerning early the deepening derangement of modern liberalism that reached supercritical mass with the arrival of Donald Trump. One of his favorite jokes in the early 1990s punctured the irrational character of the left better than a treatise from a clinical psychologist: "Conservatives stand for family values, law and order, low taxes, a balanced budget, a free market economy, and a strong national defense. In other words—*hate!*" He would have been completely unsurprised at the dimensions of Trump Derangement Syndrome, and whatever reservations he might have had about Trump's personality or comportment, he would have surely cheered Trump's vigor in challenging the left as well as Trump's entirely justified contempt for the media.

His modesty and lack of typical Washington self-promotion is one reason he isn't more widely recalled just seven years after his passing. There's also an element of confusion; even when he was in his heyday, he'd sometimes be confused with Rowland Evans, Robert Novak's writing partner for the prominent Evans & Novak syndicated column. Although they were not related, Stan Evans and Rowland Evans had similar journalistic styles, emphasizing plain, direct prose and reporting facts over opinion. Stan Evans did joke from time to with Michael Novak (no relation to Robert Novak) about teaming up to write their own "Evans and Novak" column just to confuse everyone.

This relative neglect is additionally ironic given that "Stan" has become a popular slang term among millennials, meaning "a fan of," leading to the social media phenomenon whereby a

Twitter fan site is known as a "Stan account." The term originated in a 2000 song called "Stan" by the rapper Eminem, and although Stan Evans thought "rap music" is an oxymoron, if anyone deserves a "Stan account" among young conservatives, it is our Stan. Another popular term he disliked was "role model," though few people better exemplify that term rightly understood. In recent years Yale University Press has published a special *Why X Matters Series*, with titles on various subjects and past literary figures of political consequence like George Orwell (*Why Orwell Matters* by Christopher Hitchens), Lionel Trilling (*Why Trilling Matters* by Adam Kirsch), and others. This book could easily have been called *Why Stan Evans Matters* as he left behind not merely a body of work that will stand the test of time but an example worthy of close study by anyone seeking the right mix of a brilliant career and a life well lived.

CHAPTER 1

EARLY LIFE AND EDUCATION

Medford Stanton Evans was born on July 20, 1934, in Kingsville, Texas. He was named for his father, Medford Bryan Evans (hence his use of his first initial M and middle name so as to avoid confusion with his father), and his mother, Josephine Stanton Evans. His father, a Texas native, was a man of considerable literary and polemical reputation himself having been a *magna cum laude* graduate of the University of Tennessee before earning a PhD in literature from Yale (which included passing language exams in Latin, French, and German), where he wrote a dissertation on Samuel Johnson's coverage of the parliamentary debates of the 1740s. Medford Evans was described as being a soft-spoken, courtly southern gentleman. Stan always called him "Pop" and in later years described him as "the gentlest and kindest of human beings," who possessed "indomitable courage" and "sweetness of character," all descriptions that would later be applied to Stan in equal measure, showing that Stan was his father's son. Medford became a conservative as the modern movement took shape, joining the masthead of *National Review* at its founding in 1955. Stan wrote of his father: "What was most distinctive politically about my father was that he brought verbal skills and intellectual force to bear on behalf of, rather than against, traditional values and common sense. This was extremely rare when he started out."

Stan's mother, a Mississippi native, was also highly educated, having graduated with honors from the University of Mississippi. Fluent in Greek and Latin, Josephine Evans taught classics in public schools in the various locations the family lived during Stan's youth. She was also a devout Methodist, from which Stan derived his own religious affiliation, though accompanied with his usual quips. He liked to tell the old joke that "A Methodist is a Baptist who has learned to read." Following his mother's death in 2005 at the age of ninety-seven, for which she had requested a high church Episcopal funeral service, Stan joked that he was facing difficulties "finding an Episcopal priest who has leanings towards Christianity."

At the time of Stan's birth in 1934, his father was teaching English literature at the Texas College of Arts and Industry, today better known as Texas A&M, but within weeks of Stan's birth the family relocated to Chattanooga, Tennessee, where Medford took up a teaching post at his undergraduate alma mater, the University of Tennessee. He taught at Chattanooga from 1934 to 1942 and then for the next two years at the University of the South in Sewanee. He published both poetry and prose in *The Sewanee Review*, and H. L. Mencken cited one of his philological articles ("The Southern 'Long I,'" published in *American Speech*) in his treatise on *The American Language*, which is perhaps surprising since Evans had taken after Mencken harshly in an article in *The Southwest Review* in 1929. ("Is Mencken simply the victim of a sort of latitudinal Sadism not dependent upon real defects in the object of his cruelty?"[1])

During his years teaching literature, Medford observed the decline of liberal education that was already underway and issued alarms that sound familiar to our own time. "It is my considered opinion," he wrote in the late 1950s, "that the average graduate of a non-elite college today knows less than the average graduate of an accredited high school knew thirty years ago. You may ask: Less of what? If so, I reply: Less of almost any field you care to name... It is sometimes assumed that we have substituted science for the classics. But in the mass institutions this is certainly not true. We have abandoned the classics, but we have not put science in their place."

His dismay at the decay of higher education may account for the abrupt change in his career in the late years of World War II, which deepened his existing conservative inclinations. In 1945 he joined the new Atomic Energy Commission at Los Alamos as an "organizations and methods examiner" during the late stages of the Manhattan Project and later moved to a post as chief of training with the AEC Washington, DC, through 1952. Thus Stan Evans spent his middle school and high school years in suburban Maryland and likely acquired his lifelong fondness for baseball from his little league coach Bill Moffitt, who was the father of tennis great Billie Jean King and major league baseball pitcher Randy Moffitt. Jackie Jensen, then a star with the Washington Senators, lived in Evans's neighborhood and was married to Olympic medal winner Zoe Ann Olsen, a sports celebrity in her own right. Evans and other teenage boys would hang out near Jensen's home hoping to catch a glimpse, and perhaps an autograph, from the glamorous couple as they came and went.

In later years Stan took an abiding interest in nuclear power, both on the merits and in disgust at the way the left attacked nuclear energy in the 1970s. This is only one aspect of the ways in which Stan was his father's son, though not in every respect. Stan revered his father, calling him at the time of his death "the finest man I have ever known," in part because "every son should love and admire his father." But like all sons of famous or strong fathers, Stan would carve out his own independent existence (although his writing style was similar to his father's in some ways). At the time of his father's passing in 1989, Stan wrote: "I well recall the many times when, after I had favored some conservative group with what I thought was a ringing oration, some member of the audience would patiently wait to say to me: 'I just want to tell you—I'm such a fan of *your father!*'"[2] This is likely an exaggeration but the kind of filial piety consonant with a proper conservative disposition.

Medford acquired a reputation as a supposed extremist for his anti-Communist views and his later association with the John Birch Society, an easy designation to get in that time of liberal hysteria over Joe McCarthy. As we shall see in Chapter 4, Stan walked a fine line with regard to the controversial group. At the Atomic Energy Commission in Washington, part of Medford's portfolio as chief of training was overseeing security education, and he resigned in March of 1952, charging that none of his security recommendations were being adopted. Medford had not thought of himself as a self-conscious conservative prior to his time at the AEC. It was this experience at the AEC, Stan said later, that "conservatized" him.

He moved back to Texas in 1953 to resume his teaching career, by which time Stan had started at Yale University. But before returning to academia, Medford wrote an article for *The Freeman* entitled "Are Soviet A-Bombs Russian?", which he later turned into his first book appearing later in 1953, *The Secret War for the A-Bomb.* James Burnham wrote the introduction. The uproar over the Rosenberg spy ring that had conveyed our atomic bomb technology to the Soviets was still running at high pitch, and Evans had met Klaus Fuchs, one of the conspiring scientists, during one of his many visits to Los Alamos. In his *Freeman* article, Medford expressed skepticism that the transfer of technical knowledge alone could account for the Soviets' rapid development of actual warheads. Among other things, there was little evidence that the

Soviets had the industrial capacity to produce sufficient fissile material. How had the Soviets managed to produce a working A-bomb before the more advanced British? Had some fissile material been diverted from American stocks along with A-bomb plans? "It is easier to imagine Communists stealing bomb parts from American plants and relaying them to Russia," Medford wrote, "than it is to imagine the Russians going through the whole industrial process themselves." Stan would take up the general theme of overestimating Soviet capacities early in his journalistic career, as we shall see.

Medford was appalled at the lassitude of American security services—and political leadership generally—that had prompted his resignation from the AEC, and he wondered whether we had in fact rolled up all the Soviet penetration of our advanced weapons programs. There was a studied incuriosity about the many anomalies of the treason that stole and conveyed our nuclear secrets to the Soviet Union and of the wider problem of Soviet espionage in the U.S. There seemed to have been little follow-up after the conclusion of the Rosenberg trials in 1951. He also asked a question that has come full circle in our current age of terrorism: if the Soviets can steal components, might they also assemble and plant bombs *inside the United States*, thus solving the delivery problem of that time before intercontinental ballistic missiles were developed? Medford was not alone in wondering about this seemingly outlandish possibility. Among its approving readers was former President Herbert Hoover. Robert Maynard Hutchins, the legendary president of the University of Chicago, wondered before the Soviet A-bomb arrived in 1949 whether the next war "will be won by atomic bombs planted by agents." Could we be defeated by our own bombs? Medford also took as a sign of American naiveté the widespread enthusiasm in the late 1940s and early 1950 for the Baruch Plan and other schemes of international control of nuclear technology, schemes which, had they come to fruition, would surely have been violated by the Soviet Union. What, aside from sheer stupidity, could account for the elite support of such foolishness?

The Secret War for the A-Bomb was cogently written, capaciously argued, and its circumstantial case copiously documented, the very qualities that would later define the work of Stan Evans as well as suggest a bridge to some of Stan Evans's later historical works, such as *Stalin's Secret Agents* (coauthored with Herbert Romerstein). Despite the fact that eminent people like Hutchins had expressed similar concern about whether our leaders had thought through potential vulnerabilities, most reviewers were too accepting of the conventional wisdom and could not bring themselves to entertain Medford's counterintuitive style of questioning that ought to be near the heart of any serious counterintelligence process. J. Robert Oppenheimer and other prominent scientists from the Manhattan Project were furious over the book. *The Nation* magazine attacked Evans for his role in Oppenheimer's security difficulties and for lending credence to Joseph McCarthy and J. Edgar Hoover. Evans said in reply, "I was never so flattered in my life." But he had made no specific charges or insinuations against any individual scientists; his target was a lax overall security system, indifferent materials control, and the vulnerability it presented. Sidney Hook attacked the book in *The New Leader*, acknowledging that Evans "cannot be dismissed as a man wholly without credentials" but nonetheless finding the book to be not just "bad" but "reprehensible."[3] Edward A. Shils blasted the book in an excessively long review in the *Bulletin of the Atomic Scientists*, saying that Medford was mired in "conspiratorial paranoia," while the *Bulletin*'s editor, Eugene Rabinovitch, called the book "slanderous abracadabra." Shils attempted to shame James Burnham for lending his imprimatur to this "intellectually and morally irresponsible phantasy" and tried to have Burnham expelled from the American Committee for Cultural Freedom (the U.S. offshoot of the Congress for Cultural Freedom, a principal rallying point for liberal anti-Communism.)

If the book was so self-evidently ridiculous, why such an extended review that only had one point to make? Shils's review fit the pattern of the high tide of the McCarthy controversy, which, as we shall see, set the template of acceptable opinion for successive decades: this is not the *right kind* of anti-Communism, and certain questions are out of bounds. Stan Evans would make much of his career taking up "out of bounds" questions. At the time of his father's passing in 1989, Stan wrote of this episode: "On all the major issues at stake, I would say that history has vindicated Pop, and then some."[4]

Stan summarized his father's example: "He provided literary firepower for the right on internal security and other issues at a time when the left was claiming a monopoly of 'intellectuals.'" Medford wouldn't necessarily have accepted the compliment at face value. In a 1957 article in *Human Events*, Medford explained "Why I Am an Anti-Intellectual." Modern intellectuals, he said, are "treacherous and stupid. . . . They come into being as a result of civilization and proceed to turn civilization over to the most convenient horde of barbarians. . . . Thus the trend of intellectual training in the United States is toward the liquidation of the sovereignty of the United States." He went on to suggest that "intellectual" was a better term than "liberal" to describe the ruling elite because "it is as a class that they behave. Without dignity, honor, or intelligence, they are moved by appetite, controlled by mob spirit, and guided by flashes of cunning from a few leaders who, cowardly as Hobbes, are attracted to what they take for Leviathan. . . . These people are authoritarian, dogmatic, irrational, tendentious, and obscurantist."[5] In other words, Medford anticipated the idea of modern "intellectuals" as a "new class" years before Irving Kristol popularized the term. He was a man ahead of his time.

• • •

Following in his father's footsteps on the security issues of the early Cold War was many years in the future. Evans later said he first became a conservative when he read, as a high school student in 1949, George Orwell's *1984*. "It was about communism," Evans told Adam Clymer of the *New York Times* shortly before his passing; "I said: 'Well, I'm against communism. What am I for?'"[6]

While Medford Evans's excursion into the thicket of Soviet nuclear espionage was going on, Stan had entered Yale University, emulating his father again with a major in English literature. He began at Yale in the fall of 1951, just a few months after William F. Buckley Jr. had graduated and at the same time Buckley's famous first book, *God and Man at Yale*, appeared. By his own telling, Evans arrived at Yale "a bewildered freshman"—bewildered that Yale didn't live up to its reputation of true openness to all points of view. "The Yale of 1951," Stan wrote a few years later, "was a community in which Liberalism, among faculty and undergraduates alike, ruled virtually without challenge....Yale's fidelity to 'free inquiry' was peculiarly selective."[7]

Stan's experience tracked exactly what Buckley had concluded in his book, finding for example that many professors in Yale's religion department didn't appear to believe in God, teaching that "the Judeo-Christian religion is simply an anthropological construction." The leading textbook for economics was Paul Samuelson's *Economics: An Introductory Analysis*, which was "an unblushing brief for Keynesian interventionism." The head of the political science department, Cecil Driver, taught that the coming of socialism was inevitable. Stan wrote a long account and critique of Driver's class in one of his first feature articles for *The Freeman* after he graduated in 1955. "This was no dry lecture; the subject exuded emotion... The realization of 'meaningfulness' mounted steadily, and when Professor Driver concluded his lecture, the entire class of four hundred students (with one exception) rose and delivered a thundering ovation."[8]

It is not difficult to guess who the "one exception" was, though typically Stan did not direct the spotlight to himself, leaving it instead to the reader to intuit. Stan delighted in the opportunity to lay out a detailed critique, attacking Driver's selective facts and thinly disguised Marxist dialectic of inevitable *progress*:

> The implied lesson of Professor Driver's lecture is that we are caught in the grips of an impersonal deterministic force which directs history, independent of human choice. At best, this is Marxian hogwash. At worst, it is plagiarism of Marxian hogwash. If we are caught in the grips of anything, it is the dishonesty of our "leaders," and the craft of the "intellectuals" who aid and abet that dishonesty at every turn.

"Such was the Yale of the early 1950s," Stan wrote on another occasion. "It was a world in which a student of conservative inclination found himself badly in need of help, counsel, and information."

In due course Stan followed in Buckley's footsteps and built out a self-conscious conservative presence on campus. Buckley was a frequent visitor to the Yale campus in the aftermath of his book and met frequently with Evans and the handful of other conservative Yale students. Edwin Meese, later a key figure in Ronald Reagan's political odyssey, was two years ahead of Stan at Yale, but Evans's closest classmate was Lewis K. Uhler (also

Yale '55), best known subsequently as a leader in the tax revolt in the 1970s and for founding the National Tax Limitation Committee. Stan and Lew roomed in the same residential college at Yale (Vanderbilt), and Stan traveled to Uhler's home in southern California one summer during their Yale years. At the end of the summer, they had to ride a bus from Texas back to New Haven after their car blew an engine outside Dallas. Uhler discovered on the ride that Stan was handy with a ukulele as he entertained fellow passengers along the route.

"Stan was always the movement organizer," Uhler recalls, who "decided we had to build a conservative infrastructure at very liberal Yale."

Serendipity played the usual role in charting Stan's intellectual and organizational course. He recalled one important "chance encounter" in his first book:

> Late in my freshman year I wandered into Liggett's drugstore on the corner of York and Elm. Browsing at the newsstand, I came across a magazine called *The Freeman*. From its format, the magazine looked like any number of "little" periodicals, and I assumed it was yet another Liberal publication. To my amazement, I found it was strongly anti-Communist, and an eloquent proponent of free market economics. It was something of a landmark—the first time I had ever laid eyes on a conservative periodical of any sort.[9]

It was through *The Freeman* that Stan became acquainted with the first major outside influence on his intellectual course: *The Freeman*'s editor Frank Chodorov. While many thinkers of that era are still recalled prominently today, Chodorov has become neglected and unjustly forgotten. He was an important figure in the earliest years of the postwar conservative movement.[10] As such he deserves a brief digression here to highlight his importance, both to the conservative movement and in shaping Stan's distinctive, mature thought as well as boosting Stan's early career after college. In his history of postwar conservatism (*The Conservative Intellectual Movement Since 1945*), George Nash wrote that Chodorov "began to shape directly the intellectual development of the postwar Right, especially in helping the libertarian Remnant to attain self-consciousness and intellectual coherence." Stan said later than Chodorov "probably had more to do with the conscious shaping of my political philosophy than any other person" and that Chodorov "opened up more intellectual perspectives to me than did the whole Yale curriculum." Chodorov was also instrumental in the early career of William F. Buckley Jr, who wrote that "It is quite unlikely that I should have pursued a career as a writer but for the encouragement he gave me just after I graduated from Yale."[11] While Albert Jay Nock's influence on Buckley is well known, the influence of Chodorov is mostly overlooked. Another person Chodorov inspired was the young Murray Rothbard, who wrote later "I shall never forget the profound thrill—the thrill of intellectual liberation—that ran through me the first time I encountered the name of Frank Chodorov...Frank was *sui generis*."[12] To Chodorov above all may be attributed the growing split in the 1950s between libertarians and traditional conservatives. He once said, "anyone who calls me a conservative gets a punch in the nose."

Chodorov was the son of late-nineteenth-century Russian immigrants and shortened his name from Fishel Chodorowsky. He was an entirely self-made thinker. Although he graduated from Columbia University in 1907, he wasn't engaged in intellectual life in his early adulthood, working in several business ventures as well as teaching high school for a time. By his own admission, he "wandered through the years." Chodorov's epiphany came when he picked up Henry George's *Progress and Poverty*. "A young man must have a cause," Chodorov would tell students in later years, and in reading and rereading George, Chodorov felt himself "slipping into a cause."

George, remembered mostly for his advocacy of a single tax on land, was for Chodorov more of a general inspiration than the source of specific doctrine. Chodorov ran with the implications of George's underlying philosophy, which he described as "free enterprise, free trade, free men" along with awareness of "the moral degeneration of a people subject to state direction and socialistic conformity." He joined the fledgling Henry George School of Social Science in New York City (which still exists), becoming its director at the age of fifty in 1937. One of the byproducts of the George School at that time, *The Freeman* magazine, became an important fixture at the beginning of the postwar conservative movement. Founded by Will Lissner the same year Chodorov became director of the school, *The Freeman* initially published some left-leaning writers, including John Dewey, George Bernard Shaw, and Bertrand Russell along with libertarian stalwarts such as Albert Jay Nock. (This was actually the second iteration of *The Freeman*; Nock and Francis Nielson produced a short-lived magazine of the same name in the early 1920s, though the George School's version was not a continuation. There would be a third iteration, as we shall see.)

One aspect of Chodorov's anti-statism that figures prominently among libertarians then and now was his fierce antiwar stance. He embraced the famous lesson of Randolph Bourne that "war is the health of the state," writing as early as 1938 that "war destroys liberty." His antiwar writings in *The Freeman* after the U.S. entered World War II became controversial, leading the trustees of the George School to oust him as director and editor of *The Freeman* in the spring of 1942, while he was on an out-of-town trip, with the terse announcement that "Mr. Chodorov has retired from the editorship."

Chodorov's firing plunged him into deep depression. He later said that he was nearly suicidal but for the support of his mentor, Albert Jay Nock. Chodorov eventually picked himself up and struck off on his own, launching a tiny monthly magazine called *analysis* (in deliberate lower case) in 1944. Although *analysis* only attracted four thousand subscribers at its peak, it was well regarded. Although few copies of *analysis* survive, a number of his essays from *analysis*, such as "Let's Teach Communism," are minor classics still in circulation among libertarians. He also wrote several short books that Stan Evans read as a student, including *The Income Tax: Root of All Evil*, where Chodorov ranged far beyond a merely economic and political critique of income taxation and made moral objections the center of his argument. Far from being merely an engine of centralized government growth, Chodorov thought the income tax changed the essential nature of American government and offended basic Judeo-Christian principles. He thought the necessary remedy was the straight up repeal of the Sixteenth Amendment. One hears the distinct echoes of Chodorov in Stan Evans's jokes about abolishing the income tax and also his emphasis on the Judeo-Christian elements of American liberty.

Chodorov's theological bent (and influence on Stan) was even more pronounced in his 1952 book, *One Is a Crowd: Reflections of an Individualist*. Stan later said *One Is a Crowd* was the first libertarian book he ever read and that it "opened up more intellectual perspectives to me than did the whole Yale curriculum."[13] Part personal memoir and part manifesto, the book was Chodorov's most complete statement of his philosophy of "individualism," which was, at that moment, the preferred term in opposition to collectivism or socialism. (It is worth recalling that Buckley used "individualism" rather than "conservative" in his debut book, *God and Man at Yale*. Chodorov and Nock probably deserve credit for Buckley's choice of term.) Although proud of being born a Jew, Chodorov went from being irreligious to anti-religious in college. By degrees he came to appreciate that what he had regarded as "flubdubbery" and "persiflage" was in fact at the root of human liberty and individual rights. Although Chodorov never aligned with a specific denomination, he embraced an understanding of natural law close to that of Thomas Aquinas and the American founders.

Another turning point came in 1951, when Chodorov merged *analysis* with *Human Events*—originally a newsletter founded in 1944 by Frank Hanighen, Felix Morley, and Henry Regnery—and became an editor. (Early subscribers and backers of *Human Events* included Cecil B. DeMille, Herbert Hoover, Robert Taft, and Col. Robert E. Wood.) This required Chodorov to move to Washington, DC, the last place by temperament he ever wanted to live. (Stan would make the same move—twice, in 1956 and 1975—and with the same attitude.) There he kept arguing for a noninterventionist foreign policy and dissented from the conservative embrace of Cold War internationalism, a position that sharply divided the right.

In one of his last essays for *analysis* in 1950 (reprinted in 1952 in *Human Events* and as a standalone pamphlet), Chodorov planted the germ of a vital conservative initiative that would also feature prominently in Stan Evans's career. Ruminating on the defects of higher education already evident, Chodorov thought there needed to be an organized effort to reach college students with serious counter-socialist arguments presented by visiting lecturers and through reading materials. It was hopeless to think campuses could be reformed or that the faculties could be influenced because "the professorial mind is by and large beyond redemption." Chodorov actually had a left-wing college organization from the early twentieth century in mind: the Intercollegiate Socialist Society (ISS). What he proposed was reverse engineering the ISS and starting clubs of individualists on as many campuses as possible. "If Socialism has come to America because it was implanted in the minds of past generations, there is no reason for assuming that the contrary idea cannot be taught to a new generation. What the Socialists have done can be undone, if there is a will for it." It took the socialists fifty years to get traction; a countereffort would take at least as long; hence the article's title, "The Fifty-Year Project."

J. Howard Pew of Sun Oil read Chodorov's article and sent an unsolicited check for $1,000 to jump-start the idea. Other substantial contributions soon followed, and Chodorov's article became the catalyst for the founding of the Intercollegiate Society of Individualists (ISI) in 1952, with William F. Buckley serving as the titular president and Chodorov as the real leader of ISI as vice president. ISI's first mailing yielded forty students interested in joining a campus ISI club, which quickly grew to six hundred. But what to do for those students? Chodorov soon linked up with Leonard Read, head of the Foundation for Economic Education (FEE), which two years later took over *The Freeman*. Read agreed to supply ISI with books and articles to distribute to students and convinced Chodorov that ISI should sponsor speakers to visit campuses. Within two years ISI had expanded its student membership to over 2,500 (and 4,200 by 1956) as Buckley, Chodorov, and other conservative thinkers started regular campus visits. Eventually ISI founded its own journals—*The Individualist, Modern Age,* and *The Intercollegiate Review*—to which Stan would eventually become a regular contributor as well as being a frequent campus lecturer. (After an internal controversy about the term "individualist" in the organization's name, ISI rebranded itself as the Intercollegiate Studies Institute in 1966, the name by which ISI is known today.)

In the fullness of time, FEE, *The Freeman*, and ISI would loom large in Stan's early professional career, but at this point he was finishing up his first year at Yale. Stan spent the summer of 1952 after finishing his first year at Yale back home with his parents in Abilene, Texas, working a summer job for the West Texas Utilities Company, "busting rocks, moving transformers, drilling holes, and hanging around highly dangerous electrical wires in the 110-degree heat... That experience had a lot of impact on my decision to go into journalism." Back on campus, Stan recalled his first exposure to ISI and FEE. It came after he had tangled in class with philosophy Professor Paul Weiss over the subject of states' rights. (Weiss, incidentally, was no leftist; an old-fashioned European-style metaphysician, he was critical of Marxism and most modern approaches to philosophy.) Stan's argument with an eminent professor must have been notable because "afterward," Stan recalled a few years after graduation, "a student came up to me and handed me a card. It contained two notations: 'Intercollegiate Society of Individualists' and 'Foundation for Economic Education.' 'These groups think along lines like yours,' he said. 'You might want to get on their mailing list.'"

Stan devoured the books and articles available from FEE and ISI. "This literature offered welcome information—but it was more than that... The slight quantity of materials then available to a conservative student may not seem impressive. But to me, it was a discovery beyond price; for it meant that I was no longer alone." Equipped now with intellectual material, Stan began organizing Yale's conservatives. "By the time I reached my junior year," he recalled, "we had gathered together a little nucleus of conservative-minded students." Among the initiatives Stan led included founding in 1953 the Party of the Right as a subgroup within the Yale Political Union (Ed Meese was president of the

Union at the time), which still exists today. Stan thought a new conservative organization was necessary because "we considered the Young Republicans at Yale something of a lost cause." (He would later think much the same about many not-young Republicans.) At its founding the Party of the Right only attracted about ten fellow students, and so naturally, as Stan described it in droll fashion, "the first thing we had to do was have a dispute about doctrine. We had some people in that club who would not support Joe McCarthy. Right there was a problem." (Uhler recalls that he and Stan watched some of the televised McCarthy hearings in the Berkeley College lounge in 1954, though Stan later said he was too preoccupied with his studies to pay close attention.) "And we had some other people who would not support the repeal of the income tax. So we decided that those were the animating principles of our group. You had to be for Joe McCarthy—not only his goals but also his methods—and you had to be in favor of repealing the income tax. And if you didn't believe that, you were out of the club."

As we shall see, Stan was only half-joking about these two items, though it is unknown whether these rules were actually enforced. Although the Party of the Right failed in an attempt to take over the Yale Political Union, Stan and his fellow-traveling conservatives were not discouraged.

Stan also followed Buckley's footsteps by working at the *Yale Daily News* as a reporter, where he found the senior leadership to be uniformly left-leaning, "adhering to an impeccable policy of Liberalism." Stan delighted in challenging the editors' hypocrisy of calling for objectivity in reporting while practicing clear bias themselves. Stan recalls one specific episode:

> I took occasion at one editorial meeting to protest a headline blatantly loaded against the *bête-noire* of the early fifties, Senator McCarthy. The head[line] described McCarthy as "invading" a

college campus (i.e., going to a school to deliver an address). "We have been told," I said, "to be objective in handling controversial news. It seems to me this headline prostitutes the front page to innuendo against McCarthy."

The managing editor was irate. "I am glad to prostitute my front page if it hurts Joe McCarthy."[14]

As the *Yale Daily News* was less than hospitable to conservatives, Stan and the Party of the Right decided to found their own publication, *The Independent*, whose principal mission was to critique Yale's liberalism. "As students, we were not equipped to pontificate on world and national issues. But we did consider ourselves authorities on one thing—the type of course material we were receiving in class." Like Buckley's *God and Man at Yale*, *The Independent* provoked campus controversy and a flood of irate letters to the *Yale Daily News* but also some favorable comments from a handful of Yale faculty, including the dean of the law school, Eugene V. Rostow.

The Independent spawned the Independent Library, where curious students could find conservative books and literature not carried in Yale's Sterling Library. The idea came from a student and member of the Party of the Right a year behind Stan, Gridley Wright. Wright had gone to a local co-op bookstore in search of some conservative literature, but the proprietors had never heard of any of the titles Wright sought. "We need our own library," Wright argued, and Stan jumped to action. (Gridley Wright was a curious figure of some notoriety. After being a conservative campus activist at Yale, following graduation and a brief stint on Wall Street, he became enamored of eastern mysticism, then in the 1960s he took up the cause of consciousness raising through LSD and finally founded a series of what can only be described as hippy-dippy communes in—where else?—California in the late 1960s. He died in India after being stabbed by a psychotic Australian in 1979. In short, Wright went wrong.)

The Independent Library was housed in the basement of the Vanderbilt residential college hall, and although it was well stocked with the leading conservative books of the time, such as Hayek's *The Road to Serfdom*, Henry Hazlitt's *Economics in One Lesson*, and Richard Weaver's *Ideas Have Consequences*, it didn't do much lending business. "It was something of a failure" as a traditional library, Stan wrote, but outraged liberals liked to drop in to argue, and it became the locus of activity for the Party of the Right.

The overall experience deepened Stan's attachment to books. Stan later recalled hearing directly from Weaver that what conservatism needed was "unshakeable books," which Weaver certainly supplied. Whittaker Chambers's *Witness* and Russell Kirk's *The Conservative Mind* came out during Stan's Yale years and quickly found their way to the Independent Library. Stan later said he read Weaver for the first time either in 1956 or 1958 (he was uncertain of the exact year), saying that *Ideas Have Consequences* was "the book that had the most impact on me when I first read it; I ordered 10 copies and sent them to 10 people, saying 'You must read this book.' I'd never done that before, and I've never done it since." As we shall see in due course, Weaver belongs alongside Chodorov as a formative influence on Evans's thought.

One lesson of Stan's education at Yale is that the decisive things are learned as much through self-education outside the classroom as through what is presented in formal courses. Stan's habit of challenging campus orthodoxy, both in the classroom and in extracurricular activities, prepared him well for a lifetime occupation battling liberalism. And like Buckley, he left a wake at Yale. Neal Freeman recalled, "When I arrived on campus as a college freshman, Stan's aura was very much present, even though he had graduated some years earlier."

While Stan was leaving the campus, the campus did not entirely leave him as higher education became an early focus of his career and his first book.

CHAPTER 2

THE MAKING OF A YOUNG JOURNALIST

Stan Evans's journalistic career got off to a fast but uneven start. Following graduation from Yale with Phi Beta Kappa honors in the spring of 1955, Frank Chodorov, who had recently taken over as editor for the revival of *The Freeman* at the Foundation for Economic Education, hired Stan to be an assistant editor for $325 a month. *The Freeman* was based out of New York City, so Stan took an apartment in Tarrytown that he shared with Donald Lipsett, a recent graduate of Indiana University who had also been active in ISI as a student and whom Chodorov tapped to be the business manager for *The Freeman*. Evans and Lipsett became fast friends and close collaborators, with Lipsett later going on to be the long-time executive director of the Philadelphia Society after its founding in 1964.

Victor Milione, who was running ISI's day-to-day operations, visited the duo from time to time and related that the Evans-Lipsett apartment was a scene of bohemian living and intellectual pursuit, with sports and rock and roll substituting for the pretentious artistic and musical tastes of the liberal literary-political community in New York. Lee Edwards wrote that "Milione enjoyed the long philosophical conversations with his young roommates but did not share their enthusiasm for rock and roll music and Indiana University football."[1] "Vic said the music was blaring, and it's the Beach Boys, and things like that. And Vic is strictly Mozart and Beethoven, and here is this. He goes into the bathroom, and looks over at the bathtub, filled nearly to the rim with dirty clothes. They weren't going to go to the laundry! If you need more clothes you buy some." There were also barbells strewn around the apartment; Stan was apparently "buffing up" in those days. Milione decided to make "other arrangements" for future visits.[2]

Evans also enrolled in the graduate program in economics at New York University, where he attended seminars with Ludwig von Mises. Von Mises, Evans recalled, would come into the room with a single sheet of paper, on which he'd written down just a short list of terms, typically "capitalism, socialism, interventionism." Evans marveled at how "von Mises would hold forth for 45 minutes, without a pause."

But it was Chodorov who was the important immediate influence on Stan's professional course. Though Chodorov was known as an exacting and uncompromising libertarian ideologue, as a mentor, Stan said, "He was so generous to me. The main thing about him was that he was a great editor. I was just fresh out of college, and like most graduates I thought I was a pretty good writer." Stan's maiden piece for *The Freeman* in the September 1995 issue, a book review of an early memoir by West German Chancellor Konrad Adenauer, displays early his ability to notice how conventional American liberals didn't perceive how Adenauer's essential anti-Communism was tempered by West Germany's tenuous geographical position. Instead of projecting American liberal confusion onto Adenauer, Evans praised Adenauer's patriotism and subtle realism, whose central aim was fending off Soviet ambitions, adding, "Were our own statesmen to bring themselves as readily to grips with the realities of the world situation, were they as forthright in seeking to protect the interests of their own country, we would in the long run have very little to fear from the Soviets."[3]

His second piece was also a book review of the quirky and nowadays obscure artist Wyndham Lewis, whose prose style is a challenge for readers. Although regarded as a leading modernist in the art world, Lewis was a scourge of radical subjectivity in modern art. Through Lewis's circuitous prose, Evans caught the main thread: "Implied in his assault is a condemnation of the real sickness of modern society—which is relativism gone wild. For it is relativism which refuses to allow the existence of any objective standards, either moral or aesthetic. It is the toxin which has corrupted our cultural as well as our political existence. Because it is itself disorderly and soggy, it inevitably gives rise to some horrendous dictatorship. Allowing everything, it can disallow nothing. Thus it is impotent to crush the harbingers of malevolence and the despotism of nonsense."[4]

Very promising prose from a twenty-two-year-old, though Stan would later attribute his early progress as a journalist to the tough tutoring of Chodorov. "I'll never forget the first time I handed in one of my elaborate manuscripts to him," he said in a 2002 interview. "It came back with these big 'Xs' through the first three pages. And he said, 'Your lede is on page four.' I started learning real fast from him what it was to be a professional journalist as opposed to a student writing an academic paper." One suspects that this specific memory is connected to Evans's first major feature piece for *The Freeman*, "Yale's Four Hundred," that appeared in the December 1955 edition. The article (mentioned briefly in the previous chapter) offered an extensive, point-by-point critique of the historicism of the socialist argument taught to Yale students (i.e., the Hegelian view that socialism was the natural endpoint of human social evolution). Stan displayed early a feature of his later mature writing on political economy, namely, that a market economy is superior to socialism not on the typical economic grounds of abundance or efficiency but on moral grounds. Sounding more like Whittaker Chambers than F. A. Hayek, Evans understood that socialism's appeal stemmed more from its supposed moral appeal than its economic promises.

When this essay appeared, however, Evans had moved on from *The Freeman* to *National Review*. At the time of its launch in the fall of 1955 (with Stan's father Medford listed on the masthead as a contributing editor), Buckley had grand ambitions for *National Review* to be a weekly publication with initial hopes for 500,000 subscribers and eventually rivaling *Time* magazine's multimillion weekly circulation at its peak. Buckley wanted to emulate *Time* and other major news organizations by having regional bureaus (and perhaps even regional editions or supplements), and thus he recruited Evans in November 1955 to move to Louisville, Kentucky, to be *National Review*'s Midwestern correspondent.

National Review's ambitions to be a major circulation weekly didn't progress according to plan, nor did Stan's position. His first and only bylined article for *NR* from this period appeared in December 1956: "The Liberal Against Himself." It was a critique of the godfather of anti-Communist "containment," George Kennan. Kennan was widely revered as a supreme intellect and even something of a conservative, but Evans was having none of it. He detected not only the subtle weaknesses of Kennan's superficial anti-Communism but moreover how his seemingly careful hedges about the Eastern bloc revealed an underlying ignorance that belied his reputation as our leading "expert" on the Soviet Union. His skillful arraying of Kennan's many contradictions, vague generalizations, and outright errors in prediction was less an attack on Kennan than it was an indirect shaming of the foreign policy establishment and journalists who endlessly lauded Kennan for his supposed brilliance. If *Kennan* was the prime example of intellectual leadership in the Cold War, we were in deeper trouble than we thought.

With *NR's* ambitions scaled back, Stan moved on to *Human Events*, rejoining his mentor Frank Chodorov as contributing editor on a four-person staff in Washington under editor in chief Frank Hanighen, who was one of the cofounders of *Human Events* in the 1940s. (The fourth member of the *HE* staff was publisher James Wick.) In those days *Human Events*, ISI, and *The Freeman* were joined at the hip (even though *The Freeman* was owned by FEE), with Chodorov editing *The Freeman* concurrently with his work at *Human Events*. Throughout the 1950s *Human Events* appeared in a two-part newsletter format, offering one bylined feature article, usually four pages long, and four pages of unsigned reporting and editorials on the political scene. (One of the frequent feature contributors in those years was a former conservative Republican congressman from Nebraska, Howard Buffett, father of Warren Buffett.)

Evans undoubtedly wrote much of the unsigned material, though it is impossible to know today which specific pieces owe to his pen. He surely contributed to developing the blunt and sometimes slashing style that became the signature of *Human Events* reporting as it expanded in size and circulation in the late 1950s and early 1960s. An unsigned piece from August 1957 conveys *HE's* distinctive style and focus that was markedly more pugilistic than *National Review's* more high church tone: "Senator 'Jack' Kennedy ruffled supporters who have billed him as a 'conservative' when he unfurled his true colors on the floor of the Senate last week. Kennedy submitted a bill, S. 2828, which would give the Palace Guard unlimited authority to pump foreign aid funds to Communist countries such as Poland and Yugoslavia."

A large number of the unsigned reported articles in *Human Events* in the late 1950s offer a portal into conservative divisions and uncertainty over how to think about the Eisenhower administration and the direction of the Republican Party still laboring in the shadow of the New Deal. Although *Human Events* was scrappier than the erudite *National Review*, it was less hostile to Eisenhower. Everyone in the *Human Events* circle was resolutely hostile to the New Deal and was often frustrated with Eisenhower's feeble challenge to it. At the same time, *Human Events* was enthusiastic about Ike's secretary of state, John Foster Dulles, and hopeful about Vice President Richard Nixon's chances of succeeding Eisenhower as a more committed conservative. *Human Events* reported frequently and favorably about Nixon's activities and statements and conversely reported frequently and unfavorably about Nixon's likely rival for the 1960 GOP nomination, New York Governor Nelson Rockefeller.

But a new figure was starting to attract the attention and enthusiasm of *Human Events*: Arizona Senator Barry Goldwater. In his first term in the Senate after his upset victory in 1952, Goldwater had started to make his mark as a critic of labor unions, publicly feuding with radical auto workers union boss Walter Reuther. By degrees Goldwater increased his criticism of the Eisenhower administration for not fighting more vigorously to cut government spending. His reelection in 1958 galvanized conservatives as he had been considered an underdog. Major support from the two leading Arizona newspapers owned by conservative publisher Eugene C. Pulliam, the *Arizona Republic* and the *Phoenix Gazette*, helped Goldwater's campaign, which is likely a link in the chain that would bring Evans to Pulliam's attention the following year. (One liberal critic complained, "If Goldwater recited 'Mary Had a Little Lamb,' the Pulliam press would make it the banner story of the day."[5])

A few weeks after Goldwater's reelection, *Human Events* led with an article about Goldwater entitled "A New Leader Arises."

Although unsigned, it reads like a product of Evans's typewriter. Goldwater said he supported Nixon "as of this moment," but in a passage of remarkable prescience, the story added that "if Nixon should equivocate, it would make it much more difficult for Goldwater to support the Vice President. As for Nelson Rockefeller, the Arizonan says he isn't going to buy 'a millionaire in a poke.'"[6]

Evans was promoted to managing editor of *Human Events* in April 1958, appearing on the masthead in that position for the first time on April 14. During his three-plus years with *Human Events*, Evans only published three bylined features, though this is not surprising given the publication's modest page count at the time. Two examined the political character of the Americans for Democratic Action (ADA), the premier liberal interest group founded in 1947 ostensibly to advance broad-spectrum liberalism. (Hollywood actor Ronald Reagan was an early dues-paying member.) Like his lèse-majesté toward George Kennan, Evans was having none of the "moderate liberal Anti-Communist" pretensions of the ADA: "Its claim to anti-communism is one of the more grotesque phenomena of current political life," in large part because Evans could discern no serious opposition to the advancement of Soviet interests abroad or socialist policy in America.

In October 1956 Evans's first article, "ADA on the Brink of Power," explained why it should be understood differently than a typical liberal interest group like labor unions: "The organization is not nearly so interested in selling itself, or its name, as it is in selling its ideas. This it does with considerable skill." ADA's real aim, Evans thought, was functioning as "the master strategy board in a campaign to impose a program of piecemeal socialism on the United States." It "seizes every opportunity to promote the growth of the Federal bureaucracy." He trained his sights on the ADA again nearly two years later in a June 1958 feature,

"ADA—The Enemy Within: How the Left Achieves Its Political Victories." Building on his first article, Evans explained how all facets of the ADA's highly disciplined activities, which combined intellectual combat, media influence, and direct electioneering efforts, added up to something more comprehensive and purposeful than most political organizations. "ADAers may be few in number (43,000 members are claimed), but they get around." Its aim was nothing less than taking over the Democratic Party or at least becoming a decisive power broker in the party.

In the mid-1960s Evans would expand this mode of analysis onto a wider field in his third book, *The Liberal Establishment: Who Runs America…and How*, which will be treated in due course. For now, however, it is sufficient to notice how Evans and subsequently the postwar conservative movement came to see that it needed to emulate the ADA if it wished to be an effective political force instead of merely a critical faction. One of the first efforts to emulate the ADA's modes was Americans for Constitutional Action (ACA), founded in 1958 in Chicago, but Evans never had any association with it. The more substantial replica of the ADA on the right would await the founding of the American Conservative Union (ACU) in 1964, which will be explored more fully in the next chapter.

His third and final bylined feature article in *Human Events* displayed his fierce anti-Soviet side, writing about the Soviet downing of an unarmed American military transport plane on the Russo-Turkish border in September 1958, which killed seventeen American crew members and passengers. Written jointly with retired airman W. B. Hicks, the article "Massive Humiliation" observed that this outrageous aggression caused only a momentary ripple of indignation in the media and a flaccid response from the Eisenhower administration, which exacted no reprisal of any kind. Worse, this incident was merely the latest in a long string of postwar incidents in which American citizens were abandoned by their government overseas. "The system today amounts to this: the soldier is required to be loyal to his country, but his country is not loyal to him. If some civilian bureaucrat finds his well-being inconsistent with international harmony, or with State Department yearnings toward appeasement, then he is simply sacrificed."

One other aspect of Evans's career story arc appeared in this early period with both *The Freeman* and *Human Events*: his disposition as a teacher and recruiter of talent for the conservative movement. Had he continued his graduate studies with Von Mises at NYU instead of pursuing journalism, he would likely have become a conventional academic. As a journalist he nonetheless kept up with serious intellectual life. He participated regularly in seminars and conferences of the Foundation for Economic Education (FEE—publisher of *The Freeman*) sometimes as discussion leader, which brought him into frequent contact with leading conservative and free-market thinkers. FEE president Leonard Read (author of the classic essay, "I, Pencil") recorded in his diary about a September 1955 seminar in which Evans participated in "a thorough beating up" of a proposal for a value-added tax.

At *Human Events* he took on a semi-official role as the teacher of young apprentices. If conservatives were ever going to challenge the dominance of liberalism in the mass media, it would need to generate conservative journalists. ISI was already providing college students with free subscriptions to *Human Events* (seven thousand subscriptions by 1957), but in 1957 ISI decided to launch a scholarship program in political journalism to bring students and recent graduates to Washington, DC, to learn journalism at *Human Events* and work as interns on Capitol Hill. The program was unofficially known as the Human Events School of Journalism. The interns "are given assignments 'covering the Hill' by the *Human Events* staff; they attend press conferences, interview members of Congress, and study the workings of the Government and the major political parties."

The first three interns selected showed the promise of such programs, as all three went on to become significant figures in the media and the conservative movement. Each was only nineteen years old but had already displayed precocious conservatism. They were Douglas Caddy, a student at Georgetown's School of Foreign Service who had proven himself an effective campus agitator for conservative causes; David Franke, junior college student from Texas who had edited the school paper with a conservative flair; and William Schulz, a student at Antioch College who had also shown early talent in writing columns and radio commentaries for Fulton Lewis Jr. (Lewis can be considered the Rush Limbaugh of his day as his radio program appeared on more than five hundred stations, reaching an audience estimated at sixteen million.) Caddy went on to become one of the founders and principal activists of Young Americans for Freedom, Franke went on to become an editorial assistant to Bill Buckley at *National Review*, and Schulz became a DC legend in his later career as the Washington editor of *Reader's Digest* (as much as for his long convivial lunches at The Palm restaurant on 19th Street as for his journalism, which was equally prodigious).

Although only a few years older than the interns, Evans was their hands-on tutor in the craft of journalism. Franke recalled that "*Human Events* was Ground Zero in Washington conservative circles, and Stan Evans was our gatekeeper to that tiny but exciting world. Soon after the three of us arrived in Washington, Stan gave us our instructions on what we were going to do as activist journalists: "First, we take over the Young Republicans. Then we take over the Republican Party. Then we take over the nation. And then we defeat world communism."

For the next several years, we three students would have daily contact with Stan as our teacher and mentor, our friend, and our on-and-off roommate. Stan was a serious teacher when it came to style and accuracy, and I vividly remember his red-ink changes on my copy. Seeing all that red on your copy really caught your attention. Stan's most important advice, however, was: "The hardest part of writing is gluing your ass to the chair in front of the typewriter and actually starting to write."[7]

As the *de facto* housemaster to the interns and other young conservatives floating in an out of Washington, Stan's rented DC housing, in a largely black neighborhood near Capitol Hill, boasted the same kind of chaotic and a bohemian atmosphere as his New York apartment he had shared with Don Lipsett. Franke called it "a flophouse," adding that "Stan used to love telling the story of how he returned from a weekend trip to find a stranger in his apartment living room. Who are you? he asked. The person gave his name and explained: 'David Franke has left your apartment, and I have taken his place.' Out-of-towners would use Stan's apartment as their home away from home." Stan, Franke reports, got into the occasional bar fight in those years (Harrigan's Bar on Capitol Hill and Martin's Tavern in Georgetown were favorite—and frequent—watering holes for Evans and his young entourage), on one occasion defending the honor of Barry Goldwater in the presence of the always buttoned-down William Rusher, who was horrified.

Franke related one particular episode demonstrating that Evans's legendary dry wit was an early trait:

Life was never dull at *Human Events*. I remember the time an elderly woman dropped in at our office and complained to our receptionist—an older, sweet relative (aunt?) of Chuck Colson—

how she had been abducted by aliens, they had implanted something in her head, and she was in constant pain. We were her last hope for help! The nonplussed receptionist came to Stan for assistance, and got it. Stan impulsively picked up some aluminum wrap (now where did he get that!) and soothed the woman. "Put this around your head as a hat," he explained, "and it will block out the alien signals that are causing your pain." She walked out a renewed and happy woman.

The ISI fellowships that brought Franke, Caddy, and Schulz to *Human Events* were, Evans recalled later, "an embryonic National Journalism Center." And this is where the aforementioned Don Lipsett comes back into the timeline at the pivot point to the major breakout moment of Evans's career. After Evans left *The Freeman* for *National Review* and then *Human Events* in 1956, Lipsett relocated to Indianapolis, ostensibly for a day job with the Indiana Manufacturers Association (and later a stockbroker with Dillon, Read & Co.) but also to become ISI's regional director to organize ISI's campus growth in the college-rich Midwest. Lipsett quickly fell in with Jameson Campaigne, the editor of the *Indianapolis Star*, the morning daily owned by the aforementioned conservative publisher Eugene C. Pulliam. Evans later described Pulliam as "the last of the old-time press moguls in the mold of Hearst, Pulitzer, and Colonel McCormack." *Time* magazine gratuitously pegged Pulliam as "somewhat to the right of Warren Gamaliel Harding." At his peak, Pulliam's Central Newspapers owned forty-five papers, chiefly in the Midwest but also including the *Arizona Republic* and the *Phoenix Gazette*. (Pulliam was also Vice President Dan Quayle's grandfather.)

Pulliam was especially interested in having robust conservative editorial pages. After Buckley's *God and Man at Yale* appeared in 1952, Pulliam tried to lure Buckley to Indianapolis to be the chief editorial writer for the *Star*, and after Buckley declined, Pulliam hired Campaigne. Campaigne had caught Pulliam's eye several years earlier with an article Campaigne had placed in the *Saturday Evening Post* while still a service Marine staff sergeant entitled "What's the Matter with the USA?" By 1959 Pulliam was looking for someone to lead the editorial page of his evening daily, the *Indianapolis News* (which at the time had a larger circulation than the *Star*), and Lipsett brought Evans to the attention of Campaigne and hence to Pulliam, who were impressed with Evans's work to date. Evans left *Human Events* at the end of May in 1959 to join the *Indianapolis News* initially as an editorial writer.

In retrospect it is hard to imagine a location and position more congenial for Evans to flourish and to develop a national reputation. While most histories of postwar conservatism tend to focus on sunbelt locales such as Southern California or Texas, in fact Indiana was a hotbed of conservative intellectual life and political activism. Clarence Manion, the conservative dean of Notre Dame's law school, hosted a popular local radio show (later moving to television) called the "Manion Forum," where he was an early booster of Barry Goldwater, among other figures generating enthusiasm on the right. Indianapolis businessman Pierre Goodrich established the Liberty Fund in 1960 to promote the publication of classic books of the Western canon as well as sponsor small gatherings of intellectuals for unstructured leisurely conversations on serious topics or thinkers. *The American Spectator* magazine began in the mid-1960s as a student publication called *The Alternative* at Indiana University and soon built a national following. The Lilly Endowment, a major charitable foundation born out of the pharmaceutical company fortune, was a substantial funder of several conservative institutions. And then there were the Pulliam newspapers. We can observe Evans in these early years working out his central ideas and lines of analysis that dominated his mature work for decades to come. The motto above the masthead of the *News* read: "Where the spirit of the Lord is, there is liberty." Evans's more mirthful description was that the morning *Indianapolis Star* and the evening *Indianapolis News* made Indianapolis "the only city in America with stereophonic reaction."

It didn't take long for Evans to demonstrate his energy, ability, and immense productivity. His method of operation wasn't limited merely to merely sitting at his desk in the newsroom and banging out copy. His first day on the job, May 27, found him covering an evening speech by FEE president Leonard Read. Evans's first article in the *News* was not an editorial but a straight news story on the Business page about Read's talk before forty businessmen in the suburb of Lafayette: "Government Is Blamed for Inflation." Two days later there appeared an unsigned editorial, which Evans certainly wrote, offering a favorable endorsement of Read's views. He called Read "a persuasive gentleman" who understands "the virtues of the free market system" and was thus an antidote to the "'planned economy' advocates in Washington [who] tell us that only through government manipulation of the national wealth can the nation prosper."[8] Evans often generated editorials and bylined columns based on a visit from a political figure or thinker passing through Indianapolis.

While it is not always possible to identify positively which unsigned *News* editorials came from Evans's typewriter, many bear his exacting style and eye for the telling detail and often found their way into subsequent books. Another early Evans editorial was "Wrong Way on Foreign Aid" on May 29. It noticed that a reported reduction in foreign aid (never popular in heartland states then or now) was really a budgetary sleight of hand that involved cutting military aid and increasing "economic" aid that "is simply another means of advancing collectivism" and "is strictly for public consumption." (Sniffing out government budgeting tricks was one of Evans's stocks-in-trade.) But the next short editorial that day, "Champion of 'Peace,'" also sounds like Evans—a sarcastic rendering of the awarding of the Lenin Peace Prize to Soviet dictator Nikita Khrushchev.

Writing editorials every day might have seemed less demanding than writing and reporting several unsigned pieces each week as he had done on the skeleton staff of *Human Events*. "People who have not done that kind of thing think, 'Gosh, that sounds awful,' but actually it's not that hard," Evans recalled. "Any journalist knows that the deadline is your friend, because there's no ifs, ands, or buts—you're going to get it done. And when you think about it, you have eight hours to write one editorial. The writing is often the least of it. It's getting the information." He was likely being modest again as a look at the editorial page often reveals his own bylined columns running alongside an unsigned editorial that bore all the markings of an Evans-written piece.

Indiana suited Evans temperamentally as well as philosophically. As he told *Time* magazine the following year, "I think my philosophy is pretty close to the farmer in Seymour, Indiana. He believes in God. He believes in the U.S. He believes in himself. The intuitive position is much closer to wisdom than the tortured theorems of some of our Harvard dons." And it was clear he was a good fit with Pulliam. Working for Pulliam, he said, was "gratifying, because I was able to write things that I believed in. He would never require or ask an editorial writer to write anything that he or she did not believe. That's the way he was. So I was able to write what I believed to be true and important."[9]

It is not clear if hiring Evans for the editorial page was consciously intended as a tryout to be the editor in chief of the *News*, which had been operating without one since Pulliam acquired it in 1948. Pulliam had served as the de facto editor for a decade, frustrated in his search for an editor with both ability and compatible ideology. "I've combed the whole goddam country," Pulliam told *Time* in 1960. "There are lots of good journalists around, but they're all cockeyed left-wingers." Evans described Pulliam in a 2002 interview as "a very strong, entrepreneurial type person. Very strong opinions. He cared deeply about the stands that his papers took on issues. He wasn't one of these corporate types that said let's see what the polls show and we make the paper correspond to that. He had certain ideas. And these papers expressed those ideas."

Within eighteen months Pulliam had seen enough and decided to name Evans as editor of the *News*. His appointment was announced on the front page on September 13, 1960. He succeeded C. Walter McCarty, who was near retirement but was kicked upstairs for the time being to a new post as "executive editor." Evans was only twenty-six, making him the youngest editor of a major daily paper in the nation. He would stay in the position until he was forty-one.

CHAPTER 3

AT THE INDIANAPOLIS NEWS

S tan Evans may not be accurately described as the "man about town" with the usual stereotype of the dapper dandy gracing fancy restaurants, nightclubs, and paneled salons. His style, as related by long-time friend and colleague James Roberts, ran more to "lounging around on the sofa in a pair of old khakis and an undershirt, chomping on a loaf of Wonder Bread, washed down by a bottle of Big Grape, while watching Roller Derby on TV." And by other accounts occasionally yelling back at the TV, "There's no way that pitch was a strike!" He was also known during his Indianapolis years for being the instigator of casual evening bonhomie, sometimes in a pool hall but usually in an upstairs room at the Italian Village restaurant on Meridian Avenue. Known informally as Stan's "Beer and Pizza Marching Society," his entourage consisted of other *Indianapolis News* editorial page staff such as W. W. "Dub" Griffith, David "Luky" Warner, and local conservative activists Don Cope, John Ryan, Dan Manion, and Fred Andre. In later years several of the student founders of *The Alternative* (which became *The American Spectator*) attended, as did a young man starting out in local politics named Dan Quayle. It was, *American Spectator* publisher Ron Burr recalls, "always the scene of laughter and high spirits all night long."

But these descriptions go too far in the other direction. While he delighted in his anti-elite "lifestyle" preferences, he can't be lumped in with the stereotype of the grizzled, cynical, ink-stained wretch of the newsroom (though the smoking and drinking image are partly accurate—he liked to joke in later years that journalism started downhill when newsrooms removed the built-in ashtrays from their desks). *Time* reported in its story about his *News* appointment that Evans attended the Robert Park Methodist Church and "spends hours poring over [conservative] literature in his third-floor walkup apartment just around the corner from the *News*."[1] This description barely hints at his energy and peripatetic practices.

While Evans was a voracious reader, many evenings would find him out at a community meeting of some kind, giving a talk to a local civic organization or student group at a nearby college or just gathering the news. Partly this was an expression of his philosophy of journalism. As he explained to Bill Dennis in a retrospective interview in 2002:

I didn't want to just sit in the office. I'm not a 'shoe-leather' reporter, but I definitely wanted to get out and learn about the community I was living in. To be able to comment intelligently on what is happening here. One of my beliefs, and it was certainly one of Mr. Pulliam's beliefs, is that the first duty of a newspaper is to cover your own back yard. It's very easy to sit in your office and write an editorial about what is happening in Bosnia, and a lot of people do that sort of thing, but it has no impact, and you're not really changing anything. I try to teach to my students that you write about the community you're living in, you know much more about it and you're able to have more impact on it. And also you're more accountable. I could say anything about Bosnia, and no Bosnian is going to show up on my doorstep the next morning and say, 'That was wrong.' But when I wrote about the school board in Indianapolis and got something wrong, there would be somebody on my doorstep the next morning.

He spoke to just about any civic or professional group that invited him, and the *News* usually promoted his appearances with a short notice, sometimes on the front page. The civic and other organizations Evans spoke to included the Jordan YMCA on "The Decline of Freedom"; the Mothers Council of Butler University; the Indiana University Conservative League; the Alpha Phi Sorority on "Communism and American Youth," the Illini Club, the Crossroads Rehabilitation Center ("Entertainment at the 6:30 p.m. meeting will be provided by Miss Katherine 'Kit' Field, Miss Indiana of 1968"), the Kappa Alpha Theta sorority, the Better Government Association of Terra Haute, the Columbus Junior Chamber of Commerce "bosses' night" on "the future of free enterprise," the Indianapolis Council of Women on "The Road Ahead for Indianapolis" (underneath the main story for the page, "Area Rugs Popular," by the paper's "home furnishings editor"), the Kiwanis Club, etc.

One of his earliest speaking appearances provides a portal into an important aspect of his distinctive journalistic insight, where he showed himself to be contrarian even about some standard conservative views. "Editorial Writer to Address Club" was the small note on page 41 from October 8, 1959: "Stan Evans, editorial writer for *The News*, will speak at a meeting of the Indianapolis Legal Secretaries Association Monday at 6 p.m." If a group of legal secretaries seems like an unlikely audience for an editorial writer, his topic may sound even more unlikely: "The Soviet Missile Hoax." On this particular topic, we can see a good example of Evans's independence of mind and original thought.

Although Evans was a fierce anti-Communist Cold Warrior, he didn't accept Soviet claims at face value as did many conservatives who were often prepared to believe the most pessimistic "news." Months before John F. Kennedy began touting the fictitious "missile gap" between the U.S. and the Soviet Union as part of his presidential campaign, Evans was on to the deceptions of

Soviet claims for its missile prowess and many other things, as expressed in several columns and news stories that relate to this particular evening talk. It was an extraordinary contrarian perspective coming amidst the aroused state of public opinion that became known as our "Sputnik moment," in which the nation was nearly in a panic that we were falling behind the Soviets in science and technology. In a rare step, Evans wrote several front page straight news stories about reasons to doubt Soviet claims in their announced breakthroughs in rocketry based on original reporting from several expert sources. A September 18, 1959, front page news story was headlined "Radio Fake in Red Moon Hit Hinted." "The Soviet lunar rocket that shook the world this week could have been faked by bouncing radio waves off the moon, creating one of the most spectacular hoaxes in history." He cited several experts who laid out detailed grounds for this skepticism. A follow-up story four days later (September 22) was headlined "2 Scientists Take 'Show Me' Attitude on Luniks": "Two top American scientists said today Russia's Lunik II has yet to be proved or disproved. But both made unexpected comments suggesting that the first Soviet Lunik, announced in January and 'confirmed' by the American government, was never authenticated." Although the Lunik launches were later authenticated as our monitoring technology (and some direct CIA spying inside the Soviet Union) improved, Evans was not alone in suggesting Soviet claims about this or other matters should be treated with suspicion. If Soviet grain harvest announcements were always wrong and deliberately deceptive (along with their frequent boasts to have invented the radio and the airplane), why not their announcements about rocketry too? Congress actually appointed a subcommittee to hold hearings about Soviet rocketry claims in the spring of 1959, taking testimony from several of the same scientists Evans interviewed for his news stories.

In 1961 Evans in his columns and unsigned editorials regarded the Soviet manned space program as a likely hoax, referring to Yuri Gagarin's "alleged spaceflight." Although Gagarin's flight was genuine, many of Evans's doubts were subsequently vindicated as over the years details gradually emerged of deceptions and coverups in the Soviet space launches and landings. At the time Evans noticed numerous anomalies and implausible claims in the Soviet announcements and photographs (why was Gagarin photographed exiting the landed capsule wearing different headgear than appeared in his launch photos?), providing another instance of the uncritical acceptance of "news" from the Soviet Union by both the media and government.[2] He persisted in his skepticism of a Soviet "breakthrough" in space, asking as late as 1965 "Did the Soviets Fake Their Walk in Space?"[3]

Not surprisingly the bylined opinion column Evans started at the *Indianapolis News,* appearing at least twice a week, was called "Skeptic's Corner," and the subject of our misprision of both Soviet prowess and our neglect of Soviet espionage were frequent topics. One early "Skeptic's Corner" column took aim at Soviet displays of advanced submarines, aircraft, and missiles: "It is known that the Reds have a penchant for tossing together creaky prototypes—like the delta-winged planes that wobbled over Moscow, never to be seen again—to throw a scare into the West."[4] Another column took direct aim at the CIA's analytical biases that placed too much credulity in Soviet claims and the passive groupthink of too many American observers, such as George Kennan. "As was suggested in this space some weeks ago, U.S. 'intelligence' has practically no idea of what is going on in Moscow, and has to mix double helpings of the Kremlin's own say-so into its planning estimates." This column went on to assemble independent estimates that, among other things, showed—correctly as it turned out—that the Soviet economy was actually falling further behind the U.S.[5] "Factual support for Kremlin tall talk is practically nonexistent," Evans wrote in still another column. He devoted at least seven columns and two news stories to this topic between 1959 and 1961 and ran op-ed columns by other authors pursuing the same skeptical line.

On the surface his suspicion about Soviet capabilities seems surprising as it resembles the left's frequent critique of America's defense and intelligence estimates over the decades as being too hawkish or overestimating the Soviet threat to the West for the sole purpose of pumping up military spending. Indeed, one of Evans's sentences—"there is no necessary connection between increased production of military hardware and winning the cold war"—could almost have come from the pen of a leftist like Gabriel Kolko or I. F. Stone. But his independent skepticism provides an important clue to how his mind worked and why his journalism stands out. It is not so much that he was a natural contrarian; rather, he regarded most of what today we call "mainstream" journalism to be superficial and thought it always paid to probe deeper into the facts and reject groupthink, whether in a newsroom or government agency.

Beyond a more thorough practice of journalism, we can see that Evans had a more profound grasp of the Cold War scene. Evans took dead aim at the consensus view that "we ought to accept Red assertions at face value anyway, in order to be on the 'safe' side." He discerned that Soviet disinformation served an obvious strategic purpose that escaped the grasp of the conventional foreign and defense policy establishment (and still does to this day in many ways): it deterred the West from acting more forcefully to defend against Communist expansion, and it demoralized the West. "If we simply 'assume' the Soviets to have everything they claim, we are yielding them the object of the deterrence game at the outset." The dynamic of the Cold War at this time, he thought, "more closely resembles a clinch in a prize fight, in which a boxer adept at infighting punishes an opponent who can hit with nothing but a long punch from the outside."

This theme is found repeatedly in his work during the Eisenhower-Kennedy years. "The image of Soviet power has many uses," he wrote after Kennedy took office. "For the Communists, it is a handy way of intimidating the West, impressing the wobbly sovereigns of Asia and Africa, and building internal morale. For American liberals, it is a powerful argument for appeasement, federal spending to 'catch up' with Moscow, and vast foreign aid projects to purchase the affections of the 'uncommitted.'"[6] (Needless to say, foreign aid was another frequent target of the *Indianapolis News* editorial page.) Above all, Evans pounded away at the failure to perceive that actual Soviet advances depended on Western trade and aid (when it didn't involve outright theft and espionage) and thus the folly of continuing to think the Soviet Union would "mellow" through expanded economic ties with the West. Over the next two decades, Evans took frequent aim at technology transfers and other vital economic assistance to the Soviet bloc that he thought were propping up our enemy. It was a view that was embraced and vindicated two decades later under President Reagan.

Evans discerned the germ of the liberal strategic vision that unfolded rapidly in the 1960s, in which the doctrine of mutual assured destruction (MAD) led to the acceptance of "coexistence" with the Soviet Union and the wishful thinking of "convergence" between East and West. The folly of arms control, based on the premise that our fundamental differences could be bridged by reducing them to technical differences that could be neatly split through diplomacy, followed closely behind. Only someone who took seriously the ideological dimension of the Cold War, recognizing that the ideological competition was more important than the competition in armaments, could perceive how disinformation served to reinforce the false assumption that the Cold War was a stalemate. The inverted presumptions of Western grand strategy ceded the initiative to the Communists. "By granting every claim that Moscow makes," Evans wrote in another column on the topic, "by 'assuming' something we do not know in fact, we are playing into the Kremlin's hands. The Soviets are conducting a successful campaign to terrorize the globe, and our own officials are helping construct the image of power with which they do it." In another column taking dead aim at Kennedy at the climax of the 1960 campaign, he wrote: "The argument about Soviet growth is an intellectual farce. Yet it is Senator Kennedy's principal claim to 'greatness,' and the chief issue on which he has staked his campaign...It uses the resulting confusion as a pretext for statism."[7]

Thus Evans perceived that, as he put it in a 1961 column, "The principal danger of the United States today is not Communism, but a strange amalgamation of confusions known as the 'liberal' mind...I say it because the record demonstrates that Communism, in and of itself, is not powerful. Under its own steam, it has made very little headway anywhere in the world. But it has made vast strides where it has confronted 'liberalism' as its adversary, or when 'liberalism' managed to give it a helping hand."[8] Liberalism, in other words, was a creed of self-defeatism.

A perfect example of the kind of defeatism he had in mind was a previous favorite target: Kennan.

A sample result of the current crusade for "safety": Former Ambassador George Kennan allows that, if somebody were to ask him whether our bumbling, inefficient country "has, over the long run, good chances of competing with a purposeful, serious, and disciplined society such as that of the Soviet Union, I must say the answer is 'no.'"[9]

It was not at all surprising then to see Evans resisting John F. Kennedy's famous claim about a "missile gap" between the U.S. and the Soviet Union in 1960. The conventional account that persists right up to the present day is that Kennedy was trying to burnish his credentials as a tough-on-Communism Cold Warrior by running to the right of Nixon on national defense. Although it remains useful to point to this disposition of JFK's as a benchmark against which to compare the succeeding generation of liberal Democrats like George McGovern who drifted back to the Henry Wallace view of the Soviet Union, Evans understood that this kind of fabrication played into the Soviets' hands. As early as July 1960, as the presidential campaign was just heating up, Evans argued in his column that the "missile gap" claim was "one of Russia's greatest propaganda weapons," which made it *less* likely that a Democratic administration would contest the Soviet Union vigorously. An unsigned editorial the same day, which Evans likely wrote, argued that "there is little if any evidence that Soviet performance is even remotely comparable to our own."[10] Evans thought neither party understood the problem seriously enough. The editorial page returned to the issue frequently after Kennedy's election, with Evans supplementing his own writing and house editorials (such as "The Missing 'Gap'") with columns and features from Ralph de Toledano ("The 'Missile Gap' Looks More Like a Kennedy Gap"—February 1, 1961), David Lawrence ("Shabby Politics Behind Missile Gap Myth"—December 8, 1961), and Fulton Lewis Jr. ("That Political Scarecrow, the 'Missile Gap'"—February 23, 1962).

Evans's unique perception of the consequential error of overstating Soviet power can be seen as a pregame warmup for his later extreme distaste for and direct clashes with Henry Kissinger and the defeatist détente of the 1970s. (See Chapter 8.) At the time, however, Evans approved of Kissinger, citing him in support of his skeptical thesis in a 1961 column "How We Have 'Assumed' Moscow Into Space Lead." Calling Kissinger "one of America's most sophisticated military strategists," Evans noted Kissinger's most recent book arguing that the Soviets were succeeding in frightening other nations into aligning with or appeasing them: "'If a victim of Soviet pressure comes to believe—rightly or wrongly—that the aggressor is militarily superior to the United States,' Kissinger points out, 'it will seek an accommodation regardless of our resolve to resist.'"[11] (A separate column responded favorably to a report that President Kennedy was reading Kissinger's book, *The Necessity for Choice*.[12])

The influence of his father, Medford, can be seen in Stan's skepticism about Soviet capacities as expressed in Medford's 1953 book, *The Secret History of the A-Bomb*, along with his parallel disdain for near-universally acclaimed establishment "experts" like Kennan, though there was also some distance between Stan's outlook and Medford's. Around the time Stan Evans arrived at the *Indianapolis News*, his father became embroiled in a political controversy that surely reinforced Stan's perceptions of establishment groupthink.

In the fall of 1958, former President Herbert Hoover asked William F. Buckley Jr. for recommendations for new trustees for the Hoover Institution at Stanford, and Buckley suggested Medford Evans, who was just completing his fourth year of teaching at Northeast Louisiana State College. The prospective appointment ended up involving the FBI at the very highest levels. A January 1959 memo by FBI director J. Edgar Hoover details his conversation with former Atomic Energy Commission chairman Lewis L. Strauss, then serving as the acting secretary of commerce in the Eisenhower administration and for whom Medford Evans had worked at the AEC. J. Edgar Hoover's memo recorded:

Strauss stated that Evans over the years has been a defender of Strauss whenever the Oppenheimer issue arose and has written several articles for "Human Events" and "National Review." It appears that Mr. [Herbert] Hoover mentioned Evans to Strauss and asked for his opinion and Strauss stated that he had not seen Evans for a long time but he thought Evans was all right. Mr. Strauss stated he then got in touch with Evans and had him come to New York and meet Mr. Hoover and Hoover evidently was favorably impressed and intended to recommend Evans.

Indeed Medford Evans had written at length about the Oppenheimer controversy and defended Strauss from his critics. In March 1957 Medford wrote an eleven-page feature article in *National Review*, complete with footnotes: "An Open Letter to Dr. Oppenheimer." Medford started that, despite the circumstantial and direct evidence of his Communist ties, he believed Oppenheimer was a patriotic American but asked that he offer a more complete explanation of why he had opposed the development of the hydrogen bomb and what he knew about clandestine espionage in America's nuclear weapons program. "Nobody," Medford wrote, "who knows anything about your case, Doctor—nobody I know—doubts that if you really did break and tell all you know, the whole picture of the national defense and security of the United States would light up like a used-car lot. If you are patriotic and humanitarian, why don't you turn on the lights."[13] Oppenheimer did not respond to the invitation.

A year later, in May 1958, Medford took up the cudgels on behalf of Strauss, who was under attack from the left for his role in stripping Oppenheimer of his security clearance. In "Will They Get Strauss?", Medford went through a detailed chronology of Strauss's good deeds as head of the AEC against opponents of the H-bomb, including Oppenheimer. "If Strauss had not taken his stand in the AEC in 1949, the United States would not have hydrogen weapons today," Medford wrote. "It is fair to say that without him the present defenses of this country would not exist."[14]

But Medford's appointment to the Hoover board never happened. J. Edgar Hoover's memo goes on to hint at the reason why it was scuttled:

> According to Mr. Strauss, Evans told him that after making a speech in Boston some months ago in which he stated the plain facts regarding Oppenheimer it got back to the campus and Evans was informed that his tenure there was over and at the end of the term in June he should look for another job. Mr. Strauss stated that Evans had asked for the reason for this action but was not advised. Mr. Strauss stated that Mr. Hoover would not want to settle for a man with some blemish and wanted to learn the reason for this action. Mr. Strauss thought this could be viewed as an investigation of a consultant for him and he would appreciate one of our agents calling on the Dean and finding out why Evans' term at the University had come to an end.

That the FBI would involve itself in such a matter is only possible because of the prominence of Strauss at the time. It appears that Strauss, and subsequently Herbert Hoover, got cold feet about Evans because of his growing links with the John Birch Society, which by the late 1950s was fast becoming the bogeyman of the liberal establishment.

A closer look at the whole scene supports the conclusion that Medford was a victim of the growing anti-McCarthy hysteria and the timidity of the administration of Northeast Louisiana State as well as the FBI. In the fall of 1957, Evans had applied for nine weeks paid leave from the college to travel to Washington to work on a chapter on espionage for a book project of the House Un-American Activities Committee entitled *Facts on Communism*. Despite some controversy on the academic council that Evans had not been at the college long enough to merit a paid leave, the request was granted in early March 1958. Such requests typically carry the obligation that the faculty member return to teaching for at least one year after a leave, so it came as a shock when, in late April, the college notified Evans that it was not renewing his contract for the following academic year. The college cited declining enrollment in Evans's courses (which he easily refuted) along with "changing needs" of the curriculum, a vague charge that was weak as applied to Evans in any case. As he put it in his affidavit challenging the college's stated reasons, "The case against me at this point begins to assume an air of the preposterous." His appeals to the college proved unavailing, and the real reasons for his dismissal appear to have been both budgetary and political. "I confess to having been controversial," Evans noted in his affidavit.

Judging by the FBI documents that are available from a FOIA search, it appears the New Orleans field office performed a brief and cursory investigation that involved interviewing a handful of individuals who were offended by Medford's supposed "extremism." One witness told the FBI that she suspected Medford was actually a deep cover Communist agent infiltrating the ranks of anti-Communists, an indicator of the Keystone Cops–level cluelessness of the FBI inquiry. Investigators also reviewed some news clips and the forty-page affidavit that Medford had supplied to Northeast Louisiana State College in protest of his dismissal. There was no firm conclusion to this "investigation" because there was no alleged federal crime involved, nor was this a case of a prospective federal appointment that would involve a standard background check. But the John Birch Society soon entered the fray, with the Society's flamboyant president Robert Welch charging that Evans had been fired because of his anti-Communism. Welch launched, with much fanfare, a Committee to Protest the Firing of Medford Evans. It is likely that Lewis Strauss, who reviewed the FBI findings, got cold feet about Evans's prospective appointment to the Hoover board on account of the Birch Society's hostility to President Eisenhower. The bitter irony is obvious: Strauss had played a key role in the decision to revoke J. Robert Oppenheimer's security clearance in 1954 on account of Oppenheimer's earlier association with the Communist Party. One of Medford's appearances that seems to have heightened controversy at Northeast Louisiana State was his appearance at a Harvard debate in the spring of 1958 in defense of the Oppenheimer security clearance decision. (His teammate for this debate was Willmoore Kendall. Harvard's administration attempted to scuttle the debate, but the hosting student group, the Harvard Conservative Club, persevered.) While the dominant narrative then and now was that McCarthyism was a threat to academic freedom and the careers of liberal professors, the case of Medford Evans shows that the opposite was closer to the truth.

Following this unfortunate turn, after which Medford never found academic employment again, he began writing regularly for *American Opinion* and other John Birch Society publications while continuing as a contributing editor to *National Review*. Medford resigned from *National Review* in 1962 in protest of Buckley's famous attack on the Birch Society. Stan, however, remained on the masthead. Buckley kept his distance from Medford ever after, mentioning him once in a 1976 letter: "Medford Evans is of course a fine man and a scholar, but he is nuts."[15]

Stan Evans seldom spoke or wrote of his father's political controversies, though they remained personally close, with the *Indianapolis News* once noting on the Society page that "Dr. and

Mrs. Medford B. Evans are here from Jackson, Miss., for a Thanksgiving reunion with their son." The *News* editorial page walked a careful line on the Birch Society. Stan's bylined column seldom waded into Birch Society controversies, but several unsigned editorials, some likely written by Stan, did.[16] One unsigned lead editorial in 1961 distanced itself from some of Robert Welch's more outlandish statements—especially his accusation that President Eisenhower was a Communist agent ("the quotations from Welch concerning President Eisenhower cannot be deplored too vehemently")—but defended the Society on its core belief that internal Communist subversion was a serious issue as well as defending the Society from the left's more sweeping charges. "There is, in short, nothing in the literature or program of the John Birch Society to justify the charge of 'Fascist.' . . . We are therefore puzzled by the outcry of those who, while allowing every 'right' in the book to admitted Communists, are so eager to destroy this organization."[17] The editorial page also ran many letters both in support and critical of the Society, while its straight news pages prominently covered Birch Society statements and events both nationally and in Indiana. ("John Birch Society Stirs Controversy" ran a front page news headline in March 1961.)

National security and the Cold War weren't the only domains where Evans's contrarian streak manifested itself in those early days at the *Indianapolis News*. Environmentalism is another example of Evans anticipating the shape of leftist issues far in advance—along with their refutation. More than a decade before Paul Ehrlich's *The Population Bomb* and the first Earth Day propelled the environmental movement into national consciousness, Evans was onto the defects of Malthusian ideology at its core. In "Malthus Rides Again," appearing in *National Review* in 1960, Evans took dead aim at an obscure book (*People!* by William Vogt, a director of Planned Parenthood) making the Malthusian

case for population control. More than two decades before Julian
Simon demolished the neo-Malthusianism of contemporary
environmentalism, Evans had their number. Evans wasn't sure
which was the worse defect of the argument: the resource and
economic claims or the moral claims.

> What Malthus left out of his equation was the impact of technol-
> ogy. Increased use of tools and scientific principle has enabled
> men to produce more goods with less effort, and has allowed
> production to move far ahead of the growth of population…As
> economic understanding has of late declined, the Malthusian
> specter has risen from the grave and once more stalks among us.

But unlike Simon and other critics who later made devastating empirical critiques of neo-Malthusianism, Evans understood
that the moral claims of the environmental movement were more
insidious, in part because they depend on attacking traditional
religion, especially Christianity. Here again Evans anticipates
years in advance Lynn White's infamous argument in *Science*
magazine in 1967 that Biblical religion is responsible for mankind's
supposed degradation of the planet. Vogt confined his criticism
to pro-natalist Christian (and especially Roman Catholic) views,
but Evans was having none of it.

> I admit to some surprise that a man can dismiss the ethical heritage
> of Christianity as superstition, yet become gravely concerned about
> the moral aspect of fintailed automobiles…If one has received the
> moral precepts of the West, he will not be corrupted by General
> Motors or BBD&O. If he is particularly resolute in his convictions,
> he will not even be corrupted by Mr. Vogt.[18]

Evans also caught early what has become a prominent feature
of liberal politicians who happen to be Catholic. In a January 1960

column, Evans noted the "poetic justice" of the contradictions of Sen. John F. Kennedy shortly before he announced his presidential candidacy, "whose Catholic faith rejects artificial methods of birth control" yet who supported foreign aid for birth control in developing nations because of the "population explosion." Beyond anticipating the two-step of liberal Catholics following *Roe v. Wade* more than a decade in the future, he also noted the increasing liberal fixation with distant problems whose dimensions always require the expansion of government power now: "Loud concern about this future menace comes somewhat strangely from people who view present dangers—for example, the Communist takeover of Cuba—without notable alarm. But there is always a natural human tendency to avoid the stress of the real and the immediate by conjuring up 'problems' considerably more distant."[19] Evans returned to this subject repeatedly over the next several years with several columns attacking the "clichés" of the "population bomb," taking the recurrence of this popular theme as a reason to repeat his patient tutorials about the inherent defects of Malthusianism.[20] As we shall see, he was well-equipped to debunk the shibboleths of environmentalism and especially the "energy crisis" when they rocketed to prominence in the 1970s.

Evans balanced his reportage and commentary on national and ideological issues with equal attention to local Indiana politics. His "Skeptic's Corner" column took aim at local labor union activity, the defects of Indiana's unemployment insurance system, local public school issues, and how Indiana's congressional delegation voted on key issues. He was a friend, fan, and booster of Donald Bruce, who served two terms in the U.S. House of Representatives from 1961–1965 before becoming the first chairman of the brand-new American Conservative Union. Stan appeared with Bruce at a 1961 rally in support of Rep. Bruce's House resolution calling upon President Kennedy to produce a public strategy for the defeat of Communism (popularly known as the "Victory over Communism" resolution). More than once *News* editorials ("Bruce Is Right," for example, "congratulates Bruce for his courageous vote") or Stan's column took up the cudgels defending Bruce against "liberal Democrats loading their mudguns for Don Bruce."[21]

There were two basic criteria for gaining Evans's journalistic seal of approval: opposition to increased taxes and spending, and opposing Communism directly and without equivocation. Being a Republican didn't cut much ice for him, and he didn't hesitate to praise Democrats who he thought were sound on foreign policy. Conversely, there were many Indiana Republican grandees who never impressed him, like William Ruckelshaus, Otis Bowen, and especially a rising young local politician named Richard Lugar. In later years, Evans liked to say, "You can always count on Dick Lugar's vote, except when it really counts." "Marion County GOP Tilts Left" was a typical Evans column headline (in this case, from 1969) bemoaning weak Republican legislators who publicly abandoned Governor Edgar Whitcomb's attempts to constrain state spending. (More on Evans and Whitcomb in due course.) In conversation Evans often referred to conventional Indiana Republicans as "the Machine," and he unsurprisingly supported insurgent conservatives in primary election contests.

Other columns about federal regulation often included a local angle, such as how railroad regulation needlessly increased costs for Indiana. As he explained later, typically deflecting credit for himself:

> The papers themselves—based in the state capital, the biggest city in the state, two newspapers in this city, so [Pulliam] had enormous influence on what happened in the state of Indiana. It was an education to be part of that activity. And on occasion it would have some impact on what happened. Like taxes—we were

always fighting against tax increases in the state legislature. That issue never went away. We were staunch against that.

Upon becoming editor of the *News* in the spring of 1960, he changed the name of his column from "Skeptic's Corner" to "The Editor's Corner." He was fast becoming a reader favorite. From time to time, the paper ran fan mail in the letters to the editor section. "In Stan Evans you have a truly conservative constitutionalist," said one letter under the heading "Turn Him Loose." Another read, "This man of yours—Stan Evans—is on the ball. Please, let us have more copy by him."[22] The letters section didn't run only fan mail; it also ran critical letters, which likely made Evans smile. One letter complained of Evans's "xenophobia," while another indignant critic called Evans "an illiterate, ignorant halfwit...Is there any doubt in the world that conservatives like Goldwater and Evans had their counterparts in ancient times bemoaning the breakup of the feudal system or the passing of bleeding with leeches?" Another letter attacked Evans for his "irresponsible...defense of a Fascist totalitarian state" whose "malicious propaganda" should be banned from the pages of the paper. Moreover, the writer concluded, there should be "democratic controls over newspapers." Evans didn't let this pass, attaching an editor's note that the paper's critics were demanding "a slave-state press."[23] Some letters were directed at unsigned editorials that Evans likely wrote, such as the reader who complained that the paper's anti-Communism was "a bore." This particular letter also drew an editorial response: "Editor's note: *The News* believes that there should be more, not fewer, efforts to awaken the American people to the perils of Communist propaganda and infiltration."[24] On another occasion he was pleased to quote in his own column an attack on him from the Communist *Daily Worker* newspaper: "The truth is Evans and his ilk are not conservative at all. He does not wish to 'conserve' American democracy, to the contrary, he wishes to destroy our democratic and social gains."[25]

In between mixing his interest in national and international politics along with his granular coverage of state and local politics, Evans also displayed his extraordinary range and intellectual depth by exposing his readers to the best conservative thinkers of the time expressed in columns reporting the views of Ernest van den Hagg, Edward Banfield, Hugh Kenner, Thomas Molnar, Milton Friedman, P. T. Bauer, and Russell Kirk, among others. Drawing on his undergraduate studies in literature, he wrote a fine obituary to T. S. Eliot at the time of Eliot's passing. While noting the "obscurity" of "The Waste Land" through its "leaps in sequence and learned symbolism," Evans notes that once Eliot's broader critical philosophy—and especially religious faith—are understood, he emerges as "the apostle not of obscurity, but of clarity—of bold economy in language, of meaning so condensed that every line bristles with multiple significance."[26]

On another occasion, Evans found himself seated on an airplane next to actress Debbie Reynolds on her way to a performance in Indianapolis, so naturally he interviewed her on the record for a column. It turns out the mother of Princess Leia was a conservative. "It's much more political than many people realize," Evans quotes Reynolds. "The Communists said they would destroy us from within and never have to go to war to bring about our destruction. They've had years to infiltrate and they're doing what they said. As far as I am concerned we ought to bundle them up and send them to Russia." Good advice, but merely a warmup for what might regain currency in our "defund the police" moment:

> "Living in a day and age when we call the police 'pigs' I think we're
> sick. If I saw my kids do that I'd take a baseball bat and hit them

over the head." At this point she paused and turned to her son, Todd, who was kibitzing the interview. "And you know I would, too," she asserted. Todd allowed as how she would indeed.[27]

Reynolds wasn't the only A-list Hollywood celebrity with whom he had a close encounter. In 1966, he appeared on a TV talk show in Chicago while promoting *The Politics of Surrender*, where one of the fellow guests was Michael Caine. Evans explained the strategic doctrine of mutual assured destruction (MAD) that deliberately left the American population undefended against nuclear attack. The idea was still sufficiently new at the time that it provoked "civil incredulity" among the other panelists, though Caine remained silent. "They suggested I had been smoking funny cigarettes. All too obviously, the United States could not have such a policy. The matter was dropped and discussion moved on to *Alfie*."[28]

Very rarely did his column hint at his wicked wit. But one early column lifted the veil: "How To Deal with Political Bores" took the familiar setting of being cornered at a cocktail party with someone equipped with tiresome 1950s liberal clichés, such as "too many people are watching television, too many people have cars with fins on them," and so forth. (It is largely forgotten today how many liberals in the late 1950s were obsessed with tail fins on American sedans; they seemed to be a secular substitute for the horns of Satan—or perhaps as symbols of Satanic capitalism.) Evans called his antidote the Bore Baffler, "a hellish instrument guaranteed to hold even the most insistent bore in check, befuddled into refreshing silence."

It works as follows: When you have been harangued into a coma on the subject, "Society's Responsibility for Juvenile Crime," rouse yourself, turn on your tormenter, and say: "You know Phil"—this is the more disconcerting if the adversary's name is not actually Phil—"You know, Phil, the way I size it up is this: There is no such thing as a delinquent parent. THERE ARE ONLY DELINQUENT CHILDREN." (The gaze must be level, and the tone one of belligerent sincerity.) The Bore Baffler is guaranteed to put you down in Phil's book as Unconcerned, but it should produce a quick change of subject.

He rolled out for perhaps the only time in print what may have been his most famous jest. When subjected to "a long eye-glazing monologue on 'McCarthyism and McCarthy's Methods,'" you cut short with your Baffler with, "Personally, Phil, I didn't like what McCarthy was trying to do, BUT I DID LIKE HIS METHODS." And if the liberal bore should retreat to the "looming catastrophe" of quoting Voltaire's famous cliché about defending disagreeable ideas, Evans recommended responding with: "Phil, I disagree with what you have so say—so shut up." "You will settle your problem for good and all; you will no longer be invited to cock-tail parties."[29]

For all of his sophistication and depth, Evans never shed his association with the views of "the farmer from Seymour" he described to *Time* magazine. One of his most legendary stories from his Indiana years dealt with the confusion of a Republican state legislator about the National Endowment for the Humanities, which was brand-new in the early 1970s. This legislator, whom Evans supported in his "insurgent" bid against the Republican "machine" in the 1972 election cycle but whom he admitted was "not very well versed in the issues," called up one evening to ask Evans about the "National Endowment for the Human Itties." In his telling of the story, Evans referred to the legislator a "Vernon Wormer," the fictional name of the dean of Faber College in *Animal House*. One night he called up and said, "It's 'Vernon Wormer.'" (The actual person was State Rep. Byron K. Fowler [d. 2006], a former tool and die maker.) He said "Stan—have you ever heard of something called the 'National Endowment for the Human Itties'?" Initially confused, Evans finally realized he meant "huMANities"—one word, with the proper emphasis on the second syllable, with a short-a.

Stan: "You mean hu*man*ities?"

'Wormer': "Yeah, whatever. They're trying to bring it into Indiana University, and other universities. I don't like the sound of it."

"I said, 'I don't either. Federal money—we don't need it. Get it out of here.'"

"I'm going to find out about it, because Thursday there's a budget hearing."

"Okay 'Vernon,' good luck. But remember—hu*MAN*ities."

The next Sunday, Evans opened up his morning *Indianapolis Star* and turned to the "Behind Closed Doors" column that reported on gossip and internal machinations of state politics, where he found a short item headlined, "What's This 'Human-Itties'?"

> Fowler was soon back to Ryan [IU President John W. Ryan], wondering whether IU was 'in the hotel business' through the purchase of the Poplars Hotel. Fowler got a few titters later when he asked Ryan whether he knew what the 'human-itties" was.
>
> It turned out to be the 'humanities," a reference by Fowler to literature mailed from IU's Owens hall that Fowler said attempted to get 'anybody to think of ways to spend money.' Ryan said he figured Fowler was talking about the state chapter of the National Endowment for the Humanities.[30]

Of course Evans wasn't content to let the matter be understood in conventional terms. As he embellished from memory:

The presidents of all four state universities were stunned Thursday morning from an onslaught by State Representative 'Vernon Wormer,' demanding to know, 'What's this here human-*itties*?'

I'm sitting here just thinking of this scene, with the presidents of all four state universities, in front of the budget committee—this guy is sitting on the committee and holds the power of life and death over their budgets. And they're trembling beneath the steely gaze of State Representative 'Vernon Wormer.'

And I thought to myself—'*YES!* This is America, man! Get used to it.'[31]

Despite his growing profile as a premier journalist, Evans's career was about to take on an additional dimension. About a year after his arrival at the *Indianapolis News*, he was thrust to the center of one of the key turning points in the forward march of the modern conservative movement.

CHAPTER 4

FROM JOURNALIST TO ACTIVIST

"So it happened that, in its hour of triumph, Liberalism felt the earth begin to shift beneath its feet...Liberalism will not do because it is a bore."

—MSE, REVOLT ON THE CAMPUS

Evans was already, in his first year at the *News*, gaining a wider reputation beyond the Indianapolis metro area. In 1959 he joined the masthead of *National Review* as a contributing editor alongside his father and began contributing long-form book reviews and feature articles more frequently. As noted in the previous chapter, *Time* magazine took note of his appointment as editor of the *News* in the fall of 1960. Earlier in the year, *Wall Street Journal* editorial page editor Vermont Royster tried to hire Evans away from the *Indianapolis News*, even going so far as to ask for Leonard Read's help. (Whether the *Journal*'s interest in hiring Evans played a part in Pulliam's decision to name him editor in chief of the paper is unknown, but it is reasonable to suspect it.)

By degrees Evans was branching out beyond journalism. Local civic groups weren't Evans's only or even primary venue for his speaking activity. As Evans became better known and in higher demand in the 1960s, he began to require honoraria for campus appearances, but he had a policy of always speaking for free at any college in Indiana, and it was not unusual for him to donate his honoraria to a sponsoring student group, provided it was a conservative group.

Many of his campus appearances were at the behest of ISI. As previously mentioned, moving to Indianapolis reunited him with Don Lipsett, his roommate in New York during his time with *The Freeman* four years earlier. Lipsett made heavy use of Evans in his project to build out ISI student chapters on campus. Evans recalled his close collaboration with Lipsett in 2002:

> We spent many an hour operating from Indiana, as guerillas on the campus. There was no money, no budget, no nothing, and he was in contact with students at Ohio State or Dennison or anywhere, IU, Purdue, Michigan State, and they would say, 'We need a speaker—we need to get a conservative speaker. And he would sign me up as the speaker. He'd come by in a great big old car—I don't even remember what it was—at the end of the workday and pick me up at the front door of the paper and we'd drive to Columbus. I would give a talk, and after the talk was over the more conservative kids would come up and he would sign them up to be members of ISI. And we did that a lot. I can't remember how many times. That's what he did."

"Lipsett was a born organizer," Evans said. "He was totally dedicated to organizing things, and getting people together. He never stopped organizing meetings." Evans recalled one meeting Lipsett prodded him into arranging and hosting in 1959 in Nashville, Indiana, whose principal participants were Milton Friedman, Frank Meyer, and Richard Weaver, on the subject "Conservative or Libertarian—Which Are We?" (Weaver's paper presented at that meeting, "Conservatism and Libertarianism: The Common Ground," likely had a strong influence on Evans or at least can be seen as a strong reinforcement of his already developing fusionist views.[1]) That particular meeting was financed by Indiana businessman Pierre Goodrich and was a precursor to the colloquium format of the organization Goodrich later founded and endowed, the Liberty Fund.

As Evans visited more campuses and met with conservative students, a theme took shape in his mind that led to his first book, *Revolt on the Campus*. Published in 1961, on the surface its headline prediction that the then-rising generation of students would tilt to the right in the coming years seems mistaken. The dominant narrative of the 1960s presents the student New Left as the most significant and consequential youth activist movement, and certainly there is much to be said for the standard account. The antiwar segment of the New Left toppled a sitting president and transformed the Democratic Party. But very few historians have taken note of conservative youth politics of the time, although it was arguably just as significant in the long run as the New Left.[2] But like Evans's subtle contrarianism on the Cold War, it pays to look closer at the details of his argument as it may suggest some parallels with our current moment as well as show the depth of Evans's mind.

In later years Evans regarded his first book with fondness, and deservedly so. It is misleading to regard the book as merely a journalistic prediction of how young people would trend in the short run, for the book is much more profound. It is possible to see the core of Evans's comprehensive critique of modern thought and the germ of his synthesis of liberty and free government that eventually finds its complete development in *The Theme Is Freedom* (1995—see Chapter 13. In fact, *Revolt on the Campus* could almost be updated for our present moment with only the names changed and the central arguments updated to reflect the rhetorical form of today's liberal clichés, which differ only in degree but not in kind from the arguments Evans confronted sixty years ago.

In his opening survey of the intellectual scene of the late 1950s, Evans deftly turned on its head the liberal theme prominent at the time that Americans were "conformist." "If we may believe what we read," Evans began, "the United States today is a nation oppressed by conformity." He offers a compact survey of the main parts of the liberal argument about conformity then given prominence by the leading thinkers of establishment liberalism at the time, including David Reisman, Lionel Trilling, Jacques Barzun, William H. Whyte, Vance Packard, and John Kenneth Galbraith. Evans held some of these thinkers in high regard (especially Reisman, Trilling, and Barzun) as having "complex sensitivity and discriminating minds" faithfully committed to "the canons of excellence, and of freedom," unlike many leading liberal thinkers today. Far from attacking these liberal legends, Evans was indignant that no one in the "mainstream" intellectual or literary firmament would acknowledge that thinkers like Chodorov and Nock had made the same arguments more than a decade before: "Neither Nock nor Chodorov could receive the time of day from important publishers or major journals of opinion."

Evans caught sight of the changing nature and direction of liberalism that has only grown more pronounced and radical over time: a commitment to maximal individual autonomy liberated from any moral traditions combined with aggressive statism in government policy. This two-pronged liberal argument prominent in the late 1950s involved a paradoxical construction of individualism. On the one hand, fifties liberalism deplored "rugged individualism" (the most capitalist kind), which they thought was not actually individualistic since too many American "individuals" aligned with "groups" (especially their big business employers, e.g. Reisman's "other-directed man" or Whyte's "organization man") and derived their "belongingness" from conformity to groups or groupthink. Individualism had been transplanted into this potted soil because it was increasingly cut off from its natural roots in religion and traditional morality.

The most prominent formulation of the time was Reisman's concept of the "other-directed" man, who took his cues from larger social forces. Evans offered this succinct critique:

> As prescribed by Reisman, it is generally associated with a loss of inner conviction; other-directed people are tolerant because they have no firm opinions about anything. That mood of ethical indifference has been fostered by a number of influences in American thought, and has been variously urged under the rubric of nominalism, positivism, pragmatism. The generic term for such attitudes is 'relativist.' Their common characteristic is the rejection of general propositions which are morally binding.[3]

Although the problem of dogmatic moral relativism was not unknown at the time, Evans was early in connecting it to the larger philosophical trends of the early twentieth century, anticipating the much more detailed treatment of the problem twenty-five years later by Allan Bloom. (Elsewhere in *Revolt on the Campus*, Evans quotes C. S. Lewis's *The Abolition of Man*, which was somewhat unfamiliar to American readers at the time and was another sign of Evans's capacious reading habits.) There is something else hinted at in his observations. Nothing is more evident today than the limits of leftist relativism. There is no relativism when it comes to the categorical moral wrongness of racism, sexism, or colonialism, for example. There is also no hesitation in categorically denouncing conservatives or excluding conservatives and conservative ideas from the prevailing understanding of "diversity." But these limited moral convictions are not based on anything. A relativist who comes in contact with someone with grounded convictions sees such a person as a direct threat, hence the strident reaction against conservatives, the people most likely to exhibit grounded convictions.

The consequential logic of this drift in liberal thought didn't begin to manifest itself more clearly until the middle of the 1960s. The more specific problem for political liberals of the time when Evans wrote was that the oxymoronic "conformist individualism" amounted to a "privatism" that made it harder for "society" (whatever that is) to organize itself deliberately for the "common good" or some other "national purpose." (It is mostly lost to memory now that the Eisenhower administration set in motion a Commission on National Goals, whose mission was to find common projects for the nation to pursue together.) On the other hand, early cultural liberalism—the dominant kind today—celebrated creative individuality, which means in practice the deliberate rejection of traditional social and moral traditions. But the ill effects of this kind of liberalism wouldn't become clear for another decade or so. At the moment, the liberal political project was effective in delegitimizing private-oriented individualism, as Evans explained in this compact summary:

> That we are at once *permissive* in matters of ethics, *statist* in matters of public policy; that we have become the second because we became the first; and that the two feed upon one another in baleful symbiosis.

In other words, although Evans didn't stress the point too directly in *Revolt*, he understood that rootless individualism could not find an adequate anchor in purely secular and non-transcendental values of social structures. (He saved the full development of this point for later books.) Hence modern individualism *weakened* the individual, thus paving the way for the advance of "collectivist" (a favored term then for "statist" or "socialist") government. In other words, liberals attacked individualism as an obstacle to their desired statist ideals while understanding that the defects of modern individualism would increase the acceptance of statism. Because "socialism" was a dirty word in American politics in the late 1950s, redistributionist philosophy went by a number of euphemisms, such as "the common good" or "national purpose." In the hands of writers like Galbraith, "common good" was the cover phrase for the socialist halfway house of Keynesianism.

But reformist liberals are always in a hurry, and in the late 1960s, on the cusp of John F. Kennedy's campaign of self-conscious generational change, liberal leaders thought the youth of America should rebel against the faux-individualist conformity of the time. Who else but youth could "get the country moving again"? They could do this by joining noble causes that just happened to coincide with the liberal agenda: nuclear disarmament, abolishing the House Committee on Un-American Activities (to remove the lingering stain of McCarthyism), campaigning for civil rights, and supporting neo-socialist economics.

Then as now, there was nowhere this liberal litany ran more loudly than on college campuses, which meant, as Evans pointed out, that liberal opinion represented the real conformity of the time. It was hardly rebellious to sign a petition for nuclear disarmament or to end segregation. "By some law of political oscillation," Evans wrote, "young people tend to rebel against the going order—or at least the more aggressive and resourceful young people do... [Students] are enacting the time-honored rites of youth, kicking up their heels against the reigning conformity. As *Life* observed, they are fed up with the 'dull orthodox Liberalism of the academic scene.'"

Evans observed that "the most depressing part of being a conservative student is the feeling, artfully enforced by the opposition, that one is so terribly alone." That had been his feeling starting out at Yale a decade before. But now nearly every campus Evans visited showed signs of conservative vigor and organizational effort. Campus efforts like ISI helped end the isolation of conservative college students, but Evans provided a long inventory of student leaders, publications, clubs, and political activism. Conservative speakers were starting to draw large audiences. Buckley was already drawing hundreds to his campus visits, long before he became a regular presence on television. With encouragement from Evans, ISI conducted a student survey, whose results Evans explored in detail in *Revolt*. (Evans offered a quote from a conservative law student at the University of Kansas that one can easily imagine a student today voicing about our acronymical world of "diversity and inclusion": "All of the alphabetical asininity which appealed so much to our parents is being recognized by fresh young minds for the hodge-podge of illogic and fallacy which it has always been.")[4]

Thus, liberals and the media were stunned in 1959 and 1960 to discover polls reporting that college students favored Nixon over Kennedy by as much as a two-to-one margin. It is also confusing to a degree, as it occurred at a time of turmoil in the Republican Party between critics of Eisenhower's plain oatmeal Republicanism who desired the GOP to be more forcefully conservative while at the same time fearing Nelson Rockefeller's drive to pull the GOP toward an affirmative embrace of the welfare state. Vice President Nixon, whose anti-Communist bona fides at least were in good shape, looked like a safe halfway house. But a lot of young conservatives, even if willing to vote for Nixon against JFK, were having none of it.

It is not recalled much today that the populist movement behind Barry Goldwater's ascent in the late 1950s that culminated in his nomination in 1964 was primarily a youth movement anchored in campus activism. The surging enthusiasm for Goldwater began with some single-issue efforts that proved ideal for organizing activities. Two of Evans's proteges from his program for young journalists at *Human Events*, Douglas Caddy and David Franke, were instrumental in one of the more significant efforts, the quixotic-sounding National Student Committee for the Loyalty Oath. (With his typical modesty, Evans didn't mention that he'd been a mentor to Caddy and Franke.) From this single-issue endeavor, there came a great acceleration of organized conservative activism.

A high-profile cause célèbre in the late 1950s was abolishing "loyalty oaths" that were regarded as a relic of McCarthyite oppression. By then the campaign to expunge the vestiges of the McCarthy era portrayed the loyalty oaths required for national security clearances, which had been reiterated in the National Defense Education Act passed in the height of the Sputnik panic. NDEA required that all students who accepted scholarships through the program would have to sign a loyalty oath. As would occur a decade later when many universities canceled their ROTC programs to protest the Vietnam War, several leading universities (Harvard, Yale, the other usual ones) declined to participate in the NDEA scholarship program in protest of the oath, and Sen. John F. Kennedy sponsored legislation in Congress to remove the oath. It passed the Senate in the spring of 1959 and was widely expected to pass the House. Evans blasted the Senate vote in his column as "a sound beating for the forces of anti-Communism, and a victory for the forces of softness and 'accommodation'... telling the world America's will to resist advances had been lowered another notch."[5]

Working primarily through ISI and College Republicans chapters in 1959, Caddy and Franke encouraged students to start chapters of the pro–loyalty oath committee on their campuses.

Within a few weeks, there were thirty campus chapters (including at Yale and Harvard) that Caddy and Franke could advertise at a formal press announcement. "It was not quite Man Bites Dog," Evans wrote, "but Student Bites Liberalism would do." Soon a stream of petitions, letters, and even visits from pro-oath students arrived on Capitol Hill. "It was a new experience for these legislators: voice of agitation being raised, by young people, on behalf of conservatism. They had never seen anything like it," Evans continued. Senator Kennedy's repeal bill died in a House committee.

What to do for a sequel after this taste of victory? The existing enthusiasm for Goldwater was an obvious rally point. The exact beginnings of Youth for Goldwater for Vice President are hard to pin down, but the formal effort emerged from debates and power struggles within several College Republicans and Young Republicans clubs in several states. Once again Evans had a front row seat as his proteges Caddy and Franke were in the thick of it. Pushing Goldwater for *vice president* was not just a concession to the reality that Nixon was certain to be the nominee; it was seen as a way of exerting pressure on Nixon, the GOP platform, and opposing Rockefeller—a trifecta. By May of 1960, the organization was up and running with student-based groups on sixty-four campuses in thirty-two states. Goldwater, however, was unenthusiastic about the idea, saying "One of the most effective ways to silence a man is to make him vice president." But the excitement around him on account of his sensationally successful book *Conscience of a Conservative*, published in March 1960, was unstoppable.

Evans attended the Republican National Convention in Chicago in late July, where Nixon had the votes but Goldwater had the spontaneous enthusiasm, especially from the young. Evans noted the media coverage of this and related his conversation with a taxi driver:

"You up here to cover the convention?"

"Yes," I said.

"Want to know who the people at this convention *really* want?"

"Who do they like?"

"This Goldwater guy," he said. "Everywhere you go, you see huge pictures of him—look, there's a couple over there."

The climax of the convention was the demonstration in the hall when Goldwater's name was placed in nomination for president. Swept away with enthusiasm and mindful that Goldwater didn't want to be the running mate, conservatives struck on the idea of nominating Goldwater for president instead. The idea actually attracted some delegate support such that the Nixon campaign organized a boisterous floor demonstration that lasted twenty minutes when his name was placed formally into nomination. Evans, on the convention floor, wondered if the Goldwater youth might lose heart for fear of embarrassment if their demonstration paled in comparison. But when Arizona Governor Paul Fannin placed Goldwater's name in nomination a few minutes later, "A great wave of sound exploded into the vaulted reaches of the stockyards. The demonstrators charged through the rear entrances. Delegates leapt to their feet."

Then Goldwater appeared and approached the dais, which sent the demonstration into a higher gear. He then followed with his withdrawal from consideration and his memorable charge "Let's grow up, conservatives" and take the party. Evans wrote that "The demonstration, by any standard, was a stunning success...And, as it put Goldwater on the map, the demonstration put young conservatism on the map."

Goldwater ended his speech with the charge "Let's get to work." He met with some of the leaders of Youth for Goldwater at the end of the convention, telling Doug Caddy that they should "turn your group into a permanent organization of young conservatives."[6] This was all the encouragement Caddy and his associates needed. How to follow up? Someone—no one now recalls but probably Marvin Liebman—suggested approaching William F. Buckley to see if he would host a planning meeting at his home in Sharon, Connecticut, and he readily agreed. (Liebman, a public relations executive and a friend of Buckley's, was at the Chicago convention along with Buckley.) An Interim Committee for a National Conservative Youth Organization was set up, bolstered by a $500 contribution from Charles Edison, chairman of the McGraw-Edison Electric Company, former Democratic governor of New Jersey, and son of Thomas Edison.

The subsequent meeting at Great Elm, Buckley's estate in Sharon, over the weekend of September 10–11 and attended by over ninety young conservatives succeeded in founding Young Americans for Freedom (YAF). The founding of YAF represented an important turn in the conservative movement, from ideas to political action. And although it clearly leaned toward the Republican Party, with one of its first internal debates concerning whether to endorse Nixon in the election (it ultimately decided against an endorsement), it was important that it had an independent identity.[7] Not endorsing Nixon, Evans thought, "was crucial, for it established the organization as authentically nonpartisan, and authentically dedicated to the advancement of conservatism, irrespective of party labels." (As we shall see in the following chapter, Evans had already acquired a distrust of Nixon before the Sharon conference.) YAF understood itself to be clearly distinct from the Young Republicans organizations. Though organized in state and local chapters, the Young Republicans as a whole were thought to be too close to the GOP party establishment, and as there were still a large number of conservative Democrats at the time (such as Charles Edison), it made sense to set out with a nonpartisan identity. It also reflected the practical problem that attempts to take over various Young Republicans organizations had met with mixed success. In 1957, according to David Franke, Evans had told his first pupils at *Human Events* that the object of young conservatives should be "First, we take over the Young Republicans. Then we take over the Republican Party. Then we take over the nation. And then we defeat world communism." Evans had run for a senior position in the Washington, DC, Young Republicans, recruiting Lee Edwards to come to the meetings with the promise that "there will be pretty girls there," but he came in second.

The YAF founding meeting had its share of lively debates about everything from choosing the organization's name to what doctrines it should stand for, exhibiting some of the ideological fault lines endemic to the right, most revolving around the familiar axis of libertarians (or "individualists," as the preferred term was at that time) and traditional conservatives of a more Burkean disposition (often called at that time either "trads" or the more pejorative "authoritarians"). The resolution of the debate came from Evans, who was selected to lead a committee of three to draft a state of principles for YAF.[8] Once again it is not clear who first thought of Evans for the assignment; it was likely Buckley or Liebman as it turned out that Evans wrote a first draft on an Eastern Airlines flight en route to Sharon before the meeting began.

The resulting product was the now legendary Sharon Statement that in the compass of just 368 words expressed a synoptic statement of the twelve principles that "We, as young conservatives, believe."

> In this time of moral and political crises, it is the responsibility of the youth of America to affirm certain eternal truths.

We, as young conservatives, believe:

That foremost among the transcendent values is the individual's use of his God-given free will, whence derives his right to be free from the restrictions of arbitrary force;

That liberty is indivisible, and that political freedom cannot long exist without economic freedom;

That the purpose of government is to protect those freedoms through the preservation of internal order, the provision of national defense, and the administration of justice;

That when government ventures beyond these rightful functions, it accumulates power, which tends to diminish order and liberty;

That the Constitution of the United States is the best arrangement yet devised for empowering government to fulfill its proper role, while restraining it from the concentration and abuse of power;

That the genius of the Constitution—the division of powers—is summed up in the clause that reserves primacy to the several states, or to the people, in those spheres not specifically delegated to the Federal government;

That the market economy, allocating resources by the free play of supply and demand, is the single economic system compatible with the requirements of personal freedom and constitutional government, and that it is at the same time the most productive supplier of human needs;

That when government interferes with the work of the market

economy, it tends to reduce the moral and physical strength of the nation; that when it takes from one man to bestow on another, it diminishes the incentive of the first, the integrity of the second, and the moral autonomy of both;

That we will be free only so long as the national sovereignty of the United States is secure; that history shows periods of freedom are rare, and can exist only when free citizens concertedly defend their rights against all enemies;

That the forces of international Communism are, at present, the greatest single threat to these liberties;

That the United States should stress victory over, rather than coexistence with, this menace; and

That American foreign policy must be judged by this criterion: does it serve the just interests of the United States?

Evans's draft was accepted with only minor modifications, but not without some vigorous debate on a few points. There were some objections to the invocation of God in the third sentence, and according to Lee Edwards's recollection, a vote to include the deity passed by a narrow 44–40 vote.[9] William Rusher, the long-time publisher of *National Review* who was at the YAF conference, said later that "nowhere else, for many years, did anyone attempt so succinctly and comprehensively, let alone so successfully, to describe what modern conservatism was all about."[10]

In recounting the Sharon Statement in his own narrative of YAF's founding in *Revolt on the Campus*, Evans typically made no mention of his hand in crafting the document. Partly this was a reflection of Evans's natural modesty, but it was also in part because he understood that the ideas he expressed were not original to him but were timeless, universal principles derived from God and nature. Evans reflected to historian Greg Schneider more than thirty years later: "[The Sharon Statement] wasn't the Declaration of Independence, it wasn't the Gettysburg Address—it was a very common sense statement, I think, of what American conservatives believed then and believe now." David Keene summarized the significance of the Sharon Statement at a memorial tribute in 2015: "The Sharon Statement accelerated and gave substance to the infant movement of which we are all a part. His embrace of fusionism helped cement the coalition that allowed the movement to unite conservatives into a political force no one would have imagined possible before 1960."

Evans was more expansive, though still modest about his own role, in his reflections on the tenth anniversary of the Sharon Statement in 1970 in an essay that summoned his philosophical and literary depth:

> The first section deals, rather elliptically, with the metaphysics of the case; the middle paragraph take up the political and constitutional issues; and the final portion considers the role of government in questions of domestic economy and world affairs. The implicit argument is that a proper metaphysics will lead us to establish government on its right foundation, which in turn will make a regime of liberty possible.

Although YAF got off to a flying start, organizing some successful large youth rallies (including a 1962 rally that drew eighteen thousand young people to Madison Square Garden, where Evans appeared on stage with John Wayne), assisting in the nascent Goldwater for President effort, and mounting a spirited challenge to the liberal-dominated National Student Association (a story

Evans relates fully in Chapter 8 of *Revolt*), by degrees internal factional fights prevented YAF from living up to its full potential. By the end of the 1960s it began unraveling as an organization, though offshoots of YAF exist to the present. Evans joined YAF's advisory board at its inception, and as it struggled in its early years, Buckley asked Evans to take over YAF and sort it out, but he declined and resigned from the advisory board at the end of 1963. The full story of YAF is both fascinating and entertaining, and interested readers should see any of several full-length accounts of YAF's history by Gregory Schneider, Wayne Thorburn, John A. Andrews III, Lee Edwards, and George Nash.[11]

While YAF didn't endure, the Sharon Statement did. It is still reprinted today and offered as a statement of conservative principles applicable to all times and places, even if the "international Communism" referenced in 1960 no longer exists. The Sharon Statement deserves comparison with the more famous Port Huron Statement of 1962 that launched the "New Left" Students for a Democratic Society (SDS). Unlike Buckley, Evans generally eschewed long words, but one exception was his occasional use of "lugubrious," which certainly applies to the presumptuous, repetitive, guilt-ridden, and self-referential Port Huron Statement. Tom Hayden, the principal author of the Port Huron Statement, is said to have read the Sharon Statement.

Whereas the Sharon Statement is less than four hundred words, the Port Huron Statement rambles on for almost five thousand words, which, by its very length, defends itself against the risk of being read widely or carefully. Writing on its fiftieth anniversary, Daniel Akst of the *Wilson Quarterly* observed, "The Sharon Statement seems to be everything its counterpart on the left is not...a model of brevity and coherence" next to what Akst described as Port Huron's "leftist logorrhea." And does anyone still read the Port Huron Statement today?

Some representative samples: "Our work is guided by the sense that we may be the last generation in the experiment with living... today, for us, not even the liberal and socialist preachments of the past seem adequate to the forms of the present... The decline of utopia and hope is in fact one of the defining features of social life today." Beyond taking over the universities as a base for seeking power, one will search the Port Huron Statement in vain for an intelligible principle or agenda for practical policy direction.

And although the SDS and the New Left it helped birth got most of the attention as the 1960s progressed, over the long haul both YAF and the ideas it promoted ought to be judged as more successful and significant. Some New Left leaders and fellow travelers ended up in consequential political roles in later years (such as the Clintons), but most, such as Hayden, who topped out as a fringe California state senator, never reached the pinnacles of power they sought nor achieved the revolution they demanded. Many went to ground in academia and other pursuits that fell far short of their revolutionary goal of seizing power and bringing about utopia. Some switched sides and became conservatives. By contrast, of the ninety-plus students and young activists assembled at Sharon in 1960, a high number became consequential leaders in conservative politics, serving as senior appointees in the Nixon and Reagan administrations, appointed to federal judgeships, contributing to serious conservative literature, and leading important conservative organizations. Some even went into academia!

The role of YAF and the development of conservative ideology and activism that it propelled has by now been recorded in many histories, but *Revolt on the Campus* was the first and in some ways the best account of the whole scene. It was the culmination of Evans's intellectual and professional interests of the time and represented a turning point for him as well as for the conservative movement. He was surely unsurprised that *Revolt* drew a sneering review in the *New York Times Book Review* by its education editor Fred M. Hechinger. "What this country needs is a Society for the Prevention of Cruelty to Conservatives inflicted by such books as *Revolt on the Campus*. There is a clear and present danger that extremists on the right will give conservatism a bad name…It is a revolt out of character with American tradition. It lacks compassion. It appears to confuse rugged individualism with rugged selfishness."[12]

Kirkus Reviews was similarly dismissive: "*Revolt on the Campus* is a very young work by a rather young man in defense of a hoary crusade: the Conservative revival."[13] Russell Kirk, reviewing *Revolt* in the *Annals of the American Academy of Political and Social Science,* was typically quirky and slightly cranky about Evans's neglect of conservative student activism in Britain and insufficient genuflection to Edmund Burke. The whiff of "individualism" in *Revolt* seems to have set off Kirk's dislike of libertarianism. Writing in the *Western Political Quarterly,* Marcella Miller said *Revolt* was written with "high-pitched and frequently dramatic prose," "a tendency to both oversimplify and to overgeneralize," and "an intolerant, and indeed, a distorted perception of others." A reviewer for the *AAUP* [American Association of University Professors] *Bulletin* huffed indignantly about the book for 2,500 words, dismissing it as a "hodgepodge of ideological lumber" and attacking Evans as an agent for "sick men, con men, self-seekers, and haters."[14]

Most of the reviews took no notice of and offered no argument against Evans's central analysis about the philosophical roots of liberal conformity on college campuses or his synthesis of intellectual conservatism in the later chapters of the book—just like today. Hence, the challenge Evans posed at the conclusion of

Revolt is even more salient today: "The reigning orthodoxy claims to abhor 'indoctrination.' Why then should not conservatives argue along the lines suggested by Peter Viereck—You profess to favor free inquiry, why not let it take place?"[15]

The day after Evans returned from Sharon in early September, the *Indianapolis News* announced on the front page that he was the new editor in chief.

CHAPTER 5

FROM SHARON
TO SAN FRANCISCO

A s editor in chief of the *Indianapolis News*, Evans generally kept to a hands-off practice toward the straight news pages (except for his own occasional reporting for the news pages). The paper mostly used wire service copy for national stories while encouraging local beat reporters to get out in the community for careful coverage of Indiana news. The editorial page was Evans's chief interest, and it was arguably the most consistently conservative editorial page in the nation. In addition to his own bylined columns, the page regularly featured several of Evans's favorite syndicated columnists, especially Ralph de Toledano, Raymond Moley, Morrie Ryskind, Fulton Lewis Jr., and John Chamberlain. Liberal columns never appeared, though as previously mentioned the page printed critical letters and sometimes opened its op-ed page for a long reply from a figure or institution it had attacked, though this was invariably followed by a surrebuttal from the paper. The editorial voice of the *News* was distinctly Evans, and it is easy to make out his unsigned house editorials by the style and particular arguments. But in many cases it is not necessary to guess as some favorite terms and phrases would appear separately in his bylined column, and much of his unsigned editorial material showed up later under his name in a series of books.

The first order of business upon returning from Sharon was getting into high gear covering the 1960 election campaign between Nixon and JFK. There were four main aspects of Evans's thought and journalistic work during the campaign and subsequent JFK presidency. First, Evans's low regard for and distrust of Richard Nixon hardened into place during this period after he previously thought Nixon good enough to merit conservative support. Second, he sought actively to debunk the view, especially prominent today, that JFK was a center-right Democrat on both domestic and especially foreign policy. Third, he counterattacked early on the theme just starting to emerge in 1960, and which became more pronounced following JFK's election, that the "radical right" posed the most significant threat to the American political order. (Readers will immediately recognize the revival of this theme today in the aftermath of Trump.) And finally, Evans was early to the Goldwater bandwagon that culminated in Goldwater's nomination in 1964, and he bestowed lavish news and editorial page coverage of Goldwater going forward.

"The net result of the [1960 GOP] convention was to move the entire spectrum of Republican politics to the right," Evans wrote in *Revolt on the Campus*. "The most surprising aspect of the Goldwater movement...was the deep conviction of youngsters who had grasped the intellectual message of conservatism." But one person who seemed not to perceive this was Nixon. It should have been obvious to Nixon that Goldwater and his supporters had the energy and momentum. Yet Nixon's most notable political maneuver around the time of the convention was placating Nelson Rockefeller through the infamous "5th Avenue Compact," through which Nixon agreed to Rockefeller's demands for a more liberal GOP platform. A pre-convention column took aim at Rockefeller's "Svengali-like magic over the mind of Richard Nixon," and a column written during the convention ("Nixon's

Left Turn Risks Revolt") noted that the struggle of the convention was "for the soul of the Republican party—and for the mind
of Richard Nixon...In thus moving out to embrace Rockefeller,
Nixon is running a real risk of revolt from the conservatives who
have backed him down the years."[1] An unsigned editorial that
same day attacked Nixon's likely running mate, Henry Cabot
Lodge Jr., as "an 'ultra-liberal' Republican" and that "Lodge
the Vincible"—the editorial's headline—"would be the worst
possible choice for a GOP vice-presidential nominee." Another
post-convention column took direct aim at "modern" Republicanism, the "threadbare fable...that the Republican Party can rally
mass support only if it becomes as 'liberal' as its opposition." His
rebuttal can be summarized in one word: Goldwater. (In addition
to Evans's columns touting Goldwater, the *News* began running
Goldwater's own newspaper column regularly.)

Kennedy had begun his political career with solid anti-Communist rhetoric. Evans noted later than "Jack Kennedy had entered
the hardline anti-Communist lists before the 1950 arrival of
McCarthy. Denouncing Owen Lattimore, John K. Fairbank, the
Institute for Pacific Relations and the Acheson policy on China
in terms McCarthy himself could not have faulted." But well
before the 1960 campaign, Evans had detected that Kennedy was
either insincere in his previous pronouncements or was moving
to the left, and he was not fooled by Kennedy's tough talk on the
Cold War in the 1960 campaign. Adding to Evans's doubts were
JFK's straddle on domestic policy, especially economic policy.
Though he never directly said that he thought JFK a callow man
consumed wholly by ambition, he did note the convenience with
which JFK shed a lot of his previous positions and statements
as the 1960 election drew near. One 1962 column employed the
device of quoting an "anonymous statesman" commenting on
the Kennedy administration's liberal ideology. "How long can we

continue deficit spending on such a large scale with a national debt of over $258 billion?", this "statesman" was quoted. Or concerning the centralization of power in Washington: "The scarlet thread running through the thoughts and actions of people all over the world is the delegation of great problems to the all-absorbing Leviathan, the state...Every time we try to lift a problem to the government, to the same extent we are sacrificing the liberty of the people." Through this catalogue of conservative-sounding sentiments, the alert reader might have guessed Evans's closing reveal: "The name of the anonymous statesman who so vigorously opposed the programs now advocated by President Kennedy: Senator John F. Kennedy (D-Mass)."[2] Evans also had great fun mocking the JFK-image-making PR machine, already in high gear in 1961: "In a flood of magazine stories and television documentaries, we learned he was a powerhouse of energy and a fount of wisdom. No task was too Herculean, no detail too intricate, for him to tackle. He solved cosmic dilemmas with a single thrust, chewed up Gordian knots for breakfast, slew dragons of discontent between appointments with the photographer...Our omnipotent magistrate was blessed with a sensibility so exquisite as to leave ordinary humans breathless with wonder."[3]

Evans thought JFK's veneer and easily shifting positions revealed not a mere opportunistic pol but someone who was consumed with a desire for power above all and abetted by a circle of advisers and hangers-on who wanted the same. Evans was a fan of Victor Lasky's 1963 book, *JFK: The Man and the Myth*. "When we peel away the surface trapping of family glamor and exalted utterance to discover what core of philosophy lies beneath, we find only a great emptiness," Evans wrote in a review. "The tinseled wrapping is pure Madison Avenue, but what it conceals is just as implausible—a yawning void of ambition, unadorned by visible convictions on any major political issue."[4]

He was relentless in his attacks on JFK and his circle in his bylined column and in unsigned *News* editorials for both their statist economic disposition and superficial anti-Communist rhetoric. During the 1960 campaign, for example, Kennedy protested that he wasn't an ADA-style liberal (Americans for Democratic Action), but Evans pointed out that he appointed thirty-four ADA members to senior posts in his administration. Despite Kennedy being the son of a multimillionaire business- man and appointing a Republican, C. Douglas Dillon (scion of the Dillon-Read Wall Street investment banking house), to be his Treasury secretary, Evans drilled into the signs that JFK and his entourage were closet socialists or at the very least presumptuous planners heedless of the economic lessons of thinkers like Hayek and Von Mises. Evans likely didn't know until much later about JFK's private comment that "businessmen are sons of bitches" (which JFK attributed to his piratical father), but he knew from New Deal history that Democratic Party hostility to business was less about economics than it was about diminishing a rival power base. And power, he thought, was the central object of Kennedy's ambition. He wrote numerous articles attacking JFK's circle of advisers and senior appointees, pointing out their statist leanings from their prior statements and records. He especially liked to bash Arthur Schlesinger Jr., whom he debated on a radio show two days before 1960 election. Schlesinger had been a principal political adviser in JFK's campaign and an important bridge for JFK with the party's left wing, which had distrusted him. As a founder and eminence of ADA, he was influential in peeling off Adlai Stevenson supporters to JFK in the 1960 nomination contest.

Evans came out swinging, shocking Schlesinger with the charge that modern "liberalism" (Evans put liberalism in scare quotes in his written account) was a movement bent on the destruction of freedom. But Evans didn't give an inch, recalling several of Schlesinger's previous statements such as that the only defect of the New Deal was that it didn't spend enough money. And Schlesinger went on oblivious to how his comments ratified several of Evans's judgments about his "intoxication with government." Throughout their debate Evans threw back Schlesinger's favorite liberal clichés of the time, such as how government needs to "discipline aggressive private interests" and why government needed to "prevent special interests from absorbing the communal surplus which ought to be dedicated to communal, not private, interests." Evans especially liked to recall a 1947 statement of Schlesinger's: "There seems no inherent obstacle to the gradual advance of socialism in the United States through a series of New Deals." Schlesinger tried to dismiss this line of attack by saying that the GOP idea that government is the enemy was mere "propaganda." Evans concluded: "When the agents with subpoenas drop around to 'discipline' you a little, remember that the idea of government-as-enemy is just a figment of Republican imagination."[5] Evans asked in a separate article after the election: "Is it likely that President Kennedy would choose for such a position [as senior White House adviser] a man who held such radical opinions? The answer, apparently, is 'yes.'" (A year later Evans debated the avowed socialist author Michael Harrington, finding "there is little to distinguish Socialist Harrington from New Frontiersmen like Chester Bowles and Arthur Schlesinger Jr."[6])

At the root of Evans's critique of JFK's New Frontier political economy was not so much its concealed Fabianism as its basic economic illiteracy. As he wrote later, "In matters of economics, Schlesinger's writings are invariably a superficial confection of whatever happens to be prevalent among the liberal intelligentsia."[7] An egregious instance of liberal economic illiteracy for Evans was Kennedy's bullying of the steel industry in the fall of 1961, demanding that major producers roll back price increases.

Kennedy's public letter "in effect says price increases in steel are responsible for inflation" while, naturally, supporting wage increases for steelworkers. Evans was early to the insights of Milton Friedman that inflation was a monetary problem (he'd hosted Friedman in Indianapolis shortly before JFK's predations against steel) and pointed out in his column that "Neither the steel manufacturers nor the steel unions can increase the money supply. Only government can do that—and the Kennedy administration, by enacting a hefty deficit, is doing so with all possible speed. Kennedy and his resident economists are simply using the steel industry as a scapegoat for a profligate policy."[8] The view that "price increases cause inflation," Evans taught his journalism students ever after, "is like saying wet sidewalks cause rain," a trope of journalism that lasted well into the 1980s despite the growing expert consensus about the centrality of monetary policy from the late 1960s on.

Because of his previous perception of Soviet deception about their early space program, Evans was immediately dismissive of JFK's campaign claim of a "missile gap" that was supposedly the result of President Eisenhower's strategic shallowness, writing in July 1960: "U.S. defense officials in official testimony have questioned whether we were behind the Soviets at all." Accepting this claim "thus becomes one of Russia's greatest propaganda weapons."[9] When it became clear after the election that the "missile gap" was a myth, Evans made sure to call out the perfidy of the claim: "Kennedy created it, and then, by their insistent campaign to downgrade American strength, forced it on the intelligence community."[10]

Likewise JFK's claims about Cuba. Kennedy attacked the Eisenhower administration for losing Cuba to the Soviet orbit, saying that the rise of Fidel Castro was "an incredibly dangerous development to have been permitted by our Republican policy makers." Evans pointed out JFK's earlier statements that either supported Eisenhower's handling of Cuba or called for accommodating Fidel Castro.[11] Neither was he impressed with the supposedly strong anti-Communist reputation of JFK's pick to be secretary of state, Dean Rusk. Once again Evans thought the media and the political class weren't closely scrutinizing Rusk's past statements and views.

"Who Is Dean Rusk?" asked an unsigned *News* editorial Evans wrote. Evans delighted in pointing out that Rusk had succeeded Alger Hiss as the head of postwar planning at the State Department and was associated with the dubious Institute of Pacific Relations that had been the base of operations for suspected Communists Owen Lattimore and John K. Fairbank. (More on both of these figures in Chapter 9.) Evans went back to many of Rusk's statements from his time in the Truman administration, where Rusk expounded the naive idea that indigenous Communist movements might evolve independently of the control or interests of the Soviet Union and that the Chinese Communist revolutionaries could be compared to the American revolutionaries of 1776. He was, the editorial said, "an integral part of the Achesonian surrenderbund." Evans picked at one detail that was used to burnish Rusk's anti-Communist bona fides: his opposition to summit meetings. Evans read more carefully, noting that Rusk's criticisms of summit meetings were purely procedural or technical and not based on the substance of the inherent political conflict between East and West. In other words, Rusk's anti-Communism was technocratic rather than moral, the common malady of postwar liberalism. Evans predicted—correctly—that a U.S.-Soviet summit meeting would be an early objective of JFK's foreign policy. In a series of columns, Evans ran through the views and records of numerous JFK subcabinet appointments, finding them no better. In a separate bylined column, Evans said,

"There can be no expectation of a vigorous anti-Communism from his regime."

All of Evans's criticisms and doubts about JFK's foreign policy acumen were confirmed by the multiple disasters of 1961, starting with the humiliation of the botched Bay of Pigs expedition in April and the simultaneous surrender in Laos that marked a turning point toward the terminal confusions of our Vietnam strategy and the disastrous Vienna summit meeting with Soviet Premier Nikita Khrushchev in June and culminating in the erection of the Berlin Wall in August. The *News* used scare quotes in its scornful copy about the Vienna meeting ("summit") and concluded that "the summit exchange must be chalked up as a net loss for the cause of freedom." The editorial page paid close attention to the Kennedy administration's vacillation over Laos. Although the Kennedy administration initially talked tough about keeping Laos out of Communist control, it was evident to the *News* that the momentum toward a supposedly "neutral" Laos with a "coalition" government would end up being a strategic defeat for the West. For Evans it was a simple case of what social scientists call "pattern recognition."

Evans and the *News* editorial page had long deplored the course of the Cuban revolution from well before Kennedy took office, attacking the accommodationist rhetoric of liberals taken in by Castro's deceptions alongside the limp response of the Eisenhower administration. Even before the Bay of Pigs fiasco, the *News* had called for a military blockade of arms shipments to Cuba and was properly appalled at Kennedy's flinch in the April 1960 expedition.[12] "As a case study of Liberal foreign policy," Evans wrote later, "it would be difficult to improve on Cuba." He saw our naivete about Cuba's revolution as a continuation of our misprision of China's revolution of 1949, and he would see this pattern repeated in the next two decades in Africa and Latin

America (especially Nicaragua during the Carter administration). The *News* called for a more vigorous American intervention in both Cuba and Laos, and yet there is a slight hint of restraint or an inclination toward the disposition of the Old Right from the Taft era against direct military involvement that reflected both the heartland attitudes about foreign affairs as well as the residue of Frank Chodorov's influence on Evans:

> We believe that the United States should "intervene" in both of these crises, immediately, to insure victory for the forces of freedom. But we do not believe it is either desirable or necessary for that intervention to take the form of American troops.[13]

We should emulate the Soviet Union, Evans thought, and use proxy forces. Friends and associates of Evans say he held sympathies for the Old Right view of foreign intervention, but if he seldom expressed this view directly, it was likely out of prudent calculation that public counsels of restraint would only aid the inclination of liberals toward capitulation and appeasement.

Evans's initial reaction to the Cuban Missile Crisis of October 1962 was muted in part because it appeared JFK was finally stiffening up (and we finally got the blockade the *News* had advocated for two years) and also because it was not known until much later that JFK had made a secret side deal with the Soviets to remove NATO missiles from Turkey, which made the Cuban settlement a significant strategic defeat for the U.S. But even lacking knowledge of that later element, Evans was suspicious of the immediate follow up, pointing to credible reports that Soviet arms were being hidden in underground bunkers in Cuba and even the possibility that some of the missiles were never removed at all. (The *News* had been warning for at least a year before the Cuban Missile Crisis that the Soviets were likely to ship larger weapons systems to Cuba in the aftermath of the Bay of Pigs capitulation.) The main point of Evans's skeptical inquiries was not to stoke conspiracy theories or paranoia but rather to point out the unseriousness and credulity of America's defense and intelligence establishment. "By unveiling the confusion and disagreement which racked the administration," Evans wrote in a column on "The Real Lessons of Cuba" a few weeks after the dust had settled, "it showed how totally unprepared our leaders are to cope with the exigences of the Cold War."[14] In a chapter reviewing our Cuba policy in his 1966 book, *The Politics of Surrender*, Evans cites extensively from CIA assessments of potential Soviet-Cuban deception that our foreign policy establishment simply denied could be possible along with abandoning any serious policy aimed at curbing or liberating Cuba. The public steps of the Kennedy and Johnson administrations were "designed to show the American people that something was 'being done' about Cuba; in fact nothing was being done at all."[15]

Hence Evans expected that the unfolding American involvement in Vietnam would feature the same confusion, self-delusion, and weak-mindedness combined with a presumption of omnipotence. He noted that all the same clichés from the loss of China and Cuba showed up for duty, including hand-wringing over the problem of corruption and human rights violations by the South Vietnamese government, the need for American-style "reform," and hope for "negotiations" that would surely follow the Laos model of disguised surrender. With his tacit reluctance about committing American armed forces abroad, Evans admitted that a vigorous strategy regarding Vietnam was "a difficult proposition," but he could see that the "strange policy ambivalence" that emerged after the Gulf of Tonkin episode in 1964 was certain to be unsuccessful. (Lost to history, incidentally, is the fact that the John Birch Society thought early on that the Vietnam War was a mistake, a Communist trap for America to dissipate its military power.) Evans did not write often about Vietnam in his bylined column, but unsigned editorials he supervised (and likely wrote most of the time) frequently attacked the Johnson administration's military and diplomatic strategy. Evans also featured frequent columns on Vietnam from de Toledano, Fulton Lewis Jr., and other regulars.

Whatever his private views about the heavy American military commitment in Vietnam, he was clear and direct about how American attempts at conciliation would only lead to more aggression from North Vietnam and how a feckless military strategy would not just lead to defeat in the field but contribute to a weakening of American resolve in the world. Evans anticipated the "Vietnam Syndrome" long before anyone thought of the name.

The other main line of Evans's distinctive thought of the 1960s involved the confluence of two conceits of the media and established liberalism. The first conceit of established liberalism at the time was that the chief threat to the American political order came from the "radical right" or the "fringe" represented especially by the John Birch Society and other "extremists." The Kennedy administration and other prominent liberal voices widely promoted the idea of the "threat" from the "radical right." Out in California, the state attorney general Stanley Mosk issued a breathless report about the John Birch Society that, on the one hand, originated the famous description of its members as "little old ladies in tennis shoes" but also offering the overwrought conclusion that the JBS represented a clear and present danger to American democracy.[16] Although there were few direct predictions of violence, the discourse around the "radical right" depicted it—and by extension all conservatives—as a "paranoid fringe" (though "lunatic fringe" was another common phrase).

As mentioned in the previous chapter, the *Indianapolis News* walked a careful line on the John Birch Society on account of its shared beliefs about Communism and the defects of American foreign policy and also on account of the strong support the society had in Indiana. Within a few years, established liberalism would be taken by surprise when the "paranoid fringe" of the New Left emerged, with serious violence following shortly after. Evans made a point of noting the lack of any concern that there was a potential "danger on the left." "The problem, the American people are told, is exclusively a problem involving conservatives." Noting how the liberal narrative of the JFK assassination couldn't let go of its fixation with right-wing extremism, Evans wrote several columns on the point in the weeks after Dallas.

> Memory does not recall an episode of equal scope in which men whose task it was to discern the shape of things had been so stunningly wrong. The moralizers of government, press and pulpit had exorcised a spirit of little substance and ignored the demon familiar at their elbow. They had fixed the nation's gaze upon an illusory danger on its right, and ignored the all too corporeal danger on its left.

Anticipating the thesis expounded in James Piereson's 2007 book, *Camelot and the Cultural Revolution,* Evans concluded with suitable scorn:

> Never before had America been called upon so blatantly to translate grief at a President's death into partisan energy; but, then, never had tastelessness and cormorant zeal been so perfectly mated in the citadels of orthodoxy. Liberalism had been called upon to review its preconceptions by the rude light of fact, to unite the wounded nation in its hour of pain. It was no contest. Prejudice

triumphed over proof; the nation was dismissed in the rush for advantage; the heart yielded not compassion by a nameless horror.[17]

But beyond correcting the ideological slanders directed against the JBS and conservatives generally, Evans turned the presumption of liberalism on its head: the real "fringe" in American society wasn't conservatives on the outside but "the fringe on top" of our establishment institutions, with liberals being the real "fringe" element in America because their opinions were out of harmony with most Americans. The *News* ran an editorial series under the banner "The Fringe on Top," later collected into a now-overlooked 1962 book *The Fringe on Top: Political Wildlife Along the New Frontier*. As Evans described it:

> These essays suggest that there is indeed a menacing "fringe" element in American society; but that it does not consist of the various conservative groups which have banded together for the purpose of promoting free enterprise and opposing Communism. It consists of the *soi-disant* "intellectuals" and self-confessed power seekers who favor a planned economy and a program of softness toward the Communist threat. The "fringe" which threatens to undo America is not clamoring to get into power; it is already there. That is why it is dangerous.[18]

The detailed critiques of prominent liberals and their mindset in his column and in *The Fringe on Top* were extended at greater length in his next two major books of the mid-1960s, *The Liberal Establishment: Who Runs America...and How* (1965) and *The Politics of Surrender* (1966). Evans was early to the problem that we know today as the "administrative state" or the "deep state." In a column in September 1960, "Who Really Runs America's State Department?", he noted that it is not really the secretary of state

who determines foreign policy but the "unknown policy planners and memo-makers" on the fourth floor at State "who fill the
Secretary's in-basket." While many (though not all) the issues
he confronted in the 1960s are dated, his general description in
The Liberal Establishment is just as applicable today:

> An establishment is, then, guided by a kind of informal junta by
> which a community is guided in all those things that matter. It is
> defined by large areas of agreement among its members on key
> social and political questions, and the remarkable adhesion they
> display in action when their views are tested by political resistance
> or the friction of ideas... Members of the Establishment know
> where they stand on major issues before the issues come up,
> because the Liberal ideology supplies them with a whole agenda
> of set answers to political problems... [There is] a common idiom
> and portfolio of tactics.[19]

As with all establishments throughout history, the American
liberal establishment, with the full cooperation of an aligned news
media, constantly seeks to enforce conformity with its outlook.
Three specific aspects of liberalism's stampeding herd mentality about the "threat" posed by the "extremist right" especially
caught his attention in the early 1960s.

The first was the liberal attack on the House Un-American
Activities Committee (HUAC), which conservatives had rushed
to defend. In May 1960, student protesters attempted to disrupt
three days of hearings HUAC was holding in San Francisco on
the subject of Communist influence on the West Coast. After
police forcefully removed protesters from the hearing room in
City Hall, the protest escalated outside into a riot, with eight
police officers and four students injured in the melees that
followed. The protesters charged police brutality; the police

and city officials claimed the protesters started the violence. Subsequently HUAC produced a film, *Operation Abolition*, that assembled the evidence drawn partly from FBI reports that known Communist agitators were responsible for organizing the protest and provoking the riot.

From the reaction of liberals and the media, you'd think *Operation Abolition* was a Leni Riefenstahl film. In those days the psychological term "projection" had not caught on, but the liberal attack on the film included every trait that liberals threw at McCarthyism: innuendo, distortions, character attacks, misstatements, and facts torn from context. Evans wrote about the *Operation Abolition* controversy several times in his column in 1961 and then contributed a long chapter reconstructing and critiquing the entire scene for *The Committee and Its Critics: A Calm Review of the House Un-American Activities Committee* that William F. Buckley and *National Review* put together in 1962. Evans's chapter carefully reviewed the facts, media coverage, and counterclaims of the critics, and while finding some errors and defects in the film, he concluded that "the evidence sorts itself out clearly in favor of the central allegations made by *Operation Abolition*: That the demonstrations were indeed 'Communist-inspired and Communist-led,' and that the students, not the police, were responsible for the violence."[20]

The liberal fuss over *Operation Abolition* was a mere warmup for a larger project generated by several Democratic members of the House called *The Liberal Papers*, which appeared in 1962. *The Liberal Papers* is a museum piece example of liberal presumption and censoriousness of nonconforming views. Seldom has the phenomenon of anti-anti-Communism been stated more directly. Evans focused on this statement from the opening chapter of the book written by David Reisman and Michael Maccoby: "As the cold war continues, it becomes increasingly difficult for decent Americans, humane enough to prefer peace to an egocentric national honor, to be outspokenly and genuinely anti-Communist." Quite beyond the slur that conservative anti-Communists are "indecent," the book contained a program of complete appeasement of the Soviet Union and China on the naive ground that our good-faith concessions would be reciprocated. The book, Evans wrote, "might better have been entitled 'Essays in Appeasement.'" Partly due to Evans's relentless publicity for *The Liberal Papers*, a number of Democratic congressmen who had been associated with the project moved to distance themselves from it. Evans noted that several authors and congressional staff who worked on *The Liberal Papers* project ended up with senior appointments in the Kennedy administration.

The last related liberal conceit that provoked Evans concerned the future of the GOP and was related to the liberal campaign against "right-wing extremism." Following Nixon's defeat in 1960, many media voices immediately proclaimed that Nelson Rockefeller was the obvious GOP frontrunner for 1964. And if not Rockefeller, the media suggested the GOP look to either Pennsylvania Governor William Scranton or auto executive George Romney, who was then gearing up to run for governor of Michigan. But it was obvious to Evans and any other unbiased observer that Goldwater and the conservatives had the momentum coming out of the 1960 election cycle. Romney, Evans wrote in late 1961, would be "another Wendell Willkie. (Do we really need another one?)"

Because of President Kennedy's charisma, popularity, and media sympathy, Evans thought that JFK would only be vulnerable to an authentic conservative challenge and that Goldwater was the only national figure who could do it. "There is today a real possibility that the Republican Party may nominate a conservative in 1964—a step which would for the first time in years put liberalism's handiwork to a true test at the polls," he wrote in the summer of 1963. He predicted exactly what came to pass the following year: "an all-out campaign to 'expose' conservatives as the minions of 'hate.'"[21] (The parallels with our current moment are plain to see. Little seems to have changed in the minds of liberals in the nearly sixty years since.)

In his own column, op-eds by other columnists, unsigned editorials, and straight news coverage, the *Indianapolis News* went all-in for Goldwater. "Goldwater Backers Begin Drive" is a typical Evans column headline from 1963. The preexisting "right-wing extremism" threat was ready-made for the media before Goldwater even announced his candidacy. It was an intimidation racket, all the more enraging when liberal Republicans like Rockefeller fell in line with it. As Evans concluded one column attacking Rockefeller: "As for the charge of 'extremism,' this tells us more about the people making the allegation than those against whom it is made. It signifies the liberal intention of smearing and belittling those who resist East Coast control of the GOP."[22]

As the 1964 campaign began in earnest, Evans pushed back aggressively against liberal Republicans and media bias in equal measure. Beyond the bias that expressed itself in the charge that Goldwater was an extremist was the habit of the media to denigrate Goldwater's momentum toward the nomination. Walter Cronkite reported on CBS, for example, that Goldwater's 65 percent of the vote in the Illinois primary was "disappointing," while the Chicago *Daily News* ran the inexplicable headline "Illinois Voters Buried Barry." This summoned one of Evans's most effective counterattacks in the form of a parody report printed in the straight news pages rather than on the editorial page that he filed from the GOP convention in San Francisco:

Barry Losingest Winner Again

By Stan Evans
Editor of the News

SAN FRANCISO—It was a crushing defeat for Barry Goldwater.

The Arizona conservative, in one of his worst showings to date, managed to marshal only 67 percent of the vote on yesterday's first ballot of the Republican presidential nomination. Although enough to gain victory for Goldwater, this margin was described as "disappointing" by a majority of TV commentators and Eastern journalists interviewed at the Cow Palace . . .

The drab results, so runs the press box survey, constituted what was perhaps the worst drubbing for Goldwater since the Illinois and Indiana primaries, in which he managed to scrape up only 65 percent and 67 percent of their respective vote totals.

Indeed, those earlier defeats were directly contributory to the latest one. Owing to Goldwater's weak race in Illinois it is pointed out that he managed to pick up only 56 of the state's 58 delegate votes and succeeded in winning only 32 of Indiana's 32.[23]

The day before the election, the *News* unsurprisingly endorsed Goldwater in "A Clear Choice." It should be noted, however, that the *News*'s sister morning paper, the *Indianapolis Star*, endorsed Johnson. Eugene C. Pulliam had a cordial relationship with Johnson going back to the 1950s, and Johnson worked hard to court Pulliam's favor. Pulliam had backed LBJ against Kennedy in the Democratic nomination contest in 1960 and was pleased when LBJ was picked to be JFK's running mate. "Pulliam liked being close to those in power," his grandson Russell Pulliam wrote in a biography.[24] Pulliam had been unenthusiastic about Goldwater's candidacy from the beginning, fearing he was a certain loser in

1964. But Pulliam allowed Evans to give the *News*'s endorsement to Goldwater, and in Arizona, Pulliam's *Arizona Republic* endorsed the home state favorite Goldwater.

Pulliam's tolerance for Johnson was one manifestation of a widespread confusion about the political scene at that moment. Because of Lyndon Johnson's reputation as both a southerner and a westerner, many observers argued that Johnson was actually a "conservative" and a more responsible conservative choice for president compared to the "extremist" Goldwater. There were even some conservatives who bought this line. Evans naturally thought this argument preposterous, which led him to write a nearly thirty-thousand-word broadside pamphlet entitled "Goldwater or Johnson: Does It Really Matter?"[25] As a literary matter, Evans was duplicating the same approach Arthur Schlesinger Jr. had taken in 1960 with his article "Kennedy or Nixon—Does It Make Any Difference?" Schlesinger had written his to keep liberals unenthusiastic about Kennedy on side, and Evans's task was similar. "Some conservatives," Evans noted, "see this year's presidential campaign as a battle between two conservatives, two men of the American West who, despite certain variations, are cut from the same kind of temperamental and ideological cloth...It is this author's belief that, whatever Lyndon Johnson may or may not be, he is not a 'conservative.'"

Evans's brief was extraordinary for discerning every major aspect of Johnson's personal and political character that later came out in both the unchained liberalism of the Great Society and LBJ's personal petty corruption. He defended Goldwater and his record at length: "Goldwater is a serious man. He has a certain reserve, an unwillingness to exploit cheap emotional appeals for political gain, an unwillingness to parade his sentimentality about in public in order to woo votes."[26] He also defended Goldwater against the "extremism" charge: "There is a sense in which 'extremism,' in the words of Senator Goldwater, is not a vice but a virtue: Intensity of commitment to principle, willingness to go down the line for what one believes."

This long essay displays several things, starting with Evans's own intensity about understanding politics in depth: the confusion, relative disorganization, and impotence of the nascent conservative movement and the power of the mainstream media to influence the public against a conservative presidential candidate. One long passage in the essay demonstrates how Goldwater got generally favorable media coverage—until he became a realistic prospect for president, whereupon the media wheeled on him viciously. Donald Trump experienced the same treatment fifty-two years later. Evans was under no illusion that LBJ was heading toward a substantial victory and that conservatives needed to be sober about the lessons to be learned from it. Evans didn't cite Goldwater's own words from the 1960 GOP convention—"Grow up, conservatives!"—but this was the subtext to this and many other articles Evans wrote during this period. There was a lot more work to do.

In 1962, the midway point in the Sharon-to-Goldwater time window, Evans got married to Sue Ellen Moore. It was a newsroom romance; Moore, an Indiana native and graduate of Indiana University, was an employee at the *News*. Don Lipsett was the best man, with Congressman Don Bruce and Bill Schulz as groomsmen. They divorced in 1975, when Stan moved to Washington. His private life was truly private, and he seldom if ever spoke of the end of the relationship even to his closest friends, nor did he ever make any of the typical "my ex-wife" jokes or give any hint of unpleasantness or bitterness. It is possible to make out a genuine case of "irreconcilable differences" as Stan's casual habits and plain tastes clashed with what Evans's friends describe as Sue Ellen's more refined fondness for the opera and other high society circles. His heavy travel and long work hours were said to be a source of unhappiness for both, though his home life during those years seemed to be a picture of ordinary neighborliness. Some years later Evans recalled, "We had a front lawn that was very inviting, and two young boys, about 10 or so, were throwing a football to each other on it. They were getting the spiral all wrong so I came out to show them how to do it. The next day they came to my house, rang the doorbell and said to my wife, 'Can Stan come out and play?'"

James Roberts, a student at Miami University in Ohio in 1967 who later worked for Evans in the mid-1970s in Washington, relates a story that offers a small clue. As head of a conservative club on campus, Roberts invited Evans to debate the leftist economist Robert Theobald. (Theobald, a socialist, was one of the leading advocates at the time for a guaranteed annual income, and Evans relished attacking Theobald's statement that "We must recognize the fact that the society's needs may be more important than those of a single person.") Roberts recalls that "Stan opened his brief case and his prepared remarks were not there. So he had to wing the whole thing. He pulled it off without a flaw." Roberts also related:

> Sue Ellen was very elegantly dressed, including a fur stole. After the debate I took Stan and Sue Ellen over to the Sigma Nu house for a Q & A for the brothers. We had a mascot—a huge Saint Bernard dog named Floyd, who was, despite the name, a female. And also crazy, as you can imagine living in a house with 80 college guys. Well, Floyd spied Sue Ellen and her fur stole, bounded through the room, leaped into the air and landed on her lap and proceeded to gnaw on the fur stole, with heavy growling.

Evans never remarried, though he was often seen around Washington accompanied by attractive younger ladies, showing that he never lost a certain youthful disposition. In the meantime, Goldwater's defeat meant that the conservative movement, to borrow Goldwater's own words from 1960, still needed to grow up, and Evans was in the thick of the next steps.

CHAPTER 6

REGROUPING
One Step Back, Two Steps Forward

In later years one of Evans's favorite jokes was reminiscing about how in the mid-1960s—back when there were no TV remotes and you had to get up off the couch and walk over to the TV to change channels, and when shopping malls were *uncovered*— young conservatives "had to recover from Barry Goldwater's landslide defeat *without grief counselors.*" But in the aftermath of Goldwater's crushing defeat, Evans was said to have been dejected and downcast. Evans knew that Goldwater was going to lose the election: everyone understood that after JFK's assassination the year before, it was unlikely that a Republican challenger could beat Lyndon Johnson. But the depth and breadth of the defeat for the Republican Party and conservatism (including a Democratic sweep of the major offices in Indiana) dashed hopes for even a partial breakthrough. The one-sided media campaign that amplified the Democratic Party strategy of calling Goldwater an "extremist" had been effective. "I had to stay up all night watching the returns come in because I had to write an editorial about it. I was miserable," Evans told Bill Dennis in 2002. "But we got up and pushed the stones away, and we have to get back at it."

The editorial Evans wrote for the next day acknowledged that "It is obvious that both the Republican Party and the conservative movement have been jarringly set back for long months to come."

We can't know how deliberate was Evans's choice of the phrase "long months" instead of "years" in this sentence, but it perhaps contains a hint of the resilience of the still-young conservative movement. The editorial closed with a familiar editorial trope: "Time will tell whether the GOP and the conservative movement are capable of regrouping for a comeback."[1]

It didn't take long for Evans to regain a Churchillian fighting spirit, and by 1968 he was excited about conservative prospects, more so than ever, in fact. In his columns and unsigned editorials in the *News* over the last few weeks of 1964 and into 1965, he walked a fine line between calling out the liberal Republicans who lent no assistance to Goldwater (when they didn't actively undermine his fall campaign) and calling for restoring GOP party unity and leaving past battles behind. The first cut at the subject, a week after the election, noted: "It was to be expected that various wings of the Republican Party would be involved in a round of mutual accusations following last week's electoral shellacking. This is a natural tendency within any defeated political party, and to a certain extent a necessary one." But the editorial hoped to avoid infighting, counseling that it would be "wise for Republicans of all stripes to drop the recriminations and backbiting for a while."[2]

Two weeks later in a column entitled "The Conservatives Bounce Back," Evans observed the ebullient spirits he encountered among conservatives on several college campuses and in other cities he visited in the month after the election. He quoted one "seasoned" GOP operative: "The Goldwater candidacy wasn't the end of something, it was the beginning of something. It represented the first try of a new coalition of conservative strength in America." He concluded that "the conservatives who stormed the Cow Palace in July of this year will be back in force in 1968."[3] (This column, incidentally, contains what may be Evans's first-ever reference to Ronald Reagan, who had written about Goldwater's defeat in *National Review*. Evans had watched Ronald Reagan's "Time for Choosing" TV speech on Goldwater's behalf a week before the election and said to his wife, Sue Ellen, "That's the guy who should be running for president *right there!*")

By early December Evans had come full circle with an editorial entitled "Keep Fighting" that blasted the Rockefeller wing of the GOP and calling for its repudiation: "It becomes increasingly apparent that there simply isn't room in the GOP for both the conservative forces of Goldwater and the liberal minions of Nelson Rockefeller…The conservative movement has emerged from the debris of last month's election, miraculously, intact and vigorous. Now is the time for all who believe in that movement to dig in and keep fighting."[4]

With the pundits and academic "experts" proclaiming the death of the Republican Party and the end of the road for conservatism, it took some willful optimism to recognize that Goldwater's rout of the long-dominant Rockefeller wing of the GOP represented a watershed moment in American politics, that an effective movement had come into being that could be built upon for the future. Despite this significant progress, liberals still had conservatives badly outgunned in institutional and political strength. As Evans and other conservatives sorted out the scene, three tasks came into focus: how to build up further intellectual heft and more political infrastructure and—looking ahead to 1968—how to regard the possible reemergence of Nixon as the GOP standard bearer. He might be preferable to Rockefeller, Romney, or Scranton, but opinion was divided on this point. Evans was in the middle of all four subsequent efforts, in word and in deed. On top of these internal challenges was the general problem of how to go about opposing Lyndon Johnson and his aborning Great Society welfare state and abortive Vietnam strategy.

The first two steps, advancing intellectual and political organization, took shape hard on the heels of the election almost
simultaneously: the founding of the Philadelphia Society and the
American Conservative Union. Although Evans was only periph-
erally involved in the initial efforts to found both organizations,
both incorporated the ideas and actions he had been urging for
several years, and before long he was in the thick of both.

One thing Goldwater's doomed campaign made clear was
that conservative candidates needed outside support, much the
way liberal candidates enjoyed support from labor unions and
umbrella groups like the Americans for Democratic Action (ADA).
"The left liberal block has been winning," reads the discussion
memo for the meeting, "mainly because it has had planning,
it has had coordination and it has had purpose. We have lost
because we have had no long range planning and almost complete
lack of coordination, and only recently any identifiable sense of
purpose." The author of this memo is unknown, but it sounds
like something Evans could have written as he had long thought
conservatives needed their own equivalent of the ADA. Five days
after the election, a small group convened to found the American
Conservative Union (ACU) with the intention of copying the
ADA's methods, including producing policy studies and above
all developing a vote-scoring system for office holders, which was
one of the ADA's most notable activities. Although the ADA was
the structural model for the ACU, the effort didn't just have the
ADA in its gunsights; it also wanted to counter the influence of
the liberal Ripon Society inside the Republican Party.

Robert Bauman, later a congressman from Maryland, organized the meeting, and although Evans did not attend the initial
planning meetings, the key people in attendance were a who's
who of the conservative movement and close associates of Evans,
including William Rusher, Carol Bauman, Rep. John Ashbrook

(R-Ohio), Jameson Campaigne Sr., Brent Bozell, Frank Meyer, John Dos Passos, and William F. Buckley Jr. Another key figure at the founding was former Indiana Congressman Don Bruce, Evans's close friend whom he had supported frequently on the *News* editorial page but who had surrendered his House seat in an unsuccessful Senate bid in 1964. Bruce became the ACU's first chairman, crisscrossing the country in the ACU's first year in an attempt to build up a membership base, with considerable success; within a year the ACU had 6,500 contributing members. Within a few months, the omnipresent and seemingly omniscient Don Lipsett had been hired on to be ACU's chief administrator. ACU's initial board of directors included another close Evans friend, Ralph de Toledano, along with future congressman Phil Crane and Brent Bozell. (One surprising member of the initial seven-member board was Garry Wills, who later defected to the left.)

ACU also launched an advisory board of nearly fifty people, including many familiar conservative names, but Evans initially declined to join the advisory board, waiting to see if ACU would take off. A previous effort that Evans had promoted at the *News*, Americans for Constitutional Action, had failed to gain traction and was eventually folded into ACU. Evans wrote to Don Bruce in early January 1965: "If things work out in the direction you indicated, I would be happy, as I said, to reconsider the question of going on the advisory board."[5] (Ronald Reagan also declined Bruce's invitation to join ACU's advisory board because, as he said, "until I make a decision regarding the upcoming California [governor's] race, I can't do anything about becoming a board member.") The early growth and momentum of ACU impressed Evans sufficiently that a year later he accepted an appointment to ACU's board of directors. Bruce had stepped down as chairman by that point, but Evans was enthusiastic about his successor as chairman, John Ashbrook.

Almost simultaneous with the founding of ACU was the founding of a new purely intellectual effort: the Philadelphia Society. The organization had actually been launched on a modest scale in the spring of 1964 as a special project of ISI, holding two small and lightly attended regional meetings with a limited agenda of speakers. After Goldwater's defeat, its founders decided on a more ambitious role. Evans was part of the reorganizing committee in December 1964 along with Buckley, Milton Friedman, Henry Regnery, Frank Meyer, Glenn Campbell (the Hoover Institution director, not the singer), Edwin Feulner, and several others. Once again Don Lipsett was in the middle of its creation (and became its long-serving executive director), while Buckley lent the new organization $100 for the legal filing fees.

The Philadelphia Society is sometimes lumped with the Mont Pelerin Society founded in 1947, and although the two organizations share many members in common, two differences stand out: first, the Mont Pelerin Society is an international organization (in fact, it tries to limit the proportion of American members) while the Philadelphia Society is America-centric; second, while Mont Pelerin focuses chiefly on political economy from a predominantly libertarian point of view, the Philadelphia Society is a broad-spectrum or interdisciplinary organization, deliberately mixing philosophy, political science, economics, literature, and culture in its topical menu. It was the ideal vehicle for the "fusionist" intellectual project Evans and Frank Meyer championed, and thus it came as no surprise that Lipsett tapped Evans to write the statement of purpose for the Society:

> To sponsor the interchange of ideas through discussion and writing, in the interest of deepening the intellectual foundation of a free and ordered society, and of broadening the understanding of its basic principles and traditions. In pursuit of this end we shall examine a wide range of issues: economic, political,

cultural, religious, and philosophic. We shall seek understanding, not conformity.

Evans chaired the first panel at the first national meeting of the revamped Society in February 1965, which featured Milton Friedman, Frank Meyer, and Stanley Parry of Notre Dame, on "The Problem of Philosophy."[6] The fusionist ambition of the Society can be seen in this panel and also the in final panel of that first meeting that paired Meyer and Russell Kirk, with whom Meyer had been at dagger's draw for several years. Evans joined the Philadelphia Society's board of trustees in 1966, at the same time he joined ACU's board, and was a prominent figure in the life of the Society for the rest of his life.

Evans was greatly encouraged by these developments in intellectual and political capacity on the right. While admitting that "conservatives have been outclassed by the liberals in presenting their case to the public," he celebrated the rapid progress of the conservative movement in these terms:

> Conservatism has become not merely a temperamental but a philosophical interest. The "old guard" variant was not strongly ideological, and while it featured many men of high intelligence— Hoover and Taft most prominent among them—it operated in terms of certain unstated assumptions about American life which were not sustained by scholarly endeavor. It was a "seat-of-the-pants" kinds of conservatism, strong on history and precedent, but not suited to the rigorous demands of a highly verbal age. The new Right in America is marked by the confluence of intellectual and political energies.[7]

While the conservative movement worked on building out the new modes of its infrastructure, back at the *Indianapolis News* Evans turned his attention to the new scene under the triumphant

Lyndon Johnson. Johnson was wholly different than JFK in his personal attributes but no less an avatar of the establishment. Evans wrote: "A former outsider, he is now so far 'in' that he is in danger of coming out the other side." That Johnson kept on many of Kennedy's senior appointments, such as Defense Secretary Robert McNamara and Secretary of State Dean Rusk, meant that there would be considerable continuity.[8] Less clear is whether Evans perceived whether Johnson would move to the left on his own conviction or as a result of Democratic Party pressure.

If Evans went relatively easy on Johnson in the aftermath of Kennedy's assassination, it is tempting to speculate that he might have held some residual regard for a fellow Texan, leavened by the fact that Evans had previously considered conservative southern Democrats as potential allies in the larger conservative cause. Little remembered today is the image Johnson still enjoyed in 1964 as a conservative Democrat, so much so that prior to Kennedy's killing there was rampant speculation that JFK might dump him from the 1964 ticket for a more congenial liberal. Opinion surveys in the 1964 campaign found that half of voters thought Johnson was conservative while Goldwater was characterized as "radical" or "extreme" rather than conservative. It would not be until 1968 that Evans categorically lumped Johnson in as a full-blooded liberal: "In the fourth year of Lyndon Johnson's term, the image-world shattered by the Kennedy assassination had in large measure righted itself. Johnson the apparent middle-of-the-roader stood fully revealed, in all domestic matters at least, as a President fully as liberal as Kennedy."[9]

In the meantime, Evans trained his critical fire on the liberal policies that LBJ and his administration proposed. Evans wrote little in his column about the first major LBJ political initiative, the Civil Rights Act of 1964, though unsigned editorials about the CRA and companion legislation often put "civil rights" in scare quotes or described the "warped notion" of civil rights, suggesting a prescience about the pernicious way civil rights law and politics would unfold over the coming decades. The *News*'s house editorials about the Voting Rights Act of 1965 noted the partisan motivation of the Act's vote dilution features that read especially fresh in the aftermath of the 2020 election.[10]

Evans was early to attack the Great Society, which he wrote was "a fiasco" as early as the summer of 1965: "There is hardly an aspect of the program—from its original conception to its detailed performance—which is not open to the most withering criticism." The *News* editorialized that the "war on poverty" would "not end in 30 years—or ever." Evans also bore in repeatedly against the liberal cliché that "poverty causes crime" and why further expansions of welfare spending and "urban renewal" would cause further increases in crime.[11]

Evans noted that the Great Society, besides being the brainchild of an avowed socialist (Michael Harrington), was already turning into a sinecure for the "caring" professionals of the welfare state, complete with lavish salaries that absorbed as much as two-thirds of the funds appropriated for local programs and poached staff from local government and nonprofit charities.[12] Sargent Shriver, director of Johnson's Office of Economic Opportunity, wrote a letter to the editor complaining about Evans's columns and the *News* editorials that reinforced rather than rebutted the criticism: "I am confident that the new importance of the War on Poverty is giving to the helping professions will have a beneficial effect both locally and nationally on the often inadequate salaries in those fields."[13] Evans answered with a point-by-point rebuttal in an editorial the same day.

Another topic of Evans's most prescient columns and editorials from the time concerned Johnson's proposed Medicare and Medicaid programs. His early training in Austrian economics under von Mises led him instinctively to know that introducing government as a major third-party payor of health insurance would lead to distortions in the entire health care system, public and private, hence assuring explosive health care cost inflation in the future. The subject was another of his initially contrarian perspectives that has been fully vindicated over time, and health care policy became one of his specialties all the way through the Hillarycare debacle in the early 1990s. In later articles in the 1970s and beyond, he frequently included a chart of health care cost inflation before and after Medicare's enactment, with a visible upward kink in the line starting *exactly* in 1965.

Before the Philadelphia Society in 1967, Evans went beyond the policy defects of the Great Society to describe it as antithetical to the principles of the American founding: "The Great Society measured against the American tradition is a kind of black mass. It is a total reversal and inversion on almost every general and particular point of what the American experiment is supposed to be all about." In contrast to the understanding James Madison pointed out in *Federalist No. 45* that the powers of the federal government would be "few and defined" while the powers of the individual states are "numerous and indefinite," Evans said: "The Federal government today is being conceived as a catch-all, a repository for all the powers which any government could possibly want, connected to every conceivable variety of experience, superintending every aspect of our lives down to the most minute... The Federal government which is supposed to be confined and limited is of course *de facto* unlimited." Meanwhile, Evans noted that the federal government was failing to perform its essential functions, such as ensuring domestic order:

> As the federal government sets about to doctor us, to insure us, to educate us, to feed us, to regulate advertising and packaging

and label cigarettes as poison, to harass dissenters, to regulate the airwaves, to manage the news, and to register us for living at age 18 as is now proposed—the same government that is doing all these things or trying to do all these things is defaulting on essential functions necessary to maintain order.

But Evans thought the worst effect of the Great Society was not the waste of money but the erosion of republican virtue:

> The most important of the reversals which confronts us, the most important of the inversions worked upon the American system by the ministrations of the Great Society and of the other representatives of the liberal orthodoxy which have preceded it, is the inversion which has taken place in the American character. The Founding Fathers assumed a certain character type to exist in the United States which would allow a regime of freedom to exist. John Adams put it very succinctly when he said, "Without virtue there can be no political liberty."...The Great Society reverses the equation: it assumes and encourages a lack of internal self-discipline which makes people incapable of selecting purposes and incapable of organizing their behavior...What this amounts to is a kind of infantilization of the American culture.[14]

But his main interest remained foreign and defense policy, where the problems deepened because of the two chief problems of the mid-1960s: the Vietnam War and the rapid acceleration of the nuclear arms race. Evans naturally discerned the connection between the two and why the liberal establishment was failing on both. There is throughout his writing on Vietnam a subtle reservation about the soundness of our intervention, a residue of his mentor Frank Chodorov along with sympathy for the Old Right noninterventionism of Robert Taft and others. (Keep in mind that

Human Events had been founded partly as a voice for noninterventionist foreign policy, and Indiana was always sympathetic to heartland isolationist sentiments.) At the same time, he discerned mistakes and fundamental weaknesses of our war policy derived from the wishful thinking of establishment liberals and technocrats like Robert McNamara who thought force could be "calibrated" to send "messages," thinking that the conflict could be resolved through good-faith diplomacy. And naturally Evans had no sympathy at all for the anti-war left, whose opposition to the Vietnam War he knew was just a species of anti-anti-Communism (if not open sympathy for our enemies), and as such any criticism of the war effort he might have had required walking a fine line so as not to lend aid and comfort to the left.

Evans thought from the beginning that the Kennedy administration's tentative steps in Vietnam were wrongheaded and immediately judged that the JFK-approved overthrow of Ngo Dinh Diem in 1963 was "the worst single blow struck by our government against the anti-Communist Vietnamese we were supposed to be supporting." But he seemed have some hope that President Johnson would be better, writing in 1966 that "despite nagging questions," Johnson "represented an improvement over the performance of the Kennedy regime."[15] Evans offered editorial praise for Johnson's statements on the war at various times, writing in July of 1965 about Johnson's first war speech following a major deployment of troops: "Johnson delivered a proper rebuke to those voices of appeasement who would have us lay down our arms and retreat before the Communist adversary…They sum up, as concisely as it has ever been, the essence of a correct foreign policy in a world beset by Communist aggression…a masterful statement on the realities of the Cold War."[16] Evans also defended LBJ from his critics on the left from time to time. He devoted one column to dishing on Walter Lippmann's criticism of Johnson, pointing out Lippmann's own past inconsistencies: "If President Johnson is to be criticized for reversing himself on the subject of Vietnam, Lippmann is hardly the man to take on the job."[17]

At the same time, Evans detected the ambiguity or soft-headedness of Johnson's conduct of the war while noting that the bad faith criticism of the war from the left prevented a worthy debate about the conduct of the war from taking place:

> The Johnson Administration has been taking a commendably strong line in Vietnam…But what, ultimately, is to be the objective of our stand in Vietnam? Are we there to win, to seek stalemate, or to negotiate some kind of "neutralist" settlement? These were the unanswered questions which hung so forbiddingly over our involvement in the Korean War. They are questions which badly need to be asked now.[18]

As the war escalated from 1966 to 1968 with no clear end in sight, Evans grew more exasperated with the confusions of the Johnson administration, though he took out his frustration more often on the senior figures behind the war, such as Defense Secretary Robert McNamara (who he said in 1967 should be fired) and Johnson aide Walt Rostow. By 1968 he was disillusioned with the failure of Johnson and his team to recognize that the Vietnamese Communists were not going to reciprocate the repeated bombing halts and entreaties to negotiate. "Communist hostility to the West cannot be disposed of by peace missions, 'pauses,' or the remonstrances of conversation," he editorialized as early as 1966, repeating this point several more times through to the end of the Johnson Administration. After LBJ's final bombing pause days before the 1968 election, Evans commented on "this sad but familiar story: Once more the Communists have met conciliation with aggression." Evans pointed out that even after the Tet

Offensive and Johnson's shock withdrawal from seeking reelection, public opinion polls showed majority support for taking a tougher line in Vietnam such that challenger Eugene McCarthy derived some of his support in the Democratic primaries from voters who wanted to express their frustration with Johnson's lack of a strategy for *winning* the Vietnam War.[19]

If Evans didn't seem as antagonistic toward Johnson as he was toward Kennedy, or as jingoistic as the "win-or-get-out" point of view popular on the right, it is because Vietnam was a mere symptom of a much deeper and longer-lasting problem with liberal foreign and defense policy as it unfolded rapidly in the 1960s. While many of his columns and editorials were written under the tight deadlines of an evening daily paper and were necessarily short, his extended treatment of these issues in his books, especially *The Politics of Surrender* (1966), show Evans at his best, with memorable turns of phrase and incisive summaries of the problems. (It would be fair to say that Evans's editorials and columns for the *News* were the first drafts for his books.) He paid attention to detail, especially the ideas of certain influential liberal intellectuals that the mainstream media overlooked but whose ideas were by degrees determining what Evans thought was an ominous turn in America's strategic outlook. His assessment in the mid-1960s foresaw how the debate over the Cold War would harden into the flabby détente of the 1970s and 1980s.

It will sound shocking to summarize Evans's position by saying that he was less afraid of Soviet Communists than he was of American liberals. As he put it starkly in *The Politics of Surrender*:

> The radical disjunction between Liberal ideology and the shape of the world we live in is the most serious problem confronting the United States today…We have been surrendering the globe to an enemy whose true character Liberalism refuses to

acknowledge... The Communists have not in fact been winning the Cold War so much as we have been losing it.[20]

The fundamental error of liberalism was that "The Liberal believes Communists are at bottom not too different from ourselves, and that the Cold War is the result of misunderstanding." From this core intellectual error flowed a number of disastrous policies, in particular the idea that stability would be best obtained by an equality of strategic power between the U.S. and the U.S.S.R. In other words, accepting the idea that peace would be best secured through the acceptance of the mutual assured destruction (MAD) doctrine meant deliberately surrendering American strategic superiority. Our deliberate embrace of MAD and military equality, along with expanded trade with the Soviet bloc, would lead to a "convergence" of interests in which the Soviets would "mellow." Ultimately, the most deluded liberals thought, the embrace of mutual terror and population hostage taking would lead to disarmament.

The most alarming immediate consequence of this doctrine was the purposeful rejection of missile defense, which Evans supported early on. In a 1966 column "Rejecting the Ultimate Weapon," Evans argued that "it could be the most important piece of military hardware ever invented" and "could revolutionize warfare and win the Cold War for America."[21] For the liberal, the idea of "winning the Cold War" was precisely the problem. Evans cited chapter and verse from leading liberal foreign policy intellectuals promoting the line that a robust anti-ballistic missile defense would be "destabilizing" and prevent progress toward disarmament. One of his main targets was the now-forgotten Jerome Wiesner, a science adviser to Kennedy and Johnson who opposed missile defense because it would be "de-stabilizing" and recommended that "if it appears possible to develop one, the [arms control] agreements should explicitly prohibit the development and deployment of such systems." "In other words," Evans concluded, "production of a vital defense system has been sacrificed on the altar of disarmament."[22] Sure enough, the Johnson administration and its successors decided against a serious missile defense development program and codified this self-chosen weakness under President Nixon in the Anti-Ballistic Missile Treaty of 1972.

This arms control orthodoxy survived until the 1980s, when President Reagan upended the Svengalis of arms control by reviving the idea of deploying a robust ballistic missile defense system (his Strategic Defense Initiative), which caused the left to go ballistic. The left didn't have to work hard to find the off-the-shelf arguments against it; they had been developed in the 1960s.

Speaking of Reagan, another leading preoccupation of Evans was the course of the 1968 presidential race. Despite Goldwater's triumph in gaining the GOP nomination in 1964 and thereby breaking the monopoly over the moderate east coast GOP "establishment," it was not clear whether the forward momentum coming out of that breakthrough would carry forward to 1968 or whether the east coast old guard would reestablish control. After all, Goldwater had lost in a landslide; party moderates were arguing that only a return to the center would succeed in 1968.

In addition to crusading against Rockefeller, Romney, Sen. Charles Percy, New York City Mayor John Lindsay, and other potential liberal Republican candidates, Evans began to take notice of Gov. Reagan out in California as an alternative to Nixon, whom he still distrusted even as many other conservative leaders were lining up in support of Nixon. Reagan's landslide victory in California was proof to Evans of the electoral appeal of unvarnished conservatism. In mid-April 1967, when Reagan had barely been in office for four months, Evans took his first editorial notice of the idea of a Reagan presidential bid the following year. Reagan was "a formidable and authentic candidate" who would scramble the Democrats' strategy.[23] For one thing, Evans had pointed out the fact that Goldwater had run well in southern states in 1964 and that a liberal northern Republican like Romney or Rockefeller (or Nixon) would squander the GOP's incipient gains in Dixie, especially if Alabama Governor George Wallace ran as a third-party candidate. The circumstances called for running another Sunbelt candidate. It is largely forgotten today that even with Goldwater's opposition to the 1964 Civil Rights Act, almost no one in the Republican establishment in 1964 thought he could make inroads in the south against an incumbent Democratic president from Texas. Evans argued directly that Reagan was the only potential Republican who could fend off Wallace.

Evans filed several more columns over the next few months, such as "Reagan Strength Growing Rapidly" and "The Makings of a President?", reporting Reagan's surge in polls of GOP primary voters (especially in Indiana) and how having California's large delegation easily in his pocket would put him in a strong position to contend for the nomination. By the time the 1968 campaign arrived in earnest, Evans was all-in on the Reagan-for-president idea. This set him apart from many other leading conservatives, such as William F. Buckley Jr., and even his close colleagues at *Human Events*, such as Allan Ryskind, who fell in behind Nixon as the most electable and acceptable Republican. "We supported Nixon because we didn't think Reagan was ready," Ryskind recalled years later. Evans replied: "I didn't think Nixon was ready."[24] Evans was proud in later years to declare that he had only voted for Nixon once, in 1960.

In March 1968, with Reagan's half-hearted campaign trying to find its footing, Evans produced a slim sixty-one-page tract, printed in a three-by-five format perfect for a shirt pocket, entitled *The Reason for Reagan*. Evans was fond of several solidly conservative Indiana politicians, but he positively swooned for Reagan, whom he regarded as the clear successor to Goldwater:

> The rise of California Governor Ronald Reagan as a major national figure constitutes one of the most remarkable stories in the annals of American politics... The evidence suggests that, more than any other public figure, he expresses and embodies a powerful new tendency in our politics... The evidence further shows that the currents running beneath the surface could rejuvenate the Republican Party and change the shape of American politics. It suggests that, if Ronald Reagan or someone like him were to be the GOP nominee in 1968, powerful new forces could be brought into the Republican fold, reviving a party which has long needed a fresh infusion of strength.

His tract recited all the main aspects of Reagan's political ideology and mass appeal that became familiar to everyone over the next twenty years and may have been the first to use the term "Reagan Revolution" to describe his potential. He drew back slightly from this effusive embrace in his next book, *The Future of Conservatism*, which appeared later in the year before the GOP nomination contest was settled in Nixon's favor. "It is tempting to suggest that, if Ronald Reagan did not exist, conservative Republicans would have to invent him," Evans wrote in the penultimate chapter of the book. "Tempting, but mistaken."[25] The larger point of *The Future of Conservatism*, which was one of the first synoptic histories of the right taking the story all the way back to Robert Taft, is that conservative *ideas* are more important than any individual political leaders.

The Future of Conservatism showed Evans at his virtuoso best, combining history, detailed political analysis, and intellectual substance. He took note of the rise of conservative intellectual milestones from figures in economics such as Milton Friedman and George Stigler to serious thinkers in other disciplines, such as James Burnham, Russell Kirk, and Forrest McDonald. He even notes certain center-left figures who were starting to defect from narrow partisan orthodoxy in interesting ways a decade before "neoconservatism" became a conscious category. While the names and issues in the book are dated, certain aspects of it still read fresh today, which points to the permanence of certain features of American politics. His early chapter "The Two Americas" can be repeated today with perfect application, starting with the "first" America we read about in the media:

> In this favored land, political issues are cut and dried—in favor of the liberal position. Major societal questions have long since been determined, and everyone is agreed on the proper goals of political action. These consist of increased governmental services from the Federal authorities in our quest for social justice...
>
> The second America is different. This is a nation one can discover by putting down his magazine, turning off his TV set, and walking out the front door. It is the America you discover by taking to your neighbors, by tracing the accumulation of political detail in various local communities, by noting the daily shape of American social life and American ideas.[26]

Overall the book paints an optimistic picture of the potential for conservative advance, but only so long as conservative candidates speak unequivocally to the interests and opinions of the second and not the first America. And it is just here that his implicit doubts about Nixon come into play. This book about the *future* of conservatism spent a good deal of time revisiting the intraparty Taft-Dewey fights of the 1940s and early 1950s, in which the Deweyite liberal or "mainstream" Republican Party always came out on top. Evans argued that Taft would have won either in 1948 or 1952 and that "The Eisenhower victory signaled, not the beginning of new Republican strength, but a continuation of the old decline."[27] Evans thought that Nixon, despite his anti-Communist bona fides, represented a continuation of the Dewey-Eisenhower Republican establishment that regarded itself as handmaidens to liberalism.

The delicate balance between the post-Goldwater insurgency and the establishment old guard was still up in the air on the eve of the Republican convention in Miami in August 1968. It was actually a three-sided story, with Reagan representing the conservative movement, Rockefeller as the old-guard candidate, and protean Nixon, the narrow front-runner, in the middle somewhere. In early August Evans wrote a long front-page article in *Human Events*, "Moving Left Courts Election Disaster," which tacitly conceded that Reagan's late bid was unlikely to succeed, and thus he cautioned that conservatives feared that a Nixon nomination would ensure a rerun of the 1960 election if he capitulated once again to the Rockefeller wing. Evans took aim at the media-abetted narrative and superficial poll numbers that Rockefeller, Charles Percy, and other liberal Republicans cited to bolster their point that if Nixon were the nominee, he needed to pick a liberal Republican running mate—thus ruling out Reagan or Texas Sen. John Tower—and move to the "center" to attract more urban votes. The Rockefeller-Percy circle actually tried to boost New York City Major John Lindsay to be Nixon's running mate.

Evans's attack on this conventional wisdom was a tour de force, knocking down the media narrative and shortsighted political analysis of the party moderates: "In the Rockefeller incarnation, the Eastern approach makes the Republican party non-Republican, indistinguishable from Democrats...This sort of approach gives the Republican party no reason for being, with a demoralizing effect on the GOP rank and file and consequent corrosive effects on the existing party base."[28] Evans could sense that Nixon was trying too hard to thread a needle that he would have been be better off ignoring.

After the convention, Evans offered an upbeat assessment in "The Meaning of Miami." Rockefeller and the eastern establishment had been routed. The decisive fact was that Nixon's nomination depended on the help of South Carolina's Strom Thurmond, Texas's John Tower, Barry Goldwater, and other conservative forces. Reagan's late insurgent candidacy, which on the surface threatened to split conservative forces, actually strengthened the hand of Thurmond and other key power brokers. It was, Evans reported with some measure of glee, "a massive triumph for the rightward elements of the party. With this convention, the 'Eastern Establishment' of the GOP has kept its rendezvous with oblivion."[29] In other words, whereas in 1960 Nixon thought it necessary to appease the Rockefeller wing of the party, in 1968 he knew he now had to satisfy conservatives. The Goldwater revolution had stuck. The remaining question was how vigorously Nixon would campaign as a conscious conservative.

The results of the election arguably vindicated Evans's fears. The week after the election, the unsigned front-page *Human Events* article on the election result (likely written by Allan Ryskind) expressed disappointment: "While Richard Nixon scored a fantastic personal victory in this most incredible of political years, conservatives did not." Nixon had short coattails, with Republicans making tiny gains in the House and Senate. "What, then, went wrong?"[30]

Evans had the front-page story in *Human Events* a week later: "Why the GOP Must Move Right." While he resisted the temptation to say "I told you so," the subtext of the article was that Nixon could have enjoyed a larger victory if he had campaigned more vigorously as a conservative, especially in the south. (Contrary to the currently popular refrain on the left, Nixon didn't much embrace a "southern strategy" in 1968, largely ceding the region to Wallace.) Evans took encouragement from the fact that the combined Nixon-Wallace vote represented a massive voter repudiation of Great Society liberalism upon which a durable future majority could be built—*if* Nixon and Republicans figured it out. Evans further noted an emerging electoral feature that looms large today: "The liberal cause in presidential politics has been driven into an enclave along the Eastern seaboard, maintaining a few isolated outposts in the hinterlands."[31]

If he didn't have warm feelings or high hopes for Nixon after Nixon's narrow victory in the three-way race in 1968, he was still game to counterattack the liberal narrative that implied Nixon's win was illegitimate or compromised. The 1968 election began a now-familiar pattern on the left that no Republican president can be truly legitimate because Republicans are, by definition, on the "wrong side of history." Following his election there was a steady stream of commentary in the media that he should, at the very least, liberally appoint Democrats to his cabinet and senior positions in his administration and govern as a "consensus" president. One commentary suggested that Nixon should forgo the traditional inauguration celebrations. Evans recognized this doublespeak for what it was: the special pleading of presumptuous liberalism:

> Much of this is said, of course, in a tone of sorrowful friendliness, but the intention behind it is relatively plain: To portray Nixon as a flukish president who assumes office at the grudging sufferance of the nation, and to impose upon him by psychological pressure the same liberal program that 14 million Americans voted out last week.[32]

Evans nonetheless laid down a marker: "The issue is not whether one agrees with Nixon. Although he said many fine things in the campaign, this department is not fully in agreement with him, either."

Even as Evans was writing his series of books on national and international affairs, he didn't take his eye off Indiana politics. And just as he had championed Goldwater and then Reagan, he offered vigorous editorial support for Indiana conservatives while extending the kind of attack he brought on Rockefeller-Romney Republicans to Indiana pols he thought fell short. One particular favorite was Edgar Whitcomb, who won the race for governor in 1968 on a strong anti-tax platform, while the more middle-of-the-road establishment Republican William Ruckelshaus lost his U.S. Senate bid to Birch Bayh. Whitcomb has resisted "the pressure blitz" to support higher taxes, which "cramped the style of the tax-raisers... [Whitcomb] has given Hoosier taxpayers a fighting chance of coming through the next legislature with their pocketbooks intact."[33] To gain the GOP nomination that year, Whitcomb defeated two establishment Republicans, Earl Butz and Otis Bowen, who later went on to cabinet posts under Presidents Ford and Reagan.

Evans would take up his editorial sword on behalf of Whitcomb repeatedly over the next few years as Whitcomb's resolute anti-tax and anti-spending stance caused a split in the Indiana Republican Party. While backing Whitcomb, Evans also poured scorn on less resolute Republicans. A postelection column comparing Whitcomb's win with Ruckelshaus's failure turned on a simple point: while Whitcomb campaigned on basic conservative doctrine and stayed on offense, the Ruckelshaus campaign had no philosophical center and was on the defensive during much of the campaign even though he was the challenger. "Some of the Ruckelshaus literature had a 'new politics' cast to it," Evans wrote, "seemingly aimed at the Eugene McCarthy vote."[34]

And Evans was suspicious of Richard Lugar, later known as Richard Nixon's "favorite mayor" and then a long-serving U.S. Senator in thrall to arms control dogma, from the very beginning when Lugar first ran for mayor of Indianapolis in 1967. Evans noticed that as a member of the Indianapolis school board, Lugar equivocated about whether Indiana should accept federal aid for schools (Evans was against it, naturally), sometimes claiming to oppose federal school aid and at other times hinting at a "willingness" to consider it. This was part of larger theme with Lugar, which was his presentation as someone who sought "pragmatic" and "constructive" solutions to current problems. For Evans, "pragmatic" and "constructive" were weak-minded euphemisms for "sell out to liberalism." Evans received a lot of reader blowback for his repeated criticism of Lugar during the 1967 campaign but claimed vindication when, barely a year in office, Mayor Lugar applied for federal aid: "He seems to have overcome his primary-time bias against such 'aid' in remarkably short order."[35] Evans let it all hang out when Lugar ran for the U.S. Senate for the first time in 1974 in a column entitled "Lugar Record Not Conservative." "If political terms still have any meaning," he wrote with an extra twist of the editorial knife, "Richard Lugar is not a conservative Republican but a liberal one, and is generally recognized that way by such authorities as the *New York Times*."[36]

The arrival of the Nixon presidency in 1969 coincided with Evans's tenth anniversary at the *Indianapolis News*. His career was about to take another major turn.

CHAPTER 7

NIXON'S NOT THE ONE
The Manhattan Twelve

Richard Nixon's ascension to the White House and his ultimate, ignominious exit presented a dilemma for conservatives, with Evans solidly on one side of the divide along with *National Review* publisher William Rusher, who put his dislike more pungently: "That tired, tergiversating tramp never impressed me for a moment as a conceivable instrument for any useful end." The problem, as Evans saw it, was "that once he was nominated and elected, Nixon felt, correctly as it turned out, that he had the conservatives in the bag, that they would support him almost irrespective of what he did. So he had no conservative program to speak of." That would change before his first term was out, and Evans played a key role.

Evans met Nixon only twice, the first time on a campaign swing Nixon made through Indiana in 1968 and the second time at the Republican National Convention in Kansas City in 1976 (Nixon was a furtive presence in the background at that first post-Watergate convention), where he remembered Evans and asked, "Are you still in Indianapolis?" Evans marveled at Nixon's memory. As previously mentioned, William F. Buckley Jr. and several other senior figures at *National Review* and *Human Events* supported Nixon, as did many other leading conservatives. Evans set it down to "trauma resulting from the '64 defeat

[that] convinced a number of conservatives that it was time to go pragmatic: that rather than trying to get a hardcore philosophical conservative nominee it would be much better to take a man who is perceived to be a centrist, moderate conservative, and therefore presumably more electable than a philosophical conservative of the Goldwater-Reagan type."[1]

Nixon's reciprocation toward conservatives was equivocal. While aligning himself more closely with conservatives in the run-up to 1968, Nixon privately said he thought "Buckleyite" conservatives were a menace. Concerning Buckley's important support for Nixon, Evans later told Buckley biographer John Judis that "He perceived himself as a bridge between us and the administration and not as someone being in opposition."[2]

Nixon offered many aspects encouraging to conservatives, such as his emphasis on "law and order" amidst the chaos of urban rioting and the antiwar protest movement and his disposition not to "cut and run" from Vietnam. He was culturally conservative in many ways, or at least anti-liberal. His administration included a number of conservatives in senior positions; he had given general signals of wanting to pare back Johnson's Great Society programs and to appoint conservatives to the Supreme Court to swing the Court away from its excesses of the Warren Court era. Yet Nixon's lingering reputation from the 1960 campaign, along with some uncertainty about his larger foreign policy views, left many conservatives wary. Henry Kissinger's appointment to national security adviser was a wild card. His connections to Nelson Rockefeller bothered some conservatives, but as we have seen, Evans once lauded Kissinger as a source of sound thinking, and Buckley had vouched for him to Nixon.

Nixon filled out his cabinet and numerous senior staff positions with liberal Republicans, many of whom had been his critics or opponents in the 1968 campaign. Then there was the appointment of Kennedy-Johnson veteran Daniel Patrick Moynihan to be the principal domestic policy adviser. Moynihan's appointment raised eyebrows all around, from Democrats who regarded him as a traitor to the party to conservatives who worried he would pull Nixon to the left on social policy. As early as February 1969—barely a month in office—some conservatives were already sounding the alarm, including long-time Nixon supporter (and close friend of both Evans and Nixon) Ralph de Toledano. "The 'conservatives' won the election for Richard Nixon—and they are losing the election to him. It can no longer be denied that those to the right of center who carried the election for Nixon have gotten less than the back of his hand for their efforts."[3]

Evans held his fire for the moment. In several columns in 1967 and in his 1968 book, *The Future of Conservatism*, Evans had noted that Moynihan and several other liberal figures, including Richard Goodwin and Nathan Glazer, had started to express public doubts about the centralizing aspects of liberal governance and bureaucratic rule. But Moynihan was the person Evans thought the most conspicuous "man overboard" because of his shocking (to liberals) 1967 speech to the Americans for Democratic Action, in which Moynihan said that "Somehow liberals have been unable to acquire from life what conservatives seem to have been endowed with at birth, namely a healthy skepticism of the powers of government agencies to do good."[4] In the same column, Evans singled out one figure in particular for starting the wave of second thoughts: "Perhaps the first recorded instance of a liberal spokesman assembling these discontents into a critique of the liberal program was an article in *Harper's* back in 1963, by journalist Irving Kristol." He devoted a whole chapter of *The Future of Conservatism* to "The New Consensus." In explaining how the old liberal consensus was falling apart under pressure from the right as well as from the critiques of thoughtful liberals, Evans had discovered "neoconservatism," though the term had not caught on yet.

And then there was Vice President Spiro Agnew. As governor of Maryland, Agnew had been regarded as a liberal Republican, and he had supported Nelson Rockefeller for the GOP nomination in 1968. But Nixon campaign aide Pat Buchanan had noted Agnew's tough law and order stands amidst the riots of 1967 and 1968 and helped convince Nixon that the unknown Agnew, coming from a border state, would bolster Nixon's electoral appeal in the mid-Atlantic and border states region. What no one counted upon, not even Buchanan, is that Agnew would become a conservative champion in the Nixon White House. If running mates are usually assigned the "attack dog" role in campaigns, Agnew didn't really come fully into the role until after the election. In a series of speeches in 1969 and 1970, Agnew became a conservative hero with several strong speeches attacking the news media (his most recalled phrases about the media being "nattering nabobs of negativism" and "an effete corps of impudent snobs") and the antiwar protest movement. The attack on the media and the controversy it sparked contributed to opening new doors for Evans.

The major media outlets Agnew attacked by name, such as the *New York Times*, the *Washington Post*, and the TV network news programs, responded strongly against Agnew's charges, calling them attempted intimidation or threats of censorship. But opinion polls showed strong public sympathy with Agnew's criticism. As a long-time critic of media bias, Evans came out fully on Agnew's side, writing in one editorial that "In our opinion he was right as rain" and in another that "Agnew's criticism on this score was all too obviously correct...Can anyone name a conservative newsman on network television?"[5] He also mocked the major media for their thin-skinned reaction to Agnew's criticism:

In what, then, does the "intimidation" consist? Quite simply in the fact that the Vice President has dared to criticize the media at all... What is actually being suggested by the liberal spokesmen is that the commentators and pundits may lambaste Nixon or Agnew or anybody else at interminable length, but no one in turn may criticize them. The Huntleys and Sevareids and Smiths may sit in judgment on the nation, but no one may sit in judgment on them. In short, they can dish it out, but can't take it.[6]

Between Nixon's "silent majority" speech and Agnew's attacks on the media, there began the same kind of anthropological media expeditions that became the rage after Donald Trump's surprise victory in the heartland states in 2020—a rush to "explain" what existed outside the media bubbles of New York and Los Angeles. *Esquire* magazine published a long feature article by Tom Ferrell in May 1970, "If the Silent Majority Could Talk, What Would It Say?"[7] The title alone betrays the elite media condescension toward the 59 percent of Americans who told pollsters they thought of themselves as belonging to the silent majority. The article covered four conservative media figures who *Esquire* clearly regarded as exotic, saying of one of them, broadcaster Paul Harvey, *"Variety* reports: 'Harvey appears popular everywhere except along the Eastern seaboard.' A sinister pattern emerges: there is one America that knows and loves Paul Harvey, and another, smaller America that doesn't." That smaller America, however, is the one that lives in Manhattan; Washington, DC; and Hollywood.

The other three media figures *Esquire* covered were George Putnam, a popular LA TV broadcaster and friend of Ronald Reagan; S. L. A. Marshall, a controversial broadcaster and columnist based in Detroit; and Evans. One wonders whether *Esquire* had any self-consciousness about producing a feature article whose effect would only reinforce conservative animosity toward the "prestige" media. Describing Indianapolis as "America's innermost boondock," the beginning of the section about Evans opens thus:

> Republican virtue is unlikely to perish in Indianapolis so long as the editorial offices of the Indianapolis *News* continue to confront University Park and the hitherto immortal marble of the Indiana War Memorial. Behind the window, M. Stanton Evans (as his books and *National Review* articles are signed) or plain Stan Evans (his by-line in the *News*) watches over the editorial pages of the only afternoon paper in town…Evans' desk faces autographed pictures of Barry Goldwater and Strom Thurmond, who in turn face Evans and, beyond him, the War Memorial. The air conditioner carries a bumper sticker: Keep Cool with Coolidge.

One of the aspects of media bias that Evans pointed out to *Esquire* was the skewed view of the opinion spectrum: "In the talk shows, for example: I remember one where the people they presented consecutively as sort of guests to discuss issues at large were Pete Hamill, Jimmy Breslin, and some girl who's leading the women's liberation front, and that was it, that was the ideological portion of the program. There was no indication that these were not thoroughly representative spokesmen for American society, these interesting people that they brought out there."

Evans was used to eastern media regarding Indiana as not even attaining the level of a provincial backwoods. Washington-based columnist Joseph Kraft described Indiana as "One of the last backwaters in America," though it is not clear whether Kraft visited the state in offering this judgment. A 1967 Evans column took aim at a *New York Times* article on Indianapolis by an obscure writer named Robert Gover: "According to a recent issue of the *Times*, Indianapolis is worse than a cornfield. It is a cultural wilderness populated with sullen conformists—what

Mencken used to call a 'Sahara of the bozart.'"[8] Evans, always on guard against what he called "ventriloquist journalism" (see Chapter 10), was safe in assuming that *Esquire*'s Farrell would make no difference. Now, nearly three years later, he returned to that column with Farrell:

> "The people of Indiana are self-conscious of themselves as Hoosiers, as Midwesterners," he says; "a certain hostility toward the East may be assumed. Indiana is generally selected out for reproach by visiting *New York Times* correspondents and people like that, and of course we always argue with them a lot. Robert Gover, the guy who wrote these Kitten books, came out here and did an article in *The New York Times Magazine*, a sort of Menckenesque treatment of Indiana, the Sahara-of-the-Bozart type thing, putting down Indiana for corn-fed characteristics, and of course we immediately took issue with this and denounced him, and so forth. Indiana has in some ways become symbolic to people in the East of something that they don't like, and vice versa, and there's a natural antagonism. But to my knowledge that kind of thing has never come up in a political context. This was Nixon's strongest state in '68. The Republican candidate doesn't have to come in here and say, aha, vote for me and defeat the evil powers of the East. When Nixon speaks here, generally he speaks in generalizations, you know, like 'get out and do good for America,' or something like that, and it carries the state."

Farrell also quoted Evans noting how the media ignores conservatism on college campuses while lavishing attention on every leftist student agitation that happened.

Farrell added that "Evans is not impressed by signs that the networks may now be trying consciously to balance their content," but major media organizations were stung by Agnew's attack—and likely more so by the favorable public reaction to it—and decided to take a few steps toward balance. In addition, as Nixon took office, the Federal Communications Commission had finalized new regulations for the "fairness doctrine" requiring equal time for opposing viewpoints on broadcast media. CBS Radio decided to broaden its range of viewpoints with a new radio commentary program called "Spectrum" and signed Evans in 1971 to be one of six print journalist commentators who contributed five-minute segments three times a week.[9] It was the beginning of Evans's electronic media career. He contributed to "Spectrum" until 1980, when he moved on to become a commentator for National Public Radio and later in the 1980s for Voice of America. Although he principally appeared on radio, CBS used him from time to time on television news specials.

The first thing Evans did upon signing on with CBS was join William F. Buckley Jr. in a lawsuit against the compulsory labor union for broadcast media, the American Federation of Television and Radio Artists (AFTRA), advancing the argument that compulsory union membership violated their First Amendment rights. Both Buckley and Evans wrote frequently about the case, as did several other conservative writers. After winning at the trial court level in 1973 (the trial judge agreeing with the First Amendment arguments), the case dragged on in appeals until 1978, when the case was settled with the stipulation that AFTRA had to notify members that they weren't required to join the union but still had to pay bargaining dues if they worked under an AFTRA-negotiated contract. Both sides claimed vindication from this compromise, but Buckley and Evans have the stronger case as a union couldn't compel them to observe strikes or submit to other union "orders" or disciplinary measures. Evans thought it an important victory: "You cannot be expelled from a union to which you don't belong; or if you do belong, an employer can't fire you just because you are expelled."[10] Evans and Buckley were correct to see the case as the first step in a long line of cases that step-by-step eroded coercive union power over the next three decades.

Signing up with CBS was the first step in becoming known to a wider national audience beyond just the conservative press. The next important step came in 1973, when the *Los Angeles Times* syndicate picked him to write a thrice-weekly column. While Evans's media career was stepping up into a higher gear, he also took time to attend the launch of Apollo 12 at Cape Canaveral, where he sat in the viewing stands with Frank Sinatra and Vice President Agnew.

The other major step forward came when a series of events led Evans to became chairman of the American Conservative Union in 1971. The ACU had been on a roller-coaster since its founding in 1964. The first chairman, Evans's good friend Don Bruce, resigned after a year of frenetic activity getting ACU off to a fast start, traveling the country giving speeches and taking meetings almost nonstop. Ohio Congressman John Ashbrook succeeded Bruce as ACU chairman, and the organization branched out in several new directions. William Rusher moonlighted as ACU's political director, and Frank Meyer supervised a series of ACU policy studies and helped launch an ACU newsletter, *Battle Line*. By degrees ACU began to lobby and electioneer more directly, if still on a modest scale. In 1968 there was internal debate about whether to endorse George Wallace's independent candidacy. *Human Events*, practically joined at the hip with ACU (Tom Winter, the editor and publisher of *Human Events*, was on ACU's board by this time), ran a rare two-page editorial arguing why conservatives shouldn't vote for Wallace and endorsed Nixon, and ACU's board ultimately rejected the Wallace idea and endorsed Nixon too.[11]

Despite ACU's endorsement of Nixon, they didn't have to wait long to find fault with him and to start edging into a critical stance. One early effort aimed at blunting a proposed constitutional amendment to abolish the Electoral College, which had significant Republican support in Congress and the tacit blessing of the White House, although the president plays no formal role in the constitutional amendment process. (With the Electoral College once again under criticism after the 2000 and 2016 elections, it is worth recalling that the reason for the bipartisan support for abolishing the EC in 1969 was to prevent a rerun of George Wallace's independent campaign, which plausibly threatened to deprive either Nixon or Humphrey of an electoral college majority, at which time Wallace intended to broker a pro-segregation deal from one of the candidates in return for his pledged electors.) Jeffrey Bell, a young activist who later worked for Governor Reagan in California, wrote a confidential eight-page memo ACU distributed to Republican Party leaders warning against the idea because it would disadvantage Republican presidential campaigns in the future. The amendment passed the House easily but later died in the Senate. Bell's memo persuaded several conservatives who had backed the amendment to change their minds.[12]

The most significant early breach with Nixon occurred in the summer of 1969 when Nixon proposed a federal guaranteed annual income, the "Family Assistance Plan" (FAP). The proposal, a brainchild chiefly of domestic policy adviser Moynihan, divided the right. On the one hand, it appeared to follow Milton Friedman's long-time proposal for a "negative income tax" as a substitute for the patchwork social service and gap-ridden income support programs of the New Deal and Great Society. On the other hand, FAP represented a centralization of welfare in Washington (although the existing welfare system derived from a federal mandate, states were allowed considerable leeway in designing and managing their federal welfare obligation and, most crucially, benefit levels), and moreover FAP didn't abolish any existing social programs such as food stamps or housing subsidies.

FAP also divided the left, which thought Nixon's proposed benefit levels were too low. Ultimately the left had as much to do with killing FAP in Congress, though it took several years, than opposition from conservatives. In his columns and editorials, Evans tried to steer a middle ground during Nixon's first year, offering praise for Nixon's statements on Vietnam and defense policy generally, and initially expressed mild skepticism about FAP. In his first *Indianapolis News* column after FAP's announcement, Evans liked the general principle Nixon articulated of a "new federalism" that would return power and revenue to the states, but he expressed skepticism of the program's proposed work incentives while suspecting that once in place, there would be constant political pressure to raise benefit levels. But the column was relatively restrained; it did not conclude that FAP should be opposed outright.[13]

Evans's measured tone toward Nixon in the *Indianapolis News* may partly reflect Nixon's high popularity in Indiana; no editor wants to get too far out of line with the opinions of readers. He was more directly critical of FAP in his writing about it elsewhere, such as in his "At Home" column in *National Review Bulletin* and in *Human Events*. *Human Events* published a long front-page feature article attacking FAP as "the most expensive welfare program this country has ever produced...Republicans need to ask themselves: do they want to be known as the party which put 23 million [more] people on welfare?"[14] By early 1970 ACU decided to go into active opposition to FAP, producing a critical study by economist Henry Hazlitt called "Solution or Socialism," which concluded that FAP would double the number of

Americans on welfare. ACU accompanied this with a public relations drive to generate thousands of letters to Congress opposing FAP. (It further helped that Governor Reagan decided, practically alone among the fifty state governors, to oppose FAP vigorously.) ACU founded a special project to lobby state legislators on both FAP and the electoral college amendment, the American Legislative Exchange Council (ALEC), which was later spun off into an autonomous entity that thrives today. "So effective was the special ACU report," ACU boasted in March 1970, "that White House aides openly admitted it had shaken up the prospects for the enactment for the Nixon legislation."[15]

FAP eventually failed in the Senate, though it took almost four years, during which time the Nixon Administration also proposed a federal child care add-on program that enraged conservatives further. Other areas of Nixon's domestic policy were arousing conservative anxiety. Federal spending was rising fast, producing a record budget deficit, and inflation was taking off, with mounting support for wage and price controls, including from some Republicans. Nixon initially resisted the idea, and Evans wrote several columns and editorials attacking wage and price controls while channeling Milton Friedman's teaching that inflation was a problem of loose monetary policy. Wage and price controls, he argued in 1969, "will do nothing to halt the spiral but would do a great deal to crush the freedoms of Americans and make our economic and other problems even worse than they are."[16]

Media coverage of inflation was one of Evans's favorite examples of economic illiteracy. Saying that rising costs ("cost-push" inflation it was called) were a primary cause of inflation was like saying "wet sidewalks cause rain." This common media trope confused cause and effect: "It is silly to argue that 'cost push' from any particular wage or price is 'causing' inflation. Price increases can result from inflation, but they cannot cause it. If the money supply were not being inflated, a dollar more spent for a General Motors car would simply be a dollar not spent for something else."[17] It took a decade for the media to begin to understand this basic fact. In the meantime, his many columns and editorials on the subject during these years were a virtual seminar in basic economics. In the meantime, despite Nixon's disclaimer, Congress passed legislation granting the president power to impose wage and price controls anyway.

Relations between conservatives and the Nixon administration continued to deteriorate. The Nixon experience generated one of Evans's most recalled rhetorical questions: "Why is it that whenever one of us gets into a position of power to do some good, he's no longer one of us?" Evans started joking that "There are only two things I don't like about the Nixon Administration—its domestic policy, and its foreign policy." (An alternative version, told at a speaking appearance in San Francisco, ran as follows according to a local newspaper account: "'I can total the good things and the bad things. First I can total the good things. I'll do that.' He stood silent for several seconds, then said: 'Now I'll list the bad things.'")

In January 1970 ACU produced a broadside attacking Nixon written by Evans, Frank J. Johnson, and Henry Hazlitt, "The Nixon Administration: The Conservative Judgment." Despite some positive signs on domestic policy, there was, as *Human Events* summarized the ACU report, "a genuine unease about the Nixon Administration...We don't accuse the Nixon Administration of being truly liberal, or even blindly middle-of-the-road. More often than not, it appears confused and at cross purposes with itself. Too frequently it seems as if the President has no real philosophy."[18] The ACU report concluded, "conservatives get the words; the liberals get all the action."

As conservatives wrestled with their unease over Nixon

throughout 1969 and 1970, the American Conservative Union moved toward a changing of the guard. ACU wanted to step up its activism across the board, from raising money to spend on behalf of candidates and causes, more lobbying on Capitol Hill, and outreach to the wider world. The current chairman, Rep. John Ashbrook of Ohio, was in the midst of a divorce, on top of which there was some sentiment among ACU leaders that having an elected official as chairman of the organization was less than ideal. Evans had recently joined ACU's board of directors along with several close colleagues, including Tom Winter of *Human Events* and other ACU stalwarts such as William Rusher convinced Evans to succeed Ashbrook as chairman in February 1971. "I have a hard act to follow," Evans wrote of his predecessor, Ashbrook, about whom he was always enthusiastic. ACU enjoyed significant growth in scope and influence in the 1970s under Evans's leadership (which ran until 1977) despite the usual ups and downs of nonprofit organizations that struggle with erratic fundraising and infighting.

FAP and other domestic issues continued to fester throughout 1970 and into 1971. Evans in particular was dismayed at Nixon's lack of spending restraint. Shortly after Nixon introduced his proposed deficit-heavy budget in early 1971, he made the infamous comment that "We are all Keynesians now," a phrase that could scarcely be exceeded in its capacity to annoy conservatives. It is possible to trace the ebbing support of conservatives by the banner page-one headlines in *Human Events*: "Conservatives Step Up Attacks on Nixon Policies" (July 25, 1970); "Disturbing Trends in Domestic Policy" (March 6, 1971, in *HE*'s largest font size). Evans wrote of the scene on the thousand-day mark that the Nixon administration's "presentation of liberal policies in the verbal trappings of conservatism has become the distinguishing ploy of the

Nixon government" and that it "used conservative energies to sustain a further national movement to the left."

The priority Evans placed on government spending and the growth of the bureaucracy is best revealed in a comment he made in 1975 about the midterm election of 1970, where Nixon campaigned vigorously for Republican candidates but with disappointing results on election day:

> One would think the Republican Party's experience under Richard Nixon would be a sufficient lesson here in terms of ethics and politics alike. Especially memorable was the 1970 by-election in which the GOP defaulted the economic critique of the liberal welfare state to concentrate on "social issues"—meaning drugs, permissiveness, crime, and so on. The result was a predictable disaster, since this left the economic issues to the time-dishonored promises of the liberal Democrats.[19]

On the surface this may seem a curious position given the growing significance of social issues to the improving conservative and Republican electoral fortunes in the 1970s and beyond. Evans here sounds like many libertarian and centrist critics of the "religious right," but Evans was no pure libertarian. He wrote frequently about crime, social disorder, sexual permissiveness, and against abortion on demand in his *Indianapolis News* columns. But as previously discussed, he discerned the connection between the rise of social permissiveness and unmoored individualism and the growth of government. The logic of his position, still not widely appreciated, is that a truly limited government would have a reciprocal influence on the virtue of the people. In other words, the most practical way to promote virtue is to cut federal spending dramatically. This position was as exotic then as it is unfamiliar today. It was his equivalent of Cato's refrain in the Roman Senate: *Carthāgō dēlenda est*—Carthage must be destroyed!

But it was foreign policy that ended up being the cause that propelled the conservative unease with Nixon to the breaking point. Many leading conservatives doubted that Nixon's strategy for extricating the U.S. from the war would work but were more concerned about the direction of arms control policy, insufficient defense spending, and questionable European diplomacy, most ominously, at the time, the apparent blessing of West German Chancellor Willy Brandt's attempted appeasement of the Soviet bloc along with rumors of seeking an opening to Red China.

Then came the bolt out of the blue: Nixon's surprise announcement on July 15, 1971, that he would travel to China the following year, thus ending two-plus decades of American policy that regarded the Communist giant as a pariah regime. In Evans's case, one of his chief criticisms of President Kennedy's foreign policy had been that it was weak toward China ("conniving to put Red China in the United Nations," he said in an August 1961 column), and now *Nixon* was sending us down that road. Henry Kissinger attempted to convince conservative leaders, including Buckley and Governor Reagan, that Nixon's trip didn't represent a major strategic shift, let alone a betrayal of the free Republic of China on Taiwan, but no one bought it. Evans agitated immediately for conservatives to step up their public pressure on Nixon, writing a few days later that "The President's centrism, by its very nature, brings him out at the vector sum of forces. When all the forces are surging from the left, and none from the right, he will be increasingly driven in a leftward direction."

Although the idea did not originate with Evans, ten days later Buckley convened a meeting of conservative leaders at his Manhattan residence to decide how to respond publicly. The senior editors of *National Review* and *Human Events* were both well represented along with the leaders of several conservative activist groups, including the Young Americans for Freedom, ACU, and the New York Conservative Party. As chairman of ACU as well as a prominent contributor to *National Review* and *Human Events*, Evans was not only there, but as had been the case so many times in the past, he was tapped to draft the formal statement for the group over seven hours of discussion. Participants included Frank Meyer, James Burnham, and William Rusher from *NR*; Tom Winter and Allan Ryskind from *Human Events*; Randal Teague from YAF; Daniel J. Mahoney, chairman of the New York Conservative Party; John Jones and Jeff Bell from ACU; Anthony Harrigan of the Southern States Industrial Council; Neal McCaffrey from Arlington House Publishing; and Neal Freeman. In 1968 among the assembled group only Evans and Rusher had been hostile to Nixon; at the Manhattan meeting nearly everyone had turned unfavorable.

Evans's initial draft included a full indictment of both domestic and foreign policy, but Buckley and a couple other figures resisted extending the attack to domestic policy and favored limiting it to foreign affairs. There was additional wrangling over some general terms. Evans wanted the statement to declare that conservatives were "repudiating" Nixon, while Buckley wanted it to read that they were "suspending support." Buckley also wanted their policy positions to be called "planks," while Evans and others preferred "demands." Buckley's position won out on all of these shadings, chiefly because of his preeminence.

According to John Judis's account, Evans was angry at times during the meeting but understood the importance of keeping Buckley on board. "The only thing that really gave us credibility was Buckley," Evans told Judis.[20] The resulting document acceded to all of Buckley's conditions. It concentrated on foreign policy matters, saying that "We touch only lightly on the failures of Mr.

Nixon's Administration domestically." It stopped short of opposing Nixon's 1972 renomination and ended as follows:

> We do not plan *at the moment* to encourage formal political opposition to President Nixon in the forthcoming primaries, but we propose to keep all options open in the light of development in the next months. We reaffirm our personal admiration—in the case of those of us who are his friends or who have been befriended by him—our affection for Richard Nixon, and our wholehearted identification with the purposes he has over the years espoused as his own and the Republic's. We consider that our defection is an act of loyalty to the Nixon we supported in 1968. [Emphasis added.]

In other words, Nixon was on probation.

The declaration of the conservative "suspension of support" for Nixon bore twelve signatories, who instantly became known as the "Manhattan Twelve": Bell, Buckley, Burnham, Harrigan, Jones, Mahoney, McCaffrey, Meyer, Rusher, Ryskind, Teague, and Winter. It was decided that they would neither invite nor accept any endorsements from office holders.

Conspicuously missing from the signatories was...Evans even though he had been the principal author of the declaration. Most accounts say Evans withheld his signature out of annoyance that Nixon's domestic offenses were omitted, but it is possible that as editor of the *Indianapolis News*, he didn't want to embarrass or offend his publisher, Eugene C. Pulliam, who was a strong Nixon supporter. And as Indiana was one of Nixon's strongest states, it didn't pay to put too much distance between yourself and your readers.

If the Manhattan Twelve declaration sounds like a quixotic stand, the White House didn't see it that way. Pat Buchanan had been quietly encouraging conservatives in their criticism of the administration, and recalling how the defection of the left had cost Lyndon Johnson a chance at reelection in 1968, the matter became a four-alarm fire. Buchanan attempted to intercede with the Washington-based conservatives such as Ryskind and Winters, while Henry Kissinger was dispatched to try to appease Buckley. Buckley convinced Kissinger to meet with the Manhattan Twelve, and half of them turned up at the White House on August 12. That Kissinger would devote ninety minutes to a group of conservatives he likely considered mere scribblers is evidence of how seriously the Nixon White House regarded their vulnerability to their right flank. Such a circumstance would have been unthinkable under Eisenhower.

As previously mentioned, Evans had once held Kissinger in esteem, but in later years Evans would say that he only met Kissinger three times and that each time Kissinger lied to him. Although it is not clear when Evans began to have doubts about Kissinger, the August 12 meeting was surely the point of no return. Evans had requested a meeting with Kissinger in June, but there was no response until after the Manhattan Twelve declaration was issued. Kissinger allowed Pat Buchanan to broker the meeting on the condition that Kissinger's remarks to the group would be strictly off the record. Kissinger's memorandum of the conversation runs for fourteen single-spaced pages and is of such detail that one suspects Kissinger taped the meeting. (The memo was declassified in 2004.) Although the group included several prominent and vocal conservatives, Evans did most of the questioning and arguing with Kissinger. The participants included William Rusher, publisher, *National Review*; Allan Ryskind, editor, *Human Events*; Jeffrey Bell, editor, ACU *Battle Lines*; Dan Mahoney, chairman, NY Conservative Party; Bill Schneider, staff, Sen. James Buckley; John Fischer, American Security Council; Randal Teague and Ron Docksai, Young Americans for Freedom; Frank

Shakespeare, director, United States Information Agency; Gen. Alexander Haig; Pat Buchanan, White House Communications.

Kissinger started out polite but was direct. He began with a long recitation of the strategic difficulties Nixon had inherited from his predecessors, including especially the loss of America's nuclear superiority over the Soviet Union during the middle years of the 1960s, on top of which the Vietnam War had further strapped the latitude of President Nixon. Kissinger patiently laid out Nixon's strategy to rebuild America's strategic position, resting on pushing through a program to develop anti-ballistic missile defense and the first Strategic Arms Limitation Treaty (SALT). He attacked the permanent foreign policy bureaucracy, explaining how he and Nixon were going around the State Department in their dealings with Moscow. Finally, he vigorously defended Nixon's opening to China: "I take it that no one is prone to accuse the President of excessive sentimentality, especially *vis-a-vis* Communists." He went on to explain the benefits he thought would come from treating with a nation with no nuclear missiles against a neighbor who had 1,500 of them, especially since the latter nation (the Soviet Union) was most responsible for unrest in the world. Far from damaging what relations we had with the USSR, the China opening had gotten the Russians' attention. "The fact of the matter, gentlemen," Kissinger said, "is that up to July 17 [Soviet Ambassador] Dobrynin and the Russians were insolent in their dealings with us. Since July 17 we have had their full attention. Necessity has brought us together with the Chinese, and necessity will dictate the future of our relationship." Apparently Kissinger believed that Nixon's opening to China would actually strengthen Taiwan's position in the UN, though it is hard to credit someone of Kissinger's intelligence with such a naive position.

After this strong beginning, Kissinger took up a complaint

about a lack of support from conservatives that an unbiased observer might consider whining, and the meeting went downhill from there.

> The previous administrations had moral support from the Establishment at large, from the respectable public. This Administration, gentlemen, is the loneliest administration imaginable. The intellectual Establishment turned on me, you know, only after it became clear that I wouldn't turn on the President. During the marches on Washington, for instance, we got no comments, no calls of support. During the Bay of Pigs affair, I know the Administration under Kennedy received telegrams, letters, phone calls, and the like. We don't get that kind of support, and, to be quite frank, we don't hear that kind of support from conservatives.

If Kissinger thought this attempt at shaming would work, Evans quickly disabused him:

> First, just a general comment, Dr. Kissinger. You have loosely covered the areas in which conservatives have supported the Administration—namely: ABM, the demonstrators, Cambodia, and Vietnamization. Frankly, your criticism of conservatives on that score does not seem to me to be appropriate.

From there Evans began to lay out a criticism of Nixon's foreign policy that involved a direct challenge to Kissinger's portrayal of it, concluding with: "The Johnson/Kennedy foreign policy theory seems to have taken over in the Nixon Administration." He went on to offer a direct challenge to the mutual assured destruction (MAD) doctrine at the core of American strategic defense planning: "I consider it a scandal to allow our population to be used as hostages in the Defense sense."

Kissinger parried with a recitation of the political difficulties of getting Congress to fund a serious missile defense program and having to settle for a minimal missile defense that only protected America's retaliatory capability. He didn't address the problem of MAD that Evans brought up, and Evans wasn't impressed, repeating that this understanding was no different from that of the Kennedy/Johnson liberals. Kissinger continued to use the excuse of political problems in Congress: "We have a problem of governing here. We can't fight with the bureaucracy all the time on all the issues. We have to get what we can get. We are the poor people in Washington." At this point Kissinger dissembled at length about the fast-improving capacities of Soviet intercontinental missiles in what seems to have been an attempt to wear down his critics with technical detail. At one point, General Alexander Haig, still a serving Army officer seconded to the National Security Council, came to Kissinger's aid with still more technical details.

Kissinger had a valid point that the Vietnam War had badly distorted America's defense spending and strategic planning. But the Manhattan Twelve delegation wasn't swayed or set back in the least, pressing Kissinger on why Nixon didn't "make a personal appeal to the people of the nation" on these questions. Kissinger demurred on these more direct "political" questions as though he were a mere technician.

From there the conversation moved on to Nixon's China initiative and arms control questions involving several other participants from the Manhattan Twelve delegation, with no satisfaction found on any point. After describing several fine points of the administration's strategy in the arms control talks with the Soviets, Evans returned to the fray to press Kissinger directly on what Evans regarded as their lack of courage:

EVANS: You have confirmed my belief that the Administration responds quite dramatically to immediate pressure.

KISSINGER: On defense?

EVANS: No, in general.

KISSINGER: Our basic Vietnam strategy, I can assure you, has not been affected by the media. Our basic defense strategy, similarly, has not been affected by the media. You know that in Congress the situation is simply impossible, now that Senator Russell has died. We have no Senator who can deliver votes. Senator Stennis is a decent man, but he is no fighter. Under conditions of incipient civil war in Washington we have...

EVANS (interrupting Kissinger): If the press is a factor, and I think it should be less of a factor than it is, my conviction is that the *Washington Post* and *New York Times* do not represent American public opinion.

KISSINGER: But every Congressman and Senator reads the *Post* columnists more eagerly than he reads classified documents. We must deal with that fact. Wherever there has been a real challenge, as in Cienfuegos, and as in the Middle East, we have been tough. We went to the very edge of war in the Middle East. One must view the Moscow/Peking developments as diplomatic counterweights of the same sort. I can assure you the Russians do not think we are going soft.

It is difficult to imagine a worse answer to attempt with Evans, as he made clear in the sequel:

EVANS: The media reaction has been an orgy of congratulations, for the Administration and the media itself. Old China experts have been resuscitated and dragged before Congress. We have seen the media distort the White House action, perhaps but still...

KISSINGER: If it hadn't been for the China initiative in the papers, you know it would have been Ellsberg and the Pentagon Papers, or the Vietnam War. You must consider the alternatives in May and June of this year.

EVANS: You don't mean that the China initiative had anything to do with Daniel Ellsberg?

KISSINGER: No, the China trip was scheduled anyway, but the press impact had that effect.

Sensing the increasing tension between Evans and Kissinger, another member of the group (not identified in Kissinger's memorandum) broke in to change the subject back to arms control questions and U.S. clout in the United Nations, where Kissinger assured the group that "Ambassador [George H. W.] Bush says he can get the majority for us," especially on the question of keeping Taiwan in the General Assembly. This and other answers on arms control did little to mollify the visiting conservatives.

Then Evans broke in again to draw the meeting to a close:

EVANS: I thank you, Dr. Kissinger, for being candid. I can appreciate the difficulties the Administration faces. But I must be candid myself, and say that my prior opinion still holds...And that opinion is, on the whole, the Administration has a different strategic analysis from the one I support...All we can do is go on what you *do* in the Administration.

KISSINGER: We need pressure from the Right and we appreciate it. But you are too harsh on the Administration. Without our Administration there would be no MIRV development, no ABM, no Army modernization.

EVANS: I was not referring simply to defense matters.

KISSINGER: You are right; you must judge us on our actions. I recognize your group, and hope you know we are listening. I also hope that the worst criticism that you will have of us is that we haven't moved far enough in defense matters. I just hope you will stop yelling at us, and start yelling at our enemies. I must say to this group that I have never spoken with this degree of candor before. I must emphasize that none of these matters can appear directly or indirectly in print. Please, you cannot discuss this with people.

It was evident that the meeting had changed no minds among the Manhattan Twelve. Two years later, in a feature headlined "The Trouble With Henry Kissinger," Evans made oblique reference to the essence of this meeting: "Quizzed about such matters, Kissinger and his proponents reply that he is doing the best he can for hard-nosed anti-Communism amid impossible circumstances. The 'doves' are rampant in Congress, the American people indifferent to vital questions of defense and foreign policy. What can one do? The measures promoted by Kissinger are the most that can be obtained in default of sensible public attitudes. That explanation has persuaded certain hawks and conservatives, who come away believing Kissinger shares their own distress and is battling valiantly against enormous odds. It is, however, unconvincing."[21]

Three days after the Manhattan Twelve meeting with Kissinger, Nixon announced a wage-and-price freeze and an end to the gold standard. Evans didn't crow, "I told you so," but he could have.

By the fall the conservative fury at Nixon had not subsided. Amidst speculation that Nixon might dump Agnew from the ticket in 1972, ACU endorsed Agnew but not Nixon for the ticket

("Agnew Must Stay" read the front page headline of ACU's *Battle Line* newsletter in June 1971), while YAF endorsed Reagan for president for 1972 in September. The media dismissed the Manhattan Twelve with the view that unhappy conservatives had "nowhere else to go." Evans disputed this: "A number of indices suggest this complacent slogan is mistaken, and that if the Nixon strategists continue to operate in terms of it they will succeed in generating a very large conservative defection indeed."[22] (Before the 1972 election cycle was over, a few conservatives openly argued that they'd be better off voting for McGovern, so deep was their estrangement from Nixon. Evans didn't go that far. One of his favorite quips around the time was "That government is best which McGoverns least.")

Behind the scenes the White House did not take the conservative discontent lightly. The Manhattan Twelve continued to meet and refine their demands. Evans, Buckley, and Ryskind were deputized to restate the positions of the Manhattan Twelve and resume discussions with the White House. Evans was successful in restoring an emphasis on domestic policy concerns that Buckley had insisted on downplaying in the initial July meeting and changing their description to "demands."

In early November Ryskind met Charles Colson at the White House and presented the updated list, included killing FAP and the child-care proposal, guaranteeing Agnew's retention as the running mate in 1972, higher defense spending, and a less accommodating arms control strategy. The group's last meeting with White House staff occurred on December 1, and by Pat Buchanan's account, it went poorly. A long Buchanan memo to chief of staff Bob Haldeman and Attorney General John Mitchell said that "From the White House point of view, the convocation was the least constructive to date. They were not dissatisfied with the Administration response to their 'demands;' they were outraged."

Buchanan included Evans as among the small subgroup that "are now so anti-Nixon that they cannot, under conceivable circumstances, be brought back into the fold." Because of his preeminence among the conservative Nixon critics, Evans supposedly ended up on the infamous Nixon "enemies list," according to ABC News, though this may have been a case of mistaken identity as his name does not appear on any available reconstructions of Nixon's various enemies list (there was more than one), while columnist Rowland Evans does.

"This seems a fairly serious problem," Buchanan added in an understatement.[23]

By the end of December 1971, John Ashbrook decided to mount an insurgent challenge to Nixon, and Evans was all in. His optimism of 1968 that Nixon and the Republican Party would become a reliably conservative party was gone. In the January 1972 edition of ACU's monthly newsletter *Battle Line*, Evans devoted a full page to touting the Ashbrook challenge: "The Ashbrook race makes it plain that there is a body of opinion to Nixon's right which can no longer be dismissed by either the Administration or the media." Evans was under no illusion that Ashbrook would succeed in derailing Nixon's renomination, calling the venture "problematical," but he nevertheless thought merely mounting a challenge to an incumbent Republican president was a breakthrough. And it achieved some measurable results. Nixon vetoed "the so-called 'child development' bill" that the Manhattan Twelve had attacked and publicly defended Agnew from media critics. Evans concluded early in the new year: "The President is willing to make concessions to the right when there are pressing reasons to do so. The Ashbrook candidacy in a few short weeks has achieved more notable results for traditional GOP principles than have three years of going along to get along by other conservative Republican leaders."[24]

Ashbrook's challenge didn't end up making much of a dent in Nixon's 1972 reelection drive, but Evans's career entered a new and higher phase at the moment Nixon's unraveling caused a crisis for both the Republican Party and the conservative movement. Evans played a central and still largely unsung role in the recovery of both out of the ashes of Watergate.

CHAPTER 8

THE WATERGATE CONUNDRUM

The all-consuming "Nixon question" in the run-up to and after Nixon's forty-nine-state landslide in 1972 presents several provocative counterfactual scenarios to ponder. Nixon rolled over the Ashbrook challenge easily in the opening months of 1972, and when North Vietnam launched an offensive against the south in the spring, by which point most American ground combat troops had been withdrawn, Nixon responded with the kind of serious bombing campaign that hawks had long urged. The radical left's capture of the Democratic Party and George McGovern's nomination further alarmed conservatives and drove most back to supporting Nixon despite the misgivings over the first arms control treaties with the Soviet Union, the capitulation to China, and Nixon's domestic liberalism. Then, following the election, Nixon gave signs of shifting sharply to the right with a robust determination to control federal spending and confront the permanent bureaucracy.

What might have happened if George Wallace had captured the Democratic nomination instead of McGovern (Evans had taken note of Wallace's strong showing with GOP crossover voters in the Indiana primary shortly before he was shot) or had the Democrats nominated a conventional liberal like Edmund Muskie or Hubert Humphrey instead? It is doubtful that Nixon would have lost, but more conservatives might have stayed home (or voted with enthusiasm for Wallace) and made the outcome much closer. As it was, Nixon once again failed to have any coattails, with Republicans once again making meager gains in Congress. What if Watergate had never happened and Nixon had been able to carry on with his intended confrontation with the permanent government, almost surely rallying the right behind him?

As chairman of ACU as well as a journalist of national reputation, Evans had two front-row seats from which to observe and influence events. He attended the national conventions of both parties in 1972 (both held in Miami), filing daily columns in the *Indianapolis News.* In his usual contrarian mode, Evans noticed that the dominant narrative of McGovern's juggernaut supposedly built on populist enthusiasm among the young was a "simplistic fable" that overlooked several factual defects, starting with the fact that Hubert Humphrey actually received more primary votes than McGovern and that McGovern only received half the share of the Democratic primary electorate as Goldwater had in 1964, though the media portrayed Goldwater as "weak" and McGovern as a popular icon. Evans was not about to let this obvious contrast in media coverage slip by: "The conservative Goldwater was treated as a minority candidate although he was the clear choice of his party; the leftist McGovern is treated as the people's choice although he is clearly a minority candidate."[1] McGovern's victory, Evans observed, "was much more the result of the organizational finesse than it was of massive popular backing."[2] About the legendarily chaotic Democratic convention that nominated McGovern, Evans marveled that McGovern actually fought off attempts to push him even further to the left, with radical proposals on abortion, gay rights, and expanded welfare programs: "McGovern forces sent down the word that various far-out planks were to be defeated, although simultaneously wig-wagging to the radicals that McGovern was with them in spirit."[3]

But if the disarray and radicalism of the McGovern Democrats left the door open for a Republican landslide, Evans didn't think Republicans were aware of their opportunity. In several columns and editorials filed from Miami the next month, Evans sounded the alarm on the persistence of liberal Republicans to weaken the party platform and change the convention rules to augment their influence for the 1976 presidential election cycle. The GOP was "schizophrenic." "Behind the scenes," he wrote in a dispatch the day before the convention opened, "a bitter struggle to control the destiny of the GOP is being waged by party liberals and conservatives."[4] Evans was the kind of journalist who sat through hours of tedious rules committee proceedings at conventions—this one ran almost twelve hours, ending past 1:00 a.m.—because he knew that's where a lot of the key struggles were decided. "Reformist" party moderates like Charles Percy, Mac Mathias, and Bob Packwood urged including quotas for women and minority delegates and disproportionate delegate allocations favoring northeastern states rather than the sunbelt states where GOP voting strength was growing fastest. For Evans, this represented an attempt at "McGovernizing" the GOP. Fortunately, the conservatives held despite the relentlessness of the liberals ("a multiple offense that would put the Dallas Cowboys to shame"), which may not have been to their advantage. As Evans noted with barely suppressed glee, "Percy's oratory seemed in general to have a negative impact; the more he and other liberals jawed about the delegate matter, the fewer votes they received."[5] He was, however, pleased that Vice President Agnew's position in the party was strengthened at the convention; Evans predicted that Agnew now had the inside track on the 1976 GOP nomination. (Agnew had granted an interview to Evans at the convention.) One name was conspicuously missing from both Evans's coverage and the convention in general: Nelson Rockefeller.

About the GOP platform, Evans remained unimpressed: "To put it as gently as possible, the Republican platform is a bag of mush. From start to finish, it is almost totally devoid of anything which resembles traditional Republican principles." An unsigned editorial at the *News* (almost certainly written by Evans) touted Henry Hazlitt's presentation on economic issues (sponsored in part by the ACU) to the GOP platform committee, which the committee ignored.[6] The *Indianapolis News* offered the most tepid and backhanded endorsement of Nixon on election eve in November. Noting that the polls showed a Nixon landslide coming, the best the paper could do was say, "In our opinion the predicted outcome is the proper one...At home and abroad, the McGovern position is simply too radical."[7]

Once again Evans claimed vindication from the election result, a personal landslide for Nixon with only tepid gains for down-ballot Republicans on all levels (actually *losing* two Senate seats). Although Nixon claimed a mandate—who wouldn't upon winning forty-nine states?—Evans thought the result was more a rejection of McGovern than it was an affirmation of Nixon, whose more conservative campaign rhetoric didn't match up very well with its first-term record: "Republicans at this point must question the wisdom of the Nixon strategy which staked everything on getting the largest possible margin for the President while virtually ignoring candidates for Congress. Defeated aspirants for Senate and House would have been a great deal happier with a Nixon margin of less majestic proportions and a victory for themselves. In any event, the congressional GOP is in pretty bedraggled condition."[8]

Nixon's aborted second term will always be defined by Watergate and Watergate alone, though the larger story is important as it presents enduring problems with the conservative challenge to the institutionalized left that persisted through the Reagan and Trump presidencies (being the only other Republican presidents after Nixon who attempted to confront the permanent bureaucracy). Nixon began his second term intending to carry out a serious confrontation with Congress over federal spending along with a trial balloon for a sweeping reorganization of the executive branch to give the president more control over the bureaucracy. Both initiatives were quickly engulfed in the Watergate scandal, and Nixon soon reverted to his previous form, attempting to appease liberals with a universal health care proposal, a revival of FAP-style welfare reform, and new government regulation for the "energy crisis" that erupted in 1973.

Despite sharing Nixon's objectives in confronting a spend-thrift Congress and the permanent bureaucracy, Evans was, at best, ambivalent about Nixon's early second-term moves because of his general dislike of the aggrandizement of executive branch power going back to the New Deal and before. His most complete analysis of the scene is presented in his 1975 book, *Clear and Present Dangers: A Conservative View of America's Government*. Like his previous books, Evans was able to extend, in much more elegant prose and complete argument, the ideas he didn't have the space or time to dilate in his short-form, workaday editorials and columns. *Clear and Present Dangers* is a true tour de force, with the first third of the book offering a synoptic account of the idea of human liberty as it emerged from antiquity to the republican design of the founders' constitutionalism.

While the book did not comment directly on Nixon's designs to subdue the government, his extended treatment of liberal hypocrisy over executive power carries a clear implication: any enhancement of executive power in service of short-term policy wins would backfire in the hands of a future liberal president.

At that particular moment, liberals were decrying "the imperial presidency" (the title of Arthur Schlesinger's book). Evans
reviewed the history of liberals supporting increased executive
power going back decades, demonstrating that their newfound
concern over presidential power really amounted to objecting
to a Republican like Nixon using it. Liberal hypocrisy about
presidential power was especially evident when it came to the
specific issue of executive privilege, the contested doctrine
that dates to the Washington administration in the 1790s and
which Nixon invoked to resist Congress during the Watergate
investigation. Liberals who had championed executive privilege when Truman and Eisenhower invoked it against Sen. Joe
McCarthy, or President Kennedy against Congress in the early
1960s, suddenly found Nixon's claim outrageous and a threat
to the Constitution.

And even this contingent stance was selective and incomplete:
"Despite the rhetoric about restraining the President in matters
pertaining to Indochina and Watergate, the liberal instinct when
confronted with a serious problem in American society was to
make the President's power even greater...Rather than cutting
down executive power, we should leave it as it is, or even increase
it, and count on the President to be a reasonable fellow who will
behave himself. Roosevelt and Kennedy were such good fellows
and in general to be commended; Nixon was not and therefore
needed to be thrashed."[9]

This was mere prelude to his soaring fugue:

After one has encountered enough such distinctions, their common thread becomes apparent: when the exercise of presidential
power conflicts with what liberals want, then it is both immoral
and illegal; when the exercise of presidential power conforms to
what the liberals want, it is right and proper. The rule of thumb
is therefore not a constitutional guideline, a counterpoise of pow-

ers, or a diminution of presidential authority: *It is simply to have officials do what the liberals want.* Such is the liberal conception of a "strong presidency within the Constitution." The founding fathers had another name for it—a government of men, and not of laws.[10] [Emphasis in original.]

Following the lead of his *National Review* colleague James Burnham in Burnham's neglected 1959 classic, *Congress and the American Tradition,* Evans lamented the decline of Congressional lawmaking in favor of what he called executive legislation. Evans had an early grasp of what is today called the administrative state, noting the main problems that are commonplace today: the erosion of the status of Congress as the primary deliberative body that is now more subservient to the executive branch, the erosion of the separation of powers, and the progressive premise that this upending of the Constitution is a consequence of the necessity for "expertise" in policy making.[11] Some passages read like a preface to the later work of John Marini (to pick just one leading example):[12]

Confusion on this point [as to which branch is responsible for lawmaking] is closely tied to the idea of government as the preserve of "experts" weighing technical issues in which the goals are to be sought are already known and debate is reduced to a question of how best to achieve them. In this conception, Congress is thought to be in need of expert counsel, and the executive bureaucracy with its complement of experts is seen as the superior instrument of policy. The founders' view was of course quite different. The truly important questions, again, are not *technical* but *political*— not *how* we do something, but *what* we are to do.[13]

Thus Evans was not impressed with Nixon's 1973 proposal for a sweeping executive branch reorganization that would have created a small "super-cabinet" with increased White House control of the bureaucracy (though he did not write directly about it), knowing that such an aggrandizement in the hands of a future liberal president would make the constitutional deformation worse than it already was.

Clear and Present Dangers also includes two fine chapters on the problem of the judiciary, much on the mind of conservatives after the predations of the Warren Court a few years before. Once again Evans displays his breadth of learning and supreme ability at concision, drawing from the thought of leading legal figures past and present, from Edward Coke, William Blackstone, Oliver Wendell Holmes, and Edward Corwin to Felix Frankfurter, Robert McCloskey, Paul Freund, and Herbert Wechsler. Evans traces out a number of familiar issues of jurisprudence, especially the incoherence of the two-tiered treatment of civil liberties over economic rights and the presumption of judicial supremacy. He anticipates the shape of the conservative debate over "originalism" (a term that had not come into use at the time Evans wrote), in particular the idea that today goes under the banner of judicial engagement. Evans comes down fully on the side of basing judicial review on the old tradition of natural law and the common law, implicitly rejecting a simple stance of judicial restraint. "It is true that certain conservative spokesmen have executed the same maneuver [as the liberal judicial activists] in reverse—favoring judicial review in the 1930s, opposing it in the 1950s and 1960s. They are wrong, too" he wrote.[14] He also thought Congress should not be shy about exercising its constitutional power to confine the jurisdiction of the courts.

Even as the floodtide of Watergate was rising, Evans wasn't cutting Nixon any slack. A prominent target was deficit spending, which was soaring. Nixon's proposed 1973 budget made him "the biggest deficit-spending president in American peacetime history... The truly mammoth spending hikes have been for social welfare and other domestic giveaways... If the deficits are alarming, the bland explanations put forward by the Nixon regime are even more so."[15] Evans relished going toe-to-toe in the ring with Nixon's fiscal stewards. Although the Nixon of the opening months of 1973 was vetoing spending bills and impounding funds Congress had passed over his veto (before Watergate caused Nixon to retreat), Evans noted that Nixon's own budget proposal for 1973 was hardly the picture of fiscal rectitude. He wrote a long broadside against the Nixon budget in the February 1973 edition of ACU's *Battle Line,* arguing that "the runaway spending the President now professes to combat has been in considerable measure the work of his own administration."[16] He noted that there were several leading *Democrats* who were criticizing profligate spending.

In March 1974 Evans wrote directly to Nixon in his capacity as chairman of ACU, passing along the dismay of thirty-five Republican members of Congress over continued spending growth. Evans was direct in his criticism of Nixon's motivations:

> In view of the stern fiscal tone that you set in the first months of your present term, one can only conclude that this year's inflated budget has been designed in part to assuage your liberal critics who have grown progressively more strident since Watergate broke into the news. On past political history, it seems likely any such course is doomed to failure. It will fail to placate your long-time enemies on the left and, more importantly, it will alienate the conservative rank and file who have been your most loyal supporters.[17]

Nixon made the mistake of referring Evans's letter to budget director Roy Ash for a response, and Ash had no idea what he was letting himself in for. His letter made the usual Washington excuses: Congress and the courts made us do it!

> The fact is that the Congress has built these rapid spending increases into the budget, and the executive branch is increasingly powerless to control these costs...To conclude otherwise, and especially to conclude that this budget has been designed to assuage liberal critics, is a serious mistake.[18]

It is hard to conceive of an argument that would be less persuasive to Evans. He was on to every government spending trick, such as "current services" budgeting in which program spending grew automatically year-over-year, yielding the perverse only-in-Washington circumstance in which shaving the *growth* of a program budget was called a cut. (Reagan was fond of observing this perversity; he may have gotten the formula from Evans.) He was also familiar with budgeting tricks that concealed current spending through government accounting sleight of hand that booked the spending technically in future budget years or which committed the government to large spending increases down the road.

Evans responded with the kind of high political argument that challenged the resolve and clarity of the administration more than its technical acumen or political judgment:

> I have previously encountered the argument that enormous percentages of the budget are "uncontrollable" and that therefore the executive branch can do little to reduce the aggregate level of spending. I am frank to confess that I find this contention a little puzzling...
>
> What, exactly, is it that makes a budget item "uncontrollable"? Is it not true that what Congress and the Executive have done, they

can undo? And if so, why is it not possible, at least theoretically, to begin a mandated cutback of certain programs which are now scheduled for a mandated increase?

More specifically, even assuming the reluctance of Congress to pursue such a course, why is it not at least possible for the President to *propose* such mandated cutbacks, instead of merely accepting the inevitability of further spending hikes as if these were part of the natural order of things?...

Beyond these particular considerations, I find the whole "uncontrollable" position rather ominous for our free institutions. It seems to me this argument says the American people through their elected representatives have lost control of the budgetary process, and just be swept along by the momentum of a spending machine impervious to the ministrations of the President or anyone else. Adoption of this view strikes me as a surrender to mechanistic conceptions of government completely hostile to the spirit of representative government.[19]

Ash gamely tried to respond but dug himself in deeper with a reply several weeks later that retreated to the qualification that "the answers to your questions can be summed up by replacing the term 'uncontrollable' with '*relatively* uncontrollable' *in the short run*." From here Ash went into a long technical discussion of the structure of existing statutes that commit spending for intermediate and longer time periods. When Ash, a few months later, attempted to defend the Nixon fiscal record with the argument that, adjusted for inflation, federal spending was no higher than it had been in 1968 (Ash actually said with a straight face: "We need to dispel the shibboleth that government spending implies that government as such has been increasing"), Evans had the ACU unload on Ash in *Battle Line*: "He is engaging in a hoax the likes of which has not been seen since master showman P. T. Barnum tried to convince the American public that his phony Cardiff Giant was in fact one of a species of supersized humans who used to roam the earth."[20] By coincidence, Evans's disputation with Ash in 1974 coincided with the passage of the misnamed Budget Control Act, which further reduced the power of the president to control spending, following which there has been a step change in the rate of increasing federal spending. In other words, the "Budget Control Act" should be understood as its opposite.

And if the general weakness on spending wasn't enough to disappoint Evans, he was aghast at Nixon's January 1974 proposal for a national health care program of the kind Sen. Ted Kennedy had long demanded. Kennedy opposed Nixon's plan because he wanted national health care to be a Democratic achievement, a tactic he later confessed to regretting. But there's more to this story. Nixon's national health care plan meant "the President has relinquished all visible effort to hold the line on Federal spending and social experimentation." Worse was the motive Evans suspected: "The President is on the ropes from Watergate and apparently hopes to placate his liberal Democratic opposition by giving in to it...It seems doomed to political disappointment. It is idle to suppose the wolf-pack pursuing Nixon can be bought off with liberal social programs."[21]

The Watergate saga presented a highly complicated scene for Evans to sort out. While he remained highly critical of Nixon's policy directions, he understood immediately that the Watergate scandal involved much more than the mere partisan misdeeds and criminal behavior of the President and his circle. Evans had a three-part perspective on Watergate that he worked out during the scandal and after it reached its long, sorry end in August 1974: the hypocrisy and political motivation of the left, the foolish culpability of the Nixon White House and its connection with its lack of principle, and the way in which the abuse of government power would lead to more government power and future abuses.

While Evans never directly described Nixon's ouster as a coup, he pointed to several aspects of the deeper politics behind the matter. When the whole saga was over in 1974, Evans wrote, with a certain amount of foreshadowing of our recent impeachments:

> For the first time in history, an American President has been forced from office by an orchestrated public outcry—without benefit of trial or official defense. The precedent for the future, I should think, is fairly ominous. It is rendered more so by the fact that on the available record the offense for which the President has been deposed was no more objectionable than certain actions of his predecessors and by my assessment actually less so...My personal opinion is that we shall rue the day we permitted a President of the United States to be whipped from office in this fashion."[22]

But he also suggested only half facetiously in a column that the Watergate conspirators could turn the tables on their liberal tormenters by embracing the left's understanding of civil disobedience in service of justice. But in the end, Evans used this argument to double back against what he saw as the left's Thrasymachean argument that justice is merely the interest of the stronger.[23]

In later years Evans liked to joke that "I didn't support Nixon until *after* Watergate. I actually called over to the White House in the middle of their agony and said, 'Gosh, if I had only known you guys were doing all of this *neat stuff*, I wouldn't have been so hard on you. After wage and price controls, Watergate was a breath of fresh air!'" At the back of these witticisms (which liberal audiences always failed to appreciate) was his understanding of the hypocrisy of liberals and the media, who looked the other way at similar presidential abuses of power. He detailed how the Kennedy and Johnson administrations, at the highest levels, engaged in the exact same actions, including bugging Republican campaigns and using government agencies such as the FCC and the IRS to intimidate political opponents that were at the center of Watergate. In fact, Evans had detailed many of these executive branch abuses of power in two chapters of his 1965 book, *The Liberal Establishment*, in chapters entitled "The Silencers" and "Censorship and Muzzling." "Nothing was done, whatsoever, under Nixon that had not been done by President Kennedy," Evans said later. And of course the media came in for justified criticism: "It is noteworthy that the people who most loudly condemn this clandestine effort to gather data on the Democrats are the self-same people who think it was fine for Daniel Ellsberg to abscond with data from the Pentagon and for the *New York Times* to publish it."[24]

Of particular interest (and outrage) to Evans was the obscure case of Otto Otepka, a career security official at the State Department who ran afoul of the Kennedy administration when he acted as a whistleblower about lax security procedures. The Kennedy administration retaliated by demoting Otepka and ultimately firing him, but not before sending its version of Nixon's "plumbers" to break into his office to rummage through documents, break into his safe, and bug his telephone. The Kennedy appointees who conducted the black bag work denied bugging Otepka's phone before a congressional committee, but when presented with corroborating evidence, one of them retreated to the following novel circumlocution: "I altered the existing wiring in the telephone in Mr. Otepka's office. We then established a circuit from Mr. Otepka's office to the Division of Technical Services Laboratory by making additional connections in the existing telephone wiring system." There were no charges or disciplinary measures taken against the perpetrators, and the media buried the story. "Kind of makes you wonder, doesn't it?" Evans asked.[25] He was still bringing up the Otepka case as late as 2013 when he spoke about political scandals over the years.

The second aspect of his Watergate perspective was the connection he drew between the philosophical weakness of the Nixon White House and the "moral vacuum" that enabled such a "boneheaded venture" as the DNC HQ bugging. The source of this "moral vacuum" was one of Evans's favorite targets: pragmatism, in the high Deweyite sense of the term and also its more commonplace usage. "The trouble with pragmatism," he liked to joke, "is that it doesn't work." At the heart of the dreadful mistakes of Watergate, Evans wrote in May 1973 when the scandal was starting to gain momentum, was "a mood of technical pragmatism in which the resources to bug existed and principled reason for failing to bug did not...A purely 'pragmatic' conception of politics, after all, requires continual attunement of one's opinions to the supposed needs of the hour, and a steady practice in that particular art must eventually produce a blurring of the ethical vision. If everything is to be settled on a 'problem-solving' basis, who can say it is *wrong* to turn one's coat on wage and price controls, embrace the Communist Mao Tse-tung—or bug the Watergate? And which is worse? Where clear criteria of right are abandoned, such questions can be answered only by doing a sum in utilitarian arithmetic."[26]

The third and final aspect of Evans's perspective on Watergate concerns the role of bureaucratic government as an aggravating cause and how our response to Watergate made the problem of centralized government power worse. One of the now-forgotten elements connected to Watergate was the machinations of International Telephone and Telegraph Corporation (ITT) and the trade association of milk producers who attempted through large contributions to the Nixon campaign to gain favorable regulatory treatment (antitrust in the case of ITT and higher milk price supports for the milk industry). Both were regarded as clear examples of corruption on both sides of the transaction and reason for ambitious new laws to prevent this kind of corruption and influence peddling.

Evans thought the matter not so simple:

> If this series of scandals established anything, it was that the Federal government had gotten too big and arrogant and that fallible or venal men in Washington could not be trusted with so much untethered power. But what has been the liberal response? That we should concentrate still *further* power in the Federal government by imposing restraints on private participation in the electoral process and by financing political campaigns with government money.
>
> The call for this alleged remedy was prompted by contributions to the Nixon re-election effort by the milk interests and the International Telephone and Telegraph Company—supposedly showing that private interests needed stricter government control. But the actual lesson of these episodes was precisely the opposite: The common feature of these two cases was that both ITT and the milk interests were *already* subject to government control, and thus had reason to solicit favor with the controllers. Pile on still more government regulations, and the motives of business or other interests to influence the regulators will obviously be enhanced, rather than diminished.[27]

The lesson Evans thought we should draw can be stated simply: the way to get rid of corruption in high places is to have fewer high places.

In the midst of the Nixon reelection and Watergate turmoil,

Evans had a partial falling out with *National Review* and Buckley prompted partly by the status of George Will. In 1971 Will started writing the Washington-based "CATO" column for *NR*, and in 1972 Will's constant sniping at Agnew generated considerable friction at *NR* and in wider conservative circles. Will thought Nixon should dump Agnew from the 1972 ticket—a stark departure from the key demand of the Manhattan Twelve (and *National Review*) that Agnew be kept—and then in 1973 he argued in *NR* that John Connally should succeed Nixon in 1976 rather than Agnew. When Buckley named Will to succeed Frank Meyer as literary editor of *NR* following Meyer's death, a post many conservatives thought should have gone to Evans, Evans resigned as a contributing editor and regular columnist for the biweekly *National Review Bulletin*. He wrote to Buckley: "I feel increasingly out of phase with the drift of things at *National Review*, particularly the book section and the political coverage," by which he meant Will.[28]

Evans recalled in a 1974 letter to Don Lipsett:

> I first met Will two years ago on a TV discussion show, and concluded from that experience that he was not in fact a conservative at all—at least not according to my lights. What I recollect most vividly was his penchant for dressing up liberal policy stands in conservative-sounding rhetoric.
>
> Will's subsequent activities have confirmed in me my original feeling...It does not surprise me to learn his writings have exerted a peculiar fascination for the editors of the *Washington Post*, though his emergence as Washington editor for *National Review* is considerably more puzzling.

Evans's preferred *National Review* political writer, he added, was Bill Rusher.[29] Around this same time, according to one witness, Evans and Will got into a "shouting match" at an event at the University of Indiana over the question of Vice President Agnew.[30]

The estrangement between Evans and *National Review* wasn't complete and didn't last long. Evans returned to *NR*'s pages in short order with a regular column on "The Lawmakers," covering policy battles in Congress, and a regular column in the Books and Arts Section called "Dark Horses," where he highlighted obscure but worthy new books that the usual book review outlets overlooked. ("Dark Horses" showed again Evans's wide range of interests and his ability to keep up with an enormous volume of material, which often went beyond books to overlooked government reports.)

But Evans's main concern coming out of Watergate was how much damage it would inflict on the conservative movement, even if much of the conservative movement was never enthusiastic about Nixon. In the summer of 1974, *Time* magazine named Evans to its list of the two hundred Americans under age forty-five it judged would have the most impact on the future of the country. With a nationally syndicated column and radio broadcast platform, and at the pinnacle of arguably the most important conservative activist organization (ACU), Evans was about to put his shoulder to the wheel of history in a significant way: he was about to preserve Ronald Reagan's viability as a presidential candidate and then ponder whether to destroy the Republican Party on purpose.

CHAPTER 9

PREPARING THE
REAGAN REVOLUTION

The most "distressing aspect" of Watergate, Evans wrote in the summer of 1973, was "the manner in which it has blocked consideration of just about every other issue." In January 1974 he returned to this theme, saying at an ACU press conference in Washington, DC, that "Watergate is mainly a preoccupation of this city. The real issues that concern the majority of Americans are the fuel shortages, high taxes, busing, and the explosive growth of the bureaucracy, among others." Even as Watergate was devastating Republican Party prospects at the next election, Evans noted opinion polls showing that the nation continued to move in a conservative direction in general and on many specific issues. On the eve of Nixon's final humiliation in the summer of 1974, Gallup found that the number of Americans describing themselves as conservative reached an all-time high, at 38 percent, but only 24 percent identified as Republicans. In other words, conservatism was more popular than the GOP (a strange feature of public opinion that persists today). As such, Watergate was having the effect of repealing the 1972 and 1968 elections: "Watergate may be seen as a saving diversion. By exploiting it to the limit, the liberals who should themselves be standing in the dock of public opinion become themselves the attackers instead of the attacked...The blunders of the Nixon regime, itself enmeshed in liberal theorems, become the means of saving liberalism from its day of reckoning."[1]

What to do? For Evans the answer was straightforward: continue building the institutional and political infrastructure of the conservative movement, which is what he proceeded to do as chairman of ACU. The key to progress, he thought, was for conservatives and the ACU to be "unwilling to be distracted by the phobias and enthusiasms of the liberal media."[2] As he pivoted to a more direct activist role, he kept up his steady flow of journalism: columns, magazine features, and learned longer articles in *Modern Age*, *The Intercollegiate Review*, and *The Freeman* as well as speaking appearances and debates. In the fall of 1973, Evans relished debating Sen. George McGovern at Butler University in Indiana on "The Role of Government in Society," which covered the waterfront of topics from Watergate to civil rights and social welfare programs. Evans described him as "an amiable enough opponent." Other debate sparring partners included Tom Wicker from the *New York Times*. He also enjoyed poking the federal bureaucracy whenever he could with Freedom of Information Act (FOIA) requests. A 1975 letter to the commissioner of the IRS reads, in total:

> The ACA television documentary, "The IRS: A Question of Power," shown on March 21, 1975, reported that the IRS maintains a file on the American Conservative Union. I would appreciate seeing the contents of that file, and would also be interested to know the reason for the IRS's maintaining such a dossier and for ACU's inclusion in it.[3]

The 1970s were arguably ACU's heyday, and Evans is responsible for its growth and for several effective new ACU programs, many of them designed to gain publicity for ACU that he thought would translate directly into more dues-paying members and increased clout with Congress and state legislatures. Over the next few years Evans traveled to thirty-five states and oversaw the launch or maintenance of ACU affiliate chapters in thirty-eight states. Membership grew by ten thousand in 1973 alone, and Evans achieved a one-third increase in fundraising in his first two years at the helm. ACU launched a "Congressional Action Program," which sponsored expert testimony before congressional committees as well as public briefings and seminars on Capitol Hill (arms control was a favorite topic). Evans worked to expand the resources of ACU's "Conservative Victory Fund," which was the first real conservative political action committee (PAC) that employed independent campaign expenditures that are commonplace today.[4]

Evans also launched ACU's congressional vote scoring system, weighting votes according to their significance. Most rating scorecards, such as the ADA's, the AFL-CIO's, and the League of Conservation Voters's, scores all votes equally, but Evans insisted that a weighted scoring system would reflect conservative priorities better. Hence, a vote against the Family Assistance Plan would count three times as much as a vote against a public works spending bill. A Congressman could receive a high rating by voting for or against just one or two high priority bills even if he didn't vote on any other scored legislation; conversely, voting the wrong way on one or two weighted bills would limit a member's score even if he voted correctly on every other item. One of the double-weighted Senate votes in 1973, for example, was against reducing the filibuster threshold from sixty-seven to sixty votes. (Evans also launched ACU's own think tank arm, the ACU Education and Research Institute, at this time, but it will be discussed in the next chapter.)

The growing practice of interest groups issuing scorecard ratings of legislators was not popular with office holders, prompting a response that sounds familiar in today's context of demands that internet platforms and cable broadcast networks censor books and entire organizations such as Fox News. From the *Fort Worth Star-Telegram* in 1976:

> Three Texans and a hundred other congressmen would like to see restrictions placed on some consumer groups, environmentalists and others they believe "unfairly" rate member of Congress on the basis of their voting records. Reps. Dale Milford (D-Grand Prairie), Ray Roberts (D-McKinney), and James Collins (R-Dallas), joined House Republican Leader John J. Rhodes in a letter asking the Fair Campaign Practices Committee, a private organization, to "monitor and expose" the growing use of ratings based on a small number of votes.
>
> Rhodes also has asked the House Republican Research Committee and the Republican Congressional Campaign Committee to examine the possibility of placing legal restrictions on the groups that issue such ratings.

That the Republican leader of the House would entertain an idea so clearly inimical to the First Amendment underscores Evans's cynicism about the probity of conventional Republicans. But there was an illuminating detail at the end of the article that also validated his premise that the center of American opinion was considerably to the right of the center of opinion among elected officials (especially Democrats):

> Earlier this year, some freshman Democrats elected in the 1974 liberal sweep of congressional elections were enraged to find they had been given very high ratings by the Americans for Democratic Action—a very liberal group.

The freshman found that many of their constituents disliked the liberal-leaning Congress and, while they may have voted well for their district's special interests, they are having trouble living down the "radical-lib" image.[5]

A useful reminder that liberal office holders succeed by deliberately concealing their views from voters.

A similar new ACU initiative borrowed a page from Wisconsin Senator William Proxmire's Golden Fleece Award for frivolous government spending and launched its own Budget Buster Award that called out individual senators and House members for fiscal profligacy. The ACU always sent out a press release announcing the latest recipient of its Budget Buster Award, and sometimes the target would commit the blunder of disputing the award, thus giving it more publicity. One such target was Indiana's 5th District Democratic Congressman Edward Roush, who in July 1976 wrote an indignant letter to Evans declining ACU's Budget Buster Award, complaining that "I respectfully decline the award and am constrained to point out that it is undeserved." Evans was not impressed with Roush's three-page defense of his spending votes, which concluded that "I can only conclude that your singling me out…by the use of inaccurate, distorted, and outrageously deceptive figures [was] to promote my opponent because he shares your ultra conservative views."[6] Evans copped to the charge: "A key factor in choosing award recipients was their 'reelection vulnerability.'"[7] Roush's opponent was J. Danforth Quayle, who defeated Roush in November.

But by far the most lasting of the Evans initiatives at ACU was the founding of the Conservative Political Action Conference (CPAC) and the agitation to start a new third-party. CPAC is now a major conservative institution, and while the third-party initiative is now forgotten, it shouldn't necessarily be regarded as a frivolous lark or a failure. Its intangible effect was significant.

As the Watergate scene darkened in late 1973, culminating in the resignation of Vice President Agnew on corruption charges, Evans decided that what conservatives needed was a pep rally. James Roberts, whom Evans hired to be ACU's political director in 1973, recalled that "The feeling was that conservatives were so depressed because of the whole Watergate fiasco that what we needed a national event to raise morale." And thus Evans and ACU came up with CPAC. It is more accurate to say Evans revived and expanded CPAC as *Human Events* had sponsored a "conservative leadership conference" back in the late 1950s and early 1960s while attempts to revive it in the late 1960s fizzled.

Evans had scored a coup by getting Ronald Reagan, then in his last year as governor and looking ahead to his next political steps, to agree to be the keynote speaker for the late January 1974 event. ACU booked the Mayflower Hotel for the projected three-day event. But it wasn't clear that it was going to be a success. There was one big problem: how to make sure there would be a crowd. "We were just desperate to attract an audience," Roberts said. "We had never done anything like this. There was no list to draw on, and so we were in crisis mode. Out in Indianapolis, Stan was on the phone cutting deals with Reed Irvine, Phyllis Schlafly, Reed Larson, and every other conservative leader he could think of [to turn people out]. He inspired us in his daily calls with such advice as 'Bring in the winos.'" Of special importance was access to direct-mail pioneer Richard Viguerie's list of more than twenty-one thousand conservative small donors. Viguerie allowed Evans to send a letter of invitation to the entire list.

The kibbitzing paid off as seven hundred people registered for the conference while nearly a thousand attended the dinner banquet featuring Reagan. As befits any enterprise that Evans designed, CPAC was a hybrid event, combining thought and action. Although the name of the conference emphasizes "action" in its title on purpose, CPAC's program was divided more or less evenly between panels and strategy sessions on practical political organization and panels on current policy issues, such as the "energy crisis," détente, welfare reform, health care, and fiscal policy, featuring leading conservative academics such as Milton Friedman and other Chicago school economists who were favorites of Evans.

CPAC also represented an expression of Evans's "fusionism," moving from theory to practice, as CPAC emphasized building up the practical coalition of what later became known as the "three-legged stool" of conservatism: foreign policy hawks, economic conservatives and libertarians, and the fast-rising social conservatives, represented in particular by the brand-new right-to-life organizations. (ACU and CPAC's planners also took care to keep out racist, extremist, and conspiracy-minded groups such as the John Birch Society.) Evans said in his invitation letter: "We cannot permit the Conservative Movement to be badly fragmented now. This conference will be the first of its kind since the early 1960s. It will give us the much needed chance to re-unite, renew our commitment and re-focus our energies on common goals."

Speakers included a who's who of current and future leaders of the conservative movement, all of them personally invited by Evans, including Sen. James Buckley and Reps. Jack Kemp, Trent Lott, Phil Crane, John Ashbrook, Robert Bauman, and Steve Symms. Activists and thought leaders included Kevin Phillips, William Rusher, Richard Wirthlin, Paul Weyrich, Allan Ryskind, Pat Buchanan, Phyllis Schlafly, Morton Blackwell, Richard Viguerie, Lyn Nofziger, and David Keene. One person conspicuously missing was Sen. Barry Goldwater, who begged off so he could spend all his spare time when the Senate was not in session getting an early start on his reelection campaign back in Arizona. Among attendees in the audience was a former Vietnam POW, John McCain, and the newly married aspiring pol from Indiana named Quayle.

As might be expected, President Nixon came in for severe criticism at that first CPAC, not so much for Watergate but for his betrayal of conservatism, and this proved the main hook for the considerable media coverage the conference attracted. "Dismay and Outrage Over Nixon Erupt at Conservatives' Parley," read the *New York Times* headline for R. W. "Johnny" Apple Jr.'s CPAC report. This and other stories reported on the numerous speakers who were calling for Nixon to resign so that Republicans could regroup in time for the midterm election and beyond, a view that might have commanded majority support among the CPAC attendees if a survey had been taken. Evans was in the minority in arguing against Nixon's exit in a standing-room-only session of the conference, saying such a move would be shortsighted:

> If we base our analysis on what it takes to get through the 1974 election, if we improvise something to get past this crisis, but then find ourselves with a permanent situation that is itself deleterious in the long run, it seems to me we've made a very bad bargain, and this in essence is what is being suggested when we talk about deposing Nixon and replacing him with Ford so we can get by 1974. But then we have another vista of years to contemplate in which we have another centrist in office...I think that is a radical vice of political analysis and a radical vice of much conservative participation in the political process in recent years to surrender the long perspective to the short run.[8]

While Evans was always deadly serious in the formal CPAC program, after hours his mirthful side came out. Roberts recalled: "All three nights Stan could be found in the hospitality suite, engaged in serious drinking and dancing the night away." Mal Kline, one of Stan's editorial staff a few years later, tells one story that captures Evans's mirth:

Some cub reporter from the *Washington Post* got the bright idea that he could find the 18-minute gap [in Nixon's White House tapes] at CPAC. This genius went booth to booth asking for the Watergate tapes! Well, somebody, I don't know who, decided to have some fun with the guy and gave him Stan's room number and told him to show up at midnight. Stan was having a bunch of people over, playing rock and roll, with fermented beverages. So the guy from the Post knocks on Stan's door and brusquely asks, "Your name Evans?" "Well yes it is," Stan said. "I hear you got some tapes." "Well yes I do. Would you like to hear them?" Stan said. "Yeah," the guy said. So Stan sat him down and played Martha Reeves and the Vandellas.

On a following morning Evans turned up for an 8:00 a.m. panel, "stumbling through the lobby with his trademark cigarette and can of Coke in hand," Roberts recalls, "saying 'Anyone who knows anything about me knows I had nothing to do with this panel or putting me on it at this hour of the morning. I always thought there was something semi-obscene about getting dressed in the dark.'"

"It was assumed," Roberts added, "that it would be a one-time deal, but it was so successful that people said we need to do it every year. And that's when the tradition began."

Evans presided over the next five CPACs through 1977, when he relinquished the chairmanship of ACU.

Incidentally, Reagan's speech to the first CPAC received mixed reviews. In a long account of the meeting in *National Review*, executive editor Daniel Oliver wrote that it was "A rousing, lively speech, but not deep. A reflection on our heritage, very dramatically told. But nothing special for that audience... The crowd loved it. But there were skeptics, especially by the next morning, perhaps when they tried to remember what it was he had really said; what positions he had taken, how he had demonstrated the quality of leadership."[9] Given that *National Review* was one of Reagan's favorite publications, the criticism stung. Evans wrote to Reagan telling him to ignore the criticism and that he (Evans) thought the speech was the highlight of the conference. Reagan wrote right back to Evans that his letter "brightened my day" because "I have been a little upset with some of the critical reviews that seem to think I just did some flag waving oratory and that it was unsuited to the occasion. I kept trying to remember the crowd and its response which I had thought was warm and receptive, but still the criticisms were nagging." Reagan gave a good account of the reason for his broadly thematic speech: "I had decided after a lot of soul searching not to try and speak to the group on specifics as I usually do, big government, high taxes, individual freedom, etc., because I felt that all those subjects would be treated with in the various seminars."[10] Reagan's future CPAC speeches would be much more ideological and specific—and also more memorable. He also proved that he was a forgiving soul: as president he appointed Daniel Oliver to be chairman of the Federal Trade Commission (though that might be considered revenge).

Between the first CPAC in January 1974 and the second CPAC a year later, there occurred the shock of Nixon's resignation followed by the GOP wipeout at the polls in November, which forced conservatives to think about how to regard President Ford. Evans said, "The Republican Party is coming apart at the seams," while ACU's *Battle Line* newsletter asked of the GOP, "Is There Anything Left to Take Over?" William F. Buckley Jr. agreed: "Who cares, really, about the Republican Party? Its soul is the property of the Ripon Society, and a few of the older members of the Council on Foreign Relations." Along with many other conservatives, Evans thought Ford was another centrist no better than Nixon, and the fact that Ford kept on most of Nixon's senior appointees, most notably Henry Kissinger, which guaranteed a continuation of détente.

But it was the second shock that changed the character and focus of the second CPAC and brought the conservative movement to a critical crossroads. If Ford represented a continuity with Nixon's centrism, at least he might restore the status quo ante represented by Agnew by nominating a conservative to fill the vacant vice president's office. Five days after Nixon's resignation, Evans wrote to President Ford urging him to nominate Goldwater to be vice president. He pointed to a Gallup poll showing Goldwater with the most support (at 23 percent), followed by Rockefeller (18), Reagan (12), Elliot Richardson and Howard Baker (11 each), and George H. W. Bush (1). "The fact that conservatives Goldwater, Reagan, and Baker together scored 46% as against 30% for moderate liberals Rockefeller, Richardson and Bush militates strongly against the selection of one of the latter three. In sum, the situation points strongly to Goldwater as the most logical choice for vice president."[11]

Ford didn't heed this advice (in fact there is no letter of reply in the ACU archives), and a week later Ford infuriated conservatives by nominating Rockefeller to be vice president. Evans called the appointment "a shocker. If there is any single individual who is anathema to Republican conservatives, Rockefeller is definitely it…As one wag put it, 'A man who was elected by nobody has anointed a man who has been rejected by everybody.'"[12] Bringing Rockefeller back from the cold was, for Evans, worse than carrying on Nixon's fiscal laxity and détente appeasement.

Evans wasn't about to take it lying down, and he worried that Rockefeller might become the GOP nominee in 1976 if Ford declined to run again. Evans banged out a six-thousand-word manifesto attacking Rockefeller that *Human Events* published as a special supplement in early October, before Congress had voted to confirm Rockefeller's appointment. It was a comprehensive attack on Rockefeller's liberal record, defective political instincts, and—most damning of all perhaps—the fact that Rockefeller's real constituency was the liberal media. Rockefeller's appointment led Evans to "have doubts" about whether the Republican Party could be counted upon to be a conservative party and thus to entertain the idea of starting a new third party. "It seems likely that a Rockefeller-style Republican Party would cause many millions of actual or potential Republican voters to seek lodgment elsewhere."[13] It was unlikely that conservative opposition to Rockefeller could scuttle his nomination, but if enough Republicans voted against him, it would send a strong signal to Ford and the rest of the party that conservatives couldn't be taken for granted. But it didn't make a dent: the Senate confirmed him 90–7, with only Goldwater, Jesse Helms, and William Scott of Virginia among Republicans voting no.

As planning for the second CPAC in February 1975 proceeded, a new idea was gaining steam: abandoning the Republican Party and starting a new Conservative Party. At this early point in the 1976 election cycle, Reagan was being coy about his plans, and in any case it was thought difficult for Reagan or anyone else to dislodge Ford or Rockefeller from the GOP nomination if either chose to run. (Ford's own intentions were still vague at the time.) *National Review* publisher William Rusher was the most vocal advocate of the idea, publishing in 1975 a book outlining the logic of the proposal, *The Making of a New Majority Party*. Rusher had in mind who should lead this new party: Reagan and Alabama Gov. George Wallace. Reagan would attract conservative Republicans, while Wallace would bring Democrats disaffected by the increasing social liberalism of the Democratic Party but who were, as yet, not much attracted to Republicans. Rusher met with Reagan to push the idea. Reagan was noncommittal, and he equivocated about the idea in the aftermath of the GOP wipeout at the polls in November, leaving open the possibility of a new third party in remarks to reporters just after the 1974 election. (Reagan privately disliked Wallace and didn't like the idea of aligning with him.)

Evans, thoroughly disgusted with Republicans, was intrigued enough by the idea to write favorably about it in his new syndicated newspaper column in the fall of 1974 and make it a major focus of the CPAC February 1975 conference. (It may have been around this time that Evans first quipped that "It is a good thing Republican office holders are pro-life, since they spend so much time in the fetal position.") The minutes of one December 1974 planning meeting records that ACU's board concluded "that the conference resolve to appoint a New Party exploratory committee. It was felt that the conference must end on the note of 'having taken a step; putting the conservative movement into a course of action.' Mr. Evans' suggestion that a 'Committee for a New Majority' result from the conference was approved in principle, as was the general use of this vehicle . . . prior to the establishment of a New Party." More intriguing was Evans's agreement to seek out a meeting with Gov. Wallace to pursue the idea.[14]

The subsequent CPAC was sharply divided, and it debated the proposal vigorously, with many staunch conservatives arguing for it and others against. (One of the most vociferous opponents was the head of the College Republicans, a young Texan named Karl Rove.) A soundbite from Evans made the evening news broadcasts of both NBC and ABC: "I personally believe that in 1976 we need a new political party at the presidential level." Evans told the roundtable panel at CPAC:

> How one goes about doing that, what the options are in terms of candidates, these are things that need to be discussed. I realize,

talking to my Republican friends, that this presents many terrible difficulties. This is not something to be lightly considered.[15]

In his after-action report on CPAC in *Battle Line*, Evans said accurately that "almost no one at the conference had much good to say for the Ford White House." Only two Ford administration officials were even invited to CPAC: Treasury Secretary William Simon and Council of Economic Advisers chairman Alan Greenspan. Both declined. (One other detail of the second CPAC is worth including. Evans tried, unsuccessfully, to get Alexander Solzhenitsyn, whose recent snub by the Ford White House at Henry Kissinger's urging further rankled conservatives, to speak at the second CPAC, enlisting Sen. Jesse Helms to help.)

Reagan, once again the headline speaker for the conference, walked a fine line that tilted toward his reservations with his now famous formulation about "no pale pastels" that he used throughout the late 1970s while still leaving the door slightly ajar:

> Is it a third party that we need, or is it a new and revitalized second party, raising a banner of no pale pastels, but bold colors which make it unmistakably clear where we stand on all the issues troubling the people?...I do not believe I have proposed anything that is contrary to what has been considered Republican principle. It is at the same time the very basis of conservatism. It is time to reassert that principle and raise it to full view. And if there are those who cannot subscribe to these principles, then let them go their way.

Despite Reagan's less than lukewarm treatment of the idea, he did not deter CPAC and ACU from setting in motion a serious third-party exploration and organizational effort, dubbed the Committee on Conservative Alternatives (COCA), with Sen. Jesse

Helms as chairman. COCA contacted the secretaries of state for all fifty states about their third-party ballot access rules.

Evans understood that the third-party idea was dead unless Reagan led it. He wrote directly to Reagan in May 1975, attempting to persuade him that even if he won the Republican nomination in 1976, he would be saddled with the legacy of the Nixon-Ford failures and that at the very least Reagan should keep his third-party options open if he ran for the GOP nomination and lost. If the COCA effort went forward and qualified a party for the ballot, Reagan would have a ready-made structure in place.

In August Evans and Rusher traveled to Alabama to feel out Wallace, who, Rusher biographer David Frisk wrote, "may not have known who they were." Evans described the meeting to Frisk: "We were just getting to know him . . . Sort of an interview with him, to size him up, and he was very cordial to us."[16] Wallace remained aloof from the third-party effort as he was planning to (and did) run in the Democratic primaries in 1976. Evans came away favorable enough to write a positive column about his visit with Wallace. He described Wallace's incipient presidential campaign as "the hottest political operation in the United States today . . . He is soft spoken, genial, earnest. One is not surprised that he made a good impression when he addressed the recent national convention of Young Americans for Freedom." Evans concluded that Wallace represented a bona fide force on behalf of a conservative "new majority" in American politics.[17]

Evans's meeting with Wallace occurred shortly after the next big personal step in his life: he stepped down fully from the *Indianapolis News* and moved permanently to Washington, DC, in May 1975. Washington, he liked to say, "is much like the Soviet Union, without the amenities." He had already stepped down as editor in chief at the *News* (but remained a columnist) when he became involved with ACU and began his nationally syndicated column with the *Los Angeles Times*, and the third-party mischief may have helped propel his final exit. His publisher, Eugene C. Pulliam, was not in favor of the third-party initiative, and he wrote a letter to the editor of *his own paper* to express his differences with Evans. Calling the third-party boomlet "an ill-advised and premature" idea that "would do irreparable injury to the Republican Party," Pulliam added: "Leading spokesman for this movement is M. Stanton Evans, former editor of this newspaper and one of the most brilliant writers and thinkers in this country. However, he does not represent the policy of this newspaper now and he has not made any effort to do so."[18] If Pulliam's disagreement on this point, as with his likely dissent from the Manhattan Twelve declaration four years earlier, was a factor in Evans's decision to pull up stakes for Washington, Evens never let on, nor did he ever express anything less than total admiration and respect for Pulliam.

Evans joked he made the move to Washington "so I could be closer to my money," but the main reason was that his growing national media profile and activist involvement through ACU made it more congenial to live and work there even though he disdained the capital city for obvious philosophical reasons. He had long been wary of living in DC, telling *Human Events* in 1974: "Washington DC is easily the *least* typical of all American communities and therefore the least likely to sense and act upon the conservative impulse that is running in the nation…The resulting atmosphere of liberal-radical dominance inevitably takes its psychic toll, even with legislators of conservative disposition and constituencies."[19]

But if Evans was now *in* Washington, he was surely not *of* it. It was not as lax as Indianapolis about parking enforcement; giving parking violations was the one task the DC government did efficiently. Evans was constantly acquiring parking tickets and sometimes getting his car booted and towed, once with his dog Zip still in the back seat. He had parked momentarily in a delivery zone outside *Human Events* while he delivered his column—this was in the days before fax machines or email—but his legitimate excuse that he was making a delivery didn't work with DC's parking enforcement authorities. Many of his staff and loyal friends, this author included, have tales of retrieving his old VW Beetle or its successors from the city impound lot. On one occasion Evans scaled the fence at the impound lot after hours to retrieve something a lady friend had left in the car. And on another occasion, his Mustang caught fire out on the street—cause unknown—but Evans heroically rescued his copy of Macauley's *History of England* from the back seat before the car was fully engulfed.

He didn't exactly settle in like an inner-Beltway resident, however. He settled into a small, rent-controlled apartment on Capitol Hill, but before long he bought a house an hour outside DC in Hamilton, Virginia, where he spent most weekends. Its chief attraction, he said, was that it had a Hardee's fast food franchise at each end of town, so he had dining choices. This was the key to keeping a balanced diet, he liked to say: when he needed to change up his diet, he'd eat at the *other* Hardee's. In the late 1980s, he acquired the house next door in Hamilton, chiefly to relocate his elderly parents but also to house his swollen library.

While the ACU's COCA project went about gathering detailed information on third-party ballot access rules from all fifty states, three new factors scrambled the scene. First, although Reagan remained publicly coy about challenging President Ford for the Republican Party nomination the following year, behind the scenes it was understood that he was preparing to enter the race, likely late in the year. His slowness in declaring was a source of frustration and anxiety for conservatives; *Human Events* in October ran a typical blunt front-page headline, "Reagan: Time to Fish or Cut Bait." Reagan's entry diminished the chances that a new third party could get off the ground, though Evans and ACU decided to continue organizing the effort in case Reagan lost the GOP nomination but might still be open to a third-party bid in the fall. As early as September 1975, Evans was expressing doubts publicly that a new conservative party would take off. "I still think the ticket would go if they [Reagan and Wallace] would do it," he told an audience at a speech in Denver. He added that even if a third-party organizational effort failed, the agitation behind it could exert influence on both parties to move to the right.

Then, on November 4, 1975, Vice President Rockefeller announced that, at President Ford's request, he would not be Ford's running mate in 1976. There is little doubt that Ford relented to the pressure from conservatives; the fear of the imminent challenge from Reagan likely added to the decision. Speculation began immediately about who Ford might pick to replace Rockefeller, with names running the spectrum from liberal Republicans like Charles Percy all the way over to Reagan. In the end Ford picked Kansas Senator Bob Dole, who enjoyed a solid conservative reputation in his second term. But in the meantime, gaining Rockefeller's ouster took more steam out of the third-party effort.

As Reagan was gearing up to declare his candidacy, he provoked a major controversy with his controversial plan to cut the federal budget by $90 billion and transfer responsibilities for many programs directly to the states. It was a bold proposal, aiming at "cutting the Gordian knot" of federal dominance and stopping the flow of power and money to Washington. Today $90 billion is nearly a rounding error in a (normal, pre-COVID) federal budget of nearly $4 trillion, but in 1976 total federal spending was about $400 billion. Thus Reagan was proposing to cut the federal government by almost a quarter—but to cut federal taxes by the same amount (a key detail left out of much of the news coverage). The media—and the Ford campaign—savaged Reagan's "radical" idea, arguing that it would lead to state tax increases and other horribles. The author of Reagan's plan and the September speech that introduced it was former ACU employee Jeffery Bell, and even without that personal connection it was the kind of idea near to Evans's heart, so naturally he mounted the barricades to defend it.

Evans wrote a long special supplement on "The Ronald Reagan Story" for *Human Events* in January 1976 that took up eight full pages (probably close to twelve thousand words). Having repeatedly called for articulate spokesmen for the conservative cause, Evans found his man in Reagan. After reviewing Reagan's biography and record in Sacramento in some detail, Evans concluded that Reagan's record as California governor paradoxically made him "more qualified to hold the office he seeks than is the man who currently occupies it."

But the heart of the article was a spirited defense of Reagan's devolution plan on the merits of long-familiar Evans themes about decentralized government and an extension of the political logic behind the new third-party idea. Like the third-party agitation, Reagan's shadow over Ford was pushing Ford to the right: "First, it simply isn't true that Ford is as conservative as Reagan, or even that Ford as President has generally been on the conservative side. And second, to the extent that Ford these days is *perceived* as a conservative, it is apparent on analysis that his conservatism is chiefly traceable to—Ronald Reagan...On balance, it seems rather plain that Reagan could make a considerably stronger run for the White House in the fall than could President Ford." Above all, Evans argued that Reagan was the only Republican who could preempt another potential third-party bid by Wallace—unless that third-party bid consisted of Reagan and Wallace together. He took directly after the pundits and analysts who thought a Reagan-Wallace coalition was somehow unnatural or unstable with an analysis that sounds prescient of the Trump phenomenon forty years later:

> The important thing about such [Reagan-Wallace] people is not that some of them reach their political position by reading Adam Smith while others do so by attending an anti-busing rally, but that all of them belong to a large and growing class of American citizens: Those who perceive themselves as victims of the liberal welfare state and its attendant costs. All that bubble-blowing about "populism" is a convenient way of concealing the interests such people have in common, thereby assuring that the welfare blocs and social engineers continue feeding on their hapless victims.
>
> It would be foolish to suggest that there are no differences between the Reagan and Wallace forces. Of course there are differences, as there are between any two political groups, or between any two human beings. But the point of political coalitions is precisely to bring together elements that have more in common than they do apart—and that is a description that applies with perfect relevance to the followers of Reagan and Wallace.[20]

Then the third major difficulty facing a third-party presidential campaign beyond ballot access came into play but in a way that worked out well for the Reagan cause while ending, as a practical matter, any momentum for a new third party: finance. The new campaign finance rules passed in 1974 as amendments to the 1971 Federal Election Campaign Act (FECA) restricted both contributions and spending in ways highly adverse to any third-party campaign or independent expenditure effort such as ACU's Conservative Victory Fund. Naturally Evans understood that such reforms would make political corruption worse as well as being "a blatant assault on our political liberties." Evans and ACU had a plan for the new regulations, too: a lawsuit challenging the constitutionality of FECA on First Amendment grounds. Senator James Buckley of New York became the lead plaintiff in the lawsuit that became *Buckley v. Valeo*, but Evans and the ACU signed on as coplaintiffs (along with the ACLU and Democratic Senator Eugene McCarthy). Covington & Burling agreed to take on the case pro bono, with the lead brief preparation work done by a young lawyer with a bushy mustache named John Bolton. But even with pro bono representation, there were still considerable expenses for such a case (about $15,000 before oral argument), which ACU agreed to pick up.

The *Buckley* case was argued at the Supreme Court on November 10, 1975, with the Court issuing its ruling with unusual speed (likely owing to the need to settle the matter before the 1976 campaign cycle began in earnest) on January 30, 1976. In a complicated ruling with several splits among the justices over different questions at issue, the Court ruled that both campaign spending limits and independent expenditures for or against a candidate were unconstitutional violations of the First Amendment, but it upheld the strict contribution limits. ACU was now in business to agitate on behalf of Reagan's campaign, and just in the nick of time. "When the decision came down," ACU political director James Roberts recalls, "ACU's offices were in the *Human Events* building, and [publisher] Tom Winters came down with a copy of the decision and told us, 'The way I read this, ACU could do an independent expenditure effort for Reagan.' And that's where the whole idea came from."

Some early polls showed Reagan surging ahead of Ford nationally and in the New Hampshire primary. Instead, Reagan lost New Hampshire narrowly (perhaps because of the attacks on his $90 billion budget cut plan), and his campaign went downhill from there, losing the next five primaries to Ford, including the crucial Florida primary. The Reagan campaign was on the brink of final collapse on the eve of the North Carolina primary, and behind the scenes his campaign was secretly negotiating his exit from the race with the Ford campaign over how much help Reagan could get from Ford to retire his campaign debts in return for dropping out. Reagan and his senior staff left the state the day of the primary assuming they were going to lose. It looked like the end of the line (though Reagan was telling everyone who would listen that he would not drop out).

Roberts said that "we didn't think that the Reagan campaign was nearly as tough as they should have been on Ford and nearly as conservative as they should have been. And so we decided to fix that problem with our with our ads. The Reagan people were throwing in the towel [in North Carolina]." The ads centered around the theme "Reagan and Ford—there is a difference." "And then we had listed all the other differences," Roberts recalls. ACU cut two television ads, several radio spots that ran over eight hundred times, and a newspaper ad placed in twenty papers, spending $172,000 in all. Evans flew to North Carolina to announce the effort and made a tour of the state "in a little prop plane that seemed to be made out of canvas, and it was terrifying the whole time," Roberts says. "In fact, after the primary we heard the plane crashed, so it was literally touch and go."

Reagan's upset victory in North Carolina breathed new life into his campaign and is often regarded as the key moment in Reagan's drive to the presidency. Had he dropped out after a loss in North Carolina, it is unlikely he would have run successfully in 1980. Lou Cannon, the journalist who followed Reagan longer than any other, wrote that "North Carolina was the turning point of Reagan's political career."[21] Jameson Campaigne Jr. is not alone in judging that "Without Stan Evans, it is quite likely there would have been no Ronald Reagan in 1980."

ACU wasn't the only independent effort behind Reagan in North Carolina. Sen. Jesse Helms, then in his first term and working to build up his own political machine, worked hard on Reagan's behalf. In typical fashion Evans was modest about ACU's impact, telling Dan Manion in a 1977 interview: "I don't want to overstress our role. We were definitely third in line at best behind Governor Reagan himself and Senator Helms and his activities."

But beyond North Carolina, ACU was the principal independent effort. ACU stepped up its independent campaign in nineteen subsequent primaries, with Reagan winning twelve. In Kentucky ACU ads hit Ford for his support for busing. Evans traveled to Indiana, trading on his reputation there to boost the ACU effort that included more than four hundred radio spots and a special mailing of Evans's *Human Events* feature, "The Ronald Reagan Story." In Nebraska, where TV time was cheap, ACU ran two half-hour TV spots. In Ohio, a thousand radio spots. In Texas the ads hit Ford on energy and the Panama Canal issue, running over a thousand radio spots (Evans supplied the voice-over for the ads, capitalizing on his growing public radio brand with CBS News's *Spectrum* series) and thirty-five newspaper ads. ACU was running on fumes, scrounging for funds when it wasn't out in the field pushing the effort. "If this whole organization has to go under because of this, it's worth it," Evans told anyone who would listen. "This is really an inflection point in American political history."[22] Evans estimated that he and other ACU staff logged forty-three thousand miles of total travel in the course of the effort.

The *New York Times* seemed to agree about the significance of the ACU effort: "Ronald Reagan's campaign picked up extra impetus in Texas and Indiana in the form of polemical radio commercials that were prepared and paid for by the American

Conservative Union, a right-wing organization with 70,000 members." Evans took note of the slanted media coverage of the contest, pointing out that the media had practically anointed Eugene McCarthy and dismissed LBJ in 1968 based on McCarthy's 42 percent showing in one primary while writing off Reagan who beat an incumbent president in twelve primaries: "In media terms, Mr. Ford's luckiest break may be that Reagan is a conservative. If the challenger were a liberal, with that skein of victories on his belt, the President would already have been counted out."[23]

Even though Reagan lost narrowly to Ford at the Republican National Convention in July, conservatives took some consolation in the fact that the GOP platform was wholly Reaganite, down to including a repudiation of the still-serving Secretary of State Henry Kissinger. It laid down a marker that the center of gravity in the Republican Party was solidly on the right. Evans drove a hard bargain nonetheless, arguing that conservatives wouldn't lend much enthusiasm or support for Ford's fall campaign unless they got tangible evidence that Ford would hew to the GOP platform and reverse several current administration policies on arms control and the Panama Canal giveaway.

He also started to train his fire on Jimmy Carter, noting in a long feature in *Human Events* that Carter had masterfully straddled most key issues and exploited a Democratic field divided among several pure-bred liberals, leaving many voters thinking Carter was a conservative Democrat—a more presentable version of Wallace. In "The Case Against Carter-Mondale" (another ten-thousand-word *HE* special supplement), Evans wrote: "Jimmy Carter may conceivably become our next President because he has constructed the first completely Orwellian presidential candidacy the American nation has ever seen." Evans wasn't taken in for a minute, laying out a detailed itemization of Carter's essential liberalism and concluding:

It might come as a surprise to some of these voters to discover that, on every public issue, Carter is in full agreement with the liberalism that he apparently repudiates. Get behind the surface of Carter's rhetoric—which is easier said than done—and you discover that his position, on issue after issue, is impeccably liberal. His basic commitment is to big government, not against it. His economics are Keynesian to a fault, his foreign policy a lightly laundered version of détente, his views on social issues completely compatible with the enthusiasms of the leftward counterculture.[24]

Evans presided over his last CPAC as chairman of ACU in February 1977, where Reagan ratified the new conservatism in a speech that has grown in significance over time, bearing the title "The New Republican Party." Reagan described a conservative party with exactly the traits Evans had long called for, especially an appeal to working class Americans. Evans was in full agreement with Reagan that the GOP's country club reputation was a hindrance to building a majority electoral coalition.

There is one last notable act from Evans before he stepped down as ACU chairman, and it involved Barry Goldwater. Goldwater's support for Ford over Reagan in 1976 rankled many conservatives, but not Evans, whose residual admiration for Goldwater's 1964 effort remained undimmed. In February 1977, as Evans was packing up his office as ACU chairman, he invited Goldwater to join ACU's advisory board. Goldwater was flattered but surprised, writing Evans that

You rather surprise me by asking if I would become a member of the ACU Board. From where I sit, I feel that I've been rather thoroughly reprimanded by conservative groups and, in fact, have the feeling that I am no longer considered one. That, naturally, is the right of any person or group to determine, but I remain as I've always been, in my own opinion, a conservative.

If you really feel I can be of help to you and really want my name, I'd be glad to join, but make sure that some of your members will not raise an objection as soon as it is announced.[25]

Evans responded promptly:

The matters to which you refer were generated by divergences of opinion in the past campaign, in which different people with the best of motives had different readings of the situation. Such differences, I would hope, would not blind rank-and-file conservatives to your many magnificent contributions to the conservative cause, and to the nation.

Indeed, you more than any other single individual have created the modern conservative movement in America. I know that I for one shall be eternally grateful for your leadership, and proud to recall that I was one of your supporters when we fought those crucial battles for the soul of the Republican Party.[26]

Evans's lasting gratitude toward Goldwater is significant because Goldwater was already, at this early date, starting to receive "strange new respect" from liberals and the media to go along with the doubts some conservatives voiced. A *New York Times Magazine* article in 1974 proclaimed, "The Liberals Love Barry Goldwater Now," and while friction between many conservatives and Goldwater grew more pronounced in the 1980s (when Goldwater came out fully pro-choice on abortion), Evans never castigated Goldwater publicly.

It is an exaggeration to say that Evans saved the Republican Party from its identity crisis under Nixon and Ford as such party crises are never fully resolved, and many other individuals and organizations deserve major credit for the developments of the mid-1970s. But it is hard to imagine it happening the same way without him. In any case, Evans was ready to move on from saving a political party and an ideological movement to an even larger target: saving journalism.

CHAPTER 10

"A BIG BALL OF CONFUSION AND MISINFORMATION"

Modern Journalism and How to Fix It

The mid- to late-1970s were the peak of Evans's reach and influence, not just for his work building up ACU and boosting the 1976 Reagan campaign but especially for his journalism. His syndicated column and frequent special features for *Human Events* show him at his best, ahead of the curve on several hot button issues otherwise mired in deep confusion at the time. Now that he was in Washington, he began following the course of legislation on Capitol Hill with the same assiduousness he brought to the Indiana legislature during his years at the *Indianapolis News*. He began a new regular column for *National Review* about specific legislative proposals called "The Lawmakers." These columns went well beyond the typical headlines to explain the issues involved and deep background behind a bill or hearing.

Human Events always ran one of his syndicated newspaper columns in each issue—when it wasn't running an exclusive Evans feature—thus assuring that he was always in front of one regular reader of *HE*: Ronald Reagan. Reagan based one of his radio commentaries on an Evans column in 1975, referring to him as "a very fine journalist in the heartland of our country" (though Evans had just made his move to Washington several weeks before this particular broadcast).

A great example is the "energy crisis." When the first Arab oil embargo disrupted world energy markets in 1973, setting off a spiral of wrongheaded media reporting and epic bad policy even by the supposedly market-oriented Nixon and Ford administrations, including price controls and rationing, Evans took the contrary view that existing government controls on oil and natural gas were a much larger factor in energy shortages and price spikes. Equally out of favor was his rejection of the Malthusian premise that fossil fuel resources were "running out." His columns from the 1970s reviewing resource statistics, the perversity of government energy regulation, and debunking myths could make for a small book. "Why America Has Plenty of Oil" is a typical column title from this period. Energy was a frequent focus of his "Dark Horses" book reviews in *National Review*, where he kept up with the emerging body of contrarian expertise on energy and environmental topics, often in obscure places or by little-known publishers.

He never tired of debunking the myths of the media and leftist activists, such as that oil companies reaped excessive or "windfall" profits. At the very moment the media and the left were attacking oil companies for "obscene" profits, Evans wrote a *Human Events* cover story bearing the cheeky headline, "Why Oil Companies Need Higher Profits." Going beyond the media's usual glibness to examine facts, Evans reported that the oil industry's profit margin in 1972 had been 6.7 percent, compared to 9.7 percent for the office equipment sector, 8.5 percent for chemicals, and 11.1 percent for electronic instruments. And whereas big oil company profits had surged 79 percent in 1973, the *Washington Post*'s profits had gone up 249 percent, a fact that *Newsweek* (a *Washington Post* publication at that time) didn't recognize in its coverage of oil industry "greed." Evans concluded that between rising taxes and regulatory barriers, the oil industry was starved of capital.[1] His views have been fully vindicated in the fullness of time, first by the belated move to deregulate energy markets in the late 1970s and 1980s and then the long boom in hydrocarbon energy production in the U.S. He also became a champion of nuclear power, which by the late 1970s the environmental left was out to destroy. As previously noted, Evans was early in recognizing the Malthusian core of modern environmentalism and what was wrong with it. "The 'Friends of Earth,'" he wrote, "are enemies to man." And whether the touted policy was the fifty-five-mile-per-hour speed limit, the ban on DDT, or the rush to curb radon gas exposure in the home, Evans could always be relied upon to present skeptical evidence. Not surprisingly, he was an early fan of the empirical work of Julian Simon in the late 1970s that refuted the perennial resource scarcity panics, and Norman Borlaug, the agronomist whose "green revolution" demonstrated how the dynamism of human creativity could solve our practical problems.

Likewise he was far ahead of the curve on health care. By the early 1970s Evans was pointing out that increasing government involvement in health care was distorting the sector and would only get worse through any of the new proposals, whether Nixon's or Ted Kennedy's for nationalized health care coverage or Jimmy Carter's supposedly modest "cost-containment" legislation. In 1975 Evans testified before the House Ways and Means Subcommittee on Health against all the proposals then on the table (one of only two times Evans testified before Congress), previewing a theme that became prominent almost two decades later during the debate over Hillarycare: there is no "health care crisis." There is a problem of the spiraling *cost* of health care, which "results from the existing level of government intervention...In short, existing intrusions have caused the problem that supposedly requires a new intrusion." New intrusions into the medical market would lead inevitably to the rationing of medical care.

He recommended the opposite general policy: "We should be seeking ways of extracting government whenever possible from the practice of medicine."[2]

He never tired of pointing to a time series chart he included many times in his column, a two-line graph with the consumer price index (CPI) and the hospital price index (HPI) from 1945 to the present. The HPI rose in tandem, or at the same rate, with the CPI for two decades, until it suddenly kinked higher (like a hockey stick!) and began rising twice as fast as the CPI. The year of this inflection point: 1965, the year Congress enacted Medicare and Medicaid and launched the vast expansion of third-party payment for health care that obliterated the normal operation of prices in the health care sector and introduced a myriad of perverse incentives for cost explosion. "That year [1965] is the dividing line between comparative sanity in medical pricing and the runaway inflation of which the President [Carter] complains," Evans wrote in 1977. "The reason for the present mess in hospital costs is none other than the government itself."[3] Unlike energy, however, we've never reformed the heavy presence of government in health care, so this became a recurring topic for Evans through the abortive Hillarycare plan in the 1990s to Obamacare. His go-to joke about the Affordable Care Act was that "We need to repeal Obamacare so we can find out what's not in it." It was an Evans column on health care that Reagan cribbed for his aforementioned radio commentary, though it is known that Evans's writing on arms control and détente also informed and reinforced Reagan's views on these issues as he prepared to run for president again in 1980.

Evans's frequent incorporation of a data chart or table in his columns testifies to his numeracy and command of the sources of data (usually government agencies) when it came to making comprehensible the growth of government or the defects of a government program. The contemporary journalist to whom he might be most closely compared was his peer Warren Brookes, the long-time columnist for the *Boston Herald* and later the *Washington Times* who specialized in economics, also known for his fact-laden columns full of original and contrarian insight. Nearly every Brookes article contained an original chart or graph he generated from primary data sources (Brookes passed away at the too-early age of sixty-two in 1992.) Evans had a wider range than Brookes, though, as he extended his topical range to defense and foreign policy and other issue areas where Brookes seldom roamed. His understanding of how the profound weaknesses of liberalism combined with the self-interested behavior of the bureaucracy reminds both of the insights of public choice theory and the knowing perceptions of James Burnham.

Yet it was another of his big initiatives at ACU that carried forth into his time after he stepped down as chairman that defines the next phase of his career. In February 1972 ACU launched, at Evans's instigation, an in-house think tank called the ACU-Education and Research Institute (ACU-ERI as it came to be known). Although separately incorporated, it kept the ACU connection by name until very recently. At this early date, the conservative think tank ecosystem in Washington was sparse. AEI will still comparatively small and in any case deliberately aloof from Capitol Hill, and the Heritage Foundation wasn't founded until the following year. ERI was a means of expanding Evans's own reach by sponsoring serious, in-depth research reports on issues he didn't have time to work on at sufficient length to be promoted in the media and distributed on Capitol Hill. ACU-ERI studies were purposely intended to influence debate and legislation. The studies ranged from twenty to sixty pages in length, depending on the topic, quality printed with glossy covers. Topics included a critique of federal aid to education, inflation, internal security, federal housing, federal spending, human rights in China, defense preparedness, the aftermath of the Vietnam War, and mass transit. These studies were often accompanied by half-day Capitol Hill briefings featuring leading experts, sometimes in debate format, which swelled attendance. Respect for Evans was such that he was able to attract both the FBI director (Clarence Kelly) and CIA director (William Colby) for a 1976 Capitol Hill seminar on intelligence and internal security.

It was one of these ACU events that provided an occasion for another legendary Evans witticism. The ACU staged an anti–Panama Canal Treaty rally at the Capitol on the eve of the Senate ratification vote in 1977 headlined by Congressman Bob Dornan and bearing the leading slogans of the opponents of the treaty ("we built it, we paid for it, it's ours!"). The press greeted the ACU protest with a yawn. As Evans and the ACU contingent were packing up to leave, however, a small group of uniformed Nazis turned up for a protest of their own (this was around the time the American Nazi Party maintained a tiny office on Wilson Blvd. in Arlington). Reporters naturally rushed to check out the freak show. Evans's sardonic quip: "This is the last time I ever do anything with the Nazis. They're always *late*. No wonder they lost the war."

Among the many foreign issues that Evans followed closely was the Soviet-Cuban intrigues in southern Africa, which he though both the media and the U.S. foreign policy establishment didn't regard with sufficient seriousness. As he put it in a 1979 column, Communists "are winning victories in country after country, moving decisively to consolidate their strength. Just as obviously, our response is one of weakness and vacillation—or actively helping to undermine the very people the Communists are attacking."[4] Having watched governments sympathetic to the Soviets installed in Angola, Mozambique, and Zambia, Evans turned his attention to Rhodesia-Zimbabwe, where international pressure had steadily built against the minority white government of Prime Minister Ian Smith.

At length and under the pressure of economic sanctions, Smith's government yielded to an interim government led by Bishop Abel Muzorewa (a pro-Western anti-Communist) as a prelude to an election open fully to the nation's black residents for the first time. The revolutionary left, both in Rhodesia and abroad, along with black rivals labeled Muzorewa as a puppet of white interests, in part because the new constitution Muzorewa and his party settled with Smith reserved a fixed number of seats for whites in the Senate and National Assembly and a quarter of the seats in the cabinet. (This feature could be found in the constitutions of several other former colonial nations in Africa at the time.) Complicating the scene was a guerrilla faction led by Robert Mugabe, who rejected elections almost surely because he knew he could not win a free and fair election. The election, it was suggested, should be regarded as illegitimate. The run-up to the election was thick with charges of intimidation and even "terror" by state security services (Rhodesia was under martial law at the time), press censorship, ballot rigging, and fraud, with these claims receiving credulous coverage in Western media. Between unrest in the country and controversy over the interim political settlement that provided for the election, there was high uncertainty about whether the eligible population would turn out to vote.

The American Conservative Union decided to send Evans and three others to observe the election in April 1978, joining an international delegation of about two hundred election watchers and journalists. True to form, Evans came back with tales of the unusual, such as sitting next to a young lady at a bar who emptied her purse looking for a cigarette lighter and dropped a gun on the bar. During a bus tour of Harare (formerly Salisbury), the tour guide told the passengers, "Over there is the home of Joshua Nkomo," who was operating a guerrilla operation against Rhodesia from next-door Zambia. Evans asked, "But Joshua Nkomo is leading rebel forces in Zambia." The tour guide responded, "Yes, but this neighborhood has better schools." Evans traveled in a number of the "hotter zones" in the country, with a black soldier armed with a loaded rifle providing personal security.

The ACU delegation visited 36 polling places, interviewed 156 voters, and conducted 200 interviews other than those with voters at the polls, often out of sight from government officials. Evans and his entourage also snuck away to visit locations not on the official agenda for the international election monitors. Back in the U.S., the Senate voted to lift sanctions, but the House, further to the left than the Senate in those days, was more resistant. The report ACU produced and submitted to Congress concluded: "Judging by the all the direct evidence we could gather, the elections were conducted on a free and fair basis," and he noted that ACU's conclusions "are essentially the same as those reached by the vast majority of international observers and members of the media who were on the scene." The ACU report offered reasons for doubting the claims of widespread intimidation and other irregularities.[5]

Evans was the Republican witness for a hearing of the House Foreign Affairs Subcommittee on Africa on May 14, 1979 (only the second time he testified before Congress), less than a month after the election, and his testimony was notable for answering specifically six questions about the conduct of the election that subcommittee chairman Stephen Solarz (D-New York) had posed to the panel. Other witnesses for the Democratic majority disputed the ACU's conclusion without, however, directly addressing the chairman's six questions, making for a contentious hearing after the opening statements were over and the question round began.

"The Solarz hearings," Evans wrote later, "were carefully rigged to obscure this fact [of a free and fair election]."

Lord Pratap Chitnis, a prominent left-leaning British politician, was one of the Democratic witnesses who rejected the election in toto: "There is no way whatever in which these elections can be considered free and fair... The election was nothing more than a gigantic confidence trick designed to foist on a cowed and indoctrinated black electorate a settlement and a constitution which were formulated without its consent." The substance of his critique was that the election wasn't a referendum on the interim constitutional settlement, and he did not claim or offer systematic evidence that the mechanics of the election were suspect. He placed great weight on the story of a "drunken white farmer" (Lord Chitnis's words) brandishing a rifle in a bar and claimed he'd make sure all the blacks who lived on or near his farm went to vote.

Game on. Evans decided to let him have it.

> MR. EVANS: If I might respond a little bit to what Lord Chitnis has said earlier. I do not know if there are provisions in our journalistic community for a Pulitzer Prize to someone who is a citizen of another country, but I must say Lord Chitnis has astonished me because he was able to discover things that 200 members of the press and the 70 observers could not discover, combing the country for evidence of fraud. I commend you, sir, for your investigative skill.

There was one back-and-forth between Evans and chairman Solarz worth noting:

> MR. EVANS: I have with me—I did not submit it in advance because it is rather bulky—but I have the individual statements

of all our delegation, and I would like very much permission to submit those for the record if I may.

Mr. Solarz: Knowing your concern about Government spending, I hope you will try to condense them as much as possible.

Other Democrats on the committee were more direct in their hostility. Rep. Charles Diggs (D-Michigan) tried to attack Evans and the ACU for being ideologically biased.

Mr. Diggs: Your organization stands for certain policies... The question is whether or not objectivity may have been colored by the strong views that have existed. I read your publications when they come out, and I know they take some very, very strong views on some very sensitive issues. That is the reason, that is simply the only reason I raise that point.

Mr. Evans: It is a very legitimate question. I would simply say that I think the same observation, with all due respect, would apply to Members of Congress, members of this committee. I would say that it would apply with even more force to people who have stated positions on the elections who were not there. At least we made the effort to go over there and to see what happened. I wish the U.S. Congress had done the same.

Rep. Diggs didn't take too kindly to this dig, and his word-salad response deserves reproduction in full for confirming where the bias on this issue really was:

Rep. Diggs: Well, I will say in answer to the gentleman that there were many factors involved in the assessment of this issue that are outside of that area. As a matter of fact, I think that is at least part of the thrust of Ambassador Lowenstein's legitimate concern to try to reach some kind of middle ground that will reconcile all of the forces because, if one looks upon this matter as just bring confined to that area, to that election, to just simply those parties of interest that are presently there, the one is just completely overlooking the real serious dimensions to that problem which has a bearing on the entire southern Africa situation, and which has some very serious implications for U.S. foreign policy, U.S. foreign policy that has nothing to do with the humanitarian aspects of our foreign policy but goes into many more serious problems, even involving our supplies of energy and a few other things that you and I are interested in seeing our country maintain in order to be the great country that it is. So, it is much broader than that. That is my answer to the gentleman's point about whether or not someone who did not go is in a position to make some kind of assessment.[6]

Rep. Diggs resigned from Congress the following year, then served three years in federal prison on corruption charges for having extorted kickbacks from the salaries of several of his staff. Owing chiefly to the insistent of Solarz, sanctions on Rhodesia stayed in place until further international pressure and the continued guerrilla insurgency forced the transfer of power to the Marxist Robert Mugabe, who ruled for the next forty years. In a follow-up column after Mugabe's takeover was complete, Evans blasted Solarz for being "steeped in the rankest of ideological hypocrisy." The episode was a case study in the impulse of American liberals, whether through weak-mindedness or worse, to side actively with the enemies of the U.S. and its interests.

ACU-ERI became the new base for reviving Evans's passion for mentorship of students and young conservatives. As mentioned before, he formally mentored several young journalists during his time at *Human Events* in the late 1950s but wasn't able to carry on with much of this kind of outreach during his *Indianapolis News* years. ACU started a summer student internship program after he took over in 1971, and it moved into higher gear after he moved to Washington in 1975. As ERI prospered, he began expanding its staff. One of his first hires as writer and editor was Walter Olson, fresh out of Yale University in 1977, who later went on to build his own reputation with his work on legal issues for the Manhattan Institute and the Cato Institute, including several best-selling books and a popular website, OverLawyered.com (which he closed up in 2020). At ERI Olson produced a study on the folly of mass transit, a favorite boondoggle of Evans to attack in his own columns, and served as editor for other ERI publications and the work of interns. "Working for Stan definitely moved me up the learning curve" of journalism.

In 1977 ERI's modest intern program formally transformed into Evans's next big institutional contribution: the National Journalism Center (NJC), which set as its ambitious mission to train a generation of quality journalists through a hands-on internship program for college students and recent graduates interested in a career in journalism. Joseph and Holly Coors, strong supporters of the ACU-ERI under Evans, provided new funding to get NJC launched, and it quickly attracted additional support from other major conservative foundations such as Olin, Bradley, Scaife, and Earhart. The format of the program was simple: the twelve-week program was split in half, with interns assigned to work for a journalist or media outlet for six weeks and then spending six weeks working in the NJC office on Capitol Hill on a research and reporting project for the other six weeks, the best of which ERI would publish. On a typical week every Friday afternoon, all the interns would assemble at NJC to hear from a guest speaker, usually a working journalist such as Robert Novak, Ralph Bennett and Bill Schulz of *Reader's Digest*, Don Lambro of the Associated Press, Fred Barnes of the *Baltimore Sun* and later *The New Republic*, or radio host Pat Korten. For practice, interns wrote up news accounts of the guest speakers, which editors would review with each intern to improve their style and completeness.

There were three classes a year, corresponding to fall and spring semesters and summertime, and splitting the class into two halves effectively doubled the number of interns who could be in the program at once. As the program grew, it received around six hundred applications a year for seventy-five spots. Journalists and media outlets that took a steady stream of NJC interns included the *Washington Times, Harper's* magazine, *Human Events,* the *Wall Street Journal,* Fox News, the *American Spectator, USA Today, Investor's Business Daily, Reader's Digest,* the AP and UPI wire services, and several suburban papers (this writer was assigned to the *Northern Virginia Sun* daily morning paper, which ended publication in 1998). In the fullness of time, the NJC helped launch the careers of a number of notable journalists, including John Fund, Ann Coulter ("a handful" who "stood out" even then, according to other interns and NJC staff from that time), Mark Tapscott, Bill McGurn, John Hood, Chris Warden, John Berlau, Michael Fumento, Greg Gutfeld, Rick Henderson, Lisa Schiffren, Terry Moran of ABC News, Malcolm Gladwell of the *New Yorker,* John Merline, John Barnes, Susan Ferrechio, and many others. In fact NJC became a pipeline for several news organizations. Robert Novak eventually hired most of his staff out of NJC. By the time Evans handed off the NJC to the Young America's Foundation in 2002, more than 1,600 young people had been through the full-contact Evans-led program, of whom about 1,000 had gone on to media or media-related employment. NJC alums, as of 2002, had written forty books and won two Emmy awards and a Peabody.

Headquarters for the earliest years of the NJC was a beat-up second-floor walkup suite located over a liquor store on Pennsylvania Ave SE, with well-worn, uneven, creaky wood floors. (By the early 1980s, it moved to better quarters on Maryland Avenue.) The intern "newsroom" was fitted out with secondhand metal desks, each with a manual typewriter. This was well before the first word processors or desktop computers, though Evans did have an early version of a fax machine he used to transmit his column to the *Los Angeles Times*. It was a crude optical character reader device that required wrapping each page around a spinning cylinder, with an early telephone modem hookup. It took several minutes to transmit each page, at daytime long-distance telephone rates. The space also had a legacy rodent problem that interns made worse with untended lunch leftovers. Mice would run out of the rooms when people arrived first thing in the morning until the day Olson and Fred Mann placed mouse traps extensively around the office. For a few days, the snap-snap-snap sound of the traps mixed in seamlessly with the clack-clack-clack of the typewriters. Evans's three-legged dog, Zip, helped with the eradication project. It helped that the office was located adjacent to the Hawk & Dove bar, which offered an ample happy hour food spread that attracted regular attendance from impecunious interns. (This author and Martin Morse Wooster were once tossed out for over-indulging the free food buffet.) The initial NJC quarters certainly offered an authentic experience to aspiring young journalists.

But the program format and setting do not begin to capture the secret sauce of the program, which came from the deliberate understandings of Evans. Creating self-consciously conservative journalists was not the object of the NJC. "We are not in the business of training polemicists," he declared to the Philadelphia Society in a 1990 speech. "An information flow distorted from the right would be just as much a disservice as distortion from the left," he said in another 1990 lecture at the Heritage Foundation. He acknowledged in a 2001 interview with *Insight on the News* that "It's a fact that a lot of these kids want to be pundits. They want to hold forth about the issues. But we tell them, 'Pay your dues first; be a reporter.'" One small but telling sign that his commitment to substantive journalism was not primarily ideological can be seen from one of the readings he assigned to all interns in those early years: a chapter on journalism from Charles Peters's now-out-of-print book *How Washington Really Works*. Peters, the long-time editor of the vaguely liberal *Washington Monthly* magazine, was no one's idea of a conservative (he was more of a Gary Hart–style New Democrat), but the chapter in his book on the media offered a bracing description and criticism of the sensationalism and herd mentality of the Washington press corps in the post-Watergate era, when it was the ambition of every young reporter to be the next Woodward and Bernstein. The point was, you needn't be a conservative annoyed at liberal media bias to learn how to become a better journalist.

He explained the inspiration and reasoning behind his design in a 2002 interview with Bill Dennis on the eve of his retirement from running NJC:

> I came to believe that the way journalism was being done was unsatisfactory, to put it as charitably as possible. And most people when they hear that think I'm talking about bias—that there's liberal bias. And there is. But that isn't really the main problem, or at least is only one of them. What I became concerned about was journalists covering issues they did not understand, and journalists covering issues they didn't even try to understand. This has become progressively worse as the issues have become more complex. When I started out in the business, nobody was writing about global warming, or health care policy, or any environmental

issues, or technical-scientific issues. Journalists are not trained in any of those things. Most journalists have no science background, they have no economics background, they don't know anything about these matters. They're journalists because they didn't want to learn about those things!

The same errors are made over and over again. Every time there is a blip in gas prices, the media will say 'Oh, we've got to have an investigation of this,' and Capitol Hill mobilizes, and various interest groups make statements. And the media acts like this has never happened before, and they are clueless as to prices, and why prices do what they do, or why price controls are a disaster. And that is even a more serious problem than the [liberal] bias problem, or it compounds it.

We needed to have something a little bit different, in which journalists are not trained in this [superficial] way. We try need to train people to be good solid substantive reporters, as opposed to just transmission belts for quotes by politicians. That's the genesis of NJC.[7]

In other words, a bigger problem than ideological bias is simple incompetence.

Evans's critique had a number of refinements beyond just incompetence and bias, and he a had number of original terms to describe the kinds of superficial or lazy journalism that he thought need correcting. He heartily embraced the common-place criticism of "horse race journalism," in which news stories focused on whether a legislative proposal was likely to pass or which candidate would win an election rather than reporting what the bill would do or what the main arguments of the candidates might be. In 1988 Evans came to a partial defense of Gary Hart, whose presidential ambitions had come undone by a sex scandal unearthed by the *Miami Herald*. While agreeing with Hart's complaint that the media was interested in style over substance, Evans noted that no one had benefitted more from this media tendency than Hart himself: "What we are left with is irony piled upon irony: The other Democratic candidates, attempting to debate the issues in their fashion, must tune in each night to hear Hart deploring a lack of debate about the issues."[8]

He also added to the lexicon of critical descriptors of journalism. One of his vivid phrases he used in his critiques presented to NJC interns was "waterbug journalism," in which journalists flit about lightly on the surface of things, chasing shiny objects. (This might be said to be an early version of Rush Limbaugh's more famous later phrase about the "drive-by media.") He anticipated Daniel Boorstin's famous description of "pseudo-events" in Boorstin's 1962 book, *The Image*, in which Boorstin described what we today call a "media event"—that is, as Evans summarized it, "an artificial happening contrived for the purpose of getting itself reported." As Evans wrote in a 1959 column in the *Indianapolis News*, "We have now entered the era of achievement by press release, wherein miracles of science are 'proved' simply by claiming them; the typewriter has replaced the cyclotron."[9] (It is worth mentioning in passing that his discussion of Boorstin's thesis in *The Future of Conservatism* contains a footnote that reminds us again of Evans's literary bent as he says that the clearest description of the false reality of pseudo-events is found in "the novelist Walker Percy.")

Likewise Evans was on to the idea of "fake news" long before Trump made it a household phrase, though in his case it was literally made-up news close enough to real news played for laughs. Among his favorites to use in speeches: "The CDC has determined that conservatism is not spread by casual contact."

When it came to superficial journalism, Evans was especially annoyed at the recklessness and sensationalism of Geraldo

Rivera (then of ABC News), whom he mentioned often in his lectures as an example to be avoided. His real name was Gerald, as Evans liked to mention as evidence of Rivera's truth-bending ways. Rivera was an early example of the growing problem of celebrity journalism, in which the journalist was a part of—or bigger than—the story itself rather than an impartial observer reporting on events. In a 1978 interview with *Playboy* magazine, Rivera dismissed objectivity as a concept "invented by journalism schools; it has very little to do with real life." He admitted to suppressing reporting on events he was seeing first-hand in Panama because it might adversely affect the Senate vote to ratify the Panama Canal treaty, and he admitted coaching Sandinista revolutionaries in Nicaragua on how to avoid creating a bad impression for the American media during their drive to depose Nicaraguan President Anastasio Somoza. Evans wrote of Rivera: "If Geraldo Rivera did not exist, people trying to prove the leftward tilt of network television would be anxious to invent him. He is a walking caricature of TV bias in the guise of 'news.' As long as a major network has someone like this involved in 'reporting,' TV's most ardent critics will never have a shortage of ammunition."[10] ABC News tried to claim Rivera had been misquoted in *Playboy*, but by the mid-1980s Rivera didn't even pretend anymore, openly admitting that he practiced "advocacy journalism" in a speech accepting an award from Columbia University's exalted school of journalism.

The case of Rivera provided Evans with an example of the crucial difference he imparted students between bias and objectivity. Having a point of view is fine so long as your reporting is based on an objective and honest account of the facts. This is even true—especially true—for an opinion journalist like Evans: "You can tell how good a reporter any columnist is when you read the column not so much to get the columnist's opinion, but because you know you'll learn something you did not know. In fact, with most columnists you'll be able to predict what the opinion is. But if you learn a lot about what's going on from what they write or say, then to me that's the real test." (Any content review of the body of Evans's thousands of columns and editorials will see that most of them cite data or report the original views of an expert rather than just opining.)

Rivera and agenda journalists like him generated another of Evans's memorable descriptors: "ventriloquist journalism." This phrase describes the supposedly objective reporters who call up sources looking for a comment that fits a narrative story line or conclusion the reporter has already decided upon. Elite reporters are very skilled in repeating a variation of the same question until they get the quote they are looking for (this author has experienced it firsthand on several occasions). This is less reporting that narrative fiction. True journalism seeks out sources to learn special insight or facts, not to fit a preconceived story line.

He offered this description of how good journalism should be done:

> It's not just running and getting a quote. For example, we tell our students, if you are covering a hearing, *go to the hearing*—don't just pull down from the internet what someone has said. When the hearing is over, and someone like Senator Ted Kennedy has been conducting a hearing on health care, reporters will rush up and stick a lot of microphones in Kennedy's face and ask him a question and get a quote. I say to my students, "Don't do that. As you watch Kennedy conduct the hearing, there's some guy standing in back of him, leaning over, whispering to Kennedy, he's handing him documents, he's going back and forth." And I say, 'As the reporters are following Kennedy and yelling Senator!, Senator!, you follow the other guy. *He's* the guy who knows what's going

on. He's the issue expert. Kennedy's not. Nobody's interviewing
him [the staff guy]. He'll give you the information.' But if you're
not at that hearing you don't know who he is."[11]

As might be expected, the mainstream media dismissed NJC
as a mere factory to produce right-wing propagandists. "Because
everyone knows I'm a conservative," Evans said, "they assume
that the object of this program is to turn out conservative journalists. In a very important sense that is not the case because, if
a kid comes to us who is a very strong conservative and that's
all he or she brings to the table, and he's not willing to become
a good reporter, then we both are wasting our time. If a person
comes to us who isn't the most convinced conservative in the
world and, as a result of being here, that person can go out and
do an honest and accurate job, then neither of us has wasted
our time. We do not do thesis journalism. We don't believe in
starting off with a conclusion and then collecting evidence to
support it. A lot of people don't understand that about us." Evans
once went so far as to say the phrase "'conservative journalist'
is an oxymoron, like 'jumbo shrimp,' or 'Senate Ethics Committee.'" Hence NJC alumni include "mainstream" journalists
such Terry Moran of ABC News and Malcolm Gladwell of *The
New Yorker*.

"The nuts-and-bolts part of journalism—how to write a
lede—is the easy part," Evans said about the content of NJC
instruction. "What I can't do is teach remedial civilization in
six weeks. So we look for people who bring something and then
we make them journalists. I look for a strong liberal arts background. Or I look for a hard science background. We love econ
majors, but the econ majors going into journalism are few and
far between." Fortunately for the interns, Evans was skillful in
teaching some basic economic literacy in the Friday lectures he

conducted. The essence of his lectures was a restatement of the Bastiat-Hazlitt "economics in one lesson" point that "The art of economics consists in looking not merely at the immediate but at the longer effects of any act or policy; it consists in tracing the consequences of that policy not merely for one group but for all groups." In some ways this axiom applies better to the art of journalism than economics.

In his lectures for the interns, Evans always illustrated this point with current examples, in particular the perverse or unintended effects of regulation and price controls and how badly the media treat these important effects. "Economic reporting tends to focus on the government's output of official figures such as Gross National Product, consumer prices, interest rates, unemployment data, and so on, as if these were the sum and substance of economic knowledge. But in every case these figures deal with symptoms, not causes," he wrote in a 1975 column that could serve as his manifesto of why the NJC needed to be launched. It deserves extended quotation:

> Consider the general level of reporting on inflation. There is a continual dither about interest rates and consumer prices, and steady reportage that clocks the movement of these indices. But there is comparatively little information about the actions of the Federal Reserve System in expanding the money supply, the government's crowding of capital markets as it finances deficits, or how these maneuvers create inflation and push up interest rates when the alleged object is to do the reverse.
>
> Consider also the widespread belief that "business" news is an esoteric specialty, to be sequestered from the flow of political news in general. As it happens, nearly everything debated in domestic politics—jobs, inflation, urban problems, mass transit, pollution, energy, health care—is rooted in the soil of economics ...

Finally, there is no getting around the problem of bias. Much of what is said politically and editorially about economic matters reflects not only theoretical ignorance but active hostility toward American business... On these and other matters, the usual output of many major media spreads factual error on top of theoretical fallacy, leading public opinion ever deeper into economic confusion.[12]

This writer distinctly recalls, at a remove of forty years, Evans explaining to young aspiring writers the defect of news copy that said, "Inflation came in at 1 percent last month, led by increases in the price of energy, food, and housing." "This is the logic," Evans said, "that thinks wet sidewalks cause rain."

Beyond the substantive teaching, Evans also conveyed a number of practical rules and habits. The deadline is your friend because it forces you to get the work done. The hardest part of writing, he said, is sitting your butt down in the chair and typing. He would likely have been doubtful about—if not opposed to—the recent popularity of standup desks, given that he liked to joke that newsrooms went downhill when they removed the built-in ash trays from newsroom desks.

Above all, he was relentless in expounding his main lesson: get the facts. Always get the facts. He also reinforced a canon of good journalism too little observed today: "If your mother says she loves you, check it out." Another way of describing his mode is that if everyone was saying "X," look closer because the *opposite* of "X" might be closer to the truth. Rick Henderson recalls, "More than once he told us no one really cared about our opinions. What we should give the reader is information we gleaned that was grounded in timeless principles."

While NJC pointed to the subsequent careers of its alumni as its major accomplishment, interns did instigate a few major stories while in the program. Two Yale students who were NJC interns in the summer of 1994, Pat Collins and Scott Armel, got the green light from Evans to look into what had become of Texan billionaire Lee Bass's $20 million donation to Yale University in 1990 to launch a new program on Western Civilization explicitly intended to offer a counter-perspective to the raging tides of multiculturalism. At the time, the Bass pledge was one of the largest Yale had ever received. Behind the scenes, faculty opposition had blocked the idea, but Yale's administration temporized and strung along Bass, doubtless hoping to keep his money for a watered-down purpose. Collins and Armel dug into the story, unraveling how the undertow of political correctness had thwarted Bass's intent, and published the results through an Intercollegiate Studies Institute report that was mailed to select Yale alumni.

The story became an overnight sensation, with the *Wall Street Journal, Newsweek,* and the *New York Times* picking it up. Although Yale ended up taking the extraordinary step of returning Bass's donation (plus interest), it was not without a counterattack claiming that the story was a right-wing distortion from the "well-funded" ISI. NJC's role in the story was left out for a curious reason that Evans delighted in relating—what we nowadays call "not fitting the narrative":

> This effort to make the accuser the defendant is quite familiar in our politics, of course, and for anyone who knows anything about ISI and its scholarly endeavors, or campus issues generally, totally absurd. *Newsweek,* for instance, dwells on the supposed opulence of ISI and conservative students as its stooges, enjoying "material comforts" of the "right-wing life," compared to which "shoestring student organizations can barely compete."...
>
> I got a taste of this when a *Newsweek* reporter called me about the involvement of the NJC in developing the facts about Bass and

Yale. Though she was herself a Yale alum, she showed no interest in the substance of the story; her leading question was, instead, about the NJC: "Where do you get your money?"

To all of which there is a further interesting footnote, at least from my personal standpoint. The fact that Collins and Armel had researched and written their story at the NJC apparently didn't fit the pro-Yale version of the conflict. Why this should be is not exactly clear, but could have something to do with the fact that we are an independent journalistic outfit, which doesn't conform to the controlling thesis. Also, with our meager budget, modest stipends and Dickensian quarters, portraying us as fat-cats dispensing "material comforts" would be impossible.

Whatever the reasons, *Newsweek* and the *Post* deep-sixed the fact that the NJC developed and reported the story, even though they knew this was the case.[13]

Despite the omission of NJC's role in the mainstream media coverage, it was a big win for NJC. "It was like hitting a mule upside the head with a two-by-four," Evans told Rush Limbaugh a few years later.

Evans did not think the emergence of the internet was good for journalism, writing in 2003 that while it made possible a quick search of stories already written on a subject, it led to journalists rehashing them in a slightly different version. "Unfortunately, much of what is out there is of unknown value, or positively wrong. So any reporter or historian recycling this stuff is helping to repeat the legend, to be parroted by some other Web researchers in the future."

The success of the NJC would suffice to cement Evans's reputation for helping improve the practice of journalism, but it wasn't his only significant journalistic venture. In 1980 he became publisher of a specialty magazine, *Consumers' Research*, which he positioned to be an alternative to the better-known *Consumer Reports*. This is a circuitous story. The magazine dated back to the late 1920s and was loosely affiliated with *The New Republic* at its launch as it was founded by the famous Progressive Stuart Chase (the person who first came up with FDR's famous phrase "the New Deal") and F. J. Schlink, an engineer by training. Chase and Schlink thought there was no serious information about quality control for just about every consumer good that could be imagined. They set up a laboratory to "investigate, test and report reliably on…hundreds of common commodities purchased" in the new magazine. The enterprise grew quickly. By 1935 it had a staff of fifty and employed an additional two hundred outside consultants to assist in the testing program. Subscriptions grew from about six hundred at its launch in 1927 to forty-two thousand by 1932.

Then things got weird. Chase moved on to other interests, leaving the magazine and the testing lab in the hands of Schlink. In 1935 a clique of Communist agitators, for reasons that may seem strange today, decided *Consumers' Research* was a vehicle worth taking over and began agitating for a strike action among *Consumers' Research* employees. The "fellow traveler" J. B. Matthews, who broke with Communism in the late 1930s at around the same time as Whittaker Chambers, was a board member and vice president of *Consumers' Research*, and he told the story in his memoir, *The Odyssey of a Fellow Traveler*:

> For many years, the Communists took the position that consumers as such could not be organized for revolutionary purposes. It neglected, therefore, to set up any united fronts whose purpose was to exploit consumers' interests, on behalf of Moscow. In 1935, this position was reversed and the Communists decided to launch a whole new series of united front organizations for consumers.

A strike was called and a show trial for Schlink organized in a brazen attempt to force out Schlink, who, although a mostly apolitical engineer, recognized it as a political agitation rather than a genuine labor action and resisted. The whole effort failed in short order (after an attempt at mediation that involved, incredibly, Reinhold Niebuhr and Norman Thomas), with Matthews saying, "Rarely have I derived more satisfaction from a job than that which I experienced in helping to capture effective control of *Consumers' Research*."[14]

The defeated Communist faction inside *Consumers' Research* decided to set up a rival organization that became Consumers Union, which went on to publish the much larger and better-known *Consumer Reports*. For a time Consumers Union and its magazine were recognized as a radical organization. It was investigated by the Dies Committee in 1938 and listed as a subversive organization by the House Committee on Un-American Activities, but by degrees the enterprise shed its Communist character, and it was removed from the HUAC list in 1954. And although *Consumer Reports* settled down into a format providing reviews and evaluation of consumer products, it remained something of a catspaw for a "consumer movement" that was (and remains) decidedly liberal in its orientation. Ralph Nader was a board member of Consumers Union, always urging the magazine to be more explicitly political.

Evans took early note of Ralph Nader's demagoguery about protecting "the consumer" and understood that the so-called "consumer movement" was merely another front for liberalism and bigger government—even before President Jimmy Carter proposed a cabinet-level federal Department of Consumer Protection. (Apparently Nixon's Consumer Product Safety Commission wasn't sufficient.) Nader was only the most prominent figure in a "consumer movement" that increasingly sided with new schemes of government regulation that in many cases were directly adverse to the interests of consumers. He had made his fame with *Unsafe at Any Speed,* which attacked the Chevrolet Corvair as a dangerous automobile, leading General Motors to discontinue its production. A Department of Transportation study issued in 1972 that refuted Nader's claims attracted little media notice—except from Evans and a handful of similarly minded conservative columnists whom Evans published on the *Indianapolis News* editorial page.[15] Evans thought consumers were no different than other classes of citizens—quite able to perceive and protect their own interests in a competitive marketplace. (He did have one running joke lampooning the "consumerists" about buying a $7 watch at Walmart that quit working after five years: "Where's the quality?")

So when the opportunity arose in 1980 to acquire control over a consumer magazine with a disposition favorable to free enterprise and skeptical of government regulation, Evans jumped at the chance. J. B. Matthews died in 1966, but his widow Ruth Matthews remained on the board of *Consumers' Research* and served as assistant publisher. She was also involved with some special projects for *National Review,* which put her in the orbit of Buckley, and it was Buckley who put Evans in touch with Matthews as a potential successor as both she and Schlink were approaching retirement.

Now Evans had a vehicle to contest the big government "consumerism" of the Naderites. In his first issue as publisher in May 1980, Evans explained:

We intend to continue CR's product testing and reports, adhering to the methods established by Mr. Schlink and his associates. At the same time, we are broadening the scope of CR's coverage. We recognize that "consumer" interests today embrace an enormous

range of issues—and we intend to cover them…What we are after
is a balanced mix of articles that address all the real concerns of
consumers—which are often different from the enthusiasms of
"consumerists."

Schlink actually stayed on as technical director in charge of the
product testing for a few more years and lived to the age of 103.
While Schlink was not known as an ideological conservative, he
fully shared Evans's dislike of Nader, so he and Evans saw eye
to eye on Evans's design to move the magazine into commentary on public policy questions that affected actual consumers,
in contrast to the "victim consumers" of Naderism and the left.
In something of a valedictory statement, Schlink expressed his
disdain for Nader in a 1988 article for *CR*:

In the view of Nader, and indeed of many liberals, the essential
element for the aims of the consumer movement is and should
be primarily related to the "struggle" against the wicked forces
of industry and business, rather than testing and reporting on
consumer products.[16]

Schlink had come quite a way from his start with *The New
Republic* and his initial Progressive partner Stuart Chase.

Evans introduced several new regular sections to the magazine,
such as an unsigned column, "Dateline Washington," covering
actions of regulatory agencies such as the Federal Trade Commission and the Consumer Product Safety Commission. But it
was the new, hard-hitting feature articles where Evans worked
the most significant changes. The first issue Evans published
contained a nine-page feature on automobile air bags, just then
coming into use following a federal government mandate. The
unsigned article was vintage Evans as it consisted mostly of

excerpts from a report to Congress from the comptroller general on air bags that the media ignored that concluded the Department of Transportation had rushed the mandate into place with insufficient data and limited real-world testing. The DoT estimate that air bags would save nine thousand lives a year was mostly guesswork. Automatic passive restraints (front seat shoulder belts that would deploy automatically) might be more effective, the report argued. A sequel in the next issue explored the cost of air bags.

If that heresy wasn't enough, the other major feature of the first issue under his direction was a six-page feature, "Nuclear Energy: How Safe Is It?" The Three Mile Island accident had occurred the year before, and the Kemeny Commission, appointed by President Carter in the aftermath of the accident, had issued a report that largely refuted the leading scares and exaggerations. Naturally the mainstream media didn't cover the report with much care or balance. The piece included a detailed sidebar explaining the basic facts of radiation exposure, which is seldom done in media coverage of nuclear issues. *CR*'s conclusion: "Most of the specific fears and statements at the time concerning explosion and radiation hazard were wrong—although other, less dramatic problems did and do exist; and that these mistaken statements themselves were the source of the major health hazard emerging from TMI—that of 'severe mental stress.'" Two months later *CR* returned to the subject with a sequel disputing a report from the stridently anti-nuclear Union of Concerned Scientists.

Over the next twenty years that Evans published *CR*, the magazine could be relied upon to take contrarian positions on the full range of issues with a consumer angle. Think cable TV has to be regulated because competition isn't feasible? *CR* would explain why that common view is wrong. Think ATM fees are a way for banks to gouge account holders? To the contrary, they help expand consumer access to their money. In a rush to insulate your house to save energy? Not so fast: "It may come as a surprise to readers, but insulating your home could be hazardous to your health," Evans wrote. Evans noted a recent report from the General Accounting Office (GAO) on indoor air pollution, which assessed the risk of naturally occurring radon gas accumulating in home basements. The EPA estimated that higher levels of radon in heavily insulated and weatherized homes could lead to more than ten thousand additional deaths a year due to lung cancer. "In homes with relatively high, steady rates of air infiltration," the GAO report said, "the radon level is diluted and the concentration reduced."[17] A traditional conservative could have reached the same conclusion without science on the old-fashioned ground that fresh air is good for you. This kind of counterintuitive finding and wider consideration of risk tradeoffs has not slowed the drive for energy-efficient building retrofits, as every version of the Green New Deal today attests. Under Evans, *Consumers' Research* liked to debunk health and diet fads, and Evans took special note of the irrational fear of additives. Back in his *Indianapolis News* days he liked to mock the "whole grain" bread fanatics by noting that Wonder Bread had "28 added chemicals to keep you healthy!" He delighted in a 1992 study that found "white bread did not cause weight gain and improved the quality of participant's diets."

Health care was topic of special interest for Evans and *CR*. Hate HMOs and managed care? Yes, you should, though you should understand how bad government policy drives the formulas hospitals often follow that discharge patients without regard to their actual conditions. This was a special interest to Evans, and he would not have been surprised by the perverse practices of New York state during the COVID pandemic of discharging elderly patients with COVID to nursing homes. In 1986, Evans moved his aging parents from Tennessee to live next door to him out in

Hamilton, Virginia, so he could look after them more actively. Not unusual for the elderly, his father, Medford, required at least one stay in a hospital for an age-related ailment, and Stan was appalled at how quickly his father was discharged owing entirely to the reimbursement protocols of the managed care program through which his father was enrolled for supplemental Medicare coverage.

He called it out for what it was: de facto rationing of health care, which he had been warning was the inevitable result of government command of the health care marketplace. He returned to this subject repeatedly in both the pages of *Consumers' Research* and in his newspaper column, pointing out that key decisions about hospital health care had been transferred from doctors and patients to bureaucratic formulas. This was not a market failure, he argued; to the contrary, it was the result of government policy that distorted the entire health care marketplace, not just the public programs such as Medicare and Medicaid. "Private health insurance" was no longer "private" and no longer actually "insurance" as it is supposed to operate.[18]

Evans also played the consumer angle to expose the political and bureaucratic interests behind many liberal crusades, such a climate change and anti-smoking rules. Climate change policy was certain to cost consumers a lot in higher prices for energy and other products, so the scientific basis for it ought to be rock solid. Not so fast, said *CR* when the issue first rose to prominence in the late 1980s. And when the anti-smoking movement got hold of passive or secondhand smoke as a regulatory issue, *CR* ran a cover feature, "Smoking and the Tyranny of Public Health," an excerpt from Jacob Sullum's book *For Your Own Good* that noted how the EPA had to play fast and loose with its normal standards of statistical significance to justify extending smoking bans. Still other features straddled the gray areas of regulation and market idiosyncrasies, such as airline deregulation and the pitfalls of the hub-and-spoke system that legacy airlines moved to in the aftermath of deregulation, which had the character of a cartel. This issue summoned forth a long bylined feature by Evans himself. As a frequent flyer, Evans experienced firsthand the many frustrations of modern air travel arising from congestion at airports. The remedy: more competition rather than a return to regulation as Naderites were demanding in the 1980s and 1990s.

It was the height of irony that Evans came to control a media outlet originally founded by a prominent New Dealer, and that probably was part of the attraction for him. In his typically self-deprecating way, he occasionally described *CR* to friends as "small enough to be incompetent, big enough not to care." But as was always the case when you read his copy, he took its mission very seriously. His "Publisher's Note" in every issue was usually a mini-column reminding readers of the free market principles of the magazine. They bore his trademark direct headlines: "Free to Choose,' "'No' to Controls," and "High Stakes Issues."

Consumers' Research also provided another outlet for graduates of NJC and launched the professional careers of Chris Warden, who worked at the magazine and then taught journalism at Troy University, and John Merline, who went on to *USA Today* and *Investor's Business Daily* and the *Issues & Insights* website. Peter Spencer worked at *CR* as managing editor before moving on to senior staff posts on Capitol Hill. Mal Kline worked as both the in-house editor at NJC and as contributing editor at *CR* before going off to lead Accuracy in Academia. Evans ran *Consumers' Research* for twenty-two years, spinning it off on its own in 2002, the same year he passed the NJC along to the Young America's Foundation.

Both NJC and *CR* would stand as robust contributions to alternative journalism, but as the late night infomercials say,

"But wait—there's more!" As if running the NJC and *CR* along with his regular newspaper column and contributions to *National Review* and *Human Events* weren't enough, in 1980 Evans began a twenty-year career teaching journalism at Troy University in Alabama, flying down to campus once a week each semester to conduct hands-on seminars in a new journalism school that he helped climb the national rankings.

As with *Consumers' Research*, there is a story behind this initiative. In the late 1970s, the president of Troy University, Ralph Wyatt Adams, wanted to build up a journalism school whose conscious intent would be to counter liberal media bias, "something like the NJC, only at a public university," recalls Tom Davis, who became an Evans protégé. Adams was the rare conservative college president—he had been roommates with George Wallace in law school—and he first launched a program in 1972, the Hall School of Journalism and Communications, named for Grover Hall, the legendary editor of the *Montgomery Advertiser* known for his crusades against the Ku Klux Klan back in the 1920s that won him a Pulitzer Prize. The initial architect of the new program was the conservative journalist John Chamberlain, whose column Evans used to include regularly in the *Indianapolis News*. Chamberlain served as dean of the program from 1972 to 1977, at which point Adams and Chamberlain reached out to Evans about leading the program. Not wanting to leave Washington since he had just relocated there two years before, he declined but said he'd be happy to come lecture regularly at Troy. Shortly after, Troy received a major gift from a local family (the Sorrells) for several purposes, among them an endowment for a chair of journalism. Adams initially tried to recruit Pat Buchanan for the post, but after Buchanan declined, Adams approached Evans again about filling the chair, and Evans agreed. Starting in the fall of 1980, Evans flew down to Montgomery every Monday evening all three terms that the university was in session, taught seminars on editorial writing all day Tuesdays, and returned to Washington Wednesday mornings. After a few years, he started to cut back his presence slightly and recruited other conservative journalists to rotate for him, including Don Lambro of the AP, Ralph Bennett of *Reader's Digest,* and Ken Tomlinson of Voice of America. Despite changing up the format and schedule, he became a presence at Troy for the next twenty-four years, right up until he contracted his fatal illness in 2014.

Like his instruction at the NJC, Evans offered an intensive, hands-on experience for students. He didn't use any textbooks. Instead he had students read local and national papers and simulate newsroom story conferences where the students would pitch ideas and commit to writing on a specific issue. Tom Davis, who was one of Evans's first students at Troy who then went on to be an editor for Evans at NJC and *CR,* recalls the style of Evans's course: "He'd ask, 'What are you going to write? Okay, here are some of the things you need to look at,' and you'd go out and write it and bring it back to him. And then he'd sit down with you for 30 or 45 minutes or even an hour, and you got the 'atomic blue pencil treatment.' It was very intense, but he just knew so much, and you learned what you didn't know. He was always kind, but very, very detail-oriented. Also very patient; he would just sit with students for a long time and reflect on things."

When in later years Evans would sometimes come to be in residence for a semester instead of commuting for two days a week from Washington, he offered an editorial writing class that simulated a real-life newsroom in a five-week span, meeting three-and-a-half hours a day, three days a week, where all the work would be written in class. The syllabus reinforced Evans's central point about journalism: "All good editorials have one thing in common—FACTS! The good editorial writer, then, is a good reporter, gathering information on a topic and presenting it in a logical, and hopefully, persuasive way. Looked at another way, everybody has opinions, but opinions are only as good as the facts that back them up. 'Because I said so' may have worked for your parents, but it won't work on the editorial page...Writers who don't bother to explain issues, assume facts not in evidence and employ vague generalities—'Everyone knows that Democrats are for the working man'—don't persuade, they simply annoy."

Evans's presence in the journalism program at Troy was not the sole conservative influence on campus. A program in political economy led by and named for Manuel Johnson, a stalwart monetarist Reagan appointee to the Federal Reserve, was founded at Troy in 2010. (Johnson had been born and had grown up in Troy and graduated from the university.) Evans delighted in the sympathetic company and used his connections to help arrange for conservative speakers to lecture in the political economy program, Walter Williams being a particular favorite. In some senses he became Troy's ambassador to prominent conservatives. One special occasion that required Evans's intervention was a speaking invitation to Karl Rove, who for general reasons was wary of any campus invitations because the environment was usually hostile and unpleasant. Rove called Evans to ask, "Am I walking into a liberal trap?" Evans: "Karl, it's a symposium named after me. What do you think?" Rove came for the appearance, and sure enough there were some protestors holding anti-Bush signs, but as Rove approached the gauntlet in front of the building, several of the protestors said, "Good morning, Mr. Rove. It is a pleasure to have you in Troy." Even the left-wing protestors are more polite in the south.

Evans seemed very much at ease in Troy, likely because it exemplified the same kind of heartland sensibility he enjoyed in Indiana. The pace of life suited him, as did the unpretentious local cuisine and rock and roll trivia nights at local bars. His favorites were the Double Branch Lounge and the Sidelines Sports Bar at the local Holiday Inn. He turned up frequently at university sporting events, especially basketball and baseball. He rented out a local dance hall for end-of-semester parties on more than one occasion, making him a highly popular professor. "One of the best things about coming to Troy for 25 years," he told Tom Davis, "is that I don't get trapped by someone frantic to know what I think about the outcome of a special election in Iowa. I get to break away from that a little bit." Not having to run off to a radio studio, political meeting, or other typical DC obligation meant that he could relax and enjoy the simpler pleasures that appealed to him more than the typical offerings at the Kennedy Center. His fondness for the town, its environs, and its people was richly reciprocated. Tom Davis recalls that "He made friends from all walks of life. Every year, as the new school year would start, I'd be asked by people as diverse as the chancellor of the university and the owner of the local pizza place, or the public address announcer at our baseball games, 'When is Stan coming back? I just can't wait to see him.' When he passed, there were several people on the faculty and staff who were anything but conservative who said to me, 'What a great man. I really enjoyed knowing him.'"

Among the many little platoons of his fans was a small-time, rock-and-roll group of middle-aged guys who played regularly for fun at a bar in Eufaula, a little town sixty miles east of Troy where Evans and Davis often traveled just to have fun with the band. The band, it turned out, never knew fully who their friendly fan was. After Evans's passing, one of the band members called up Davis: "I never realized that 'our Stan' was M. Stanton Evans!"[19]

CHAPTER 11

FRONT ROW SEAT
FOR THE REAGAN REVOLUTION

Ronald Reagan's landslide victory in 1980 presented Evans with both a problem and opportunities. The opportunities were obvious: the politician he most admired, and with whom he had a warm personal relationship, was now president, and he could expect to have the ear of the president to some extent. The sentiment was reciprocated. The Reagan transition team reached out to Evans to see if he would be interested in formally joining the Reagan White House as a speechwriter or for some other post, but between his commitments to NJC, Troy University, and his broader journalistic career then at its zenith, he declined. (In 1982 he also declined the invitation to be the first editor in chief of the startup *Washington Times*.)

The problem arose from his understanding of Washington that gave rise to "Evans' Law: When 'our people' get to the point where they can do us some good, they stop being our people," a more elegant formulation of "going native." The bitter lessons of the Nixon-Ford experience were on his mind, along with the conclusion he propounded then: the conservative movement needs to keep the pressure on its own team. He knew that he, and the movement, would often need to be critical of Reagan. His criticism was frequently sharp, and while it upset Reagan at times,

Evans was careful never to attack Reagan directly or personally. Evans could well be considered the charter member of the "Let Reagan be Reagan Club," though that phrase owes to Reagan's close friend William Clark.

For the moment the broader conservative movement was jubilant about Ronald Reagan's landslide election victory, especially after the contest had apparently stayed close throughout the fall. *Human Events* ran its largest banner headline ever: "Victory At Last!" Evans shared in parts of this celebratory mood, seeing the election result, which swept away several liberal Senators (George McGovern, Birch Bayh, John Culver, Frank Church, and Warren Magnuson) as a vindication of his view that American opinion had been trending to the right for a long while but hadn't broken through because of a combination of contingencies that obscured these trends.

His first postelection column, "Why Reagan Won," explained that it was the "constants" of politics that determined the outcome, not the "volatility" of the day-to-day campaign events that the media fixated upon in their typical "horse race" mode:

> The demographic and other changes leading up to this year's upheaval had been evident beneath the surface for several years, but were ignored or explained away by the seismographers to whom they were repugnant. The economic and other costs of liberal government have simply become too great for most Americans fed up with taxes, deficits, inflation, regulation interference and other aspects of the welfare state, and concerned about the seeming impotence of the United States in world affairs.
>
> These impulses showed themselves as early as the 1960s, and in fact led to the Nixon victories of 1968 and 1972. But the ambiguity of Nixon's policies and his failure to carry majorities in Congress blunted the progress of the new conservatism, while the calamity

of Watergate derailed it altogether. The Carter win of 1976, against that backdrop, was an aberration—a temporary detour from a journey started two decades in the past. This year's election put the train back on the track.[1]

The unstated question for Evans going forward was whether the train would stay on track under Reagan or be derailed again as it had under Nixon. Thus he maintained a reserved demeanor somewhere between that of the triumphant conservatives who thought Reagan would sweep all before him and pessimists who worried that Reagan would succumb to the forces of the permanent government in Washington, which was resolutely against him.

Well before Reagan won, Evans was thinking ahead to the election and beyond and laying down markers. In the fall of 1979, Evans wrote a column attacking John Sears, the GOP campaign strategist who ran Reagan's 1976 campaign and was back for the 1980 campaign. Among other things, it was Sears's idea in 1976 for Reagan to pick liberal Republican Senator Richard Schweiker as his potential running mate, which not only failed to sway enough delegates to pry the nomination away from President Ford but infuriated many conservatives. As an old Nixon "pragmatist," Evans was beyond suspicious of Sears, offering a litany of details in support of the conclusion that Sears wanted to "moderate" Reagan's public views and campaign strategy: "The Sears factor presents an obvious paradox: the anomaly of the Republican Party's most famous conservative spokesman having a campaign directed, at the highest political level, by an ardent non-conservative."[2]

One of the readers of the column was none other than Governor Reagan himself, who answered a letter from a friend a few weeks later:

I, too, read Stan Evans' column and was concerned as you evidently are. So much so, in fact, that I called Stan. We have known each other for a number of years, and I think he jumped to conclusions because of some of the Washington press stories about my campaign.

Let me assure you that I feel as you do about the vice presidency, and if it should fall to me to recommend a nominee, it would not be a liberal with any idea of balancing the ticket. I don't believe in "balancing the ticket." I believe the vice president should share the president's philosophy and views.

It is also untrue that I am moderating my positions or beliefs in any way in order to get elected. If I were willing to alter my positions, there would be no reason for me to seek that office. My only purpose in doing what I am doing is to have an opportunity to put my ideas into practice. I believe what I have always believed.[3]

In a separate letter to another friend in January 1980, Reagan wrote: "I do want you to know that Mr. Sears is not determining my policy." On the eve of the New Hampshire primary the following month, Reagan fired Sears.

Evans attended his sixth Republican National Convention that July and wrote, "I can safely say the Detroit platform is the best the party has produced in my experience." Evans thought Reagan would only serve one term on account of his age and thus found the choice of George H. W. Bush to be his running mate concerning, but "the conservatives for now have triumphed, and have their best chance in decades of putting a candidate of their choice into the White House."

Another Evans preelection initiative was his launching, in the fall of 1979, an ad hoc group known as the Chesapeake Society consisting mostly of conservative staff members on Capitol Hill, whose purpose, according to one leading member of the group, was to be "a parliamentary wrecking crew for disemboweling, stopping, and delaying liberal legislation until Ronald Reagan arrived." Over the next year, the Society grew to about seventy-five regular members. After the 1980 election, Evans networked with other conservatives to attempt to influence the Reagan transition through another informal initiative that he called the Inchon Forum, a project designed to establish a beachhead of solid conservatives "behind enemy lines" in the Reagan administration. Evans was far from alone in worrying about moderate Republicans in the senior ranks of Reagan's White House, starting with Vice President George H. W. Bush and chief of staff James Baker. Evans was personally fond of Reagan and heartened by his record as California governor and as a campaigner in two cycles. He knew there would be wins and losses. But he also knew the supreme importance of the adage "personnel is policy."

If Evans seemed slightly aloof from the conservative ferment of the beginning of the "Reagan Revolution," it wasn't from any cynicism or memories of frustration from the Nixon-Ford experience but from a deeper view that the cause of conservatism can't be vindicated or achieved primarily by politics. The best statement of his views on this question is a remarkable and wide-ranging speech he gave to the Philadelphia Society in April of 1977:

> Party politics should not and cannot be our major object. If we should lose ourselves in the ephemera of politics, we would be lost indeed, without compass points or bearings... *The ends of politics cannot be politically derived.* They must come from a realm of affirmation beyond the legislature and the precinct. Yet, it has to be remembered that if we are concerned with the right ordering of our society, with protecting human freedom, combating social entropy, defending our national sovereignty, someone somewhere is going to have to do the political work—electing candidates, drafting legislation, and seeing to the administration of the laws.

> At some point the insights of the scholar must be translated into the practical functions of the lawmaker. It can be argued that we have attempted such translation prematurely, that some among us who should be spending more time on scholarly pursuits are dabbling far too much in party politics. But the fact remains that conservatives eventually must grapple with the stuff of politics in the colloquial meaning of that term. [Emphasis added.]

With the coming of Reagan, it seemed plausible that the moment had arrived for stepped up political engagement by the conservative intelligentsia. But it is clear that Evans understood that a central principle—perhaps the central principle—of conservatism was to recognize the limits of politics. Conservatives should never think like liberals do that electoral victory will deliver us to the Promised Land.

From here Evans went on to diagnose two emerging aspects of the political scene that will sound familiar and are salient for the time of Trump: the character of the "working class" (he called them "hardhat populist elements") and the rise of "neoconservatism." Evans was early to seeing the rise of neoconservatism long before the term came into currency and had been noting in his *Indianapolis News* column the liberals such as Moynihan, Richard Goodwin, and Irving Kristol defecting from Great Society orthodoxy starting in the mid-1960s. He understood, however, that the neoconservatives would always differ from other conservatives by the absence of any a priori principles, which manifested itself in their attachment to social science and an acceptance of the basic idea of the welfare state. But Evans's attitude toward the "neocons" showed again his ecumenical disposition, while his skepticism of conservative pragmatism (as he called it) ought to be recalled in today's enthusiasm for various conservative proposals for "pro-worker" subsidies, tax preferences, and industrial policy:

I think an alliance *de facto* is possible with each of these groups capable of evolving across the years into something stable and enduring—provided that conservatives in search of such alliance stick by their own principles. In the case of the populist hardhats, the fallacy of some recent theories is the notion that we should jettison some of our defense of individual freedom and limited government, to advocate for some kind of welfare state for some of our blue-collar ethnics, recirculating dollars from liberal client groups to our own. I think this is mistaken in terms of principle and in terms of practical politics as well...They should not be assailed with a pragmatic mish-mosh of Tory welfarism *cum* law-and-order that blends insensibly into the very liberalism they are beginning to oppose.

At other times Evans acknowledged the problem of the GOP reputation as the party of big business and the country club, and he occasionally applied his typical humor with a quip suitable for the Trump era: "I'm tired of hearing about what Republicans are doing for the working man—what have they done for the country clubs lately?" And: "For certain members of the Republican Party, a 'social issue' is when someone gets blackballed from a country club." He had been pointing to the opportunity for conservatives to attract the working class vote since at least the late 1960s. His best succinct expression of his perspective can be found in a 1978 *National Review* column: "The presumed hostility between conservatives and the working man is factitious. The conservative stress on productivity and expansion, after all, is much more clearly in the interest of working people than is the 'no growth' posture of the liberals."[4] In other words, stick to our principles: good policy is good politics.

Turning to the neoconservatives, Evans made the same essential point in his aforementioned 1977 speech:

I for one welcome this development and believe we should encourage it in any way we can. Some of the research and social analysis that appears in *Commentary* and *The Public Interest* is amazingly good, and as credentialed liberals these writers can reach an audience that is denied to most of us. But let us be clear: these intellectuals are moving quite clearly toward our position; we are not moving toward theirs. Their insights have become increasingly profound and increasingly accurate almost exactly in the proportion that they have come to approximate our own, whether the subject is the Cold War, internal security, the economics of health care, or the follies of mass transit...I would sum it up in a symbolic formula: Kristol is great, but Friedman is greater.

At the outset of the Reagan presidency in 1981, Evans concentrated his commentary and behind-the-scenes advocacy on a handful of issues that were long-time concerns of his but not on the front pages of the papers or atop the priority list of most other conservatives: reviving internal security efforts (including reestablishing the congressional committees on internal security that were scuttled in the mid-1970s) and stanching the flow of trade and technology to the Soviet Union. Today the Kama River truck plant is a forgotten name, but in the 1970s, Cold Warriors were incredulous that the U.S. government granted export licenses for American companies to build the world's largest truck factory for the Soviet Union that could be easily repurposed for military vehicle production (and in fact a separate American-supplied factory was used to build missile launchers).

Evans had watched with dismay in the mid-1970s as the post-Watergate frenzy ripped into the CIA and counterintelligence capacities of the FBI, culminating in the abolition of the House and Senate Internal Security Committees.[5] Sen. Ted Kennedy was behind the drive to abolish the Senate committee, but Evans was particularly out to attack liberal Republicans who not only went along with this appeasement but in some cases were assisting Kennedy in the effort, such as Oregon's liberal Republican Senator Mark Hatfield. A 1975 column criticized Hatfield for supporting abolishing the Senate committee outright, which drew a complaint from Hatfield, which boiled down to the argument that the committee's work had little serious value and that no one in the Senate wanted to keep it. Evans disputed this stoutly in reply: "At a time when domestic terrorists are blowing up airports, law enforcement officials are under increasing attack, and the KGB is stepping up its efforts to cultivate contacts on Capitol Hill, it is astonishing to see so many efforts to abolish our internal security agencies."[6]

He was encouraged when the Senate, under Republican control for the first time in twenty-six years in 1981, set up a judiciary subcommittee on terrorism and security and encouraged it to be aggressive in the scope of its investigations. "The revival is timely," he wrote, "and the new committee certainly has its work cut out for it. A peculiarity of the campaign to abolish the old internal security group and other internal security agencies of the government, was that it occurred in tempo with an upward surge in internal security troubles. The worse the problem got, it seems, the more determined the effort to ignore it."[7]

Evans was an early and enthusiastic backer of the Kemp-Roth plan to cut income tax rates 30 percent across the board that Reagan adopted in his 1980 campaign. Evans was writing favorably of Kemp and his economic ideas as early as 1977, having featured him at CPAC in 1975. But his enthusiasm for tax cuts was less for the supply-side reasons that it would stimulate economic growth and potentially increase revenue than for the general principle best set out by Milton Friedman. Like Friedman, Evans was for "cutting any tax, at any time, for any reason." One of his favorite send-ups of lazy liberal clichés was "Any country that can land a man on the moon can abolish the income tax." When Evans casually remarked that the Reagan-Kemp tax cuts weren't big enough, he wasn't joking.

Spending drew his sharpest attention, however, and was, along with what he considered to be weak or liberal personnel appointments, the main focal point of his criticisms of Reagan. If you went by the news media coverage, let alone the claims of Reagan's partisan opponents, you'd have the impression that Reagan's proposed budget cuts in 1981 would repeal the New Deal and return the nation to the supposed "social Darwinism" of the nineteenth century. (Some critics actually made both claims literally.) In reality, Reagan's proposed budget cuts in 1981 were modest (reducing food stamps by a net of $100 million) or weren't cuts at all but were merely a reduction in the rate of growth under the perverse "current services budgeting" unique to government. In some cases the "cuts" OMB director and congressional budget writers came up with were accounting tricks, pushing current spending into the next fiscal year on the ledger. The initial 1981 proposed budget cuts left untouched the main entitlement programs such as Medicare, Social Security, and several other categories of income or service maintenance programs, and the Reagan Administration abandoned early on any serious attempt to reform these programs in a fundamental way. This was a fatal mistake, which Evans would come back to repeatedly in the coming years, in part because he knew from his arguments with Roy Ash in the Nixon years recounted in Chapter 9 that entitlements were the automatic pilot of federal spending growth.

Evans knew all the tricks and did his best to counter media disinformation along with chastising the White House for not being more aggressive in trying to cut spending. Spending for the food stamp program, Evans observed in *National Review*, had *doubled* between 1977 and 1980 and had risen by 1,000 percent in the decade. When the food stamp program started in 1965, it served 442,359 recipients. By 1980, it had 23 million recipients. (Here again we see Evans's practice of reporting meaningful facts.) If the current trend continued, the number of Americans on food stamps would grow from one in ten to one in seven. (At its peak level in 2013 under Obama, the proportion of the population on SNAP—the successor name for food stamps—was...one in 6.5.) Evans scrutinized other specific budget items, arguing in detail that Stockman's knife had barely nicked the skin of many areas. As early as March of 1981, Evans wrote that "To hear the outcry generated by President Reagan's suggested reductions in the budget, you might suppose federal spending was being cut back to the marrow. Nothing could be further from the truth, as may be discovered by examining some of the enormous spending programs of the federal government, and what is supposed to happen to them in the Reagan budget. Far from going after the programs with a meat ax, the Reagan budget cutters have actually treated them with relative caution."[8]

Evans did his best to employ the budget battles for humorous purposes. At one Monday Club meeting in 1981, he declared that the Club was "dedicated to the proposition that ketchup is a vegetable." (This referred to a media firestorm over a bureaucratic proposal to save money on the school lunch program by classifying ketchup as a vegetable. Reagan suspected this was deliberate sabotage by the bureaucrats, and in the 1990s, the Clinton administration classified salsa as a vegetable in the school lunch program, with no media notice, let alone outrage.)

Evans and most other conservatives accepted the necessity of the compromise that scaled back Reagan's income tax cut plan but remained disappointed that he wasn't more successful in cutting government spending. (After leaving office Reagan said that was his greatest disappointment too.) John Lofton, Ralph de Toledano, Tom Bethell, and Don Lambro all wrote sharp articles to the effect that the Reagan budget cuts were essentially nonexistent. Evans delved deeply into Congressional Budget Office data to show that in most cases spending *growth* was hardly slowing, let alone reversing: "What Reagan has been attempting to do is to slow the rate of increase in federal spending below that proposed by Carter. The budget would continue to grow, but not at so rapid a pace. Unfortunately, even this limited objective is endangered by the freight-train momentum of the federal spending process." And the income tax cuts, good as far as they went, would barely keep up with inflation and rising taxes on the state and local level. Above all, if spending wasn't controlled, further tax cuts would be difficult or impossible.

Evans's commentaries weren't directed at only at negative developments in the Reagan administration. His column was quick to highlight and lavish praise on things he thought the administration was doing well, especially efforts at deregulation, expending domestic energy production, and in foreign and defense policy.

But by early 1982, personnel changes at the White House and talk of a tax increase caused Evans and others in his wider circle to take a more critical public stance. Richard Allen, Reagan's first national security adviser, had been pushed out, along with political director Lyn Nofziger. "The White House staff itself is heavily tilted toward the followers of George Bush (and others of even more liberal persuasion)," Evans wrote in late January 1982. He took special aim at chief of staff James Baker but also thought Secretary of State Al Haig was a bad influence. Conservative hopes at the most senior levels of the staff rested upon

Ed Meese and William Clark, who succeeded Allen at national security: "Unless Meese and Clark assert themselves strongly in the days ahead, the Reagan revolution could soon become the Bush rebellion."[9]

Alarmed that the Reagan Revolution was slipping away, in January 1982, forty-five conservative leaders, including Evans and several of the group who had formed the core of the Manhattan Twelve in 1971, gathered for a day-long meeting at the Mayflower Hotel in Washington to plot a course with respect to their growing worry. The meeting was closed to the media. After debating major aspects of the scene, the group naturally selected Evans to draft what became known as the Mayflower Statement, formally signed by thirty-six of the conservative leaders present. It was a much longer document than either the Sharon Statement or the 1971 declaration of the Manhattan Twelve, and it bore all the hallmarks of Evans's careful position of admiration for and confidence in Reagan while assailing policy mistakes and personnel problems. The Mayflower Declaration stopped far short of "suspending support," as was done with Nixon in 1971, let alone hinting at opposition. The tone was "more in sorrow than anger" from an aggrieved lover:

> President Reagan has...made a magnificent effort to articulate the case for limited government on the homefront, and a firm defense of free world interests overseas. We strongly commend him for his attempts to control the rate of federal spending, achieve tax rate reduction, and lift the burden of unnecessary regulation from our economy.

The Mayflower Declaration reviewed six broad policy areas, but the most serious charge, reiterated throughout the text, was the defect of personnel:

> By far the most urgent problem in the Administration—from which many of the others appear to stem—concerns the appointment of key personnel. In one department after another, crucial positions are occupied by people who have small history of sympathy with, or understanding of, the Reagan mandate, the principles on which it rests, or the sense of urgency that it communicates.[10]

The Declaration didn't name names, but it was clear that James Baker and others of the so-called "pragmatists" were the targets.

It was an Evans column in mid-June that got Reagan's attention: "Reagan Government a Mystery to Conservatives."

> After a year and a half in power, the Reagan government is getting mixed reviews—something between a Dunkirk and a Dien Bien Phu... Overseas, Administration policy increasingly resembles that of Jimmy Carter—in substance and in method, if not in tone... What it all begins to look like is another moderate Republican interregnum, with pragmatic attitudes dictating slightly milder versions of the policies followed by the national Democrats.

But he was again careful to exempt Reagan himself:

> Has Ronald Reagan changed? It seems doubtful. In personal conversation, the President remains as vocal on the old themes as before. He reassures those who express concern about such things that he still wants to implement the "revolution." No one who knows him doubts his commitment. Unfortunately, too many of his subordinates don't seem to share it.[11]

One of those "personal conversations" was with Evans and other leading writers from *Human Events*, which remained high on Reagan's regular reading pile in the White House despite the best efforts of his senior staff to keep it from him. Presidential counselor Ed Meese said that "Reagan puts more credence in *Human Events* than in the *New York Times*." For some of Reagan's senior staff, that was a big problem. The *Washington Post*'s Lou Cannon, who called it "the *Human Events* problem," reported: "The White House pragmatists believed he often paid more attention to articles in *Human Events*, particularly at the outset of his administration, than to the information he received in his national security briefings...Reagan liked to clip stories from *Human Events*, and aides waged a long and losing battle to keep the publication out of his hands. On the campaign plane Deaver sometimes hid it from him." Reagan solved this problem easily enough, as Cannon related. Reagan simply had *Human Events* mailed directly to the residence at the White House, bypassing his mail screeners. In fact he had *two* copies sent. Cannon: "He sometimes complained that he couldn't clip a story out of *Human Events* without ruining another story on the reverse side."[12] He continued his practice of clipping out articles and sending them to aides throughout his entire term, often with a note attached along the lines of "Is it true we [the administration] are actually doing this?"

After being stung by these repeated criticisms in *Human Events*, Reagan invited Evans and several other *Human Events* regulars to the White House in June to see if he could smooth things over and correct what he thought were distortions or omissions in *Human Events* coverage. At the meeting Reagan said to the group, "I'm reading you more, but enjoying it less." Reagan let out his frustrations in a letter to Nackey Loeb, publisher of the *Manchester Union Leader* that had stoutly supported Reagan in the New Hampshire primaries in 1976 and 1980:

> Nackey, my old friend Jeffrey Hart based his column on some misinformation plus the image that is being created of me as being packaged and delivered by staff and aides who won't let me

think for myself... [T]hat seems to be not only a theme of the liberal pundits but of the so-called "new conservatives" including some of my old friends from *Human Events*, etc. It just isn't true... None of our gang tried to talk me into giving up our tax cuts even though for a time half the columnists were saying they were on a near daily basis . . .

I tried a meeting with some of those conservatives I mentioned, John Lofton, Stan Evans, Alan Ryskind et al. and gave them chapter and verse on what the actual record is but it didn't do much good.[13]

There was little chance, however, that Evans and other like-minded conservatives could be held off from criticizing Reagan's course in 1982, the centerpiece of which was his agreement to what was advertised as a $98 billion tax increase (though not income taxes, which is a significant point) over the following five years to help stanch the federal deficit that was soaring on account of the steep recession that year. The entire story of that deal is long and complex, and it involved a pledge by Congress to cut spending $3 for every $1 of new taxes, which Reagan thought an acceptable compromise that would have the net effect of shrinking government. But of course that pledge was not kept, with one later study concluding that Congress spent $1.14 for every new dollar of tax revenue. On the eve of the passage of the deal in August, Evans wrote a *Human Events* cover story on "The Largest Tax Increase in History," which argued that the tax increase would be closer to $227 billion if the fine print were examined more closely. "All of this signals a virtual abandonment of Reaganite philosophy on taxes." In this and several other articles, Evans deliberately placed the major blame on Congressional Republican leaders, calling it "[Robert] Dole's Record Tax Hike." Reagan later admitted that the deal was the biggest mistake of his presidency.[14]

Evans and *Human Events* kept up their fine line of criticizing and praising specific actions of the administration while avoiding attacking Reagan directly. Other conservative leaders were not as charitable toward Reagan as Evans and *Human Events* were during this crucial period. *Conservative Digest* abandoned Reagan completely, asking in a summer cover story, "Has Reagan Deserted the Conservatives?" Howard Phillips of the Conservative Caucus and publisher of *Conservative Digest* blasted Reagan: "It's silly for conservatives to waste an ounce of energy anymore trying to get a 72-year-old leopard to change his spots. We've got to write this Administration off. This is not our Administration." Reagan was furious, firing off a letter to *Conservative Digest* editor John Lofton: "I believe that the July *Conservative Digest* is one of the most dishonest and unfair bits of journalism I have ever seen."

After Republicans took large losses in the midterm elections in 1982, which many conservatives blamed on the surrender on taxes and spending, conservative movement leaders gathered again for a midterm assessment. *Human Events* once again led the charge with a long front-page open letter addressed "Dear Mr. President." It was unsigned, but Evans contributed to it. Unlike *Conservative Digest* that had given up on Reagan, the *Human Events* article was careful to reiterate its respect and personal confidence in Reagan and gratitude for his many positive accomplishments, acknowledging that "we have probably not dwelt on them nearly enough, for, as you reminded us not so long ago—after wading through some of our tarter critiques—you were reading us more but enjoying us less." The article resumed its central attack on the "pragmatists" around Reagan and urged him to become more aggressive in asserting his conservative policy views.[15]

Evans escalated the pressure at the 1983 CPAC the following month. On a panel on the specific topic of assessing the Reagan administration at the midpoint of the first term, fellow speakers William Rusher and Lyn Nofziger, Reagan's former White House political adviser, were both upbeat about Reagan's performance so far and optimistic about the future. But as *Human Events* reported:

> Evans, on the other hand, vehemently maintained that the Administration has defaulted on its obligations to conservatives and that there will be no "Reagan revolution" without radical changes. He urged activists to demand the immediate resignation of James A. Baker, the White House chief of staff often accused of presenting issues and information in a way designed to moderate Reagan's basic conservatism.

But this summary doesn't capture the fullness of his attack, its effect on the CPAC crowd, or the madcap episode after. Evans named several specific people beyond James Baker whom he thought should be cashiered, including Michael Deaver, Richard Darman, and David Gergen. The crowd was agitated and cheering. Evans, caught up in the moment, offered the improvisation that "the White House treats us [conservatives] like any other special interest group, like Indians or handicapped Filipinos!" Both NBC and CBS Evening News picked up Evans's comment in their broadcasts on CPAC, with CBS correspondent Bob Scheiffer saying, "M. Stanton Evans criticized Reagan's aides, comparing White House treatment of conservatives with that given American Indians and handicapped Filipinos."

Evans said later he had no idea where he came up with "handicapped Filipinos," but the next morning at his office he was deluged with angry phone calls from Filipinos, including one from the outraged president of the National Filipino-American Association. Evans kept his cool and used some quick thinking.

"Well, that's the news media for you. They distort everything!"

The caller: "You're damned right they do!"

The conversation took a friendly turn, with Evans explaining what conservatives and Filipinos had in common, namely, shabby treatment from Washington. His caller, now charmed and appeased, followed up:

"Say, would you be willing to be the keynote speaker at our annual convention in two weeks?"

Evans accepted on the spot despite knowing next to nothing about Filipino history, culture, or interests. But he studied up, gave a well-received speech that got a standing ovation, and as a bonus crowned Miss Filipino-America at the end of the program.

William F. Buckley Jr. had long urged Evans to "show a little more leg" in his writing, and Evans did make rare use of his dry wit on a few occasions during this period to make his point about both media coverage of Reagan and how the "pragmatist" faction was fundamentally opposed to Reagan's views. In a column spoofing mainstream media coverage of Reagan's conservative appointees that some papers appended with a headnote to make sure readers understood it was satire, Evans "reported" on the "hit list" of federal officials whom Reagan intended to fire as discovered by several liberal activist groups:

> According to Americans for Democratic Action, Common Cause, the Mondale for President Committee and several other consumer groups, the 1980 balloting was invalid because then-candidate Ronald Reagan and his advisers planned a deliberate purge of high-ranking Democrats from public office. The charges were based on internal memos leaked by a disgruntled former employee of the Reagan campaign . . .
>
> At the top of the hit list were President Jimmy Carter and Vice President Walter Mondale. However, the intended purge did not stop there. It also included all members of the Cabinet, and numerous Democratic senators and congressmen.[16]

The liberal activist groups, the column continued, were compiling their own "hit list" of Reaganites compiling "hit lists," saying, "In the interests of common decency, we demand that this list of people involved in compiling a list of people to be fired be fired." A second column in the same vein presented the mock "news" that James Baker and other senior White House staff were urging President Reagan to step down so the staff could get on with the work of governing the country. Finally, in another spoof of the media, Evans reported receiving an advance copy of a forthcoming *Washington Post* article, "Move to Satanism Threatens to Split GOP":

> A decision by the Reagan Administration to embrace Satanism, scheduled to be announced this week, has caused a serious rift within the government and inner councils of the Republican party.
>
> Highly placed official spokesmen say the new initiative was bitterly opposed by hard-line conservatives in the Administration, led by Atty. Gen. Edwin Meese. Once again, however, pragmatists in the Reagan Cabinet and White House staff have had the better of the argument, successfully contending that the policy move would improve the President's negative image as being "preachy" and excessively moralistic . . .
>
> In one especially controversial move, Reagan's advisers want him to personally sacrifice a goat on the South Lawn of the White House. Former White House assistant Michael Deaver has reportedly urged this step as a major photo opportunity. "It's important," says one official, "that the President not only lead on this, but be *seen* to lead."[17]

Behind this mirth and his frustration with Reagan's moderate senior aides was his understanding that politics really was war by other means, a truth that eludes too many people of "pragmatic" outlook. The war between left and right in American politics, he explained in a speech, is really "a war between the permanent government and the elected government." In contrast to the liberals who decried Reagan's ideological disposition that they alleged "politicized" the government (which was just sneaky device to delegitimize all opponents of liberalism without having to win the arguments), Evans reflected the following year that "If truth be told, the major failing of the Reagan Administration is that it hasn't politicized the government nearly enough. It is a little-known truth that an incoming President can replace only about one-tenth of 1 percent of the federal workforce, thanks to the death grip of the civil service. Only if the new appointees are committed tenaciously to the President's program can they have much impact on the enormous machine of the bureaucracy."[18] (This would seem to be a lesson the Trump Administration understood better than previous GOP administrations. And as it happens, in a late column on a different issue, Evans wrote what could have been the Trump motto: "Instead of swatting at mosquitos, we need to drain the swamp.")

While spending and personnel issues continued as a point of friction for the rest of the year and into the next, there were other events that Evans and his friends rated more highly, especially Reagan's announcement of his missile defense proposal (the Strategic Defense Initiative) in March 1983. Evans understood immediately that SDI represented a potential turning point in strategic doctrine against mutual assured destruction, which, as we have seen, he opposed since it first emerged in the 1960s. He worried that political and bureaucratic opposition to SDI would hobble its development, and he was right to do so.

But he remained relentless in his hostility to James Baker, for one example writing in April 1983 that "It should be obvious to all and sundry that Baker has to go. If a house divided cannot stand, still less so can a White House." The personnel question finally came to a direct confrontation in February 1984. Once again, a *Human Events* front-page story upset the White House: "Reagan Budget: Worse Than You Heard." The central charge of the article was that Reagan's proposed budget for the coming fiscal year spent more than Jimmy Carter would have spent under Carter's last five-year budget plan from 1980. As always the article was careful not to attack Reagan directly, instead blaming budget director David Stockman and calling for his ouster. The unsigned article, written by editor Allan Ryskind and head *HE* writer Joe Baldacchino, contained facts and figures to bolster their argument, down to meager six-figure increases for obscure boards and commissions that ought to be abolished outright. Reagan took note of the piece in his personal diary, noting that "*Human Events* had done a feature indicating I was a bigger spend thrift than Jimmy Carter."

No doubt alerted to the piece by the president, a furious Michael Deaver phoned Allan Ryskind from Air Force One en route with Reagan on a western campaign swing, demanding that he and Tom Winter, the publisher of *Human Events*, come to the White House the next day to talk with Stockman and the president. Ryskind demurred that the following day was the deadline for putting the next issue to bed and thus they couldn't come. Deaver angrily said, "In that case, you'll never see the President again." Ryskind replied, "Well, Mike, we wouldn't like that, of course, but so be it. We just can't see you tomorrow."

Whether Reagan overruled Deaver or someone (Deaver himself or perhaps Ed Meese) had second thoughts, Deaver called back the next day and said Reagan would see them the following week. Ryskind told Deaver that he wanted to bring Evans along to the meeting because Evans was the master of budget details. Ryskind was worried that they might have made some errors in the piece; maybe they had gotten some of their numbers wrong. Evans would know the right answers. "We didn't want to be taken to the cleaners by Stockman," Ryskind recalls.

The meeting took place on Friday, February 17, a typically busy day for Reagan, with two national security council meetings, a lunch for ninety-two Republican women office holders, a reception for new ambassadors heading out to their postings, a grip-and-grin photo op with an Olympic medal winner, numerous phone calls, and capping off the day hosting a dinner for the visiting Prince Rainier, Princess Grace, and their family.

Evans, Ryskind, and Winter were ushered into the Cabinet Room late in the morning, where in addition to Stockman, they were joined by James Baker, Richard Darman, Deaver—the main four people Evans and others in the *Human Events* circle wanted fired—and Meese and several other White House staff. Stockman had prepared a lengthy memo rebutting the *Human Events* article, but he didn't dispute any of the factual claims *Human Events* had made. His response rested on spending changes that he claimed would reduce spending in following years (typically called "the out years" in budget jargon). "Stockman didn't say we had made any mistakes, but that we didn't understand the trajectory of what was happening with the budget," Ryskind says. Evans wasn't buying any of it, and he politely argued that OMB's projections and stratagems simply weren't credible and that they were misleading the president with these esoteric fiscal schemes.

Recollections vary, but at some point James Baker confronted Evans sharply and said something to the effect of, "Just say it! You're talking about me!" Evans, never one to shrink from a contest, replied coolly, "Yes, that would be accurate."

Around this time Reagan came into the room to make his appearance. The official White House diary for the day records that he only spent three minutes with the group between a

National Security Council meeting and a briefing on women's issues ahead of lunch and swearing in a new assistant secretary of Health and Human Services. He was jaunty as ever, asking, "So, did the fellas straighten you out?" Of course the group wasn't going to take up the substance of the matter with a busy president just dropping by, and Reagan knew this, too, changing focus to mention that his latest issue of *Human Events* had arrived badly smudged from the printer and with a printing error to boot, with jump pages indicated incorrectly. Reagan told a typical yarn, saying he and Nancy had held the paper up to the light trying to read a smeared article and find where the article continued.[19] This is the kind of story that, even if literally true, can be interpreted in several clever ways. While Reagan may have thought this was a subtle way of suggesting to his friends at *Human Events* that they had things out of perspective or blurred, the story also sent a clear message to the Baker circle that *Human Events* was important to him.

Evans did not cease pounding away at details of spending growth and the insidious influence of Baker and Darman in his subsequent columns. Perhaps his hardest blow was delivered in a special symposium issue on "What Conservatives Think of Ronald Reagan" in *Policy Review*, the quarterly journal of the Heritage Foundation, in the winter of 1984, just as Reagan's reelection campaign was ramping up. Reagan had some defenders among the eleven prominent contributors, William Rusher and Phyllis Schlafly in particular, but most were highly critical, including Newt Gingrich ("The Administration has had no capacity to launch strategic offenses on behalf of Reagan's vision"), Paul Weyrich ("The radical surgery that was required was not performed"), and Terry Dolan ("I expected more to happen"). But Evans turned a memorable summary phrase: "This has been essentially another Ford Administration."

It has been business as usual, not much different from any other Republican administration in my lifetime. It has been an administration populated by corporate executive types, and people with previous experience managing large government institutions, with the result that there has been no Reagan revolution.

While praising the administration's efforts to reduce regulation, Evans expressed disappointment that Reagan hadn't fought more effectively to control spending: "Real budget growth has been larger under Reagan than under Carter, and the budget is now totally out of control. If the energy used on the AWACS [airplane sale to Saudi Arabia] and a tax increase had been used on entitlements reform, the Reagan people would have gotten it."[20]

William Rusher (who wrote in the symposium that "Genuine conservatives are by and large overjoyed with Reagan, and rightly so") believed that Reagan privately welcomed some public pressure from vocal conservatives as it helped him fend off some of the pressures he received from White House moderates, the media, and squishy Republicans on Capitol Hill. But Reagan also found it dispiriting, writing to Rusher that he was bothered by Evans's "intense and continual disapproval of me" as he had been "a longtime fan and admirer" of Evans.[21]

Even though it was evident by late summer that Reagan was cruising to an easy reelection against Walter Mondale, Evans pivoted to giving Reagan active support in his columns, attacking Mondale and his running mate, Geraldine Ferraro, and correcting media misinformation about Reagan, writing in one column that "Reagan's real opponent, and it is a formidable one, is the national press corps." He celebrated Reagan's forty-nine-state landslide as a general vindication for conservatism but noted that the election "settled nothing" because the forces arrayed against Reagan were still very much in the field and

Congress remained recalcitrant. He expected "another 20 years of firefights."

In Reagan's second term, the focus of Evans's journalism shifted away from budget fights (though he actually praised Reagan's tough 1987 budget proposal) and hectoring the Baker crew at the White House and toward defense and foreign policy questions. Like the budget battles of the first term, Evans knew there were internal divisions inside the White House and in the State and Defense Departments over arms control, aid to anti-Communist insurgents such as the Contras in Nicaragua, Jonas Savimbi's UNITA rebels in Angola, and the Mujahedeen rebels in Afghanistan. Over the years he devoted dozens of columns refuting the commonplace liberal claims about defense spending, reporting the numbers showing that defense spending as a proportion of both the total budget and of GDP had been falling steadily since the Kennedy years. If anything, he argued, Reagan still wasn't spending *enough* for defense.

Like most conservatives Evans cast a wary eye on the series of summit meetings Reagan started to hold with the new Soviet leader Mikhail Gorbachev. Rightly skeptical about summits in general because of their history to date, he worried that our strategy was drifting toward "Henry Kissinger continued by other means: More arms restraint, more trade with Moscow and its satellites, more efforts to build bridges to the Kremlin." He was thrilled when Reagan announced in 1986 that the U.S. would no longer bind itself to the unratified SALT II arms treaty but hoped this was a step to the larger goal of withdrawing from the 1972 Anti-Ballistic Missile (ABM) Treaty that would eventually prevent deployment of SDI missile defense and the final overthrowing of the MAD doctrine.[22] (Withdrawing from the ABM Treaty finally occurred under President George W. Bush in 2001.)

While Evans was wary of Reagan's summitry and arms control

diplomacy with Gorbachev, he didn't go as far as many conservatives such as Howard Phillips, who said that Reagan was "fronting as a useful idiot for Soviet propaganda." Evans was not enthusiastic about the treaty Reagan signed with Gorbachev in 1987 removing intermediate range missiles from Europe, but in several columns during this period Evans allowed for the possibility that Gorbachev *might* be different from previous Soviet leaders and someone who genuinely sought internal reform and improved relations with the West. "If Gorbachev is for real," he wrote in 1988, "and if he can stay in power, then we truly may be advancing to an age of global amity, nuclear tension-easing, and the rest of it." But the proof would come from deeds, not words, such as withdrawing from Afghanistan, removing the Berlin Wall, and introducing true internal reforms. When in the fullness of time all these happy developments occurred, along with the dissolution of the Soviet Union itself, Evans was unsurprised that the media gave all the credit to Gorbachev (such as *Time* magazine's designation of Gorbachev as "Person of the Decade" in 1990 without mentioning Reagan or U.S. policy once), and he offered the contrary conclusion that Reagan's about-face in American policy, however imperfectly executed, deserved the credit for forcing the Soviet Union into a corner: "Communism is like a tapped-out gambler who suddenly finds the table stakes have doubled... It was the tougher-line policies of the '80s that pushed them to their day of reckoning. The lessons for the future should be apparent, as should the fact that Ronald Reagan, not Mikhail Gorbachev, is the authentic man of the decade—if not, indeed, the century."[23]

But that judgment wouldn't become clear for several more years. On the eve of the dramatic summit in Reykjavik, Iceland, in October 1986, Evans anticipated that Gorbachev was intending to spring a trap to get Reagan to abandon SDI, which turned out to be exactly the case. He also anticipated how the media and the political class in Washington would respond if Reagan refused, that is, attacking him as "irresponsible" for turning down a historic arms reduction deal on behalf of what the establishment—and much of his own national security staff—regarded as a wild fantasy. Evans was correct on both predictions, and he noted with satisfaction that Reagan's public approval ratings rose in the aftermath of his refusal of the deal. Reagan's refusal, he wrote, "was treated as a terrible disaster by many in the media, reported in funereal tones that would have been appropriate for the crash of the *Hindenburg* or the loss of the *Lusitania*... The American people prefer a leader who stands up to the Communists to one who gives in to them... Again, the obvious truth of the matter is that the public *agrees with Reagan* on SDI—and does so for some very evident reasons."[24]

But Evans really enjoyed poking the conventional wisdom in the eye when the Iran-Contra scandal exploded on the scene in November 1986. While the media and Washington went into full-scale scandal mode, Evans's natural independence of mind led him to take the opposite point of view. One early column on the scandal began, "The more we hear about the Iranian-hostage-Contra deal, the better it sounds. This is a perfectly serious comment, not intended to be facetious or perverse." Perhaps he had in the back of his mind his quip about not supporting Nixon until after Watergate, but he was earnest in his analysis that neither end of the intrigue violated any laws and moreover that the operations being run through the national security council was necessary to preserve secrecy. As the affair unfolded over the next several months, Evans devoted numerous columns and features analyzing the various policy flip-flops in Congress (the successive Boland Amendments, whose terms changed with each iteration) and defending the legality of the enterprise, whether wise or not. In the fullness of time, his position was vindicated by the fact that the only legal charges ever brought were on secondary matters such as the generic charge of "conspiracy" or, in Oliver North's case, accepting an "illegal gratuity" in the form of a security fence for his home.

When the Iran-Contra matter reached its climax with the dramatic hearings before a special congressional committee in the summer of 1987, Evans noted that the overall effect was turning into a victory for Reagan, and it was more evidence of the gulf between the Beltway media and the country at large: "The more the American people heard and saw of Ollie North, the less inclined they were to take the media view of things." To the shock of Washington, polls in the aftermath of the hearings showed support for Reagan's central America policy rising for the first time in his presidency. Evans took this as yet another case study of the significance of the alienation between the media and the rest of America:

> The point of these observations is not so much the spin the media imparts to stories of this type—though that is certainly a problem; nor is it the disservice that the media do to the public in their one-sided treatment of such topics. It is, rather, in this instance, the disservice the media do to themselves because they can see and comprehend only part of the story—and are thus incapable of doing their jobs in proper fashion.[25]

But it was two cover features Evans wrote for *Human Events*, one defending Reagan on the latest budget and another proclaiming "Hearings So Far Support Administration on Contras," that drew a phone call from Reagan thanking Evans for his helpful contrarian analysis. Evans followed the protracted investigation of independent counsel Lawrence Walsh into the 1990s, noting the media's pathetic and lazy coverage of the story and writing in 1993 that, after six years, it was *Walsh* who ought to be investigated for prosecutorial misconduct.

Reagan also hosted another small gathering of conservative leaders at the White House in the spring of 1987 that included Evans along with Sen. Paul Laxalt, Phyllis Schlafly, William Rusher, Ed Fuelner, Midge Decter, and several others. In part the meeting was intended to help new White House chief of staff Howard Baker (whom Evans didn't like any better than the first Baker in the job) get out ahead of conservative discontent. Evans praised Baker for calling the meeting, saying Baker "has proved a bit of a surprise in the early going for his willingness to meet with, and hear the opinions of, conservatives…The novelty of being consulted in advance is a pleasant change."[26]

Unlike previous White House meetings where Reagan popped in for just a few minutes while leaving the heavy lifting to aides, Reagan sat for an entire hour with the group—twice as long as expected—often responding to questions or comments. Evans pressed the case for an immediate breakout from the ABM Treaty and rapid deployment of whatever anti-missile technology was available to break the back, once and for all, of the MAD doctrine. Although it is known that Reagan sympathized completely with Evans's rejection of MAD, he gave no indications at the meeting what he might do.

Reagan, never one to keep a grudge, made fun of Evans in his last speech as president to CPAC in 1988:

> I got a message from Dave Keene reminding me that this was the eve of Lincoln's birthday and suggesting I go upstairs and check on the ghost in Lincoln's bedroom. I did. And what do you know, there was Stan Evans dressed as Abe Lincoln. And he kept saying, "Listen to Jesse Helms." [Laughter]

By this point in Reagan's second term, Evans was starting to look ahead to, and comment publicly on, the 1998 GOP nomination contest. Taking the long view, he counseled in early 1988 that "conservatives need to see the Reagan era not as the end of a process, but the beginning of one. It has been a 30-year struggle to reach the present juncture of events, with plenty of learning from both successes and disappointments." Although he didn't initially tip his hand, Rep. Jack Kemp was his favorite in the field despite the fact that Kemp had "strayed from the reservation a couple of times from the standpoint of conservative purists (myself among them)." Evans had been an early enthusiast of Kemp's supply-side economics platform, inviting him to featured time slots at CPAC in the 1970s and once introducing him at a black-tie dinner for Henry Regnery with the observation, "To Kemp, tax cuts are like sex; when they're good, they're great. When they're bad, they're still great."

But he worried that while Kemp was "the most electable" among a growing field of conservative candidates that included Pete du Pont, Pat Robertson, Paul Laxalt, Bob Dole, and possibly others, a split field would result in Vice President Bush capturing the nomination. Evans thought conservatives needed to unite behind one candidate. It was, however, the kind of collective action problem beyond the ability of anyone to solve, and Bush ran away with the nomination, as Evans predicted would happen in the absence of consensus within the conservative movement. Evans didn't consider Bush to be reliably conservative (ditto Dole, but he acknowledged that Dole seemed to be trying to court conservatives). But Evans also perceived early what turned out to be Kemp's fatal flaw as a candidate: he couldn't figure out how to run as a convincing conservative. Evans returned to the office after a meeting with Kemp in late 1987 and told his staff, "Well, the campaign is finished. They're predicating it on three things: cutting taxes, winning New Hampshire, and saving Social Security." (Evans had written repeatedly over the years about the long-term fiscal unsoundness of Social Security; anyone who thought it could be "fixed" in the conventional sense was deluded.)

Conservative wariness of Bush was mitigated to some extent by Bush's choice of Indiana Senator Dan Quayle to be his running mate. As previously mentioned, Evans was personally acquainted with Quayle from his time at the *Indianapolis News*, and he had helped Quayle move into an apartment when Quayle was first elected to the House of Representatives in 1976. Bush had been reaching out to movement conservatives in the spring and early summer of 1988, shrewdly making sure he could find ways to gain their enthusiastic support. Evans was part of these discussions, and he emphasized that personnel patronage was less important than *running as a conservative* on the issues. Evans kept in touch with Quayle after he arrived in the Senate in 1981 and hosted him as a speaker at ACU-ERI events on national security and arms control issues, for which Quayle had taken a leading role in the Senate even though the media usually lavished its attention on Indiana's utterly conventional senior senator, Richard Lugar. (This asymmetry in media coverage was not lost on Evans; one of his typical columns from the period bore the title "How Lugar Helps the Left.")

There followed what Evans called the media's "Great Quayle Hunt of 1988," which generated and then repeated every unfounded rumor, salacious tale, and distortion about Quayle that Evans said represented "one of the all-time low points in American journalism." And because Evans knew Quayle, he became part of the story in a way that vindicated every criticism he had ever made about media malpractice. As John Merline, an editor at NJC and *Consumers Research* at the time, recalled, "The mainstream media were so determined to get trash on him that they dug so deep into his past that they found Stan Evans!"

A prominent theme of media Quayle-bashing was that his wealthy and influential family, including his maternal grandfather Eugene C. Pulliam, owner and publisher of the *Indianapolis News* when Evans was editor, had used their influence to propel Quayle forward (a line of inquiry the media seldom if ever applies to anyone from the Kennedy family). One of the specific charges was that his family had "pulled strings" to get Quayle an entry-level job with Indiana Attorney General Theodore Sendak after Quayle finished his National Guard service and before heading off to law school. According to some accounts, Quayle had misrepresented the status of his post in the AG's office. Contacted by the *Los Angeles Times* (among other media outlets) for comment, Evans was careful to avoid the usual tricks of "ventriloquist journalism," but one of his comments was clipped and used out of context. As the *Times* story read, "'He wasn't chief of anything when he went over there,' added M. Stanton Evans, a former editor at the *Indianapolis News* who arranged Quayle's job interview with then-Atty. Gen. Theodore L. Sendak." Evans's comment was then recycled by the *Washington Post*, the *New York Times*, and ABC News, none of which contacted Evans to verify the quote or ask for context or additional detail.

Needless to say, Evans responded with a column setting the record straight, which deserves excerpting at length:

> I have found myself presented as an example of string pulling by the Quayle family...In point of fact, the episode in question proved the *opposite* of the media thesis. At the time, Quayle had just completed his six months' training in the National Guard and was entering the job market. He had an interview lined up with the Indianapolis city administration of Mayor Richard Lugar,

but wasn't sure if this was the direction he wanted to go. (And how, by the way, did he get *that* interview? I'm sure the media will want to know.)

Jim Quayle, Dan's father and a long-time friend of mine, accordingly asked if I would talk with Dan and advise him, since I was based in Indianapolis. Dan and I met over lunch, and I discovered that he was interested in going to law school and pursuing a legal career. Whereupon I suggested to him that he might be better advised to seek employment with the state attorney general's office (then looking for young people to hire), which more obviously fitted his goals…

At no point did Dan Quayle (or Jim Quayle) ask me to do any favors, pull any strings, or use any influence on Dan's behalf…

Thereafter, I contacted a staffer in the attorney general's office to find out how and where Dan should call to see about an interview. He had the interview and was hired, not into a "prestigious position" as the *New York Times* put it, but to an entry-level slot exactly like those concurrently held by scores of young people in state government—no better and no worse (and then proceeded, rather oddly for a child of privilege, to work his way through law school).

End of story—or non-story, to be precise. The conversation I had with Dan, and the job interview that followed, were exactly the same as hundreds of other conversations and referrals in which I have engaged across the years with young people starting out in journalism, government, and other professions. And, of course, such interviews and referrals occur all the time in the workaday world. I have no doubt that most of the reporters hallooing after Quayle have had such experiences of their own…

I find the ABC report a particularly contemptible piece of distortion, since the people putting it together had my entire statement in front of them, and therefore knowingly selected a snippet that could be made to fit their predetermined story line.[27]

Evans thought Bush's decisive victory in 1988—nowhere near as large as either of Reagan's landslides but still very substantial—owed to Bush running more or less as a Reaganite conservative. He held no illusions that Bush in office would govern reliably as a conservative, and he wasn't surprised when Bush abandoned his "no new taxes" pledge in 1990. In fact, Evans noted shortly after Bush's victory in November that the "permanent government" of the Beltway establishment was already lining up to corner Bush into abandoning his anti-tax stance before he'd even taken office, offering not merely a skepticism of Bush's resolve but a reminder that the Beltway is heedless of public opinion:

> What is of particular interest is the *process* we are witnessing here—and what it says about our system of representative government. Having just completed an election in which the American public resoundingly cast its ballots in favor of the candidate pledged against a tax hike, we suddenly find ourselves besieged by people (most of whom have not recently been elected to anything) clamoring insistently that such a hike must be adopted…
>
> If the newly elected President can be rolled on taxes, his prospects for winning much of anything else will be dramatically diminished.[28]

He hadn't expected much better from Bush in any case. Evans's Law ("Whenever 'one of our people' reaches a position of power where he can do us some good, he ceases to be 'one of our people'") didn't apply to President Bush because, as he said when asked later about George W., "To be utterly candid, I never considered him to be one of our people. Not that I have any hostility toward him, but considering those who lined up early for him, George W. was a considerably different kettle of fish, say, from Barry Goldwater or Ronald Reagan, both of whom were much more definitely conservative-movement leaders." Sure enough,

President George H. W. Bush's elevation of Richard Darman to be director of the Office of Management and Budget was evidence that Bush's "pragmatic" streak would be even more evident than the undertow of the Reagan White House. One of Evans's quips to the Philadelphia Society during the Bush administration was that "This is the greatest assembly of intellect since Richard Darman dined alone at the White House. Which was often." Evans called for Darman's resignation in a *Human Events* cover story in 1991, and when Bush was defeated for reelection in 1992, Evans relished placing the blame on Darman in a column entitled "Darman Tax Hike Doomed Republican Chances." He adapted Ross Perot's famous phrase assailing the NAFTA treaty to conclude: "The giant sucking sound then audible to the country [when Bush broke his "no new taxes" pledge in 1990] was the Republican Party being absorbed into the shapeless mass of Washington's tax-and-spend establishment... When President Bush agreed to the package concocted for him by Budget Director Richard Darman, he also signed his own political death warrant. It was one of the great political blunders of all time."[29]

In late 1987 Evans made a rare overseas trip to attend a conference of conservative MPs at Windsor Castle and to speak in London to the St. Stephen's Club, a conservative club dating back to the Disraeli era. Evans didn't often comment on British politics, but a column about the trip offered his highest praise for Margaret Thatcher as a model of how to be "constantly on the ideological offensive" because "Mrs. Thatcher rules with a sense of purpose... In the past, British conservatives have learned a lot from their American counterparts. Now, it is fair to say, Americans have a lot to learn by traveling to London."[30] (One brief aside from the column is relevant again: Evans took note of a speech by Labour Party leader Neil Kinnock "not yet repeated by Joe Biden.") He went on to France on this same trip, attending a conference in Paris and taking in an appearance by Henry Kissinger, who was present trying to defend the Vietnam Peace Accords of 1973 to an audience including numerous Vietnamese refugees who were not impressed with Kissinger's explanations to their question, "Why did you abandon us?" "Kissinger seemed alternately nervous, exasperated, and—dare I say it?—guilty," Evans wrote. "He was uneasy in the extreme. Yet in substance it was the same old, vintage Kissinger: It wasn't my fault; I got the best deal I could; Congress made me do it."[31] Evans resisted the temptation to say "I told you so," preferring instead to ask the question as to whether anyone had learned the proper lessons from the long Vietnam agony.

As the 1980s gave way to the 1990s, with his activist years receding in the rearview mirror and knowing that Reagan's departure meant he would not receive the same level of attention at the White House, the focus of Evans's journalism tilted back to policy wonkery on issues, including housing, homelessness, health care, taxes and spending, and occasionally science. This latter subject offers a tiny clue to the final turn in Evans's long career toward a literary legacy that deserves to stand the test of time.

CHAPTER 12

A LITERARY LEGACY

As Evans drew toward his sixth decade in the 1990s, he entered a new and final phase of his life and career. His prodigious journalistic output did not slow down. He continued writing his newspaper column, publishing *Consumers' Research*, teaching at Troy University, and running the National Journalism Center. When the *Los Angeles Times* began shrinking its syndication service in the mid-1980s, Evans moved his column to the Heritage Foundation, which had launched its own newspaper syndication service. He had also moved on from CBS Spectrum and signed on for regular commentaries for Voice of America. With the day-to-day calculations of how to engage the Reagan administration over, Evans began stoutly defending Reagan's accomplishments from the relentless media and revisionist attacks. In the early 1990s he collaborated with Ed Meese on Meese's White House memoir, *With Reagan.*

By degrees, however, a turning point can be made out. In retrospect Evans might be said to have cleared the decks for his greatest legacy as a writer and thinker. First, with the end of the Reagan administration (and the resumption of conventional Republicanism under both Presidents Bush) and the subsequent end of the Cold War, Evans began to mark out some positions slightly distinct from mainstream conservative thought, especially on foreign policy and health care. Second, his return to the theoretical questions at the heart of conservatism that animated his early work (especially the Sharon Statement) marked out the essential continuity of an integrated conservative philosophy, which has been up for grabs ever since and never more so than today. In reviewing this period today, Evans can be seen to be well ahead of the curve.

With the Soviet Union gone and international Communism an expired threat, here and there can be detected some hints of a latent disposition toward noninterventionism that was a hallmark of his first mentor, Frank Chodorov, as well as a central feature of what is still sometimes called "the old right." The existential threat of the Soviet Union had always been a problem for noninterventionist libertarians like Chodorov and cautious Midwestern conservatives who were the heirs of Robert Taft, and Evans was certainly close to both strains of thought. While Evans never directly declared himself on the question of "isolationism" or noninterventionism, it is clear he thought that much of our Cold War diplomacy, especially foreign aid, was counterproductive when it wasn't in fact perversely helping augment the power and reach of the Soviet Union. He always preferred that the United States win the Vietnam War, but here and there in the 1960s were hints of doubt about the wisdom of the enterprise in the first place. If cross-examined, Evans would likely have proclaimed himself to be a "realist" of a certain kind—not the amoral "realism" of someone like Kissinger, whom he despised, but the kind of realism that thought if America had an ample defense, no one would mess with us. His view was reflected in Reagan's axiom that no country was ever attacked for being too strong.

Thus when the first major conflict after the Cold War erupted, the Gulf War of 1990–91, Evans did not automatically jump on the prowar bandwagon. While voicing support for Israel, he wondered whether American policy in the Middle East was actually help-ful to Israel or was in America's interest at all. Evans wrote that some of the region's troubles owed to our own "myopic interfer-ence." In radio commentaries for Voice of America in the late 1980s, Evans wondered "why we were kowtowing so endlessly to Saddam Hussein, and hearing little or nothing by way of an intelligible answer." When President George H. W. Bush began assembling a war coalition in the aftermath of Iraq's invasion of Kuwait in 1990, Evans noted that it wasn't clear that the coming war was necessarily a vital interest of the United States (while also rejecting the idea that we were intervening at the behest of Israel) and moreover questioned the sudden "neo-interventionism" of the left: Where were the usual indignant cries of "no more Viet-nams," against backing foreign autocrats, and concerns about the "imperial presidency"? This skepticism of Middle Eastern policy should not be regarded as "isolationism" of the old Robert Taft variety, he argued, but rather it flowed from his long-running contempt for our hubristic foreign policy establishment. In another column Evans came close to repudiating the Vietnam War: our Middle East blunders that had helped strengthen the Baathist regimes in Iraq and Syria reminded him of "the grim effects of early Vietnam syndrome, which might best be described as creating such a mess through mistaken intervention that U.S. troops are sent in to set the situation right."[1] In the aftermath of Operation Desert Storm in 1991, Evans thought his skepticism was fully vindicated, arguing that the ambiguous post-conflict conditions in Iraq proved that U.S. strategy and messaging had been "incoherent."

Evans returned to this problem in the aftermath of September 11, 2001. He had given up his column by that point and was only writing intermittently about current issues, but *Human Events* reporter John Gizzi caught up with Evans in December 2001 to ask him about the wider war strategy then being contemplated in Washington. In particular, Gizzi wanted Evans's reaction to a comment from William Kristol in the *Washington Post*: "Whether we take on Iraq has huge implications for the U.S. role in the world and, fundamentally, it's whether we're going to take it upon ourselves to shape a new world order." Evans was not enthusiastic about the idea, telling Gizzi:

> I don't know where the idea came from that conservatives favor a 'new world order' or any variant of that notion. That sounds more like the globalism of Woodrow Wilson and FDR than the limited constitutional government U.S. conservatives have historically favored. As to conservative doctrine on such issues, my personal view is that the proper role of the U.S. government is to defend our country against attack or imminent security damage. I'm no military expert, but judging by results to date, the President and his team have done a superlative job of responding to the attacks of September 11th. I would specifically include in this their reluctance to expand the fighting in all directions.[2]

With the arrival of the Clintons in 1992, he greeted out-of-town visitors to the Monday Club and other events with the quip, "Welcome to Washington—or, as it is known now, 'Rodham and Gomorrah.'" He fully concurred with New Gingrich's assessment that the Clintons were "1960s countercultural McGoverniks." His long-time criticism of America's largely socialized health care system led him to take more than usual interest in Hillarycare, not solely on the merits but because of direct personal experience mentioned in Chapter 11. The "managed care" strategy of the Hillarycare plan would have coerced millions of Americans into Health Maintenance Organizations (HMOs), he pointed out in numerous columns, and would make the problem of medical rationing exponentially worse. "It will be a credit to Mrs. Clinton's powers," he wrote, "if she is able to repeal the laws of economics."

While he agreed with the Republican push to rein in Medicare and Medicaid spending (which contributed to the government shutdown showdown between Speaker Newt Gingrich and President Clinton in 1995–96), he thought it was a disaster for Republicans to embrace HMOs and "managed care" as the policy vehicles to control health care spending. "HMOs and care denial bid fair to be the foremost domestic scandal of the '90s—which free-market types should be investigating and opposing. Instead, many in Congress are doggedly working to put a Republican label on these horrors," he wrote in early 1996.

Both parties, Evans thought, were uncomprehending of the inherent defects of our health care system and, as usual, Republicans flinched from acknowledging the problem openly and embracing genuine reform involving changing the perverse tax treatment of health insurance. "Why Not Real Health Care Reform?" argued one 1992 column that, ironically, prefigured the later proposal of one of Evans's least favorite Republicans, Sen. John McCain. (McCain's 2008 campaign proposal would have ended the tax preference for employer-based health insurance and substituted a direct tax credit for individuals to purchase insurance on the open market.) Evans did not oppose every reform idea that did make it onto the Congressional agenda. In 1998 he urged Republicans to support a Democratic bill to regulate HMO rationing practices, however imperfect the proposal might be.[3] (A compromise bill passed the following year.)

Evans also expressed doubts about NAFTA and the way "free trade" was supposedly advancing, but not for the same reasons as Ross Perot or Pat Buchanan, that it would tilt the playing field against American industry. Rather, Evans noticed that what was being called "free trade" was in reality better understood as "managed trade," with lots of special deals and the further empowerment of national and international bureaucracies. In a 1995 column written during a trip to London, Evans drew parallels between Britain's growing accession to the European Union and the tendency of NAFTA and the World Trade Organization to affect American economic interests. In the case of the UK, Evans's observations on the loss of sovereignty this entailed for Britain and the rise of the "Euro-Skeptics" in the Conservative Party can be seen as a prescient anticipation of the Brexit movement twenty years later.

> The obvious lesson for Americans is that, just because something is called "free trade," it doesn't follow that it will enhance our freedoms. This is decidedly the case with NAFTA (which has extensive provisions empowering eco-bureaucrats and activists), GATT (which contained, to everyone's surprise, a secret tax hike), and the evolving World Trade Organization (also loaded with bureaucratic powers and "green" provisions, whose workings we can't veto). The similarities to the E.C. structure are apparent.
>
> Not, to be sure, that NAFTA-GATT-WTO among them are as scary as the European Union; the movement, however, is in the same direction, accompanied by similar bait-and-switch techniques. In both cases, a set-up promoted as "free trade" turns out on close inspection to be something else—a political structure conferring power on bureaucrats and regulators, rather than simply letting private parties go in peace. One wonders why "free trade" requires so much coercive intervention.
>
> It is unfortunate that dispute about such issues has been cast almost entirely as a battle over protectionism, since this has allowed promoters of these measures to evade discussion of deeper questions concerning bureaucracies and global regulation.[4]

This was also a minority position among conservatives at the time (though it was shared, significantly, by otherwise staunch free-trader Milton Friedman).

In all three of these areas—foreign policy, health care, and trade—along with his long-time embrace of a conservative populism, we can see in Evans's independent views a foreshadowing of the shift among conservatives that erupted fully with Trump's arrival in 2016. Evans was naturally thrilled with the 1994 midterm election landslide that delivered Republican control of both houses of Congress for the first time in forty years. That the election sweep occurred in a midterm rather than presidential contest highlighted the importance of issues and contrasts between left and right, making it more difficult for the liberals and the media to attribute the outcome to superficial personal aspects that often come into play in presidential contests. He sized up the scene in *Human Events*:

> All too obviously, the Republican landslide of 1994 was not the result of masterful handling, great photo-ops, or Teflon coating, but of the issues that divide the parties—which happen to be, with few exceptions, the selfsame issues addressed by Reagan: Excessive government spending and taxation, over-regulation of the economy, permissiveness on law enforcement and "social issues." In this regard, the wisdom of House Republican strategists in projecting their 10-point "Contract with America," and thereby helping to "nationalize" the voting, is confirmed in full (as is the obtuseness of their media critics in deriding this as a major blunder).

He was mildly encouraged that *this time* perhaps Republicans understood their opportunity and might get things right. Although enthusiastic up to a point about Newt Gingrich's Contract with

America, Evans thought Republicans would be well advised to hold extensive oversight hearings to "expose the horrors of the welfare state" before moving additional legislation.

If these discrete issue positions marked out a unique spot for Evans within the spectrum of conservative thought, it was a warm-up to his two major books he was soon to produce that establish his long-term literary legacy. While his earlier books, such as *Clear and Present Dangers*, are period pieces anchored largely to contemporaneous events, his final three books deserve a long shelf life. Having given up his regular newspaper column in 1998, Evans turned his attention to this legacy.

The three books are *The Theme Is Freedom: Religion, Politics, and the American Tradition*, a capacious theoretical account of conservatism and human freedom published around the time of his sixtieth birthday in 1994; *Blacklisted by History: The Untold Story of Senator Joe McCarthy*, a bold revisionist history published in 2007; and *Stalin's Secret Agents: The Subversion of Roosevelt's Government* (coauthored with Herbert Romerstein) in 2012. These three books made it clear that had he pursued a formal academic career—as might have happened had he continued his graduate studies with von Mises at NYU—he would surely have been a successful professor and likely a literary intellectual of the first rank mentioned in the same breath with Eric Voegelin, Russell Kirk, and Thomas Sowell. These divergent topics and genres represent not merely a capstone to his long career but the completion of an intellectual arc that traces back to his early adulthood.

Evans's capaciousness and depth as a philosophic thinker in his own right was intermittently on display from the beginning of his career. As early as 1955, only months after graduating from Yale, Evans was trying out unified theories that reconciled libertarianism and traditional or religious conservatism.

Throughout his long career, Evans made episodic contributions to the never-ending disputes over doctrinal differences within the right, starting with his first book, *The Revolt on Campus*, but most especially in this periodic long-form essays in *Modern Age* and other intellectual fora far removed from the op-ed page. As previously mentioned, Evans was a friend and follower of Frank Meyer's fusionism, writing occasional essays from the 1960s through the 1980s. Some were revised versions of campus lectures or conference presentations (often at Hillsdale College, where he was a favorite guest lecturer), including "The Conservative Case for Freedom," an essay Meyer solicited from Evans for the multi-author 1964 collection, *What Is Conservatism?*

Thus *The Theme Is Freedom* can be seen as his complete, valedictory statement of his distinct political philosophy. The book performs several unique tasks. It can be conceived as an elucidation of the intellectual background of his 388-word Sharon Statement, especially the centrality of the Western theological tradition to the cause of human liberty, an aspect of the Sharon Statement that had been controversial at the founding meeting of YAF in 1960. On the level of contemporary political thought, it establishes that the harmony of disparate conservative strains—whether understood as the "three-legged stool" of the conservative voting coalition or as the melding of libertarianism and traditionalism under the banner of "fusionism"—was no mere artifact or temporary expediency of the Cold War destined to fracture with the end of that geopolitical conflict.

The book can also be seen as an antidote to the left-wing versions of the American founding, such as Howard Zinn's risible *A People's History of the United States* (or more recently, the "1619 Project"). In fact, several of Evans's friends thought the book should have a more populist title, such as *The Secret History of the United States*, *The Civilization They Tried to Hide*, or *Everything*

You Were Ever Taught Was Wrong—all "accurate summaries of my thesis," he admitted.

The straightforward account of how Evans came to write *The Theme Is Freedom* involves the enthusiastic support of the Fund for American Studies (TFAS), its president Roger Ream, and long-time friends of Evans including Donald Devine, David Jones, Al Regnery, Tom Phillips, and Ron Robinson of YAF. This circle had been brainstorming about the need for a good new book to acquaint young people with basic conservative ideas analogous to the function Barry Goldwater's *Conscience of a Conservative* played thirty-five years earlier. As with other key moments in conservatism, like YAF's Sharon Statement, Evans was everyone's favorite choice. TFAS committed $50,000 to support the writing and marketing of the book.

But there may be a secondary instigation of the book that is only apparent upon close inspection. The arc of the book's main arguments shall be outlined in due course, but the additional aspect of its inspiration and purpose should start with Evans's reference in the book to "Tory paternalists and big government conservatives who think the state should inculcate virtue in its people." After noting certain historical advocates of this view, including Thomas Hobbes and Joseph de Maistre, he adds "There are also some devotees of this general idea around today."[5] Who might he have in mind with this comment? The answer is George Will, though his name appears nowhere in *The Theme Is Freedom*.

As previously mentioned, although Evans occasionally made sharp criticisms about types of conservatives he found defective, he never in print and almost never in public remarks named a specific individual as a guilty party. The one exception was Will, and the occasion was Will's 1983 book, *Statecraft as Soulcraft: What Government Does*. Evans wrote a long and highly critical review of the book in *Human Events*, coming as close as the gentlemanly

Evans ever did to a personal attack. Example: "Will is smitten with big government…He is, like many other products of our university system, quite sincerely confused."[6]

Will's book was controversial with many conservatives when it came out, in particular for its embrace of a "conservative welfare state," which was bound to set off Evans's alarm bells. But the thematic question of modern government as source or instructor of virtue also struck Evans as a nonstarter: "Putting down Will's book and considering the government we actually have, it is not clear how such virtue is to be imparted, or by whom. Teddy Kennedy? Tip O'Neill?"

But beyond sharing with many other conservatives a disdain for Will's fondness for the welfare state and "virtuecrats" (this author's term), he discerned a different problem that few if any other critics engaged with:

> Will's errors at this mundane level are symptomatic of the deeper intellectual error that undergirds his argument. As a self-styled follower of Burke, he would do well to recall Burke's precept that all political issues are ultimately theological. Though Will seems unaware of it, the most fundamental of all such issues, and the one most relevant to his subject, stems from the theological conflict between the pagan view of the state and the radically different view emerging from the Bible.

From here the review laid out a thumbnail sketch of the role of the Bible's "distinctive theological insight" that he thought informs modern constitutional government. Will, he concluded, "perversely casts his lot with the pagans of antiquity, most conspicuously with Aristotle."[7]

Well now, as Will likes to say: here is a different side to Evans seldom on conspicuous display—Evans the Protestant theologian and defender of religion in public life—up to a point. And as we shall see presently, *The Theme Is Freedom* is not simply a reply to George Will but a sweeping and ambitious revision to our understanding of American liberty that contests popular accounts of both left and right.

Evans took a long time—by his standards—to write the book, surely because he wanted to trace out his ideas in depth, which required a lot of new research. Max Schulz (Bill Schulz's son) recalled, "It was not uncommon for close friends—many doubting the book would ever actually be finished—to needle him about its exceedingly slow pace. Pressed on one occasion how the book was coming along, he shot back, 'Oh, just great. Just this week I finished two more chapters—one on Canadian postal reform and other titled 'Our Mineral Heritage.'"

To grasp how Evans's account marks out a contrasting perspective on American liberty, it is useful to place in the foreground the leading narratives of the ideas that dominate the histories of liberal democracy and the American founding. One strand of explanation emphasizes natural rights-based social contract theories, especially those of Locke and other Enlightenment-era theorists such as Montesquieu and Blackstone. A second strand places the American founding in the context of the classical republican tradition stretching back to pagan Greece and Rome and modified by modern political theory. Several leading histories offer a blend of both. The preeminent modern authors of these main schools of interpretation include Gordon Wood, Bernard Bailyn, Edmund Morgan, Clinton Rossiter, Forrest McDonald, Thomas G. West, and Russell Kirk.

Evans didn't think these accounts were wrong as much as they were incomplete, and hence they conveyed a distorted view that has had deleterious effects in modern times. *The Theme Is Freedom* attempts to remedy this distortion by reestablishing the centrality of Christianity to the emergence of liberal democracy.

On the surface this presents a puzzle. Evans kept a studied distance from the organized religious right in practical politics, but he was a consistent defender of the religious right and their issue positions from the persistent attacks from the left. Dating all the way back to his column and editorials in the *Indianapolis Star* in the early 1960s, Evans attacked the serial Supreme Court decisions that struck down prayer in public schools and interpreted the First Amendment's "establishment clause" to marginalize religious influence in America, and he deplored abortion and *Roe v. Wade*. In the 1970s, he defended Anita Bryant from critics of her opposition to extending civil rights protections to homosexuals, and he also leaped to defend elected officials such as Mississippi Governor Kirk Fordice in 1992, who came under fire for describing America as a "Christian nation." He also wrote periodically about the weaknesses of Darwinian evolution as an explanation for the origin of life, most notably after Governor Reagan made an offhand comment in the 1980 campaign that Darwin's theory had some problems, which the media pronounced a major "gaffe." To the contrary, Evans wrote: "Reagan's statements on this topic were altogether accurate." It was not a matter of religious faith to question Darwinian theory, and he went on to cite the work of Gertrude Himmelfarb and Jacques Barzun in support of Reagan's position. (Reagan called Evans from the campaign trail to thank him for the column.)

Some of his friends suggest that Evans's personal modesty may have played a key role in his studied distance from the religious right; as a smoker, drinker, and enthusiast of rock-and-roll, he didn't offer the most exemplary example for a leadership role. But it is also likely that his libertarian policy sympathies led him to dissent from some tendencies of the religious right toward "legislating morality" (though he'd have never seen the matter the way this phrase is used derisively and simplistically by the left). One clue to this reluctance can be seen in his contributions to a symposium issue of *Policy Review* in 1984 on the topic "Sex and God in American Politics." (Other contributors included Phyllis Schlafly, Irving Kristol, Jerry Falwell, Paul Weyrich, Sen. Orrin Hatch, and Howard Phillips.) While he declared himself fully on the side of the pro-life cause, on most questions he struck a more libertarian pose. On the question "Should unmarried couples be allowed to live together?", Evans's offered the terse reply: "This is not a matter for the law. I don't believe they should, but you shouldn't police that through the state. I believe in a state that protects people from each other rather than from themselves. I don't like intrusive government that tries to police the morals of its citizens."

He was equally wary of a greater government role in preventing child abuse: "We're moving toward the Swedish government-knows-best approach, which won't let you spank your kids, and which promotes social engineering behind the smokescreen of guarding against child abuse. Before you know it, we will have government intervening in all kinds of cases where there is no real abuse as usually understood." On homosexuality: "Homosexuality is a sign of civilizational decline. It is a form of life-denying death ethic in our society. If the homosexual ethic prevailed, that would be the end of the human race." (In one of his last public speeches in 2013, he returned to this theme, saying "Demographics spell the inevitable defeat of liberalism; to put it bluntly, liberals are aborting themselves.") But, he added, "I'm not in favor of the government policing what people do in their bedrooms...but we must resist the notion that homosexual conduct as such is entitled to civil rights protection."

While Evans had reservations about parts of the practical

political agenda of the religious right, or the "Moral Majority" as the left liked to bundle everyone together, it is evident that he was not only deeply familiar with Christian theology but took it seriously as a source of political wisdom. Hints of his theological literacy are scattered in his columns and book reviews over the years, especially in his regular contributions to the "Dark Horses" book column in *National Review*. He noted a number of otherwise obscure or out-of-the-mainstream theologians or authors treating theological subjects in complex ways that would come to inform his synthesis in *The Theme Is Freedom*. And as we shall see in the final chapter, these reflections ultimately took on a deeply personal dimension in his own religious faith.

He was, for example, a fan of Stanley Jaki, the Benedictine philosopher of science, whose "complete re-writing of our intellectual history" worked out "the close connections that exist between the religious faith of our society and its attainments in the field of science." One of Jaki's insights that stuck with Evans was Jaki's rejection of the commonplace assumption that the scientific revolution of modernity owed to or depended upon discarding or marginalizing the religious traditions of the West. (The popular presentation of the Galileo matter is the leading example of this pervasive attitude.) Quite the opposite: science owed its premise of an intelligible universe to Biblical theism.[8]

He also picked up on the idiosyncratic work of the French theologian Jacques Ellul, a figure who never caught on widely in the U.S. and whose own politics leaned left. But Ellul, sometimes described as a "Christian anarchist," perceived that the left's aggressive secularism spawned "an all-consuming hatred of the West that would relentlessly destroy the good in our society" (Evans's summary). Ellul, writing in the late 1970s, was clearly prophetic of our current moment.[9] And from astronomer Robert Jastrow's cosmological observations on how the scientific community's aversion to the implication that the Big Bang origin of the universe entailed "forces or circumstances we cannot discover," Evans drew a connection to the supposedly "science-based" hostility to other aspects of Biblical teaching.[10]

But it was Evans's interest in several controversial religious right theologians that is most notable, in particular Cornelius Van Til, Gary North, and R. J. Rushdoony. Rushdoony, in particular, has long been marginalized even in conservative Christian circles for his advocacy of "Christian reconstructionism," which the secular left portrayed as straightforward Christian theocracy, i.e., installing Biblical teaching as the basis for all positive law. Evans never declared directly on this aspect of Rushdoony, but it is easy to see why Evans wouldn't go as far as Christian reconstruction: "Rulers [who would implement such a vision] are apt to be just as imperfect as their subjects, and appreciably more dangerous." Evans ultimately grounded the idea of limited government in the Christian idea of sin. But Evans valued Rushdoony, his son-in-law Gary North, and several other overlooked writers and original sources for effectively challenging numerous aspects of the standard historical narrative in a way that only unconventional and independent thinkers (that is, non-university thinkers) would dare to do.

Drawing from their historical research, Evans concluded that the "deism" of the founders like Washington, Hamilton, Madison, Franklin, and Jefferson was exaggerated at best but mostly wrong: "On the public record the framers were overwhelmingly believers in the revealed religion of the Bible." Evans thought the "deist" thesis about the leading framers was in service of a modern impulse "to diminish the influence of religion in our public life, and... to set up a purely secular republic."

This is only one example of the broad reach Evans brought to his original and admittedly idiosyncratic account of the origins and substance of American liberty. Curious readers should see his fifteen-page bibliographic essay at the end of the book to grasp how widely Evans cast his net. Evans cites over two hundred modern scholars and 185 specific titles in addition to the dozens of primary authors such as Locke, James Madison, Adam Smith, Hume, Burke, Montesquieu, J. S. Mill, and Tocqueville along with many more from the Middle Ages and early Renaissance such as Bracton, Fortescue, and Sir Edward Coke. (He also nearly lost his volumes of Macauley's *History of England* to a car fire. His Mustang convertible ignited—cause unknown, but Evans blamed the catalytic converter—and he had to fetch the books from the back seat before the car was fully engulfed.)

"How could so many people get it so completely wrong?", he asked at the beginning of *Theme*. Although in his typical gentlemanly way, Evans did not name any specific current thinkers or writers he had in mind (he only named long-dead thinkers like John Dewey), and his criticism applied to some aspects of conservative historiography as well as to secular liberals. Even Russell Kirk's 1974 book, *The Roots of American Order*, which comes closest to Evans's synthesis, still shared what Evans regarded as the fundamental defect of attributing too much influence to the pagan tradition, especially of ancient Greece. Evans was not a fan of Plato or even Aristotelian metaphysics (though he allows that Aristotle is "in many ways the most agreeable of the pagans") even though he was familiar with, and approved of, Leo Strauss's interpretation of the profundity of the Greeks.[11] He was somewhat more favorable to the Romans and the Stoic tradition but mostly as refracted by Christianity.

Evans's beef with ancient political philosophy might be summarized by reversing the old cliché about the New York cab driver informing a prospective fare about the impossibility of a destination: "You can't get here from there"—*here* being the idea of limited government and individual liberty. "The ancients knew nothing of our ideas of limited government and personal liberty," he wrote in the middle of *Theme*, "and given their peculiar conception of the world could not have done so."

Evans's dismissal of Greek metaphysics can certainly be contested, but he is on stronger ground with his perception of how the emphasis on the role of pagan antiquity along with the bright light of Enlightenment social contract theory became bookends that mangled the nature and significance of the Middle Ages. The Middle Ages were regarded by the standard liberal and secular narrative as a long period of "gloomy superstition" whose smothering Christianity and religious wars needed to be overcome before democracy and individual liberty could be achieved. His narrative convincingly reexamines medieval political thought to establish several key propositions, that what we call "social contract theory" existed well before the leading contractarians of the Renaissance and the Enlightenment such as Hobbes and Locke and that the idea of a higher law that binds and limits the authority of princes owes its development to Christian thought in the Middle Ages. Evans pointed to sources as early as the twelfth century in support of key contractarian ideas such as consent of the governed and the translation of natural law into written constitutionalism by way of the common law.

Evans actually found support for contractarianism in the Old Testament, but it was also in the Old Testament that he traced another key concept he thought too many thinkers accorded chiefly to the Enlightenment: the idea of equality and individual rights. Evans found significant the passage Samuel I, Chapter 8 that warns the Israelites against having a king with tyrannical powers like in other nations but expands from there to point out that the concept of the limited power of the state also established the reciprocal principle of individual equality before God. "The correlation of Christianity with the rise of freedom is anything but accidental... *It was the era of the Middle Ages that nourished the institutions of free government, in contrast to the ideas and customs of the ancients.*" [Emphasis in original.]

Evans might be disputed for overlooking some classical elements of the core ideas he attributes primarily to the Middle Ages; Sophocles's *Antigone* as well as some aspects of Aristotle and Plato certainly entertain the idea of natural law that is binding on political rulers, and the common law tradition certainly owes something to Roman law antecedents. (In particular Evans avoids resolving his praise of Thomas Aquinas with Aquinas's reliance on Aristotle.) But to the extent he is correct in noting the marginalization or distortion of the Christian heritage of the classical liberal tradition, he is on more solid ground in his admittedly "completely heretical" reading of the Declaration of Independence. He does not reject the Declaration or reinterpret its meaning wholesale as some conservative and liberal thinkers do (Garry Wills comes to mind), but he thinks Jefferson's originality and authorship are overstated and that its key ideas, including even the right of revolution, can be found fully developed at least a century before Locke and in some cases much earlier than that. "This is a reversal of the accepted teaching," Evans admits. "We have been told a lot about the Declaration that isn't so... Missing the point about such matters is of course the essence of the standard history."

Evans aligns himself with a Burkean outlook in seeing human equality and individual rights derived from God rather than from equality in a state of nature or the natural right of self-preservation. By making equality and individual rights fully and solely Lockean (and therefore secular), Evans thinks the door was left open to the neopaganism of modern times. It was precisely the Christian idea of the equal, transcendent dignity of the individual before God that repelled both the Romans and Nietzsche alike, not to mention modern ideologies, gnostic in character, that pervert equality in service of redistributionism and centralized political power. (Here the influence of Eric Voegelin is evident.)

Gradually Evans's profound understanding of the harmony of traditional conservatism and libertarianism come into sharper focus. The free market is ultimately in service of limiting government as much as any specific constitutional provisions for reasons best traced not to the efficiencies of Adam Smith but to the Bible. This synthesis went far beyond the fusionism of Frank Meyer or anyone else.

He also offers an explanation for his minor reservations about the religious right. Although he generally applauds the religious right in the conclusion of the book, he adds:

> There is a class of issues on which conservatives have been partial to the centralizing impulse. These have primarily to do with 'law and order'—crime, drugs, and cultural issues of one kind or another. Under Republican administrations of recent decades, there has been a tendency to favor increased federal power in these areas, both because of the subject matter and because Republicans were sponsoring the measures. Whatever the motive for such programs, they contribute further to centralization in the system. Granted that some aspects of the problem are national in scope, dealing with crime is overwhelmingly a state and local matter, and friends of limited government should look askance at increasing federal powers in this regard, as in most others.[12]

Here Evans came full circle as this passage is a restatement of his early passage about the caution in the Old Testament's First Samuel against concentrated government power.

But any liberals who might think Evans's reserve about religion as a source of public policy provides some kind of wedge against the right would be sorely disappointed if they take in his argument in full. We shall return to Evans's views on religion in the final chapter of this book as it appears his research and reflection for this book led directly to his own final affirmation of religious faith in the final year of his life.

Though idiosyncratic, *The Theme Is Freedom* was well-received. Forrest McDonald, a preeminent historian of the American founding in his own right, called the book "a remarkable work that combines erudition with clear thinking" and noted in particular how Evans rescued the role of Christianity from the neglect or distortion of most standard histories. McDonald demurred on only one point, noting that the anti-capitalist strain of certain kinds of conservatives (especially southern agrarians) didn't fit well into Evans's framework.[13] The "review" that probably flattered Evans the most came from Rush Limbaugh. Limbaugh called Evans, telling him "I saw C-SPAN's replay of a speech you gave [about the book], and it inspired me. It lit a fire under me. And I wanted to make sure to talk to you because I think what you had to say is exactly what's missing." Evans, it turned out, was a regular Limbaugh listener.

The Theme Is Freedom, his first book in twenty years at the time of its publication, could easily have been the capstone of Evans's entire career as it completed his exploration of ideas and problems within conservatism that had interested him since his student days at Yale. But he had one more major literary project ahead of him that also represented the completion of a related early interest: rescuing the tattered reputation and correcting the distorted historical record of Joseph McCarthy. The 1960 *Time* magazine article that reported Evans's appointment as editor of the *Indianapolis News* included the detail that Evans "studied the record of the late Senator Joseph McCarthy, decided that McCarthy 'was in the main correct.'"

As early as 1960 Evans had worked out a serious defense of McCarthy from the mounting historical disdain. He gave a long lecture in 1960 that prefigured *Blacklisted by History*. The audience and exact date Evans delivered the lecture is unknown (likely a college campus). This author has only the manuscript, but it refers throughout to Richard Rovere's "recent" critical biography of McCarthy that was published in 1959. In addition to arguing that McCarthy was "preponderantly in the right" in most (though not all) of his charges, Evans added this coda: "McCarthy deserves well of history in a more metaphysical way—because he believed that history was informed by some moral purpose, that men are moral beings and as such responsible for their choices. Part of his struggle was to cut through contemporary frivolities, and to stand up for the proposition that men must be held accountable for their decisions, and so must not deal lightly with the destinies of nations."[14]

Over the years Evans intermittently kept up with aspects of the McCarthy story, writing a column whenever a new biography appeared or some news item about an episode or person from the McCarthy era emerged. McCarthy's reputation, already in tatters at the time of his death in 1957, only descended further with the passage of time and the rise of the anti-anti-Communist revisionist history in the 1970s and 1980s.

It especially bothered Evans that many conservatives whom he thought ought to know better more or less embraced the left's central thesis about McCarthy. For example, in reviewing the increasingly shabby historiography of McCarthy in a 1999 article, Evans wrote: "Even worse in some respects, because much more would be expected, is English intellectual historian Paul Johnson. His *History of the American People*, acclaimed by many on the right, also provides some odd misstatements on McCarthy, making it plain that Johnson too is sadly ignorant of the subject."[15] Evans thought it a mistake for conservatives to embrace "McCarthyism" as an epithet against the left, and he devoted a *Human Events* feature to the rare criticism of calling out conservatives by name for this sin, including George Will, Charles Krauthammer, Rich Lowry, *Breitbart News*, and several talk radio hosts. "It's usually not a good idea for conservatives to let the liberals do their thinking for them."[16]

Evans was a one-man battalion chasing after and demanding corrections of the more egregious distortions of McCarthy that continued to appear in the media. Periodically he'd weigh in with a long article based on new information or refuting a newly recycled claim. In 1987 he wrote an eight-page special supplement for *Human Events* marking the thirtieth anniversary of McCarthy's death, "History's Vindication of Joe McCarthy." In 2000 he took after the *New York Times* for an obituary of Oscar Shaftel, "Fired After Refusing McCarthy," as the headline read. The obit said Shaftel had been fired from Queens College in the 1950s because he refused to answer "some questions" from a Senate committee McCarthy supposedly chaired. Every detail of the obituary was wrong, from the name of the committee to the fact that McCarthy was not even a member of the committee that had questioned Shaftel, and it omitted the fact that other witnesses had positively identified Shaftel as a member of the Communist Party. Evans wrote to the *Times* demanding a correction, which the *Times* ignored. After he mentioned the *Times* story twice in subsequent appearances on C-SPAN and several more follow up letters, the *Times* relented and printed a grudging correction six weeks later acknowledging their factual errors, telling Evans that the correction had been delayed because of "some kind of snafu in the office" and an "editing lapse." He was less successful in pursuing corrections from error-ridden stories about McCarthy in the *Los Angeles Times, Washington Post, Roll Call,* and Reuters.

When the U.S. Senate declassified and published four thousand pages of closed-door executive sessions of McCarthy's committee in 2003 (after the fifty-year period of keeping the files sealed had been reached), Evans took after the Senate's historian, Donald Ritchie, for distorting the contents of the files in his introduction and editorial notes. As he had done with several reporters for the previously mentioned stories, Evans called Ritchie on the telephone, asking him probing questions about whether he had read the primary source material carefully or just went with the standard characterizations from (hostile) secondary sources. Ritchie wasn't very forthcoming: "I am growing very tired of this conversation," Ritchie said and hung up.[17] Nearly all of the reporters he called, Evans said, were "very testy" when he questioned their grasp of the actual facts (when they didn't refuse to speak with him at all), claiming to be "too busy to discuss the matter with me."

These attempts at correcting the record, Evans wrote, was "the equivalent of dropping a bottle into the ocean." The entire McCarthy story was surrounded by "a kind of black hole of anti-knowledge in which strange factoids and curious fables circulate without resistance" such that "the real Joe McCarthy has vanished into the mists of fable and recycled error." It took courage, though, to take on this revisionism so directly. As Evans notes in *Blacklisted by History*, "'McCarthyism' is the third rail of Cold War historiography—and of our political discourse in general—and any contact with it could prove fatal to writers trying to get their work accepted in academic or mainstream media circles."

But the end of the Cold War and the availability of new materials such as the Senate executive session files as well as material from Soviet archives made possible a new look at McCarthy's record and the countless controversies that have surrounded the historical record ever since. There's also an aspect of filial piety at work. His father Medford's concern with lax security wasn't limited to the 1940s and 1950s. He, too, was a defender of McCarthy, penning a little-noticed book in 1970 with the title *The Assassination of Joe McCarthy*.[18] He had in mind the *character* rather than literal assassination of McCarthy, and while he dismissed as "lurid speculation" scenarios of actual foul play because "I cannot prove anything," he does wonder how a once vigorous man dies at the age of forty-eight even with a reputation for advancing alcohol abuse. He also believed the motive was certainly present: "I will say this; I believe *they would have murdered him if they could have.*" [Emphasis in original.]

Medford Evans's brief for McCarthy was aimed at rehabilitating McCarthy's character (though he does not ignore or excuse McCarthy's mistakes and bad judgments) and placing the drama of the McCarthy interlude of the early 1950s in a wider context of the serious issues of security, subversion, political interest, and above all the battle for civilization itself that the Communist threat entailed, all of which he believed had grown worse by the debilitating developments of the 1960s.

Stan Evans's *Blacklisted by History* takes up a revisionist tack but with the new information not available to his father in 1970. Most significant of the new sources were the "Venona" decrypts, the highly secret Soviet cables that U.S. intelligence had intercepted between 1946 and 1981 that were finally declassified and made public in the mid-1990s following the collapse of the Soviet Union. The Venona decrypts were dynamite, making clear, as historians John Earl Haynes and Harvey Klehr put it in one of the first major surveys of the Venona cache, that there were "not a 'few,' but hundreds of American Communists who had abetted Soviet espionage in the United States" and that "the Soviets had recruited spies in virtually every major American government agency of military or diplomatic importance."[19] Venona proved beyond any remaining doubt that Alger Hiss and Harry Dexter White had indeed been Soviet assets along with several of the figures involved in the Rosenberg plot to steal our atomic secrets. In all Venona identified 349 American citizens or legal residents with ties to Soviet intelligence, and given that there were thousands of Soviet cables that Venona was unable to decipher, the real number was likely much larger. Many of the individuals McCarthy inquired about in his investigations starting in the early 1950s were among the names included in Venona, many of whom in later years were considered "innocent victims" of McCarthyism.

The decryption capabilities of the Venona program were understandably kept secret at the time and for decades to follow. Public disclosure would have tipped off the Soviets about our capabilities and cut off additional intelligence from the program. The Truman administration did in fact act on some Venona information to purge Soviet agents from government agencies and tighten up security screening, albeit quietly and with no public notice that would have risked exposing Venona or other security sources and methods. Many of the individuals revealed in Venona had been removed from their government positions well before McCarthy seized on the issue (which is partly the origin of the criticism that McCarthy trafficked in "stale, warmed-over charges"), but neither Truman nor his successor, President Dwight Eisenhower, shared their steps with McCarthy or their secret source. Still, when Venona was revealed in the 1990s, historians went out of their way to say that the Venona revelations did not offer any vindication for McCarthy.

That is exactly the kind of summary claim that Evans would never let pass without a closer look. Evans's subsequent research into the full McCarthy record in light of new information might well be the most extensive ever conducted, certainly far more extensive and in-depth than any of McCarthy's many biographers. In addition to reviewing Venona and the Senate executive session files, Evans unearthed though Freedom of Information Act (FOIA) requests thousands of pages of heretofore unexamined FBI files. Although he did most of the primary research himself, he did receive substantial research assistance from Fred Mann and Mal Kline. Kline recalls going to the FBI reading room one day looking for information on an unrelated subject, whereupon:

> The nice lady in the FBI reading room asked me if I'd like to look at the list of their available files. I did, and saw that they had several thousand pages on Owen Lattimore. I asked if I could get a copy of that list and she said I could keep that one. When I showed it to Stan his eyes damn near popped out of his head. "Well, of course, for openers, we want the file on Lattimore." I said, "I thought you might say that so I already put in a request for it." Fred Mann and I actually went down to the reading room to get it. They wheeled it out in a shopping cart.

Evans left no stone unturned. He visited the FDR presidential library in Hyde Park. He went out to the National Archives branch warehouse in College Park, Maryland, to look up State Department phone directories from the 1950s in order to refute the claims of McCarthy's critics that many of his targets were no longer at the State Department when McCarthy claimed they were. (Guess what: several of the individuals were still listed in the contemporary directories.) He acquired many of McCarthy's own papers from Ralph de Toledano. One of the curious findings of Evans's exhaustive research is how many crucial documents somehow went missing over the years. Although Evans does not say so directly, his account certainly raises the question of whether documents were deliberately removed or misfiled by someone. Around the time Evans was working on the book, we learned that President Clinton's former aide Sandy Berger had spirited original copies of classified documents out of the National Archives in his socks and destroyed them. Evans had lunch with the director of the FBI, hoping for some high-level help unearthing missing or "misplaced" files as well as access to unredacted files, but the director demurred. (That director's name: Robert Mueller.)

Among the most curious missing documents isn't a government file but the Wheeling, West Virginia, newspaper that originally reported the most notorious of McCarthy's supposed excesses: his "list" of 205 suspected Communists in the State Department. A news report in the Wheeling *Intelligencer* gave wing to this famous fact from a February 1950 speech McCarthy delivered in Wheeling, though McCarthy later claimed he said he had 57 names, not 205, though his own recollections were confused and varied over the years. (He did, however, use the 57 figure in a speech a few days later in Reno, Nevada.) The episode has remained in dispute ever since. Although the speech was broadcast on local radio, it was either not recorded or the recording was lost. Also lost were any copies of the original *Intelligencer* news story. The newspaper's own "morgue" didn't have a copy, and Evans discovered that the microfilm files for the *Intelligencer* in the local public library were missing all the editions from February 1950, as was the Library of Congress. Evans did unearth an editorial from the *Intelligencer* two days after the speech that referenced McCarthy as claiming he had the names of "over 50" suspected Communists at State along with excerpts from McCarthy's speech that did not include any figure.

Evans also noted a *Denver Post* story two days later that bore the headline, "57 Reds Help Shaping U.S. Policy: McCarthy." Where did the *Post* get that figure?

The 605 pages of *Blacklisted by History*—by a wide margin Evans's longest book—are full of meticulous reconsiderations of dozens of events, committee hearings, and cases of individuals long considered "martyrs" of McCarthy's "reckless" crusade. (His research files for the book now occupy twenty-six boxes, measuring 32.5 feet, at the Hoover Archives at Stanford.) Most or all these names and episodes are now nearly forgotten. Even aging baby boomers will have little remaining recognition of Amerasia, Owen Lattimore, or Annie Lee Moss; for millennials and later generations, Owen Lattimore might as well be William of Occam, and figures such as John Stewart Service, Solomon Adler, or Cedric Belfrage—Communists all (except William of Occam)—are even more obscure.

It is impossible even to begin a summary of the major revisions to the "established" versions of the McCarthy story contained in *Blacklisted*; suffice it to say that, like *The Theme Is Freedom*, the subtext is that "everything you think you know is wrong," including the climactic Army–McCarthy hearings of 1954 that precipitated McCarthy's final downfall. But in no way can the book be considered a hagiography or whitewash. Evans is clear and direct about McCarthy's specific errors and larger weaknesses. "His straight-ahead, take-no-prisoners views and methods did lead him to make mistakes of facts and judgment," Evans wrote. He also criticized McCarthy's "impulsive, lone-wolf side" that "made him a problem in other ways as well ... Considerations of political prudence ... were alien to his nature." McCarthy's attack on George Marshall was "a huge error in judgment." But Evans also brings out how McCarthy's agitation did in fact spur our security reviews to become more serious in the 1950s, though

McCarthy was never given any credit: "It's a remarkable but generally neglected fact that *every* major McCarthy investigation of the period 1953–54 resulted in some significant change in governmental practice."

The balance of Evans's judgment is that "McCarthy was far more sinned against than sinning, and that on the central issues he was chiefly right and his opponents chiefly in error...That McCarthy was a flawed champion of the cause he served is not in doubt (and who among us isn't?). It would have been better had he been less impulsive, more nuanced, more subtle in his judgments. On the other hand, somebody more nuanced and refined wouldn't have dreamed of grappling with the forces deployed against him. Those forces were powerful, smart, and tough, and they played for keeps. Taking them on was the task not for a Supreme Court justice, but for a warrior. McCarthy, to his dying breath, was that."

While Evans was effective in debunking countless McCarthy myths, his critics, among them some conservatives and honorable old-school liberal anti-Communists, weren't convinced that the problem of espionage was as serious as McCarthy thought or that he was the right person to lead the cause. Many conservatives have long settled into the view that McCarthy's net effect was to damage the cause of anti-Communism, starting with Whittaker Chambers in 1954 *before* the infamous Army–McCarthy hearings that were McCarthy's undoing. William Bennett wrote that "The cause of anti-communism, which united millions of Americans and which gained the support of Democrats, Republicans and independents, was undermined by Sen. Joe McCarthy...McCarthy besmirched the honorable cause of anti-communism." Even Herbert Romerstein, a former congressional committee intelligence staff member and Evans's close friend and coauthor of the follow-up book *Stalin's Secret Agents* in 2012, was a McCarthy critic, writing once that McCarthy was "irrelevant to the anti-Communist cause."

Evans treats this aspect of the wider meaning of McCarthy indirectly because his book taken in full advances a significant argument—relevant for our current moment—beyond just correcting the narrow historical record about specific controversies from seventy years ago. The second section of the book, the "Back Story" running nearly one hundred pages, explores the decade before McCarthy arrived on the scene, making a strong direct and circumstantial case for decisive Soviet influence on American foreign policy by Soviet agents or Soviet sympathizers close to President Franklin Roosevelt as well as in key positions overseas sending disinformation to Washington that misled important decision-makers. Alger Hiss was only the most famous of the figures Evans explores. Evans thinks this influence was decisive in souring American enthusiasm and support for Chiang Kai-shek, thus paving the way for the Communist triumph in China after World War II. Despite some investigations (many with missing records) and arrests in the late 1930s and during World War II, the entire phenomenon was not taken with sufficient seriousness and has been largely ignored by historians or belittled as a cartoonish affectation of the "Who lost China?" partisan political controversy of the early 1950s.

The distant echo of our confused, subverted—or infiltrated?—China policy back then is salient again just now for reasons that do not need pointing out. Some reflection on bureaucratic inertia, ideological wishful thinking, and special interest influence in the past can always be a guide to the present. Evans describes the conventional wisdom about the period with a phrase useful for any time: political astigmatism.

There is a still more important and related reason to stand up for a balanced and truthful understanding of McCarthy. The left's demonization of McCarthy through character assassination and gross distortion became the left's primary playbook ever since, the most glaring examples being the despicable charges brought against Supreme Court nominees Robert Bork, Clarence Thomas, and Brett Kavanaugh. Evans makes a compelling case for the ironic judgment that the tactics described ever after as "McCarthyism" were most fully applied against McCarthy himself.

And there's one other person on which the McCarthy playbook was run. Take in this passage from Evans:

> For most of his five years that his doings transfixed the nation, McCarthy was locked in mortal combat with the most powerful forces in the land, including two presidents of the United States, vast bureaucratic empires, formidable adversaries in Congress, relentless leftward lobby groups, and a horde of press, TV, and radio critics who made him their daily target. Even more to the point, he had been put through the wringer of endless, back-to-back investigations and repetitive charges that drained time and energy, sapped his strength, and blocked him from the mission to which he was devoted.[20]

Swap out "Donald Trump" for McCarthy and you have an accurate description of the dynamic of the opposition to Trump over the last half decade. It is surely not a coincidence. Richard Rovere compared McCarthy to Hitler in his 1959 biography, to give an early example of the tactic. And then the first parallel comes back into focus: in some ways McCarthy won on the China issue in the 1950s, and Trump has transformed the West's disposition toward China to a large extent today, even if our China policy remains hesitant and confused.

It was to be expected that the "mainstream" media would attack or ignore *Blacklisted by History*. The *New York Times* did review it, with David Oshinsky calling the book "remarkable fantasy" without disputing a single specific claim of the book (including places where Evans pointed out factual mistakes in Oshinsky's own McCarthy biography) and rejecting prima facie the strong circumstantial case Evans made for the much more widespread influence of Communist agents and sympathizers in the government's decision loops during World War II.[21] The *Wall Street Journal* did not formally review the book, but a Ronald Kessler feature article about McCarthy took a "sideswipe" of *Blacklisted* riddled with errors. The *Journal* refused to run a letter from Evans refuting Kessler's mistakes. Reviews in specialty journals ran the gamut, from mildly favorable to hostile, as might be expected. The short notice in the *Library Journal* was complimentary of Evans's use of primary sources, concluding that "His crisply written study may daunt some readers owing to length and may not win over most McCarthy critics. But it will certainly send historians to the primary sources and is recommended for academic and larger public libraries."[22] *Kirkus Reviews* said "The book is exhaustively researched and impeccably sourced...well-written and accessible. But it's highly unlikely that Evans will win any converts." A review in *American Communist History* rested its criticism chiefly on the fact that "Evans has for decades been actively involved in the conservative movement" and as such is biased, a question seldom or never raised about any of McCarthy's critics over the decades. Among the many mistakes in the review is the charge that Evans ignored or failed to cite the work of Harvey Klehr and John Earl Haynes, when in fact Evans had sent his manuscript to Klehr seeking comment and criticism before submitting it to the publisher.

And Haynes praised the book while not yielding in his opinion that McCarthy was a hindrance to anti-Communism: "Evans does an excellent job of correcting excesses in the historical record—the unthinking, near-hysterical, and far too common demonization of McCarthy...So comprehensive is Evans's research that it will be a foolish historian who does not consult *Blacklisted by History* when a question arises over some person or event that comes into the McCarthy story."[23]

Most conservative authors and publications unsurprisingly gave the book favorable notice. And then there was Ann Coulter, who described *Blacklisted by History* with her usual flamboyance as "the greatest book since the Bible."

What was startling was a hostile review in...*National Review*.[24] Ron Radosh, a former New Left writer who turned to the right in middle age and the coauthor of *The Rosenberg File,* the 1983 book that established beyond a reasonable doubt the guilt of the Rosenbergs in the conspiracy to deliver America's A-bomb secrets to the Soviet Union in the late 1940s, had nothing but scorn for *Blacklisted by History.*

While the review gave some credit for its "extensive research" that "managed to prove that many of McCarthy's main opponents themselves had a highly partisan agenda" that "totally ignored or minimized the serious issue of Communist penetration of the highest levels of government," Radosh was dismissive of the book as a whole. It was "weakened by a lack of balance, and his desire to write an unabashed tribute that seeks to exonerate McCarthy on virtually every count." He deemed Evans's assessment of many of McCarthy's minor targets (whom he did not specify with the exception of journalist James Wechsler) as "highly unsatisfactory." Most scurrilous was the insinuation that Evans plagiarized Radosh and coauthor Harvey Klehr's book on the Amerasia case. Radosh concluded: "His own exaggerations and unwarranted leaps parallel those made by McCarthy. It is unlikely that his hope to change history's verdict will become a reality as a result of this book."

Had Buckley—who had, after all, written his second book in defense of McCarthy in 1954 (*McCarthy and His Enemies*, with Brent Bozell)—still been running *NR,* or had William Rusher (also very pro-McCarthy) still presided as publisher, there is no doubt the review would have been spiked. (Buckley consulted Evans extensively for background material for one of his last novels, *The Redhunter: A Novel Based on the Life of Joseph McCarthy*, published in 1999. And Evans was still listed on *NR*'s masthead as a contributor in 2007. Radosh had also criticized *The Redhunter* when it appeared, prompting Buckley to reply: "There is no point in Radosh, burdened by his mindset, reading [the book] because it would necessarily be uphill for him, as hard going as an impotent locked in all night with a whore.")

Radosh's review appeared during the peculiar reign of Michael Potemra, a pro–Hillary Clinton liberal that *NR* editor Rich Lowry hired to be *NR*'s literary editor on the counterintuitive thought that it would make the magazine more lively and credible if it published unpredictable or critical reviews of conservative authors. Potemra evidently delivered what Lowry wanted as Radosh's rough handling of a conservative author was not the only such instance of rubbishing a conservative author in *NR* during those years.

Evans was understandably flabbergasted at the review, writing a strong letter to *NR* (though the version that appeared was not as angry as his first draft, according to friends who advised him to tone it down):

> Having been around the block a time or two, I guess nothing should surprise me, but I have to admit I was profoundly shocked by Ronald Radosh's onslaught against my work—and honor—in what professed to be a review of my new book about Senator Joe McCarthy.
>
> Had this Radosh effusion appeared in *The New Republic* or

Washington Post—where it would have been more fitting—I probably wouldn't have bothered to reply. As it appeared instead in the beloved pages of *National Review*, with which I have been connected since its inception, I can hardly let these poisonous charges against my writing, and my character, go unanswered.[25]

Evans's reply is convincing in several specifics that Radosh gave the book a careless reading, but Evans's main countercharge was that Radosh had "a nasty penchant for turning a debate about substantive issues into a species of personal slander."

Among other Radosh criticisms is the insinuendo of plagiarism of Radosh's 1996 book with Harvey Klehr on the Amerasia case—"a book from which Evans takes virtually all of his material and which he does not acknowledge." Evans handily refuted this calumny by pointing out that a check of his footnotes would have revealed that his account of the Amerasia case were derived from original research in FBI files "based on an entirely different indexing system, so that one isn't transposable to the other" and reminded readers that he had given the Klehr-Radosh book a favorable review when it appeared. Finally, Evans concluded:

I have now been a journalist for upwards of 50 years, most of them with some connection or other to *National Review*. In all that span, many things have been said about me and my work, not all of them positive in nature. But at no point in my career has anyone to my knowledge ever accused me of plagiarism, one of the most serious charges that can be leveled at a professional writer. Nor do I recall even my most determined left-liberal foes, however much they might disagree with me, accusing me of being in any way dishonest. It remained for these sinister charges to be made in the year 2007 by Ronald Radosh—in the pages of *National*

Review. What that says about Radosh, *National Review*, and me,
I leave to the judgment of the reader.

In reply, Radosh said that Evans was "overreacting" and that
"I never wrote anywhere that Evans plagiarized our book. I only
noted he ignored its findings." Strange, then, to see a hostile
third-party reviewer of *Blacklisted*, Larry Ceplair writing in the
Historical Journal of Film, Radio and Television, comment that
"I found only one negative review in a conservative periodical,
written by Ron Radosh, for *National Review*. Radosh alleges,
among other things, plagiarism from the book he co-authored
on the *Amerasia* case."[26] And the aforementioned harsh review
in *American Communist History* said, "Equally troubling is Evans'
tendency to pass of the research of others as his own...Evans
does not even cite Klehr or Radosh in the text or footnotes."
("Question," Wes Vernon of Accuracy in Academia asked in a
story about the feud: "If any author had plagiarized the work of
another author, would he have handed an advance copy of his
new book to that other author for his comment?")

A wide-angle look at the back-and-forth between friends
and critics of the book will show that much of the divide was
less over facts than the interpretation of the proximate facts and
Cold War history itself. And herein lies a parallel controversy that
led to Evans's final book, a sequel to *Blacklisted*, entitled *Stalin's
Secret Agents: The Subversion of Roosevelt's Government* (coauthored with Herbert Romerstein and published in 2012). *Stalin's
Secret Agents* went through the intrigues of policy planning and
decision-making during World War II, offering suggestive details
about how well-placed Soviet agents or sympathizers affected
U.S. policy in dozens of incremental ways intended to aid the
strategic position of the Soviet Union. Some of the policy ideas
were not that incremental: Evans and Romerstein make much of

the Morgenthau Plan to destroy Germany's industrial base after the war that FDR ultimately rejected. It had been promoted to Treasury Secretary Hans Morgenthau by several administration staff who were Communists, such as Harry Dexter White. Had it been implemented, an economically prostrate Germany would have been fertile ground for Soviet expansion. The authors also make a compelling case for Communist influence in the Allied decision to back the pro-Soviet "nationalist" Josip Broz Tito in Yugoslavia over an anti-Communist rival (whom Tito later captured and executed).

Evans and Romerstein believed that the number of Americans identified in Venona and other sources as collaborators or sympathizers with the Soviet Union in the 1930s and 1940s was a vast underestimate of the real number and that most would never be known. "We'll never know even half of it," Evans told Paul Kengor. He thought there were hundreds of books still to be written about Communist infiltration during that period, and he thought there was lots of classified material still to be revealed. Evans had planned another book himself, a critical look at Dean Acheson, who, he told Kengor, "has been viewed as this great Cold Warrior, but for a long time was anything but."

Did this influence add up to cumulative changes in American strategic and tactical decisions (what Whittaker Chambers called "the staggering sum of day-to-day decisions") that can be regarded as world-historical in scale and consequence? Evans liked to say that Alger Hiss was the only person who "knew what he was doing at Yalta." Was FDR's close aide Harry Hopkins, in particular, an active Soviet sympathizer or just naive and misguided about the Soviets? The implications of this line of inquiry called into question the consensus history of the Cold War as radically as any of the New Left revisionism of the 1960s and 1970s.

Diana West, a protégé of Evans in many respects, extended the

Evans-Romerstein thesis in her own provocative book *American Betrayal: The Secret Assault on Our Nation's Character* (2013) and touched off a sequel of the Evans-Radosh exchange of 2007. West wondered, among other questions, whether pro-Soviet influence extended as far as the decision to favor the D-Day invasion through France rather than Churchill's preferred strategy of invading from the eastern Mediterranean, which, if successful, would have cut off much of eastern Europe from Soviet conquest.

Similar to *Blacklisted*, Radosh wrote a savage seven-thousand-word critique of *American Betrayal*, and the melee was on once again, only this time a many-sided affair that drew in additional combatants to the arena, including David Horowitz, Andrew McCarthy, Conrad Black, and Evans. Evans was delighted to act as a champion for West, getting to the heart of the matter in a letter to the *New Criterion* with his usual indirect and gentlemanly manner (typically, he doesn't specifically name any of West's critics):

> Ms. West, in her approach to revisionist history, has committed *lese-majeste*—an offense against the sovereign power. She has dared to challenge the long-established and much cherished "court history" of World War II—glorifying Roosevelt, Hopkins, Marshall, et al.—and to raise the dread specter of Communist internal influence on American policy in that conflict . . .
>
> Such painting outside the lines of the "consensus" is not to be permitted, and where it occurs will be severely punished. Why Ms. West in particular has been selected for this treatment I'm not sure, but the larger lesson is there for all to see: *If you stray beyond the limits we've established, this could happen to you as well.*[27]

With the Cold War and Soviet intrigues a rapidly receding memory of a faraway time, these quarrels may seem a matter of mere historical curiosity and obsession by nonagenarian Cold

Warriors. But in his last word on the Diana West controversy, Andrew McCarthy reminds us why unconventional—even seemingly outrageous—lines of contrarian inquiry might still be *very* relevant:

> In the here and now, Islamic supremacists and their sympathizers are ensconced in significant government positions; are closely consulted on defense and foreign policy issues; are invited to provide training to our law-enforcement, intelligence, and military personnel; and are given a veto over the content of instructional materials used to educate our agents about national security threats. Those of us who have challenged those developments—and have irrefutably documented both the virulent anti-Americanism of Islamic-supremacist ideology and ties between Islamist organizations and government officials or consultants—have been demagogued as neo-McCarthyites.

EPILOGUE

> "We Christians believe that death is not the end for any man, and all men know that death may be only the beginning of a great man's historic power and influence."
>
> —MEDFORD EVANS

As Evans drew into his last decade and began the intensive work on his final two books, he spent most of this time at his country home out in Hamilton, Virginia, near Leesburg, where he took to driving a beat-up Chevy pickup truck. He delighted in his dining choices in Leesburg as there were Roy Rogers franchises at each end of town, this bringing "variety" to his diet. He gave up his regular column in 1998, though he still popped up now and then with feature articles for *Human Events*. In 2002 he handed off the National Journalism Center to the Young America's Foundation and spun off *Consumers' Research* magazine. But he continued teaching journalism at Troy University until 2012. As he drew closer to old age, Evans liked to begin most talks with a joke, his slow semi-drawl now slowing further, that ran: "There are two things that happen to you when you get older. The first is your hearing starts to go. And...I can't remember what the second one is."

Despite the rapid advance of technology, Evans persisted in continuing all his writing on a typewriter and never adopted email, though he did once claim that he was signed up for "assisted email for the elderly." "I have a dumb phone," he'd say, "which is why I can't keep up with the Kardashians. It is not easy. It takes a lot of study to keep up with what they are doing." When told that Evans didn't use email, Jameson Campaigne Jr. asked Tom Winter, "Then what have I been doing all these years sending him email!?" If an NJC intern ever claimed that "the computer lost my copy," Evans would point to his typewriter and say, "*My computer never eats my copy.*"

As many people do as they approach old age, Evans showed signs of mellowing—but not much. And he was just as sharp as ever in his political judgments. As he had with George H. W. Bush, Evans took a wait-and-see attitude about the rise of George W. Bush in the late 1990s and after the 2000 election, but his few public statements about the second President Bush lacked the latent distrust Evans held about Bush's father. He summarized his views in a 2001 interview with Stephen Goode:

EVANS: To be utterly candid, I never considered him to be one of our people. Not that I have any hostility toward him, but considering those who lined up early for him, George W. was a considerably different kettle of fish, say from Barry Goldwater or Ronald Reagan, both of whom were much more definitely conservative movement leaders...Early on, I think people with big clout decided that Governor Bush was going to be the nominee. Conservatives who didn't know a lot about him were so tired of their eight years in the wilderness that they said, "Let's go with him," and so most everybody got behind him from the outset. He was something of an unknown quantity at that point, Rorschach-like, so in a sense he's the converse of my law in that he was not perceived as being one of our people, but he's now performing much more like one than I personally would have anticipated. And some people have said, with some justice, that he's in many ways a lot more like Ronald Reagan than he is like his own father. But the jury's still out.

Goode: You sound pleased with this unexpected development.

Evans: I had a growing enthusiasm for now-President Bush when he was a candidate. But the thing that really tipped me in his favor was when I learned that, if he were elected, Alec Baldwin would leave the country. I said at the time that got my vote right there. But Baldwin has backslid on that promise; he's still here. I have suggested that we all take out full-page ads in the *New York Times*, signed by hundreds of academics, urging Baldwin to fulfill the promise he made during the campaign. And only if that doesn't work should he be deported.[1]

Evans added that Baldwin's failure to leave the country vindicated his old observation that "pragmatism doesn't work."

He kept up regular lectures and speaking appearances on college campuses and at conservative gatherings, including CPAC. In 2006 this author reminded Evans at a conference at Princeton of his 1984 comment that Reagan was "just another Ford Administration." He replied, "I still think that." Of David Brooks's presentation at the same event, Evans said to him, "I liked it better when I heard Nelson Rockefeller give it in 1958."

He was not taken in the slightest by the adulation of Barack Obama, but he directed most of his fire after the 2008 election at downcast conservatives. His message throughout the Obama years was surprisingly optimistic for someone otherwise so sober about the massive forces arrayed against conservatives in nearly all the nation's major institutions, partly because he'd seen conservatism in a much worse political position than in 2009, such as after Goldwater's defeat in 1964 and in the aftermath of Nixon's Watergate collapse. (In fact it was during this period that he began rolling out his quip that "As young conservatives we had to get over the Goldwater defeat *without grief counselors*.") His cover story for *Human Events* shortly after Obama's convincing victory in 2008 opened thus:

> Right wing pundits and politicos moaning about this year's election need to snap out if it *muy pronto* and get to work devising victories for the future. Though you could never guess it from all the breast-beating and teeth-gnashing, the conservative/Republican cause has been much further down than this, only to come back quickly in decisive fashion.[2]

This, months before the first Tea Party rally and before anyone dared believe Republicans would have a record landslide in the off-year election in 2010.

He returned to this theme after Obama's 2012 reelection plunged conservatives into a new bout of discouragement. Evans made an appearance at the 2013 CPAC, twenty-eight years after the first CPAC that he had originated. By then CPAC had become a sensational event, with attendance approaching a thousand and attracting major media coverage. It turned out to be his final public speech, and he updated what he had told conservatives after 2008. He reminded the audience that conservatives were in a much stronger position than they had ever been in after previous defeats. He spoke of a "return to first principles," not of philosophy but of political practice.

> I've spent a lot of time over the last several years researching aspects of hard-left, ruthless, revolutionary tactics. That's what we've got. That's what's going on here. This is a by-the-numbers recapitulation of every left-wing revolution that ever happened. It has nothing to do with policy; it has nothing to do with principle; it has everything to do with power. That is all it is about. You cannot deal with a revolutionary left cadre by compromise, or

trying to conciliate, or 'reach out.' That's not going to work. The only thing you can do with people like that is to *defeat them*. And to defeat them, you have to fight them. Unfortunately, looking at the great panorama of our politics today, I see lots of evidence we're not fighting them, or at least not effectively. The Republican Party seems totally defensive, hesitant, apologetic, back on its heels, not knowing what to do.

Too many conservatives were saying that because Obama won the election, they had to let him get his way...Does anyone remember when Reagan won 49 states. Did Tip O'Neill say, 'You know, Reagan won the election; we've just got to be more like Reagan.' I don't remember that. Instead, they savaged Bob Bork. They savaged Ollie North, tried to bring down Reagan.

In 1964 we were wiped out. We were crushed flat. We didn't start whining, and saying 'Oh I guess we'll roll over.'" The media was happy to say that; they said, 'You're over, you're done, conservatives." And as I've said before it was a tough time for us, because we didn't have any grief counselors. We came out of that election fighting harder. We didn't give up. And out of that election came a person named Ronald Reagan.

We are in a much better position of strength today than we were back then. We didn't have any positions of strength at all in 1965. You wouldn't know it, but we have a majority in the House of Representatives—hello! There's a 'Speaker Boehner'— not sure you you've made the connections there. But there are more Republicans than Democrats [in the House]. There are 30 Republican governors.

You are not going to win many battles by lying down on the floor, sucking your thumb, and saying "we lost, we lost, we lost." If we had had this mentality back in the 1960s, there never would have been a conservative movement.

The 2013 CPAC was, incidentally, where Donald Trump made a well-received appearance in which he embraced the conservative movement more fully than before. Evans's views on Trump, if he had any at the time, were unrecorded. But Evans did start writing about immigration around that time in accents that were fully congruent with Trump even as many leading Republicans were still flirting with "comprehensive immigration reform" that would have involved a mass amnesty. Contrary to the widely accepted cliché that Democrats have the wind of changing demographics in their favor, Evans argued that in fact demographics spelled the inevitable defeat of liberalism because liberals are "literally aborting themselves."

> The liberal-counterculture Democrats will of course continue fighting this [culture] war in the schools and through the media, but have only one major demographic weapon to counter the fertility gap that is working relentlessly against them. That weapon is illegal immigration. As the population trends move steadily conservative, the liberals must bring into the country and enfranchise new voters who will reliably cast Democratic ballots. That, and that alone, is the real issue in the battle over immigration and why the Democrats are so bent on gaining amnesty for illegals. All the rest is window dressing. It's also the reason that this is the one issue above all others on which Republicans, if they want to win, should not surrender.

In 2011 a large group of Evans's oldest friends held a gala dinner in Washington at the National Press Club, a semi-roast in format, in honor of Evans. This author made his best effort at emulating Evans's style of inverted humor in his honor and can't resist the personal privilege of including some of it:

> Start with his "lifestyle," as liberals would call it, or his vices, as

Stan's mother would have said. Winston Churchill once dismissed the socialist Ramsay McDonald, who was a pacifist, a vegetarian, a non-smoker, and, worst of all, a teetotaler, by saying that McDonald had all of the virtues he abhorred and none of the vices he admired. I think Churchill would have approved of Stan; he has all the right bad habits.

He's an analogue person in a digital age; an alpha male on beta blockers; believes that rock n' roll is forever, and that the term "rap" should be followed by "sheet" rather than "music."

Stan is a fan of America's Founding Fathers, but does them one better: he's not so sure that taxation *with* representation is such a hot idea, either. Then there was the time in 1968, when he signed on to the McCarthy for President campaign. That lasted about 48 hours, until he discovered that the candidate was *Eugene* McCarthy.

Back in 1970, William F. Buckley told *Playboy* magazine that the biggest problem facing the conservative movement was a scarcity of good writers and journalists. Stan's founding of the National Journalism Center helped address that gap, but I always wondered where he got the idea. He couldn't have gotten the idea from Buckley's *Playboy* interview because we all know Stan only buys *Playboy* for the pictures.

Evans capped off the evening with a recitation of his greatest hits that easily outdid everyone's effort to match his wit.

The spring of 2014 brought the test results that Evans had pancreatic cancer, advanced sufficiently that his doctor gave him a grim prognosis of perhaps only a few weeks to live. His immediate reaction was typically insouciant: "The good news is I no longer have to worry about my money holding out." He underwent extensive chemotherapy in a hospital in Leesburg, where he received a steady stream of visitors. He made arrangements from his hospital bed for his extensive files on McCarthy and Soviet espionage to be deposited at the Hoover Archives.

It was by all accounts a long and painful ordeal as such illnesses usually are, but he faced it, his frequent bedside visitor Ralph Bennett said, "fearlessly, with real bravery and humor. Mentally sharp to the last, he was unfailingly gracious to the nurses, doctors, hospital workers, and others who came to see him. Except for a social worker, who came to ask him some questions. He dismissed her with a kingly wave to leave the room."

Bennett said that Evans's humility was "a true Christian humility," and therein lies the tale of the final milestone of his life: his turn to devout religious faith. He began having conversations with visitors and callers about the nature of faith, and among his visitors were two Catholic priests he had known for years: Father Vincent Rigdon and Father Mario Calabrese.

Father Rigdon was Evans's kind of clergyman. As an undergraduate at Columbia University in the late 1960s, Fr. Rigdon was active in Young Americans for Freedom at the time YAF was going through a bitter internal schism that reflected the traditionalist-libertarian split. Rigdon sided with the traditionalists. "Anarchism is inconsistent with conservatism," Rigdon told the *Columbia Spectator* student newspaper in 1969, denouncing in particular Karl Hess and Murray Rothbard. Evans visited Columbia to report on the ruckus and met Rigdon, who recalled, "Stan not only reported, he gave us encouragement and hope. We felt that we were part of something greater, and it was clear that Stan Evans truly was a mentor and guide."

When the Clinton administration in 1996 issued a gag order to prohibit military chaplains from mentioning abortion in their sermons, Fr. Rigdon—then serving as an Air Force chaplain, he successfully sued in federal court to have the gag order struck down—later hosted at a meeting of Evans's Monday Club to tell the whole story. When Stan's father died in 1989, he had Fr. Rigdon lead a memorial service in the Dirksen Senate Office (the other speaker was Sen. Jesse Helms, hence the location).

Likewise Evans met the future Fr. Calabrese when Calabrese was an undergraduate at Bonaventure University in New York in the late 1990s. Calabrese had read *The Theme Is Freedom* and mustered up the courage to invite Evans to speak, which Evans graciously agreed to do. Following his usual practice, Evans followed his talk with a late night of talking and drinking with Calabrese and his fellow students at "a local rathskeller." Calabrese and Evans kept in touch over the following decade and a half. In the weeks before his passing in March 2015, Calabrese visited Evans several times in the hospital and at home in his final days after Evans left the hospital for what he knew would be the last time. In the course of their conversations about religious faith, Calabrese asked Evans if he had ever been baptized. Evans couldn't remember, and he readily accepted Calabrese's offer to make doubly sure. Calabrese also administered the sacrament and last rites for Evans, who requested a Catholic memorial service to follow his passing.

It would be a mistake to commit the commonplace assumption that Evans was enacting Pascal's wager in the face of mortality. It is hard to escape the conclusion that Evans reasoned himself into religious faith in a fashion similar to C. S. Lewis. He more than once remarked to friends that *The Theme Is Freedom* is a very pro-Catholic book, and indeed Fr. Calabrese said that it was Evans's unique presentation of Augustine and Aquinas that helped inspire his decision to study theology more closely and eventually take holy orders.

Toward the end of *The Theme Is Freedom*, Evans wrote:

From these reflections it should be apparent that we need, above all else, a reinfusion of religious precept in our national life and public custom. In this regard, the growth not only of the "religious right" but of evangelical churches generally should be applauded, as should the active engagement of traditional Catholics in questions of social value and public policy...In saying this, I am mindful that social and political questions are from a religious standpoint distinctly secondary—that our religious belief is justified not by its social effects but my its intrinsic truth and relation to the life hereafter."[3]

Brian Lamb had this exchange with Evans on C-SPAN's *Book TV* about *The Theme Is Freedom* when the book appeared in 1994:

LAMB: How much of your own religious beliefs led you to write the book?

EVANS: I guess my religious beliefs led me to ask a lot of questions. I certainly am a believer. Anyone who knows me knows that I am not a particularly pious person, and I don't consider myself to be a particularly good Christian. I'm a believing Christian. But the book is not a book about piety or theology; it's a book about politics.

It is evident, though, that Evans took piety and theology seriously and as something separate from politics even if paradoxically Christian theology, rightly understood, had the most profound political implications. One reason he wasn't a regular church goer is that he was put off by how politicized so many denominations had become in the low sense of taking the liberal line on hot-button policy issues that had little serious theological basis. The National Council of Churches had been a target in his columns from time to time, and he was disgusted by the leftward drift of his parent's Methodist Church. Mal Kline recalls, "I know that on three separate occasions, in the 80s I think, others got him to attend Methodist services. In one of these, the minister delivered an anti-Reagan sermon. In another one the minister delivered an anti-Contra sermon. In yet another, the minister pleaded for sanctions on South Africa. As you might guess, all of these pleas turned off at least one visitor to the congregation." His mother requested a high church Episcopalian memorial service to follow her passing, which summoned Evans to remark to a friend, "So I have to try to find an Episcopal priest with leanings toward Christianity."

Evans passed away on March 3, 2015, about nine months after his cancer diagnosis. He was buried in Hamilton, next to his mother and father, with his Coors cap rather than his Phi Beta Kappa key. Father Rigdon said at Evans's memorial service that "God used him as His instrument." Evans would likely disclaim such praise even though his own cheerfulness and stubborn optimism can be seen as an expression of the Christian virtue of hope. He told Rush Limbaugh some years before: "I'm getting up in years now, so I tend to see things in longer perspectives, but I think there are cycles historically, and maybe providentially, where at a certain time and occasion there are people there who are capable of doing the job."

And thus his final legacy is an army of disciples inspired by his intellectual, professional, and personal example, all capable of carrying on the job. Scot Faulkner, a long-time friend of Evans and a Reagan White House veteran, wrote in the *Washington Examiner*: "The formal obituaries declared that Stan Evans had no immediate survivors. They are wrong. Thousands of conservative activists owe their lives and livelihoods to Stan Evans. We are all Stan's descendants. Those who knew him are recalling his ceaseless devotion to mentoring young people, both through NJC and in his other enterprises. His door was always open. There was always an extra chair at any table where he ate and drank. He always answered his phone. He always had time to listen and reflect, provide advice and support, and take action to help. He was a mentor to us all."[4]

Mal Kline recalled: "He never forgot his roots. We got a call one day from a gentleman who had seen Stan on C-SPAN. He said he was born in Kingsville, Texas, 'and that's where I am calling from,' the caller said. 'I'm 84-years-old and I've lived here all my life and never knew anyone famous came from Kingsville, Texas.' I asked him for his phone number but he demurred: 'I don't want to bother him.' 'Oh, trust me on this, he will want to talk to you,' I said, and he did, for about three-quarters of an hour. In the thirty years I knew him, two decades of which I worked for him, I saw an unending brigade of people troop to his door for advice and assistance, usually the latter, and not once did I see him turn away anyone empty handed."

Evans had a regular signoff line for his speeches and lectures that is a fitting conclusion to this book: "My time is up; I thank you for yours."

A SAMPLER OF STAN EVANS'S GREATEST QUIPS

Evans liked to say that "There is no absurdity that you can invent that a liberal will not state seriously." (An alternate formulation: "Liberalism today is impossible to satirize, since there is no absurdity it will not embrace in pursuit of ideological obsession.") Herewith some of his most famous quips, many of them based on an ironic restatement of liberal sentiments and clichés.

That government is best which McGoverns least.

Liberals don't care what you do so long as it's mandatory.

I didn't like Nixon until after Watergate. After wage and price controls, Watergate was a breath of fresh air.

There are only two things I don't like about the Nixon Administration: Its domestic policy, and its foreign policy.

I didn't always care for Joseph McCarthy's *ends*, but I always admired his *methods*.

Gridlock is the next best thing to having a constitution.

I'm tired of hearing what Republicans will do for the working man. What have they done for the country clubs lately?

Washington, DC, in the Clinton years: "Welcome to Rodham and Gomorrah."

The CDC has determined that conservatism is not spread by casual contact.

About the U.S. Senate: "At least Caligula appointed the whole horse."

About members of Congress in general: "If we can't raise their pay, we can at least lower their bail."

Tax cuts are sort of like sex. When they are well done, they are great! When they are badly done, they are *still* pretty good.

Any country that can land a man on the moon can abolish the income tax.

For those of you not familiar with economic terms, when your hear 'Gross National Product,' it is not a reference to Tip O'Neill.

A paleoconservative is a conservative who has been mugged by a neoconservative.

Give a man a carp, and you feed a man for a day. Teach a man to carp, and you've created a pain in the ass for life.

We need to repeal Obamacare to find out what's not in it.

Happiness is finding a declassified list of closet Communists.

The problem with "pragmatism" is that it doesn't work.

Washington, DC, is much like the Soviet Union—without the amenities.

Living in DC is worse than communism. At least with communism you get stuff.

Mayor Marion Barry wants to turn Washington, DC, into a work-free drug zone.

Congresswoman Olympia Snowe of Maine has said there are only two things she doesn't like about Jerry Brown. His face.

The difficulty with appeasing Communist China is that a couple hours later you want to do it again.

It's a good thing Republicans are pro-life, since they spend so much time in the fetal position.

A "social issue" for some Republicans is when someone gets blackballed from a country club.

The only time I text is when I'm driving. It helps pass the time.

Anybody who has their head screwed on right should be conservative when they are young. And then as they get older, they should become ... *more* conservative.

Whenever there is a pressing public policy issue, I want to know what celebrities think. It is important for our lawmakers to hear from Bono.

Evans's Law of Inadequate Paranoia: No matter how bad you think things are, if you look closer you'll inevitably find it's worse.

I generally start every day with a cigarette (a leafy vegetable) and coffee (a legume) because my Mother always told me breakfast is the most important meal of the day.

Why is it that when one of us gets into a position of power in Washington, he's no longer one of us?

The Falklands War is a tough call. On the one hand, we like imperialism. On the other hand, we like military dictatorships.

I have started a Committee for the Prevention of Nuclear Peace. Its motto: since we already have enough nuclear warheads to blow up the world several times over, a few more won't hurt.

We have two parties, and only two. One is the evil party, and the other is the stupid party. I'm very proud to be a member of the stupid party. Occasionally, the two parties get together to do something that's both evil and stupid. That's called bipartisanship.

Conservatives stand for family values, law and order, low taxes, a balanced budget, a free market economy, and a strong national defense. In other words—*hate!*

We all know that Mrs. Clinton has complained about the vast right-wing conspiracy, and of course, she is correct about that, and we are all part of it. But when I was starting out, it was only half-vast.

President Clinton released a statement today. He said he thought it was a tragedy that 50 percent of people fell below the median.

"Senator Jesse Helms has announced that he is now for the federal government taking over sex education in public schools. Senator Helms said, "If the federal government does that as well as it does everything else, pretty soon nobody will be doing it."

You know, I bought a bottle of wine the other day and it had a damn cork in it.

I had to scrape it out with my hunting knife.

I don't read *Self* magazine but I pump Self gas.

I have the heart of liberal; I keep it in a jar on my desk.

(The Philadelphia Society has an archive of Evans's many speeches from 1964 to 2012, available at https://phillysoc.org/voices-of-conservatism/?speaker_id=4194)

EVANS'S SIX RULES
FOR POLITICAL COMBAT

Around the time Evans ended his regular newspaper column in the late 1990s and turned to his final books, he summarized his lessons for contesting politics. As a preface, Evans explained what he called "the left's standard drill," especially for environmental or other health and safety issues:

> The routine is always just the same: Build up alarm about some asserted menace to public health or Mother Nature; cite "studies" or "science" of some sort the average person can't find or fathom; bring forth a crew of activists/politicians/official spokesmen who hammer on these alleged data—all repeated at endless length in hearings, meetings and media forums. Finally, when the public has had its "consciousness raised" enough (i.e., is scared out of its wits) move to adopt the desired big spending-taxing-regulating measure.

The remedy, Evans thought, was to "stop playing goalie and go on the offensive" with the following rules in mind:

1. POLITICS ABHORS A VACUUM. Conservatives too often wait to merely oppose a liberal proposal, which leaves the initiative always in the hands of liberals. It is important to beat liberals to the lead.

2. WRITE THE RESOLVED CLAUSE. One secret of winning a debate is to decide up front what it is going to be about. Liberals seem to know this instinctively, conservatives all too often don't, which means they wind up discussing what solutions to adopt, or not, to problems that the liberals have selected. This permits the left to maintain the rhetorical offensive, define the scope of possible action, and wind up getting much of what they want. Conservatives must avoid the trap of simply debating issues as the left presents them and instead define the issue for themselves.

3. NOTHING IS "INEVITABLE." This is one of the hoariest verbal-conceptual tricks in the liberal handbook. Usually what is called "inevitable" in Washington is something leftward activists or Beltway pundits assume or want, thus encouraging their cadres while demoralizing their opponents. Conservatives should resist this dismal counsel wherever it is offered, remembering that by their own exertions and advocacy they can change the dynamics of most political situations (and have often done so).

4. FIGHTING IS BETTER THAN NOT FIGHTING. A self-evident proposition, one would think, but apparently it isn't. Nothing can more certainly assure the victory of leftward causes than the failure of conservatives, Republicans, businessmen, et al., to oppose them. This doesn't mean every battle can be won or that all battles can be fought at once. It does mean that, generally speaking, a vigorous, sustained resistance well-grounded in the facts can drastically change the feedback from the polls and focus groups that are so much relied on.

5. WASHINGTON IS NOT AMERICA. Republicans for the most part come to DC repeating this mantra to themselves, but once more there seems to be a memory problem. The enveloping atmosphere of the city, the hugeness of the government itself, the clamorous interest groups, the TV talking heads—all of this is hard to ignore or overcome. In these precincts, many liberal ideas are regarded as a done deal, something no sustained or decent person could oppose. Opinion surveys often reveal, however, that things look quite different outside the Beltway, especially after the opposition finally starts to oppose.

6. TAXES ARE TRUMPS. As all of the above suggests, the question of high and rising taxes remains what it has ever been: the gold standard of Republican issues. This is the great trump card of the GOP, a solid, powerful, and intelligible topic that can be placed against all the standard liberal promises of something-for-nothing from the federal larder. Whenever the GOP has been able to use this issue in credible fashion, most notably under Ronald Reagan, it has emerged the winner. Whenever it strays from the anti-tax position, as under George H. W. Bush, it gets itself in trouble.

This all seems pretty obvious when you write it down, but given the powerful forces arrayed against it, it can stand a good deal of repeating.

ACKNOWLEDGMENTS

Writing this tribute to Stan Evans was a complete joy from start to finish despite some difficulties getting access to archival material and conducting interviews because of COVID restrictions in 2020 and early 2021. In addition to the opportunity to pay honor to a worthy man, it was a delight to read through his entire corpus, especially some of his early work in the 1950s and then at the *Indianapolis News.*

Another delight was speaking with so many people who share the same enthusiasm, high regard, and personal affection for Stan. The conversations and interviews were as inspirational as they were informational. In a way that Stan was perhaps unaware, he touched countless lives. Scot Faulkner, a longtime friend and Reagan White House veteran, captured the essence of this in the *Washington Examiner* at the time of Evans's death: "The formal obituaries declared that Stan Evans had no immediate survivors. They are wrong. Thousands of conservative activists owe their lives and livelihoods to Stan Evans. We are all Stan's descendants."

My first appreciation owes to Neal Freeman, who first suggested the idea and then helped secure a research grant for me to pursue the project in earnest. Neal offered many excellent suggestions for aspects of Stan's story that deserve highlight as well as some specific stories. Mal Kline, Fred Mann, Jameson Campaigne Jr., and Al Regnery were indispensable guides, and they answered endless queries and follow up questions. Other figures who were personal friends, professional contemporaries, employees or colleagues, or interns at the National Journalism Center who shared memories and other information include John A. Barnes, Ralph K. Bennett, Mary Jo Buckland, Ron Burr, Bill Campbell, Tom Davis, Jason Duke, Bill Dennis, Becky Norton Dunlop, Lenore Ealy, Judson C. Edwards, Lee Edwards, John Fund, James Gaston, Rick Henderson, Mark Henrie, Paul Kengor, Robert W. McDowell, John Merline, Andrew Olivastros, Daniel Oliver, Walter Olson, Russ Pulliam, Roger Ream, James Roberts, Greg Schneider, Peter Spencer, Allan Ryskind, Lew Uhler, and Martin Morse Wooster.

I owe a special debt to Gordon Daines and his staff, keepers of the ACU Archives at Brigham Young University, for arranging access to the archives amid the COVID restrictions and for their super-competent help finding and arranging materials for me. Although some of Evans's research papers are housed at the Hoover Institution, the Hoover archives remained closed to outside researchers during renovations in 2019 and then COVID, but Sarah Patton on the Hoover staff answered several helpful research inquiries.

Last, what turned out to be the most interesting discovery of the process of constructing a life of Stan Evans was his late turn to devout religious faith. The role of Father Vincent Rigdon is related in the last chapter, and Father Mario Calabrese was also very helpful in providing insight into this most personal aspect of Stan Evans's life.

And as always, thanks to Roger Kimball and his fine staff at Encounter Books.

NOTES

INTRODUCTION

1 M. Stanton Evans, *Revolt on the Campus*, (Washington, DC: Regnery, 1961), p. 29.

2 Evans, "A Lesson in Championship," *Indianapolis News*, October 11, 1963, p. 10.

3 Lee Edwards, *Educating for Liberty: The First Half-Century of the Intercollegiate Studies Institute* (Washington, DC: Regnery, 2003), p. 35.

4 "A Conservative Case for Freedom," in Meyer, ed., *What Is Conservatism?*, p. 86.

CHAPTER 1

1 Medford Evans, "Oxford, Mississippi," *The Southwest Review*, Vol. 15, No. 1 (Autumn 1929), p. 59.

2 M. Stanton Evans, "Medford Evans: A Pioneer of Conservatism," *Human Events*, March 11, 1989, p. 8

3 Sidney Hook, "The Techniques of Controversy," *The New Leader*, March 8, 1954, pp. 15–18.

4 M. Stanton Evans, "Medford Evans: A Pioneer of Conservatism," *Human Events*, March 11, 1989, p. 8.

5 Medford Evans, "Why I Am an Anti-Intellectual," *Human Events*, January 26, 1957.

6 Adam Clymer, "M. Stanton Evans, Who Helped Shape the Conservative Movement, Is Dead at 80," *New York Times*, March 3, 2015, p. A20.

7 Evans, *Revolt on the Campus*, p. 1.

8 Evans, "Yale's 'Four Hundred,'" *The Freeman*, December 1955, pp. 773–775.

9 Evans, *Revolt on the Campus*, p. 5.

10 Much of this biographical sketch comes from Charles H. Hamilton's introduction to *Fugitive Essays: Selected Writings of Frank Chodorov* (Indianapolis: Liberty Fund, 1980).

11 Lee Edwards, *Educating for Liberty*, p. 12.

12 Murray Rothbard, "Frank Chodorov, RIP," *Libertarian Review*, Vol. 3, No. 1 (Winter 1967), p. 4.

13 Cited in George Nash, *The Conservative Intellectual Movement in America Since 1945* (Wilmington, DE: ISI Press, 2006), p. 39.

14 Evans, *Revolt on the Campus*, p. 3.

CHAPTER 2

1 Edwards, *Educating for Liberty*, p. 24.

2 Lee Edwards, interview with the author, December 9, 2019.

3 Evans, "Barricade for Freedom," *The Freeman*, September 1955, p. 664.

4 Evans, "A New Philistine," *The Freeman*, November 1955, p. 755.

5 Edwards, *Goldwater*, p. 91.

6 "A New Leader Arises; Man of the Hour," *Human Events*, December 1, 1958, p. 1.

7 Franke, "Stan Evans Is Dead; Long Live Stan Evans!", ConservativeHQ, March 4, 2015, http://www.conservativehq.com/article/19818-stan-evans-dead-long-live-stan-evans.

8 "And So It Is Today," *Indianapolis News*, June 1, 1959, p. 10.

9 Bill Dennis interview.

CHAPTER 3

1 "End of a Search," *Time*, October 10, 1960, p. 51.

2 Evans, "Where'd Those Peasants Get Lindy's Hat?", *Indianapolis News*, April 21, 1961, p. 10. See also: the same day, the unsigned editorial, "What Can You See?"

3 *Indianapolis News*, November 26, 1965, p. 10.

4 "Can We Disprove Red Missiles—or Purple Cows?", *Indianapolis News*, August 31, 1959, p. 8.

5 "Double Enigma: USSR—and CIA," *Indianapolis News*, December 1, 1959.

6 Evans, "Moscow's Dwindling Power Image," *Indianapolis News*, February 15, 1961, p. 8.

7 Evans, "Senator Kennedy's Growing Pains," *Indianapolis News*, October 11, 1960, p. 6.

8 Evans, "Not Communism,' but 'Liberalism'—That's the Danger," *Indianapolis News*, June 2, 1961, p. 8. See also: "The Danger Is Internal," *Indianapolis News*, December 29, 1961, p. 8.

9 "How Safe Is the 'Safe' Assumption?", *Indianapolis News*, December 15, 1959, p. 10.

10 Evans, "The Missile Hassle," *Indianapolis News*, July 4, 1960, p. 10; "The Real Failure" (unsigned editorial), *Indianapolis News*, July 4, 1960, p. 10.

11 Evans, "How We Have Assumed Moscow Into Space Lead," *Indianapolis News*, April 14, 1961, p. 10.

12 Evans, "A Book for the President," *Indianapolis News*, May 19, 1961, p. 8.

13 Medford Evans, "An Open Letter to Dr. Oppenheimer," *National Review*, March 7, 1957, pp. 225–235.

14 Medford Evans, "Will They Get Strauss?", *National Review*, May 17, 1958, pp. 465–478.

15 Cited in David B. Frisk, *If Not Us, Who? William Rusher, National Review and the Conservative Movement* (Wilmington, DE: ISI Books, 2012), p. 328.

16   We can reliably surmise this because several unsigned editorials in a series called "The Fringe on Top" dealing with John Birch Society controversies turned up later in an overlooked early collection of Stan's essays entitled *The Fringe on Top: Political Wildlife Along the New Frontier*. (1962)

17   "For Saner Controversy," *Indianapolis News*, March 29, 1961, p. 8.

18   Evans, "Malthus Rides Again," *National Review*, December 17, 1960, pp. 380–381.

19   "Notes in India's 'Population Bomb,'" *Indianapolis News*, January 12, 1960, p. 6.

20   "The New Cliché: 'Population Explosion,'" *Indianapolis News*, June 7, 1963, p. 10; "'Population Bomb' Exploded, *Indianapolis News*, September 27, 1963, p. 10.

21   Evans, "The Strategy Against Don Bruce," *Indianapolis News*, October 27, 1961, p. 10.

22   December 9, 1959, p.12; February 24, 1960, p. 10.

23   "John E. Shade Urges News to Ban Ackelmire, Evans," *Indianapolis News*, September 6, 1960, p. 6.

24   Evans, "Some New 'Experts' Join the Fray," *Indianapolis News*, March 15, 1960, p. 8.

25   Editor's Corner, *Indianapolis News*, January 5, 1962, p. 8.

26   "The Achievement of T. S. Eliot," *Indianapolis News*, January 15, 1965, p. 10.

27   "Debbie Has a Serious Side, Too," *Indianapolis News*, July 31, 1970, p. 6.

28   Evans, "Of Michael Caine and Mutual Assured Destruction," *Human Events*, July 27, 1986, p. 7.

29   "How to Deal With Political Bores," *Indianapolis News*, October 13, 1959, p. 10.

30   "What's This 'Human-itties'?", *Indianapolis Star*, January 28, 1973, p. 6.

31   Remarks to the Philadelphia Society, September 25, 2010.

CHAPTER 4

1   This hypothesis is cogently argued by Tyler John Snelling in *Launching Conservative Resistance: A Rhetorical Criticism of the Young Americans for Freedom* (PhD dissertation, UNLV, 2017).

2   One exception is John A. Andrews III, *The Other Side of the Sixties: Young Americans for Freedom and the Rise of Conservative Politics* (New Brunswick, NJ: Rutgers University Press, 1997).

3   *Revolt*, p. 200.

4   *Revolt*, p. 45.

5   Evans, "Loyalty Oath: Repeal by Trickery," *Indianapolis News*, June 28, 1960, p. 8.

6   Caddy quoted in Wayne Thorburn, *A Generation Awakes: Young Americans for Freedom and the Creation of the Conservative Movement* (Ottawa, IL: Jameson Books, 2010), p. 21.

7   See especially Evans's account of this debate in *Revolt on the Campus*, pp. 112–114.

8 The other two people on the ad hoc committee were Carol Dawson and David Franke.

9 Cited in Gregory L. Schneider, *The Other Sixties: The Young Americans for Freedom and the Politics of Conservatism* (PhD dissertation, 1996), p. 53.

10 William A. Rusher, *Rise of the Right*, p. 63.

11 Schneider, *The Other Sixties* (PhD dissertation, 1996); Thorburn, *A Generation Awakes* (Jameson Books, 2010); Andrews, *The Other Side of the Sixties* (Rutgers University Press, 1997); Lee Edwards, *Educating for Liberty: The First Half-Century of the Intercollegiate Studies Institute* (Washington, DC: Regnery, 2003); George Nash, *The Conservative Intellectual Movement in America Since 1945* (Wilmington, DE: ISI Press, 2006).

12 Fred M. Hechinger, "One School of Thought," *New York Times Book Review*, November 19, 1961, p. 50.

13 *Kirkus Reviews*, November 1, 1961.

14 Robert B. Heilman, "Revolt on the Campus," *AAUP Bulletin*, Vol. 48, No. 2 (June 1962), pp. 181–183.

15 *Revolt*, p. 240.

CHAPTER 5

1 Evans, "The GOP's Man of the Hour—Sen. Goldwater," *Indianapolis News*, July 29, 1960, p. 8; "Nixon Left Turn Risks Revolt," *Indianapolis News*, July 29, 1960, p. 6.

2 Evans, "An Anonymous Statesman Views Kennedy's Program," *Indianapolis News*, March 29, 1962, p. 8.

3 Evans, "Culture in the White House," *Indianapolis News*, September 21, 1961, p. 10.

4 Evans, "'Man and Myth' Critique of JFK Shatters 'Image,'" *Indianapolis News*, September 6, 1963, p. 10.

5 Evans, "A Meeting with Prof. Schlesinger," *Indianapolis News*, November 15, 1960, p. 10.

6 Evans, "Should We Have Joined Castro's Red 'Movement?'", *Indianapolis News*, November 24, 1961, p. 10.

7 Evans, *The Fringe on Top: Political Wildlife Along the New Frontier* (New York: American Features, 1962), p. 34.

8 Evans, "Kennedy Letter on Steel Opposes Economic Growth," *Indianapolis News*, Friday, September 22, 1961, p. 10.

9 Evans, "The Missile Hassle," *Indianapolis News*, July 4, 1960, p. 10.

10 "The Missing 'Gap,'" unsigned editorial, *Indianapolis News*, April 6, 1962, p. 10.

11 Evans, "Record Reveals Kennedy and Ike Agreed on Cuba," *Indianapolis News*, October 18, 1960, p. 8.

12 See in particular "It's Time for Action," unsigned editorial, *Indianapolis News*, April 22, 1961, p. 8.

13 "Cuba and Laos," unsigned editorial, *Indianapolis News*, April 20, 1961, p. 8.

14 Evans, "The Real Lesson of Cuba: U.S. Officials Unprepared," *Indianapolis News*, December 28, 1962, p. 8.

15 Evans, *The Politics of Surrender* (New York: Devin-Adair, 1966), p. 408.

16 See Stanley Mosk & Howard H. Jewel, "The Birch Phenomenon Analyzed," *New York Times Magazine*, August 20, 1961, p. 12.

17 *The Liberal Establishment*, pp. 15–16.

18 M. Stanton Evans, with Allan H. Ryskind and William Schulz, *The Fringe on Top: Political Wildlife Along the New Frontier* (Indianapolis: American Features, 1962), p. 7.

19 M. Stanton Evans, *The Liberal Establishment: Who Runs America...and How* (New York: Devin-Adair, 1965), p. 29.

20 Evans, "The San Francisco Riots," in William F. Buckley Jr., ed., *The Committee and Its Critics: A Calm Review of the House Committee on Un-American Activities* (New York: Putnam, 1962), p. 200.

21 Evans, "How to Silence Conservatives," *Indianapolis News*, July 23, 1963, p. 8.

22 Evans, "Who Was Intimidating Whom?", *Indianapolis News*, July 19, 1963, p. 6.

23 Evans, "Barry Losingest Winner Again," *Indianapolis News*, July 16, 1964, p. 2.

24 Russell Pulliam, *Publisher Gene Pulliam: Last of the Newspaper Titans* (Ottawa, IL: Jameson Books, 1984), p. 253.

25 Evans, *Goldwater or Johnson: Does It Really Matter?* (Shepherdsville, KY: Victor Publishing, 1964).

26 Among many notable passages in Evans's brief is this: "No one would suggest that Barry Goldwater is another Russell Kirk; but Goldwater reads Kirk, and Goldwater's intelligence commands Kirk's respect. Similarly, Goldwater's close relationship with such scholars as Robert Strausz-Hupe and Milton Friedman and Gerhart Niemeyer is a matter of record. Who are Lyndon Johnson's favored political theorists? What books does he read?"

CHAPTER 6

1 "Johnson's Landslide," unsigned editorial, *Indianapolis News*, November 4, 1964, p. 14.

2 "The GOP Future," unsigned editorial, *Indianapolis News*, November 13, 1964, p. 8.

3 Evans, "The Conservatives Bounce Back," *Indianapolis News*, November 27, 1964, p. 8.

4 "Keep Fighting," unsigned editorial, *Indianapolis News*, December 4, 1964, p. 12.

5 Evans letter to Don Bruce, January 15, 1965, ACU Archives, L. Tom Perry Special Collections, Brigham Young University, MSS 176, Box 14, Folder 3.

6 Scratchy recordings of the three panelists (but not Evans's introductions) are available on the Philadelphia Society's website: https://phillysoc.org/tps_meetings/the-future-of-freedom-the-problems-and-the-prospects/

7 Evans, "A Generation of Growth," *Human Events*, April 12, 1969, p. 53.

8 Worth notice on this point is a curious book Stan's father, Medford Evans, published in 1968, *The Usurpers: The Men Who Rule America—An Appeal to Those They Rule* (Belmont, MA: Western Islands, 1968). A study ostensibly of six senior Kennedy holdovers—Dean Rusk, Walt Rostow, Robert McNamara, Clark Clifford, Abe Fortas, and Nicholas B. Katzenbach—the book entertained the exotic theory, bordering on conspiracy theory, that the Kennedy assassination represented a coup d'etat on behalf of the permanent government—what today we have come to call the "deep state." Although stopping short of alleging a direct or literal conspiracy involving senior government officials, Medford agreed with some far-left figures in dissenting from the Warren Commission's finding that Lee Harvey Oswald acted alone. The main point is that the continuity of Rusk, et al., represented a permanent government interest distinct from and hostile to constitutional government, a class of administrators whose rule persists regardless of who is in the White House or running Congress. With the names and events changed, one can see parallels with Steve Bannon.

9 Evans, *The Future of Conservatism* (New York: Holt, Reinhart & Winston, 1968), p. 288.

10 "The ideology of 'one man, one vote' has been extended to the point where anyone who can get himself to the polls, or be carted there by someone else, will be permitted to vote irrespective of qualifications of any sort." "The Final Proof," unsigned editorial, *Indianapolis News*, May 28, 1965, p. 12.

11 Evans, "How Welfarism Breeds Crime," *Indianapolis News*, August 4, 1967, p. 6.

12 Evans, "'War on Poverty' Is Turning Into a Fiasco," *Indianapolis News*, July 9, 1965, p. 4.

13 Sargent Shriver, "Shriver Claims Poverty Salaries Are Justified," letter to the editor, *Indianapolis News*, July 1, 1965, p. 10.

14 Evans, Speech to the Philadelphia Society, March 31, 1967; https://phillysoc. org/tps_meetings/the-american-tradition-and-the-great-society/

15 Evans, *The Politics of Surrender*, p. 369.

16 "A Fine Statement," unsigned editorial, *Indianapolis News*, July 30, 1965, p. 8.

17 Evans, "Lippmann and the President," *Indianapolis News*, July 15, 1966.

18 Evans, "Debate Is Needed in Vietnam," *Indianapolis Star*, November 12, 1965, p. 10.

19 Evans, "What Polls Show on Vietnam," *Indianapolis News*, April 12, 1968, p. 8.

20 Evans, *The Politics of Surrender* (New York: Devin-Adair, 1966), p. 23.

21 Evans, "Rejecting the Ultimate Weapon," *Indianapolis News*, January 28, 1966, p. 10.

22 Evans, "Inside the Disarmament Lobby," *Indianapolis News*, November 24, 1967, p. 8.

23 "Looking to '68," unsigned editorial, *Indianapolis News*, April 17, 1968, p. 8.

24 Recollection of Mal Kline, interview with author, July 2020.

25 Evans, *The Future of Conservatism*, p. 271.

26 Evans, *The Future of Conservatism*, pp. 18–19.

27 Evans, *The Future of Conservatism*, p. 292.

28 Evans, "Moving Left Courts Election Disaster," *Human Events*, August 3, 1968, p. 10.

29 Evans, The Meaning of Miami," *Human Events*, August 24, 1968, p. 8.

30 "Conservative Battle Is Hardly Over," *Human Events*, November 16, 1968, p. 1.

31 Evans, "Why the GOP Must Move Right," *Human Events*, November 23, 1968, p. 1.

32 Evans, "Should Nixon Creep Into Office?", *Indianapolis News*, November 15, 1968, p. 10.

33 Evans, "Whitcomb Wages Anti-Tax Fight," *Indianapolis News*, November 1, 1968, p. 12.

34 Evans, "GOP Campaign Efforts Differ," *Indianapolis News*, November 8, 1968, p. 10.

35 Evans, "Going After the Federal 'Aid,'" *Indianapolis News*, July 26, 1968, p. 6.

36 Evans, "Lugar Record Not Conservative," *Indianapolis News*, February 15, 1974, p. 16.

CHAPTER 7

1 Evans, "How One Conservative Views '72 Scene," *Human Events*, October 7, 1972, p. 9.

2 John B. Judis, *William F. Buckley Jr.: Patron Saint of the Conservatives* (New York: Simon & Schuster, 1988), p. 261.

3 Ralph de Toledano, "Nixon Ignoring Conservatives?", *Indianapolis Star*, February 26, 1969, p. 14.

4 Evans, "Man Overboard on the Left," *Indianapolis News*, September 29, 1967, p. 8.

5 "The TV Debate," unsigned editorial, *Indianapolis News*, November 21, 1969, p. 16.

6 "Censorship?", unsigned editorial, *Indianapolis News*, November 28, 1969, p. 12.

7 Tom Ferrell, "If the Silent Majority Could Talk, What Would It Say?", *Esquire*, May 1, 1970.

8 Evans, "Indianapolis Annoys the Times," *Indianapolis News*, December 27, 1967, p. 8.

9 The other five original print journalist contributors were Jeffrey St. John, Stewart Alsop, John K. Jessop, Nicholas Von Hoffman, and Murray Kempton. Over the next several years, CBS added several additional contributors, including Ellen Goodman, James Jackson Kilpatrick, Shana Alexander, and Joe Sobran. Kilpatrick and Alexander were ultimately recruited from *Spectrum* for the "Point-Counterpoint" segment on "60 Minutes."

10 Evans, "Employee Freedom Wins in AFTRA Case," *Human Events*, February 4, 1978, p. 15.

11 "Should Conservatives Vote for Wallace?", *Human Events*, October 19, 1968, pp. 7–8.

12 Conservative columnist James Jackson Kilpatrick was one of the first to change his mind publicly, with a column entitled "Some Second Thoughts on Electoral Changes," November 26, 1969.

13 Evans, "Will the 'Work Incentives' Work?", *Indianapolis News*, August 15, 1969, p. 6.

14 "Can Nixon's Welfare Plan Work?", *Human Events*, August 23, 1969, pp. 1–5.

15 "ACU, Human Events Fight Welfare Bill," *ACU Report*, March 1970, p. 1.

16 "'No' To Controls," unsigned editorial, *Indianapolis News*, September 12, 1969, p. 6.

17 Evans, "The 'Cost Push' Inflation Myth," *Indianapolis News*, December 4, 1970, p. 10. See also "The Debauching of Our Currency," *Indianapolis News*, December 11, 1970, p. 12.

18 "Conservatives Worried: Nixon After One Year," *Human Events*, January 24, 1970, p. 1.

19 Evans, "Recipe for Ruin," ACU *Battle Line*, July 1975, p. 12.

20 John B. Judis, *William F. Buckley Jr: Patron Saint of the Conservatives* (New York: Simon & Schuster, 1988), pp. 328–330.

21 Evans, "The Trouble With Henry Kissinger," *Human Events*, September 8, 1973, p. 16.

22 Evans, "Have Conservatives a Place To Go?", *Human Events*, October 23, 1971, p. 7.

23 Buchanan memo to Haldeman and Mitchell, December 3, 1971, Contested Materials Collection, Box 3, Folder 56, Richard Nixon Presidential Library.

24 "Getting Results," unsigned editorial, *Indianapolis Star*, January 28, 1972, p. 8.

CHAPTER 8

1 "The Two Campaigns," unsigned editorial, *Indianapolis Star*, June 16, 1972, p. 6.

2 Evans, "What Produced McGovern's Win?", *Indianapolis Star*, July 13, 1972, p. 10.

3 Evans, "Sen. McGovern and the Radicals," *Indianapolis News*, July 14, 1972, p. 8. Evans made a point of attending rallies and press conferences of Jerry Rubin's Yippies.

4 Evans, "GOP Future in the Balance," *Indianapolis News*, August 22, 1972, p. 8.

5 Evans, "Chuck Percy's Liberal All-Stars," *Indianapolis News*, August 23, 1972, p. 10.

6 Evans, "But What About the Taxpayer?", Indianapolis News, August 24, 1972, p. 10; "In One Lesson," unsigned editorial, *Indianapolis News*, August 23, 1972, p. 10.

7   "For the Nation," unsigned editorial, *Indianapolis News*, November 6, 1972, p. 8.

8   Evans, "McGovern's Mandate in Reverse," *Indianapolis News*, November 10, 1972, p. 12.

9   Evans, *Clear and Present Dangers: A Conservative View of America's Government* (New York: Harcourt Brace Jovanovich, 1975), p. 68.

10 Evans, *Clear and Present Dangers*, p. 70.

11 See Chapter 4, *Clear and Present Dangers*, "The Decline of Congress," pp. 73–87.

12 See, e.g. John Marini, *Unmasking the Administrative State: American Politics in the 21st Century*, (New York: Encounter Books, 2019).

13 Evans, *Clear and Present Dangers*, p. 87.

14 Evans, *Clear and Present Dangers*, p. 96.

15 Evans, "Those Nixon Deficits," ACU *Battle Line*, March 1972, p. 8.

16 Evans, "Through the Looking Glass," ACU *Battle Line*, February 1973, p. 2.

17 Evans letter to Nixon, March 15, 1974, ACU Archives, L. Tom Perry Special Collections, Brigham Young University, MSS 176, Box 14, Folder 16.

18 Ash letter to Evans, March 20, 1974, ACU Archives, L. Tom Perry Special Collections, Brigham Young University, MSS 176, Box 14, Folder 16.

19 Evans to Ash, April 5, 1974, ACU Archives, L. Tom Perry Special Collections, Brigham Young University, MSS 176, Box 14, Folder 16.

20 "The Problem with Roy Ash Is That He Wants to Have His Bullets and Bite Them, Too," ACU *Battle Line*, December 1974, p. 1.

21 Evans, "Busting the Budget," ACU *Battle Line*, February 1974, p. 8.

22 Evans, "After the Fall," ACU *Battle Line*, August 1974, p. 8.

23 Evans, "The Perfect Defense," ACU *Battle Line*, August 1973, p. 6.

24 Evans, "The Double Standard," ACU *Battle Line*, May 1973, p. 8.

25 Evans, "A Case of Political Bugging," *Human Events*, June 16, 1973, p. 8.

26 Evans, "Pragmatism and Politics: The Lesson of Watergate," *Human Events*, May 19, 1973, p. 13.

27 Evans, *Clear and Present Dangers*, p. 67.

28 Cited in John B. Judis, *William F. Buckley, Jr: Patron Saint of the Conservatives* (New York: Simon & Schuster, 1988), p. 350.

29 Evans letter to Don Lipsett, April 18, 1974, copy in possession of the author.

30 This distaste apparently lasted after Will left *NR*. Lipsett checked in with Evans and Rusher about Will in a letter dated July 30, 1980: "What is the official party line on George Will these days? John Ryan says he is getting better. Per your orders, I have avoided inviting him to any Philadelphia Society meetings." This author was unable to find a reply but notes that Will has never spoken to the Philadelphia Society.

368 • M. STANTON EVANS

CHAPTER 9

1   Evans, "Watergate Wallow," ACU *Battle Line*, July 1973, p. 8.

2   Evans, "Progress Against the Odds," ACU *Battle Line*, December 1973, p. 5.

3   Evans letter to Donald Alexander, April 10, 1975, ACU archives, L. Tom Perry Special Collections, Brigham Young University, MSS 176, Box 1, Folder 9. If Alexander replied, his letter does not appear to have been deposited in the ACU files.

4   Not all conservative political activists were enthusiastic about Evans's aggressive initiatives through the ACU. At a small conference of conservative leaders in the summer of 1975, Evans commented that the proliferation of political committees was "dividing a limited pie" of funds. Paul Weyrich, founder of the Committee for the Survival of a Free Congress, and Terry Dolan, who had recently founded the National Conservative Political Action Committee, were both in the audience and were not pleased with Evans's perspective, complaining that ACU seemed to have "the point of view that they are the only people in Washington who really deserve to exist.

5   Darlene Schmalzreid, "Group Ratings Held 'Unfair,'" *Fort Worth Star-Telegram*, April 8, 1976.

6   Roush letter to Evans, July 28, 1976, ACU Archives, L. Tom Perry Special Collections, Brigham Young University, MSS 176, Box 3, Folder 7.

7   Evans letter to Roush, August 3, 1976, ACU Archives, L. Tom Perry Special Collections, Brigham Young University, MSS 176, Box 3, Folder 7.

8   ACU Archives, L. Tom Perry Special Collections, Brigham Young University, MSS 176, Box 113, Tape 5.

9   Daniel Oliver, "What Conservatives Are Telling Each Other," *National Review*, March 1, 1974, p. 257.

10 Reagan letter to Evans, March 1, 1974, ACU Archives, L. Tom Perry Special Collections, Brigham Young University, MSS 176, Box 14, Folder 10.

11 Evans letter to Ford, August 14, 1974, ACU Archives, L. Tom Perry Special Collections, Brigham Young University, MSS 176, Box 14, Folder 16.

12 Evans, "Rocky to Test Conservatives," *Human Events*, August 31, 1974, p. 15.

13 Evans, "The Rockefeller Revolution," *Human Events*, October 5, 1974, p. 14.

14 Minutes of Directors Meeting, December 15, 1974, L. Tom Perry Special Collections, Brigham Young University, MSS 176, Box 21, Folder 11.

15 Quoted in Daniel Preston Parker, "CPAC: The Origins and Role of the Conference in the Expansion and Consolidation of the Conservative Movement, 1974–1980," (Unpublished dissertation, University of Pennsylvania, 2015), p. 106.

16 David B. Frisk, *If Not Us, Who? William Rusher, National Review, and the Conservative Movement* (Wilmington, DE: ISI Books, 2012), p. 325.

17 Evans, "A Visit with George Wallace," *Human Events*, September 13, 1975, p. 13.

18 Pulliam, letter to the editor, *Indianapolis News*, February 18, 1975, p. 10.

19 Evans, "*Human Events* and the Conservative Movement," *Human Events*, April 27, 1974, p. 4.

20 Evans, "The Ronald Reagan Story," *Human Events*, January 24, 1976, p. S-8.

21 Cannon, *Reagan*, p. 218.

22 James Roberts interview with author, November 10, 2020.

23 Evans, "The 42 Percenters," ACU *Battle Line*, June 1976, p. 8.

24 Evans, "The Case Against Carter-Mondale," *Human Events*, August 21, 1976, p. S-3.

25 Goldwater letter to Evans, February 4, 1977, L. Tom Perry Special Collections, Brigham Young University, MSS 176, Box 2, Folder 21.

26 Evans letter to Goldwater, February 14, 1977, L. Tom Perry Special Collections, Brigham Young University, MSS 176, Box 2, Folder 21.

CHAPTER 10

1 Evans, "Why Oil Companies Need Higher Profits," *Human Events*, January 5, 1974, p. 1.

2 Statement before the Subcommittee on Health of the Committee on Ways and Means, U.S. House of Representatives, November 10, 1975, ACU archives, L. Tom Perry Special Collections, Brigham Young University, MSS 176, Box 14, Folder 21.

3 Evans, "Why Hospital Costs Keep Rising," *Human Events*, June 11, 1977, p. 8.

4 Evans, "The Pattern of U.S. Global Surrender," *Human Events*, August 11, 1979, p. 13.

5 See in particular Evans, "Eyewitness Report on the Rhodesian Elections," *Human Events*, May 5, 1979, pp. 5–6.

6 All quotations from "Economic Sanctions Against Rhodesia; House of Representatives, Committee on Foreign Affairs, Subcommittees on Africa, and on International Organizations," May 14, 1979. See also Evans's account of the hearing in "How Liberals Change Rhodesia Views," *Human Events*, June 16, 1979, p. 13.

7 "A Conversation with M. Stanton Evans," Interview with William C. Dennis, Liberty Fund Intellectual Portrait Series (DVD, 2002), 57 min. mark.

8 Evans, "Hart Proves Criticism of the Media Is Correct," *Human Events*, January 9, 1988, p. 8.

9 Evans, "Editor's Corner," *Indianapolis News*, October 27, 1959.

10 Evans, "ABC and the Geraldo Rivera Syndrome," *Human Events*, February 14, 1981, p. 9.

11 William C. Dennis interview.

12 Evans, "Our Economic Ignorance," *Human Events*, July 5, 1975, p. 7.

13 Evans, "The Mystery of Bass' Missing $20 Million," *Human Events*, June 30, 1995, p. 8.

14 J. B. Matthews, *Odyssey of a Fellow Traveler* (New York: Mount Vernon Publishers, 1938), pp. 260, 267.

15 "Egg on His Face," unsigned editorial, *Indianapolis News*, August 26, 1972, p. 10.

16 F. J. Schlink, "The Free Market and the Consumer," *Consumers' Research*, February 1988, p. 17.

17 Evans, "Home Insulation May Be Hazardous to Your Health," *Human Events*, January 3, 1981, p. 7.

18 Evans, "If You're in an HMO, Here's Why," *Consumers' Research*, December 1997, pp. 10–15.

19 Author interview with Tom Davis, December 15, 2020.

CHAPTER 11

1 Evans, "Why Reagan Won: The Constants Prevailed," *Human Events*, November 22, 1980, p. 17.

2 Evans, "'Sears Factor' Troubling to Conservatives," *Human Events*, October 27, 1979, p. 13.

3 Reagan letter to Edward Caffery, December 1979, in Kiron Skinner, Martin Anderson, and Annelise Anderson, eds., *Reagan: A Life in Letters* (New York: Free Press, 2003), p. 235.

4 Evans, "A Working Man's GOP?", *National Review*, June 8, 1978, p. 717.

5 See esp. Evans, "How U.S. Internal Security Was Destroyed," *Human Events*, August 3, 1985, p. 7.

6 "Hatfield and Evans Tangle on SISS," *Human Events*, February 21, 1975, p. 8.

7 Evans, "Who's Behind the Intelligence War?", *Human Events*, February 7, 1981, p. 12.

8 Evans, "Reagan Budget Urges Modest Cutbacks," *Human Events*, March 21, 1981, p. 9.

9 Evans, "Reagan Revolution—Or Bush Rebellion," *Human Events*, January 23, 1982, p. 15.

10 "Conservative Leaders Find Administration Officials Undermining Reagan Mandate," *Human Events*, January 30, 1982, pp. 17–18.

11 Evans, "Reagan Government a Mystery to Conservatives," *Human Events*, June 26, 1982, p. 7.

12 Lou Cannon, *President Reagan: The Role of a Lifetime* (New York: Simon & Schuster, 1991), pp. 180, 363.

13 Reagan letter to Nackey Loeb, June 28, 1982, *Reagan: A Life in Letters*, p. 595.

14 For a more complete account of the 1982 tax and spending deal, see Steven F. Hayward, *The Age of Reagan: The Conservative Counter-Revolution, 1980–1989* (New York: Crown Forum, 2009), pp. 182–213.

16 "80 Mandate Endangered by Yielding to 'Pragmatists,'" *Human Events*, January 15, 1983, p. 1.

17 Evans, "Still Another Reagan 'Hit List,'" *Human Events*, April 9, 1983, p. 15.

18 Evans, "Move to Satanism Threatens to Split GOP," *Human Events*, December 5, 1987, p. 8.

19 Evans, "Time to Politicize Government," *Human Events*, April 20, 1985, p. 7.

20 Allan Ryskind, interview with author, December 9, 2019; Lee Edwards, "Reagan's Newspaper," *Human Events*, February 7, 2011, p. 7.

21 "What Conservatives Think About Ronald Reagan: A Symposium," *Policy Review*, Winter 1984, p. 15.

22 Reagan private letter to William Rusher, cited in David B. Frisk, *If Not Us, Who?* (Wilmington, DE: ISI Books, 2012), p. 368.

23 Evans, "From SALT II to the ABM Accord," *Human Events*, June 14, 1986, p. 7.

24 Evans, "Tougher U.S. Policies Pushed Soviets Toward Collapse," *Human Events*, January 6, 1990.

25 Evans, "Gorbachev's Game Plan at the Summit," *Human Events*, October 25, 1986, p. 8; Evans, "Media Strike Out Again on Summit," *Human Events*, November 1, 1986, p. 8.

26 Evans, "Iran-Contra Hearings Show Media Alienation," *Human Events*, August 8, 1987, p. 8.

27 Evans, "A Meeting at the White House," *Human Events*, April 11, 1987, p. 8.

28 Evans, "How N.Y. Times, ABC Misrepresented Quayle," *Human Events*, September 3, 1988, p. 8.

29 Evans, "Permanent Government Seeks to Roll Bush," *Human Events*, December 10, 1988, p. 8.

30 Evans, "Darman Tax Hike Doomed Republican Chances," *Human Events*, November 14, 1992, p. 8.

31 Evans, "Mrs. Thatcher: Conservatism Done the Right Way," *Human Events*, October 24, 1987, p. 8.

32 Evans, "Henry Kissinger Meets the Boat People," *Human Events*, December 19, 1987, p. 8.

CHAPTER 12

1 Evans, "Mideast Misgivings Aren't 'Isolationism,'" *Human Events*, August 25, 1990, p. 8.

2 John Gizzi, "Right Rallies Around Bush on War," *Human Events*, December 3, 2001, p.1

3 Evans, "Why—and How—Conservatives Should Support PARCA Reform," *Human Events*, June 6, 1998, p. 10.

4 Evans, "British Experience Disproves the 'Free Trade' Rationale," *Human Events*, June 23, 1995, p. 10.

5 Evans, *The Theme Is Freedom: Religion, Politics, and the American Tradition* (Washington, DC: Regnery, 1994), p. 96 (Hereinafter cited as *Theme*.)

6 Evans, "But Statecraft Is *Not* Soulcraft," *Human Events*, July 23, 1983, p. 8.

7 There was also a long unsigned attack on Will in *Human Events* in 1996 for Will's criticism of Pat Buchanan on the issue of creationism versus evolution in the public schools that may possibly have been written by Evans or at least largely influenced by other Evans columns that overlapped the content of the

HE article. ("Columnist George Will Ridicules Creationism," *Human Events*, March 1, 1996, p. 1.)

8 Evans, "Dark Horses" column, *National Review*, June 27, 1980, p. 798.

9 Evans, "Dark Horses" column, *National Review*, August 18, 1978, p. 1037.

10 Evans, "Dark Horses" column, *National Review*, November 24, 1978, p. 1495.

11 Evans reviewed Strauss's *The City and Man* in *National Review*, noting that "Strauss brings out strongly and seems to concur in the Aristotelian notion that the purpose of political life is to train the citizens in virtue and excellence, and that the principles of right can be deduced through the systematic action of human reason upon the materials of nature." While Evans clearly respected Strauss, he was not persuaded, as the next paragraph made clear, where he offered Rushdoony as the counterpoint to Strauss: "Rushdoony argues that the pagan mentality, even if its highest form, was radically deficient in understanding the central issues of political right because it did not, and could not, grasp the notion of divine transcendence." Evans went on to summarize Rushdoony's view that became the central argument of *Theme*: "The Trinitarian doctrine of the early Church established the basis of Western freedom."

12 Evans, *The Theme Is Freedom*, p. 321.

13 Forrest McDonald, "What Makes Right?", *National Review*, October 24, 1994, p. 62–64.

14 Evans, "McCarthy and History," undated manuscript in possession of author.

15 Evans, "Joe McCarthy and the Historians," *Human Events*, January 1, 1999, p. 7.

16 Evans, "When Conservatives Parrot Liberal Lies about Joe McCarthy," *Human Events*, August 20, 2012, p. 22.

17 Evans offered a long account of Ritchie's errors in "How Senate Historian Botched Data on McCarthy," Human Events, May 26, 2003, pp. 12-14.

18 Medord Evans, *The Assassination of Joe McCarthy* (Belmont, MA: Western Island, 1970).

19 John Earl Haynes and Harvey Klehr, *Venona: Decoding Soviet Espionage in America* (New Haven: Yale University Press, 1999), p. 7.

20 Evans, *Blacklisted by History*, p. 600.

21 David Oshinsky, "In the Heart of the Heart of Conspiracy," *New York Times*, January 27, 2008.

22 *Library Journal*, December 2007, p. 133.

23 John Earl Haynes, "McCarthy, According to Evans (and Novak)," December 11, 2007, at https://www.washingtondecoded.com/site/2007/12/mccarthy-accord.html.

24 Ron Radosh, "The Enemy Within," *National Review*, December 17, 2007, p. 50.

25 Evans, "The Book on McCarthy," letter to the editor, *National Review*, December 31, 2007, p. 2.

26 Larry Ceplair, "McCarthyism Revisited," *Historical Journal of Film, Radio and Television*," Vol. 28, No. 3, August 2008, p. 410.

27 Evans, letter to the *New Criterion*, January 2014, p. 91.

EPILOGUE

1 Stephen Goode, *Insight on the News*, May 28, 2001, Vol. 17, Issue 20, p. 36.

2 Evans, "GOP: Don't Whine, Rebuild," *Human Events*, November 24, 2008, p. 1.

3 Evans, *The Theme Is Freedom*, p. 319.

4 Scot Faulkner, "R.I.P. Stan Evans," *Washington Examiner*, March 12, 2015.

INDEX

ABC News, 177, 242, 244
Abolition of Man, The, 87
abortion, 75, 346
Accuracy in Academia, 256
ACU Education and Research Institute, 229–230, 235–236, 292
Adams, John, 137
Adams, Ralph Wyatt, 257
"ADA on the Brink of Power," 49
"ADA—The Enemy Within: How the Left Achieves Its Political Victories," 50
Adenauer, Konrad, 44
administrative state, 116–117
Affordable Care Act, 5, 228
Afghanistan, 285
Africa, 230–235
Agnew, Spiro, 17, 154–155, 159, 181, 195, 201
air bags, automobile, 252–253
airline deregulation, 256
air pollution, indoor, 254
Akst, Daniel, 99
Allen, Richard, 272
Alternative, The, 55, 59
Amerasia, 327, 332, 334, 335
American Betrayal: The Secret Assault on Our Nation's Character, 337
American Civil Liberties Union (ACLU), 217
American Committee for Cultural Freedom, 29
American Communist History, 331, 335
American Conservative Union (ACU), 13, 18, 50, 75, 130–131
    ACU Education and Research Institute at, 229–230, 235–236
    backing of Reagan's primary campaign, 219–220
    Conservative Political Action Conference (CPAC) and, 13, 200–210

delegation to Africa, 231–232
invitation to Goldwater to join advisory board of, 221–222
new programs and growth in the 1970s, 198–199
opposition to Nixon's FAP proposal, 161–162
scorecard ratings and reviews of legislators, 200–201
Stan Evans as chairman of, 159, 164, 180, 187, 198
summer internship program at, 1–2, 10, 236–237
views on Nixon, 159–162, 167
American Enterprise Institute, 12
American Federation of Television and Radio Artists (AFTRA), 158–159
American Language, The, 24
American Legislative Exchange Council (ALEC), 162
American liberty, origins and substance of, 314–315
American Nazi Party, 230
American Opinion, 72
Americans for Constitutional Action (ACA), 50
Americans for Democratic Action (ADA), 49–50, 107, 130, 153, 279
American Spectator, The, 55, 59, 237
analysis, 35–36
Andre, Fred, 59
Andrews, John A., III, 99
Annals of the American Academy of Political and Social Science, 101
Anti-Ballistic Missile Treaty of 1972, 142, 286
anti-Communism. *see also* McCarthy, Joe/ McCarthyism
    Dean Rusk and, 110

George Kennan and, 46
House Un-American Activities
    Committee (HUAC) and, 71, 117–118
Joe McCarthy and, 29
John Birch Society and, 26, 70, 71–73,
    113–116
John F. Kennedy and, 105, 107, 111
Konrad Adenauer and, 44
McCarthyism and, 70–73
Medford Evans and, 26, 70–72
Stan Evans and, 5, 19, 49, 61–62, 75–78
Antigone, 317
Apple, R. W., Jr., 204
Aquinas, Thomas, 317
Arab oil embargo of 1973, 226
Aristotle, 317
Arizona Republic, 48, 54, 122
Armel, Scott, 247–248
arms control agreements, 142
Ash, Roy, 187–190, 270
Ashbrook, John, 13, 130–131, 159, 164, 203
    challenge to Nixon, 177–178, 179
Associated Press, 12, 237
Atomic Energy Commission, 25, 26, 68

Bailyn, Bernard, 310
Baker, Howard, 207, 290
Baker, James, 265, 272, 274, 278, 280–283
Baldacchino, Joe, 282
Baldwin, Alec, 341
Baltimore Sun, 237
Banfield, Edward, 78
Barnes, Fred, 237
Barnes, John, 3, 237
Barzun, Jacques, 86, 311
Bass, Lee, 247–248
Battle Line, 159, 169, 176–177, 187–189, 206,
    210
Bauer, P. T., 78
Bauman, Carol, 130–131
Bauman, Robert, 130–131, 203
Bayh, Birch, 149, 262
Bay of Pigs, 111
Bell, Jeffrey, 160, 167, 169, 215
Bennett, Ralph, 2, 4–5, 10–12, 17, 236, 258, 346
Bennett, William, 328
Berger, Sandy, 326
Berlau, John, 237
Berlin Wall, 111
Bethell, Tom, 272
Black, Conrad, 337
*Blacklisted by History: The Untold Story of
    Senator Joe McCarthy*, 11, 306, 320–325

mainstream media criticisms of, 330–335
    Stan Evans's research for, 325–327
Blackwell, Morton, 203
Bloom, Allan, 87
Bolton, John, 217
Bono, 6
Boorstin, Daniel, 241
Bork, Robert, 330, 343
Borlaug, Norman, 227
Boston Herald, 229
Bourne, Randolph, 34
Bowen, Otis, 76, 149
Bowles, Chester, 108
Bozell, Brent, 131, 333
Brandt, Willy, 166
Breitbart News, 321
Breslin, Jimmy, 156
Brexit, 304
Bridges, Linda, 4
Brookes, Warren, 229
Brooks, David, 341
Bruce, Donald, 75–76, 123, 131, 159
Buchanan, Pat, 5, 154, 303
    Conservative Political Action Conference
        (CPAC), 203
    Kissinger and, 170
    Manhattan Twelve and, 168–169, 176–177
Buckland, Mary Jo, 10
Buckley, James, 169, 203, 217
Buckley, William F., Jr., 3, 4, 12, 14–15, 17, 52,
    94, 279, 345
    American Conservative Union and, 131
    *Committee and Its Critics: A Calm Review
        of the House Un-American Activities
        Committee, The*, 118
    defense of McCarthy by, 333
    Frank Chodorov and, 33
    God and Man at Yale, 30, 36, 40, 54
    Intercollegiate Society of Individualists
        (ISI) and, 37
    lawsuit against AFTRA, 158–159
    Philadelphia Society and, 132
    recommendation for the Hoover
        Institution, 68
    on the Republican Party coming apart,
        206
    Stan Evans's falling out with, 195
    support for Nixon, 143, 151
    suspended support for Nixon, 166–167
    visits to Yale University, 31–32
Buckley v. Valeo, 217
Buffett, Howard, 47

Buffett, Warren, 47
Bulletin of the Atomic Scientists, 28
Burke, Edmund, 101, 309, 315, 317
Burnham, James, 26, 28–29, 145, 185, 229
  views on Nixon, 167
Burr, Ron, 59
Bush, George H. W., 174, 207, 264–265, 272,
  340, 359
  electoral victory in 1988, 295
  Gulf War, 1990–91, and, 301
  Stan Evans's wariness toward, 291–292,
    295–296
  taxes raised under, 296
Bush, George W., 286, 295–296, 340
Butz, Earl, 149

Caddy, Douglas, 52, 54, 91–94
Caine, Michael, 79
Calabrese, Mario, 346–347
Camelot and the Cultural Revolution, 115–116
Campaigne, Jameson, Jr., 14, 54–55, 218–219
Campaigne, Jameson, Sr., 131
campaign finance laws, 216–217
Campbell, Glenn, 132
Campbell, William, 15
Cannon, Lou, 218, 275
Carter, Jimmy, 112, 220–221, 250, 253, 272,
  279, 282
"Case Against Carter-Mondale, The," 220
Castro, Fidel, 109–110
Catholic politicians, 74–75
Cato Institute, 12, 236
CBS News, 278
CBS Radio, 158–159, 299
celebrities, 6, 78–79
celebrity journalism, 242
Ceplair, Larry, 335
Chamberlain, John, 103, 257
Chambers, Whittaker, 19, 46, 249, 336
"Champion of 'Peace,'" 57
Chase, Stuart, 249, 252
Chesapeake Society, 264–265
Chiang Kai-shek, 329
child abuse, 312
China, 166, 170, 172–174, 329, 330
Chitnis, Pratap, 233
Chodorov, Frank, 86, 112, 137, 300
  at *The Freeman,* 20, 32–37, 43, 44–45
  at *Human Events,* 47
Christianity, 19–20, 346–349
  equality and individual rights in, 317–318
  liberal democracy and, 311
  Old Testament principles in, 316–317

reconstructionism and, 314
  religious right and, 19–20, 311–313
Church, Frank, 262
Churchill, Winston, 345
Civil Rights Act of 1964, 134–135
Clark, William, 262, 273
*Clear and Present Dangers: A Conservative
  View of America's Government,* 183–186,
  306
climate change policy, 255–256
Clinton, Bill, 271, 302, 326, 346
Clinton, Hillary, 12–13, 302–303, 333
Clymer, Adam, 30
Coke, Edward, 315
Colby, William, 230
Cold War, the, 26–30, 47, 50–51
  Cuban Missile Crisis and, 112–113
  doctrine of mutual assured destruction
    (MAD) during, 65–66, 79, 141, 171–172,
    286, 290
  end of, 300, 322–323
  Evan's understanding of, 64–68
  John Kennedy and, 105
  liberal view on, 140–141
  missile defense systems and, 141–142, 170,
    281, 286, 287–288
  rejection of missile defense and, 141–142
  Ronald Reagan and, 286–288
  Soviet claims during, 61–68
  *Stalin's Secret Agents: The Subversion of
    Roosevelt's Government* on, 28, 306,
    328–329, 335–336
  Vietnam and, 113–114
College Republicans, 209
Collins, James, 200, 247–248
Collins, Pat, 247
Colson, Charles, 176
Columbia Spectator, 346
Commission on National Goals, 88
*Committee and Its Critics: A Calm Review
  of the House Un-American Activities
  Committee, The,* 118
Committee on Conservative Alternatives
  (COCA), 210–211, 213
Common Cause, 279
"common good," 89
conformity, 86
Congress and the American Tradition, 185
Connally, John, 195
Conscience of a Conservative, 92, 308
conservatism. *see also* Goldwater, Barry
  American Conservative Union (ACU)
    and, 13, 18, 50, 75, 130–131

on college campuses, 18, 89–90
Eleventh Commandment of, 16–17
Frank Chodorov and, 32–37
fusions of libertarianism and traditional,
    15–16, 84–85, 203, 307, 318
Kissinger and, 169–175
media bias against, 155–158
Nixon and, 151–153, 162–178, 273
Philadelphia Society and, 15, 43, 130,
    132–133, 136
present-day thinkers in, 17
revived after Goldwater, 142–143, 146
Ronald Reagan and (*see* Reagan, Ronald)
Sharon Statement and, 18, 20, 95–99
six rules for political combat and, 357–359
Stan Evans as recruiter for, 51–54
Stan Evans on future of, 144–146, 153–154
"Conservative Case for Freedom, The," 15
"Conservative Case for Freedom, The," 307
Conservative Caucus, 277
Conservative Digest, 277
Conservative Political Action Conference
    (CPAC), 13, 200–210, 290–291
assessment of Reagan administration by,
    277–278
discussion about a new Conservative
    Party at, 208–211
during the Obama administration,
    341–342
Trump's 2013 appearance at, 344
"Conservatives Bounce Back, The," 128–129
"Conservatives Step Up Attacks on Nixon
    Policies," 164–165
consumer movement, 250–254
Consumer Product Safety Commission, 250,
    252
Consumer Reports, 249
Consumers' Research, 299, 339
on climate change policy, 255–256
Communist agitator interest in taking
    over, 249–250
contrarian positions on various issues
    taken by, 253–254
contributions to alternative journalism,
    256–257
coverage of regulatory agencies, 252–253
founding of, 248–249
interest in health care, 254–255
on nuclear energy, 253
Ralph Nader and the consumer
    movement and, 250–252
Stan Evans on mission of, 256

Consumers Union, 250
Contract with America, 305–306
Cope, Don, 59
Coulter, Ann, 237, 332
Council on Foreign Relations, 206
COVID pandemic, 254
Crane, Phil, 203
Cronkite, Walter, 120
Cuba, 109–113
cultural liberalism, 88
Culver, John, 262

Daily News (Chicago), 120
Daily Worker, 77
Darman, Richard, 278, 283, 296
"Dateline Washington," 252
Davis, Tom, 257, 258, 260
"Dear Mr. President," 277
Deaver, Michael, 278, 280, 282–283
Declaration of Independence, 317
Decter, Midge, 290
deep state, 116–117
defeatism, 66, 67
defund the police movement, 78–79
de Maistre, Joseph, 308
DeMille, Cecil B., 36
Democratic Party, the. *see also* liberalism
    1964 presidential campaign and, 119–121
    campaign against "right-wing
        extremism," 119
    Kennedy's presidential campaign and, 89,
        104–106
    the New Deal and, 48, 108
Dennis, Bill, 60, 127, 239–240
Denver Post, 327
de Toledano, Ralph, 12, 67, 103, 153, 272, 325
Devine, Donald, 308
Dewey, John, 34, 315
Dewey, Thomas, 145–146
Diggs, Charles, 234–235
Dillon, C. Douglas, 107
Dinh Diem, Ngo, 138
"Dismay and Outrage Over Nixon Erupt at
    Conservatives' Parley," 204
Docksai, Ron, 169
Dolan, Terry, 284
Dole, Bob, 214, 276, 291
domestic order, government responsibility
    for, 136–137
Dornan, Bob, 230
Dos Passos, John, 131
"drive-by media," 241

Driver, Cecil, 30–31
Dulles, John Foster, 48
du Pont, Pete, 291

Economics: An Introductory Analysis, 30
Economics in One Lesson, 41
Edison, Charles, 94
Edison, Thomas, 94
Edwards, Lee, 3, 43, 95, 97, 99
Ehrlich, Paul, 73
Eisenhower, Dwight D., 48, 65, 146, 184
  John Birch Society and, 72–73
  Soviet downing of unarmed American
    military transport plane and, 50–51
  strategic shallowness of, 109
  Venona decrypts and, 324
Electoral College, 160
Eleventh Commandment, 16–17
Eliot, T. S., 78
Ellsberg, Daniel, 174, 192
Ellul, Jacques, 313
energy crisis, 226–227
Enlightenment, the, 316
environmentalism, 74, 227
Erie Railroad v. Tompkins, 15
Esquire, 155–157
European Union, 304
Evans, Josephine Stanton, 23–24
Evans, Medford Bryan, 23–30, 46, 255, 323,
  339
  Hoover Institution and, 68–70
  as victim of anti-McCarthy hysteria,
    70–72
Evans, M. Stanton
  ability to detect unreliable Republicans,
    18–19, 20–21
  American Conservative Union and (*see*
    American Conservative Union (ACU))
  anti-elitist lifestyle of, 6–9, 59–60
  on Barack Obama, 341–342
  battle with pancreatic cancer, 345–347
  on bias *versus* objectivity in journalism,
    242–243
  birth of, 23
  *Blacklisted by History: The Untold Story of
    Senator Joe McCarthy*, 11, 306, 320–333
  on budget cuts under Reagan, 270–271
  campus speeches by, 83–85, 198
  on Carter, 220–221
  on Catholic politicians, 74–75
  celebrities interviewed by, 78–79
  on celebrity journalism, 242

  as chairman of American Conservative
    Union, 159, 164, 180, 187, 198
  Chesapeake Society and, 264–265
  Christian faith and beliefs of, 19–20,
    309–310, 313–314, 346–349
  on climate change policy, 255–256
  concern over the administrative/deep
    state, 116–117
  on conformity, 86
  Conservative Political Action Conference
    (CPAC) and, 13, 200–210
  at *Consumers' Research*, 248–257
  on the Contract with America, 305–306
  on corruption, 193–194
  coverage of the 1964 presidential
    campaign, 120–123
  criticisms of Reagan, 261–263, 270,
    272–276
  on the Cuban Missile Crisis, 112–113
  on danger of overstating Soviet power,
    67–68
  on Dan Quayle, 292–294
  on defeatism, 66
  depth as philosophic thinker, 306–307
  diagnosed with pancreatic cancer, 345
  dislike for Nixon, 20–21, 104, 186–187
  distance from the religious right, 311–312,
    318
  enrollment at New York University, 44
  on federal government's essential
    functions, 136–137
  as first-rank journalist, 11–12, 52
  on Ford, 206–207, 210
  foresighted writing by, 17
  at *The Freeman*, 43–46, 51
  funeral of, 349
  Future of Conservatism, The, 144–146,
    153–154, 241
  on the future of conservatism, 144–146
  on George W. Bush, 340–341
  on George Will, 308–309
  on Gerardo Rivera, 241–242
  great quips of, 351–355
  on the Great Society, 135–137
  on the Gulf War, 1990–91, 300–301
  on health care, 227–228, 254–255, 302–303
  on horse race journalism, 240
  hostility toward James Baker, 280–282
  on how good journalism should be done,
    243–244, 258
  at *Human Events*, 47–55, 57, 225–226
  humor of, 3–6, 12–13, 19, 53–54, 79–82,
    351–355

on impact of the internet on journalism, 248

at the *Indianapolis News* (*see Indianapolis News*)

on individualism, 88

influence of Frank Chodorov on, 32–37, 44–45, 112, 300

interest in foreign policy, 137–138

interest in Indiana politics, 149–150

interest in nuclear power, 25–26

interest in Ronald Reagan, 142–144

invited to meet with Reagan, 275–276, 283–285

on the Iran-Contra scandal, 289–290

on Johnson and the Vietnam War, 138–140

journalism teaching at Troy University, 257–260

Kissinger and, 169–175

last decade of, 339

later career of, 299

lawsuit against AFTRA, 158–159

legacy of, 21–22, 299–300, 306–307

as less afraid of Soviet Communists than of American liberals, 140–141

libertarian leanings of, 311–312

life in Washington, DC, 212–214

love for rock and roll, 7–8, 19–20

marriage of, 123–124

on McCarthy, 319–333

on Medicare and Medicaid, 135–136

misstatement regarding "handicapped Filipinos," 278–279

modesty of, 14, 17–18, 19–20, 21, 97–98

on moral issues, 311–313

on NAFTA and free trade, 303–304

at the National Journalism Center (*see* National Journalism Center (NJC))

National Press Club dinner in honor of, 2011, 344–345

at *National Review*, 46–47, 195–196, 225, 226

on neoconservatism, 266–268

neo-Malthusianism and, 73–74

on Nixon's FAP proposal, 161

on the oil industry and energy crisis, 226–227

on the Old Testament, 316

on origins and substance of American liberty, 314–315

parents of, 23–30

peak of reach and influence of, in the mid- to late-1970s, 225

Philadelphia Society and, 132–133, 265–266

as political activist, 13–14

politicians endorsed by, 76–77

on post-Watergate changes, 268–269

on presidential impeachments, 191

on presidential power, 183–186, 191–192

on Reagan as alternative to Ford, 215–216

on Reagan's electoral victory, 262–263

on the Reagan's second term, 285

as recruiter for the conservative movement, 51–54

on rejection of missile defense, 141–142

on Republican midterm success in 1994, 305

resistance to using email and smartphones, 339–340

respect for Barry Goldwater, 207, 221–222

Revolt on Campus, The, 18, 83, 85, 87–90, 97, 100–102, 104, 307

on the scientific revolution, 313–314

on the September 11, 2001, terrorist attacks, 301–302

Sharon Statement and, 18, 20, 95–99

six rules for political combat, 357–359

skepticism about the Soviet space program, 62–68

on Soviet-Cuban interests in Africa, 230–231

"Spectrum" program with CBS Radio, 158–159

speeches to civic and professional groups, 60–61

Stalin's Secret Agents: The Subversion of Roosevelt's Government, 28, 306, 328–329, 335–336

Steven F. Hayward as intern for, 1–2, 10

as teacher of journalism, 13

Theme Is Freedom, The, 14–15, 16, 20, 85, 306–319, 327, 347–348

three-legged dog owned by, 10–11

trip to Europe, 296–297

understanding of ancient philosophies, 315–316

use of data charts and tables by, 228–229

on ventriloquist journalism, 157, 243

Vic Milione and, 43–44

on the Vietnam War, 113–114, 137–140

visit to Africa to observe elections, 231–235

at Voice of America, 299, 301

wariness toward George H. W. Bush, 291–292, 295–296

warmth and friendliness of, 3, 10–11

on waterbug journalism, 241

on Watergate, 191–194, 197–198
on why the GOP needed to move right,
  147–148
on the "working class," 266–267
worries about Reagan's presidency,
  263–264
writing style of, 3–4, 11–12, 14–16, 79–82
at Yale University, 30–42
Evans, Rowland, 21, 177
Evans, Sue Ellen Moore, 123–124
"Evans' Law," 261, 295

Fabianism, 108
Facts on Communism, 71
Fairbank, John K., 105, 110
fake news, 241
Falwell, Jerry, 312
Family Assistance Plan (FAP), 160–162
Fannin, Paul, 93
Faulkner, Scot, 349
Federal Communications Commission, 158
Federal Election Campaign Act (FECA),
  216–217
Federalist 45, 136
Federal Trade Commission, 206, 252
Ferraro, Geraldine, 285
Ferrechio, Susan, 237
Ferrell, Tom, 155
Feulner, Ed, 8, 132, 290
5th Avenue Compact, 104
"Fired After Refusing McCarthy," 321
Fischer, James, 169
food stamps, 271
Ford, Gerald, 149, 206–207, 210
  Reagan's primary challenge against,
    213–220
Fordice, Kirk, 311
Fort Worth Star-Telegram, 200
For Your Own Good, 255
Foundation for Economic Freedom (FEE),
  37–38, 43, 51, 56
Fowler, Byron K., 80–81
Fox News, 200, 237
Franke, David, 12, 52–54, 91–92, 95
Franklin, Benjamin, 314
Freedom of Information Act (FOIA), 198
Freeman, Neal, 15, 20, 41–42
Freeman, The, 51, 84, 198
  founding of, 26, 31–32, 34–38
  Stan Evans's writing for, 43, 44–46
free trade/managed trade, 303–304
Friedman, Milton, 17, 78, 84, 109, 145, 269–
  270, 305

American Conservative Union and,
  132–133
Conservative Political Action Conference
  (CPAC) and, 203
on inflation, 162
on negative income tax, 160
*Fringe on Top: Political Wildlife Along the New
  Frontier, The*, 116
Frisk, David, 211
Fuchs, Klaus, 26
Fumento, Michael, 237
Fund, John, 3, 237
Fund for American Studies, The (TFAS), 308
fusionism, 15–16, 203, 307, 318
Future of Conservatism, The, 144–146, 153–154,
  241

Gagarin, Yuri, 63
Galbraith, John Kenneth, 86, 89
Gaston, Jim, 8
General Motors, 251
George, Henry, 34
Gergen, David, 278
Gingrich, Newt, 284, 302, 303, 305–306
Gizzi, John, 301–302
Gladwell, Malcolm, 237, 244
Glazer, Nathan, 153
God and Man at Yale, 30, 36, 40, 54
Goldberg, Jonah, 17
Goldwater, Barry, 5, 48–49, 53, 55, 77, 98, 208,
  295
  1964 presidential campaign and, 119–123,
    125
  as alternative to Nixon, 90, 92–94, 104
  Conscience of a Conservative, The, 92, 308
  Conservative Political Action Conference
    (CPAC) and, 203
  conservativism revived after, 142–143, 146
  defeat of, 125, 127–130
  invited to join ACU's advisory board,
    221–222
  negative press coverage of, 122–123
  Nixon's nomination helped by, 147
  populism and, 90–91
  Stan Evans's letter to President Ford
    regarding, 207
  youth support for, 91–94
"Goldwater or Johnson: Does It Really
  Matter?", 122
Goode, Stephen, 340–341
Goodrich, Pierre, 55, 84–85
Goodwin, Richard, 153, 266
Gorbachev, Mikhail, 286–288

Gover, Robert, 156
"Government Is Blamed for Inflation," 56
"Great Quayle Hunt of 1988," 292
Great Society, 122, 129, 135–137, 148, 152, 160
Greenhouse, Linda, 15
Green New Deal, 254
green revolution, 227
Greenspan, Alan, 210
Greve, Michael, 15
Griffith, W. W., 59
Gulf War of 1990–91, 300–301
Gutfeld, Greg, 237

Haig, Alexander, 170, 172, 272
Haldeman, Bob, 176
Hamill, Pete, 156
Hamilton, Alexander, 314
Hanighen, Frank, 36, 47
Harper's, 153, 237
Harrigan, Anthony, 167
Harrington, Michael, 108, 135
Hart, Gary, 239, 240–241
Hart, Jeffrey, 275–276
Harvey, Paul, 155
"Has Reagan Deserted the Conservatives?",
    277
Hatch, Orrin, 312
Hatfield, Mark, 269
Hayek, Friedrich, 17, 41, 46
Haynes, John Earl, 323–324, 331
Hazlitt, Henry, 41, 161–162, 163, 182
health care, 227–228, 302–303
"Hearings So Far Support Administration on
    Contras," 289–290
Hechinger, Fred M., 101
Helms, Jesse, 208, 210–211, 219, 346
Henderson, Rick, 237, 246
Heritage Foundation, 8, 12, 229, 239, 299
Hess, Karl, 346
Hicks, W. B., 50
Hillarycare, 227, 302–303
Hillsdale College, 307
Himmelfarb, Gertrude, 311
Hiss, Alger, 324, 329, 336
Historical Journal of Film, Radio and
    Television, 335
History of England, 315
History of the American People, 320–321
Hitchens, Christopher, 22
Hitler, Adolf, 330
Hobbes, Thomas, 308, 316
homosexuality, 312

Hood, John, 237
Hook, Sidney, 28
Hoover, Herbert, 27, 36, 68, 70, 72
Hoover, J. Edgar, 28, 68–70
Hoover Institution, 68–70
Hopkins, Harry, 336
Horowitz, David, 337
horse race journalism, 240–241
House Un-American Activities Committee
    (HUAC), 71, 117–118, 250
"How Lugar Helps the Left," 292
"How To Deal with Political Bores," 79–80
How Washington Really Works, 239
"How We Have 'Assumed' Moscow Into
    Space Lead," 68
Human Events, 2, 12, 13, 36, 91, 166, 169,
    212–214, 237, 257, 339
    American Conservative Union and, 159
    on conservativism and Nixon, 164–165
    criticisms of Reagan, 276–277, 282–284
    on the Iran-Contra scandal, 289–290
    on McCarthyism, 321
    Medford Evans's writing in, 29
    on Nelson Rockefeller, 207–208
    on Nixon's FAP proposal, 161
    on the Reagan administration, 262,
       274–278, 282
    on Reagan as candidate, 146, 214, 215, 219
    Reagan as regular reader of, 225, 274–275
    on Republican midterm success in 1994,
       305
    on the September 11, 2001, terrorist
       attacks, 301–302
    Stan Evans at, 47–55, 57, 225–226
    support for Nixon, 143, 151
    as voice for noninterventionist foreign
       policy, 138
Hume, David, 315
Humphrey, Hubert, 160, 179–180
Hussein, Saddam, 301
Hutchins, Robert Maynard, 27, 28

Ideas Have Consequences, 41
"If the Silent Majority Could Talk, What
    Would It Say?", 155
Image, The, 241
Income Tax: Root of All Evil, The, 35
Independent, The, 40–41
Indianapolis, Indiana, eastern media on,
    155–157
Indianapolis News, 21, 54–82, 156, 165, 180, 225,
    236, 254, 257, 292, 293

coverage of the 1960 presidential campaign, 104–111
coverage of the 1964 presidential campaign, 120–122
coverage of the Johnson administration, 133–141
coverage of the Kennedy administration, 110–112
coverage of the Nixon administration, 161–162
endorsement of Nixon in 1972, 182
Evans's "Skeptic's Corner" of, 63, 75
on the John Birch Society, 115
on the liberals as the real "fringe" element in America, 116
on Ralph Nader, 251
on rise of neoconservatism, 266
Stan Evans's anti-elitist lifestyle and, 59
Stan Evans as editor in chief of, 102, 103, 319–320
Stan Evans's departure from, 211–212
Indianapolis Star, 311
individualism, 86, 88, 101
Individualist, The, 37
inflation, 162–163, 228
Insight on the News, 239
Institute for Pacific Relations, 105, 110
intellectuals, modern, 29–30
Intelligencer, 326
Intercollegiate Review, The, 37, 198
Intercollegiate Socialist Society (ISS), 37
Intercollegiate Society of Individualists (ISI), 37–38, 43–44, 84, 90
internships at, 51–54
interest group ratings of legislators, 200
International Telephone and Telegraph Corporation (ITT), 193–194
Investor's Business Daily, 237, 256
Iran-Contra scandal, 288–290
Iraq, 301
Irvine, Reed, 201
isolationism, 137–138
Israel, 300–301
Issues & Insights, 256
"Is There Anything Left to Take Over?", 206

Jaki, Stanley, 313
Jastrow, Robert, 313–314
Jefferson, Thomas, 314, 317
Jensen, Jackie, 25
JFK: The Man and the Myth, 106
John, Elton, 6

John Birch Society, 26, 70, 71–73, 113–116
Johnson, Frank J., 163
Johnson, Lyndon B., 113, 121–123, 129, 169, 220
differences between Kennedy and, 134
Vietnam War and, 138–139
Johnson, Manuel, 259
Johnson, Paul, 320–321
Johnson, Samuel, 23
Jones, David, 308
Jones, John, 167
journalism, 155–157. *see also* National Journalism Center (NJC)
bashing of Dan Quayle by, 292–293
bias *versus* objectivity in, 242–243
celebrity, 242
coverage of pseudo-events, 241
economic illiteracy of, 162–163
fake news and, 241
horse race journalism and, 240–241
impact of the internet on, 248
Stan Evans's excellence in, 11–12, 52
Stan Evans on how to do good, 243–244, 258–259
superficial, 241–242
ventriloquist, 157, 243
waterbug, 241
Judis, John, 152, 167

Kavanaugh, Brett, 330
Keene, David, 203, 290
"Keep Fighting," 129
Kelly, Clarence, 230
Kemeny Commission, 253
Kemp, Jack, 203, 269, 291
Kendall, Willmoore, 72
Kengor, Paul, 336
Kennan, George, 46–47, 49, 63, 66
Kennedy, John F.
1964 campaign and, 119–121
anti-Communist rhetoric of, 105, 107, 111
assassination of, 115, 134
Catholic faith of, 75
Cuba and, 109–113
liberal ideology of, 105–106
liberal narrative on assassination of, 115
loyalty oaths and, 91–92
multiple foreign policy disasters under, 111–113
New Frontier political economy of, 108–109
not favored by college students, 90

presidential campaign of, 89, 104–106
proposal for foreign aid, 47
on the Soviet space program, 61, 65–67, 109–110
Kennedy, Ted, 190, 227, 269
"Kennedy or Nixon—Does It Make Any Difference?", 122
Kenner, Hugh, 78
Khrushchev, Nikita, 57, 111
Kincaid, Cliff, 5
King, Billie Jean, 25
Kinnock, Neil, 296
Kirk, Russell, 16, 17, 78, 101, 133, 145, 306, 310, 315
Kirkus Reviews, 101, 331
Kirsch, Adam, 22
Kissinger, Henry, 67–68, 152, 166, 169–175, 207, 220, 286, 297
Klehr, Harvey, 323–324, 331, 332, 334
Kline, Mal, 7, 8, 11, 204–205, 256, 325, 348, 349–350
Kolko, Gabriel, 64
Korten, Pat, 237
Kraft, Joseph, 156
Krauthammer, Charles, 321
Kristol, Irving, 153, 266, 312
Kristol, William, 302

Lady Gaga, 6
Lambro, Don, 12, 237, 258, 272
Laos, 111, 112, 113
"Largest Tax Increase in History, The," 276
Larson, Reed, 201
Lasky, Victor, 106
Lattimore, Owen, 105, 110, 327
Lawrence, David, 67
Laxalt, Paul, 290, 291
League of Conservation Voters, 199
Lewis, C. S., 87, 347
Lewis, Fulton, Jr., 52, 67, 103
Lewis, Wyndham, 45
liberal democracy
    equality and individual rights in, 317–318
    modern theorists of, 310–311
    Old Testament principles in, 316–317
    origins and substance of American, 314–315
Liberal Establishment: Who Runs America . . . and How, The, 50, 116–117, 192
liberalism
    alternative versions of the American founding and, 307–308

campaign against "right-wing extremism," 119–120
changes in presidential power and, 183–185
changing nature and direction of 1950s, 86–87
college campuses dominated by, 30–32, 85
cultural, 88
as greatest danger to the United States, 66, 140–141
"other-directed" man in, 87
population control and, 73–75
on the "radical right," 113
as the real "fringe" in American society, 116
statism and, 88–89
Students for a Democratic Society (SDS) and, 99–100
welfare state and, 135
Liberal Papers, The, 118–119
libertarianism, 15–16, 84–85, 165, 307, 311–312, 318
Liberty Fund, 55, 85
Library Journal, 331
Liebman, Marvin, 94
Lilly Endowment, 55
Limbaugh, Rush, 52, 241, 248, 319, 349
Lindsay, John, 142, 146
Lippmann, Walter, 138–139
Lipsett, Donald, 43, 53–55, 84, 123, 131, 132, 195
Locke, John, 315, 316, 317
Lodge, Henry Cabot, Jr., 105
Lofton, John, 272, 276
Los Angeles Times, 2, 159, 212, 238, 293, 299
Lott, Trent, 203
Lowry, Rich, 321, 333
loyalty oaths, 91–92
Luce, Henry, 12
Lugar, Richard, 21, 76, 150, 292, 293–294
"Lugar Record Not Conservative," 150

Maccoby, Michael, 118–119
Madison, James, 136, 314, 315
Magnuson, Warren, 262
Mahoney, Daniel J., 167, 169
mainstream media. *see* journalism
Making of a New Majority Party, The, 208
"Makings of a President?, The," 143
Malthusianism, 73–75
"Malthus Rides Again," 73–74
Manchester Union Leader, 275–276
Manhattan Institute, 236
Manhattan Project, 25, 28

Manhattan Twelve
  continued demands by, 176, 195
  declaration by, 168–169
  Kissinger and, 169–175
  Mayflower Statement, 273–274
Manion, Clarence, 55
Manion, Dan, 59, 219
Mann, Fred, 8, 238, 325
Marini, John, 185
Marshall, S. L. A., 155
Marxism, 31
"Massive Humiliation," 50–51
mass media. *see* journalism
Mathias, Mac, 181
Matthews, J. B., 249–250, 251
Matthews, Ruth, 251
Mayflower Statement, 273–274
McCaffrey, Neal, 167
McCain, John, 203, 303
McCarthy, Andrew, 337, 338
McCarthy, Eugene, 140, 149, 217, 220, 345
McCarthy, Joe/McCarthyism, 5, 26, 28–29,
    39, 70–73, 80, 89, 105, 118, 184
  downfall of, 327–328
  innocent victims of, 324
  list of suspected Communists in the State
    Department compiled by, 326–327
  loyalty oaths and, 91
  other books on, 333
  Stan Evans final assessment of, 328–329
  Stan Evans research on, 325–327
  as third rail of Cold War historiography,
    322
  value of balanced and truthful
    understanding, 329–330
  Venona decrypts and, 323–325
McCarthy and His Enemies, 333
McCarty, C. Walter, 58
McDonald, Forrest, 145, 310, 319
McDonald, Ramsay, 345
McGovern, George, 67, 176, 179–181, 262
  debate between Stan Evans and, 198
McGurn, Bill, 237
McNamara, Robert, 134, 138, 139
Media Research Center, 12
Medicaid, 135–136, 255, 303
Medicare, 135–136, 255, 303
Meese, Edwin, 31, 38–39, 273, 280, 282, 299
Mencken, H. L., 24, 157
Merline, John, 237, 256, 292–293
Meyer, Frank, 15–16, 84, 131–133, 159, 195,
    307, 318
  views on Nixon, 167

Miami Herald, 240–241
Middle Ages, the, 316–317
Milford, Dale, 200
Milione, Victor, 43–44
Mill, J. S., 315
Miller, Marcella, 101
missile defense systems, 141–142, 170, 281,
    286, 287–288
Mitchell, John, 176
Modern Age, 37, 198, 307
Moffitt, Bill, 25
Moffitt, Randy, 25
Moley, Raymond, 103
Molnar, Thomas, 78
Mondale, Walter, 279, 285
Monday Club, 14, 271, 302
Montesquieu, 315
Montgomery Advertiser, 257
Mont Pelerin Society, 132
Moore, Sue Ellen, 123–124
moral relativism, 87
Moran, Terry, 237, 244
Morgan, Edmund, 310
Morgenthau, Hans, 336
Morley, Felix, 36
Moss, Annie Lee, 327
"Move to Satanism Threatens to Split GOP,"
    280
"Moving Left Courts Election Disaster," 146
Moynihan, Daniel Patrick, 153, 266
Mugabe, Robert, 231, 235
Muskie, Edmund, 179
mutual assured destruction (MAD), doctrine
    of, 65–66, 79, 141, 171–172, 286, 290
Muzorewa, Abel, 231

Nader, Ralph, 250–252
Nash, George, 33, 99
National Defense Education Act, 91
National Endowment for the Humanities,
    80–82
National Journalism Center (NJC), 1, 299,
    339
  content of instruction at, 244–246
  contributions to alternative journalism,
    256–257
  dismissed by the mainstream media, 244
  founding of, 13
  interns at, 1–3, 237, 247
  journalist training objectives at, 238–240
  Lee Bass/Yale University story by, 247–248
  Stan Evans on the need for, 245–246

subsequent careers of alumni of, 246–247, 256

success of, 246–249

National Press Club, 344–345

National Review, 2, 4, 12, 20, 48, 52, 97, 118, 169, 185, 257, 313

on Goldwater's defeat, 129

on growth of the food stamp program, 271

Medford Evans at, 23, 46, 69, 72

Nixon and, 151, 166

on Reagan's speech to the Conservative Political Action Conference (CPAC), 205–206

review of *Blacklisted* by, 332–335

Ruth Matthews and, 251

Stan Evans at, 46–47, 225, 226

Stan Evans's falling out with, 195–196

National Review Bulletin, 161, 195

National Student Committee for the Loyalty Oath, 91

National Tax Limitation Committee, 32

natural law, 317

NBC News, 278

Necessity for Choice, The, 68

neoconservatism, 145, 266–268

neo-Malthusianism, 73–74

New Criterion, 337

New Deal, 48, 108, 160, 183, 249, 270

New Leader, The, 28

"New Leader Arises, A," 48–49

New Left, 85, 99–100, 332, 336

New Republic, The, 237, 249, 252

"New Republican Party, The," 221

Newsweek, 226, 247

New Yorker, The, 4, 156, 237, 244

New York Times

on ACU support for Reagan, 219–220

attacks on Spiro Agnew, 154

Collins and Armel story on Yale University in, 247

on CPAC, 204

on Evans's comments about Dan Quayle, 293, 294

interview of Stan Evans, 30

obituary of Oscar Shaftel, 321

Reagan on, 275

review of *Blacklisted*, 330–331

on Richard Lugar, 150

Stan Evans's debate with Tom Wicker of, 198

Watergate and, 192

New York Times Book Review, 101

Nicaragua, 112, 285

Niebuhr, Reinhold, 250

Nielson, Francis, 34

1984, 30

Nixon, Richard, 5, 13–14, 18, 48, 67

1960 defeat of, 119

Anti-Ballistic Missile Treaty of 1972 and, 142

compared to Reagan, 143

Conservative Political Action Conference (CPAC) and, 204–205

conservatives' unease with, 151–153, 162–178, 273

Consumer Product Safety Commission and, 250

as continuation of Dewey-Eisenhower Republican establishment, 146

domestic policy of, 160–165, 183, 185–189

election in 1968, 148–149

endorsed by the American Conservative Union, 159–160

enemies list of, 177

Family Assistance Plan proposed by, 160–162

federal spending under, 162, 186–190

foreign policy of, 166–167

Goldwater as alternative to, 90, 92–94, 104

health care proposal by, 227

inflation under, 162–163

influence of Rockefeller on, 104–105

Kissinger and, 169–175

liberal Republicans in cabinet of, 152–153

presidential campaign of, 104–105

reelection of, 179–182

relations with China changed under, 166, 170, 172–174

"southern strategy" not embraced by, 147–148

Stan Evans's dislike of, 20–21, 104, 186–187

Stan Evans's meetings with, 151–152

Strategic Arms Limitation Treaty and, 170

Vice President Agnew and, 154–155, 195, 201

Watergate and, 5, 178, 182–186, 190–194, 201

"Nixon Administration: The Conservative Judgment, The," 163

Nkomo, Joshua, 232

Nock, Albert Jay, 33, 34, 35, 86

Nofziger, Lyn, 203, 272, 277–278

noninterventionism, 137–138, 300

Norquist, Grover, 14
North, Gary, 314
North, Oliver, 289, 343
North American Free Trade Agreement
    (NAFTA), 303–304
Northern Virginia Sun, 237
Novak, Michael, 21
Novak, Robert, 12, 21, 236, 237
nuclear arms race, 137
"Nuclear Energy: How Safe Is It?", 253

Obama, Barack, 271, 341–342
Obamacare, 5, 228
Odyssey of a Fellow Traveler, The, 249–250
oil industry, 226–227
Old Right, 18–19, 112, 137, 300
Oliver, Daniel, 3, 205–206
Olsen, Zoe Ann, 25
Olson, Walter, 236, 238
O'Neill, Tip, 343
One Is a Crowd: Reflections of an Individualist,
    35
Operation Abolition, 118
Operation Desert Storm, 301
Oppenheimer, J. Robert, 28, 69, 72
Orwell, George, 22, 30
Oshinsky, David, 331
O'Sullivan, John, 5
Otepka, Otto, 192–193
"other-directed" man, 87

Packard, Vance, 86
Packwood, Bob, 181
Panama Canal Treaty, 230
Parry, Stanley, 133
Party of the Right, Yale, 39–41
People!, 73
People's History of the United States, A, 307
Percy, Charles, 142, 146, 181, 214
Perlstein, Rick, 5
Perot, Ross, 303
Perry, Katy, 6
Peters, Charles, 239
Peterson, Jordan, 17
Pew, J. Howard, 37
Philadelphia Society, 15, 43, 130, 132–133, 136,
    238, 265–266
Phillips, Howard, 277, 287, 312
Phillips, Kevin, 203
Phillips, Tom, 308
Phoenix Gazette, 48, 54
Piereson, James, 115–116

Pilon, Roger, 3
Planned Parenthood, 73
Plato, 317
Playboy, 242, 345
Policy Review, 284, 312
Politics of Surrender, The, 79, 113, 116, 140–141
pop culture, 6
Population Bomb, The, 73
population control, 73–75
populism
    Goldwater and, 90–91
    Trump and, 18
Port Huron Statement, 99–100
Potemra, Michael, 333
presidential power, 183–186, 191–192
Presley, Elvis, 7
privatism, 88
Progress and Poverty, 34
Proxmire, William, 201
pseudo-events, 241
Pulliam, Eugene C., 48, 54–58, 121–122, 168,
    212, 293
Putnam, George, 155

Quayle, Dan, 54, 59, 201, 203, 292–294
Quayle, Jim, 294

Rabinovitch, Eugene, 28
"radical right," 113
Radosh, Ron, 332–335, 337
Read, Leonard, 37, 56, 83
Reader's Digest, 2, 12, 13, 52, 237, 258
Reagan, Nancy, 284
Reagan, Ronald, 2, 11, 14, 31, 49, 65, 149, 160,
    188, 196, 207, 295, 343, 359
    American Conservative Union and, 131
    Chesapeake Society and, 264–265
    Conservative Political Action Conference
        (CPAC) and, 201, 205–211, 277–278,
        290–291
    conservatives invited to meet with, 275–
        276, 283–285, 290
    electoral victory in 1980, 261–263
    endorsed by the YAF, 176
    federal budget under, 270–272, 282, 285
    foreign policy of, 285–289
    on Goldwater's defeat, 129
    as governor of California, 142–143, 162, 311
    "hit list" of federal officials, 279
    internal fighting in administration of,
        280–281
    Iran-Contra scandal under, 288–290

Mayflower Statement and, 273–274
midterm losses under, 277
Mikhail Gorbachev and, 286–288
Nixon's visit to China and, 166
plans for federal spending cuts, 214–215
primary challenge against Ford, 213–220
reelection of, 285–286
as regular reader of *Human Events*, 225,
    274–275
Stan Evans's criticisms of, 261–263, 270,
    272–276
Stan Evans's interest in, 142–144
Strategic Defense Initiative and, 142, 281,
    286, 287–288
tax cuts under, 269–270, 271–272
tax hikes under, 276
terrorism and security subcommittee
    established under, 269
"Reagan Budget: Worse Than You Heard,"
    282
"Reagan Government a Mystery to
    Conservatives," 274
"Reagan Strength Growing Rapidly," 143
"Reagan: Time to Fish or Cut Bait," 214
Ream, Roger, 308
Reason for Reagan, The, 144
*Redhunter: A Novel Based on the Life of Joseph
    McCarthy, The*, 333
Regnery, Alfred, 1, 308
Regnery, Henry, 36, 132, 291
Reisman, David, 86–87, 118–119
"Rejecting the Ultimate Weapon," 141–142
religion
    liberal democracy and, 311
    Old Testament principles of, 316–317
    in public life, 19–20, 309–310, 318–319
    Stan Evans and, 19–20, 309–310, 313–314
religious right, 19–20, 311–313, 318
Republican Party, the. *see also* conservatism
    1940s–1950s intraparty fighting in, 145–146
    1964 presidential campaign and, 119–123,
        125
    1972 presidential campaign and, 181–182
    Contract with America, 305–306
    CPAC exploration of new Conservative
        Party as alternative to, 208–212
    Goldwater conservatives in, 90–94,
        119–120
    liberal wing of, 48–49, 89, 104–105, 119,
        120, 129, 142–143, 146–147
    media bias against, 155–158
    midterm success in 1994, 305

populism and, 18, 90–91
recovery after defeat of Goldwater,
    127–130
Revolt on Campus, The
    critical reviews of, 100–102
    explanation of liberalism in, 18, 83, 85,
        87–90, 97, 104, 307
Reynolds, Debbie, 78–79
Rhodes, John J., 200
Rhodesia, 230–235
Richardson, Elliot, 207
Rickenbacker, William F., 4
Riefenstahl, Leni, 118
Rigdon, Vincent, 346, 349
"right-wing extremism," 119–120
Ripon Society, 130, 206
Ritchie, Donald, 322
Rivera, Geraldo, 241–243
Road to Serfdom, The, 41
Roberts, James, 59, 123, 201, 204, 205, 217–218
Roberts, Ray, 200
Robertson, Pat, 291
Robinson, Ron, 308
Rockefeller, Nelson, 48–49, 89, 104–105,
    119–120, 182, 341
    Nixon's connections to, 152
    Republican convention, 1968, and, 142–
        143, 146–147
    Stan Evans's opposition to, 129, 142–143,
        207–208
    as vice president, 214
Roe v. Wade, 75, 311
Romerstein, Herbert, 28, 306, 335–336
Romney, George, 119, 129, 142–143, 149
"Ronald Reagan Story, The," 215, 219
Roosevelt, Franklin D., 184, 329
Roots of American Order, The, 315
Rosenberg File, The, 332
Rosenberg spy ring, 26, 27
Rossiter, Clinton, 310
Rostow, Eugene V., 40
Rostow, Walt, 139
Rothbard, Murray, 33, 346
Roush, Edward, 201
Rove, Karl, 209, 259
Rovere, Richard, 320, 330
Royster, Vermont, 83
Ruckelshaus, William, 76, 149
Rushdoony, R. J., 314
Rusher, William, 15, 53, 97, 130–131, 151, 159,
    164, 211
    Conservative Political Action Conference
        (CPAC) and, 203, 208–209, 277–278

Kissinger and, 169
meetings with Reagan, 284–285, 290
as pro-McCarthy, 333
views on Nixon, 167
Rusk, Dean, 110, 134
Russell, Bertrand, 34
Ryan, John, 59
Ryskind, Allan, 7, 143, 147, 169, 276, 282–283
Conservative Political Action Conference
(CPAC), 203
Kissinger and, 169
views on Nixon, 167
Ryskind, Morrie, 103

Samuelson, Paul, 30
Satanism, 280
Saturday Evening Post, 55
Saturday Night Live, 8
Savimbi, Jonas, 285
Scheiffer, Bob, 278
Schiffren, Lisa, 237
Schlafly, Phyllis, 201, 203, 284, 290, 312
Schlesinger, Arthur, Jr., 107–108, 122
Schlink, F. J., 249–252
Schneider, Bill, 169
Schneider, Greg, 98, 99
Schulz, Bill, 310
Schulz, Max, 310
Schulz, William, 13, 52, 54, 123, 237
Schweiker, Richard, 263
Science, 74
scientific revolution, 313–314
scorecard ratings of legislators, 200
Scott, William, 208
Scranton, William, 119, 129
Sears, John, 263
Secret War for the A-Bomb, The, 26–29, 68
Sendak, Theodore, 293
September 11, 2001, terrorist attacks, 301–302
Sewanee Review, The, 24
"Sex and God in American Politics," 312
Shaftel, Oscar, 321
Shakespeare, Frank, 170
Shapiro, Ben, 17
Sharon Statement, 18, 20, 95–99, 307, 308
Shaw, George Bernard, 34
Shils, Edward A., 28
Shriver, Sargent, 135
silent majority, 155
Simon, Julian, 74, 227
Simon, William, 210
Sinatra, Frank, 159

six rules for political combat, 357–359
1619 Project, 307
Smith, Adam, 315, 318
Smith, Ian, 231
"Smoking and the Tyranny of Public
Health," 255
smoking bans, 255
SNAP program, 271
Solarz, Stephen, 232–235
"Solution or Socialism," 161–162
Solzhenitsyn, Alexander, 210
Somoza, Anastasio, 242
Sophocles, 317
Southwest Review, The, 24
Soviet Union, the, 26–28, 50–51. *see also* Cold
War, the
1960 United States' presidential campaign
and, 67
claims regarding space flight, 61–63
Cuban Missile Crisis and, 112–113
demise of, 300, 322–323
Evans's skepticism regarding, 62–68
Kennedy on, 61, 65–67, 109–110
Kissinger and, 170–175
under Mikhail Gorbachev, 286–288
Venona decrypts and, 323–325, 336
Sowell, Thomas, 306
*Stalin's Secret Agents: The Subversion of
Roosevelt's Government*, 28, 306, 328–329,
335–336
Statecraft as Soulcraft, 17, 308–309
statism, 88–89
Stigler, George, 145
Stockman, David, 282–283
Stone, I. F., 64
Strategic Arms Limitation Treaty (SALT), 170
Strategic Arms Limitation Treaty II (SALT
II), 286
Strauss, Lewis L., 68–70
St. Stephen's Club, 296
Students for a Democratic Society (SDS),
99–100
Sullum, Jacob, 255
superficial journalism, 241–242
Symms, Steve, 203
Syria, 301

Taft, Robert, 36, 137, 300, 301
Taft, William Howard, 112, 145–146
Taiwan, 174
Tapscott, Mark, 237
Teague, Randal, 167, 169

Tea Party, 342
Thatcher, Margaret, 296
Theme Is Freedom, The, 14–15, 16, 20, 85, 306–319, 327, 347–348
Theobald, Robert, 123
third-party initiative, 208–212
Thomas, Clarence, 330
Thomas, Norman, 250
Thorburn, Wayne, 99
Three Mile Island accident, 253
Thurmond, Strom, 147
Time, 12, 46, 54, 57–58, 60, 80, 83, 196, 287, 319
Tito, Josip Broz, 336
Tocqueville, Alexis de, 315
Tomlinson, Ken, 258
Tower, John, 146–147
traditionalism, 15–16, 307, 318
Trilling, Lionel, 22, 86
"Trouble With Henry Kissinger, The," 175
Troy University, 257–260, 299, 339
Truman, Harry, 110, 184, 324
Trump, Donald
  appearance at CPAC in 2013, 344
  civil service bureaucracy and, 281
  on fake news, 241
  liberal narrative on the "radical right" and, 104
  media treatment of, 123
  opposition to, compared to treatment of McCarthy, 330
  populism and, 18
  rejection of modern liberalism and success of, 21, 216, 266, 267, 305
  victory in heartland states, 2020, 155
Trump Derangement Syndrome, 21
Turkey, 112
Turning Point USA, 18
"Two Americas, The," 145

Uhler, Lewis K., 31–32, 39
Union of Concerned Scientists, 253
Unsafe at Any Speed, 251
Upside-Down Constitution, The, 15
USA Today, 237, 256

van den Hagg, Ernest, 78
Van Til, Cornelius, 314
Venona decrypts, 323–325, 336
ventriloquist journalism, 157, 243
Vernon, Wes, 335
victim consumers, 252
"Victory At Last!", 262

Viereck, Peter, 102
Vietnam War, 129, 300, 301
  Johnson and, 138–140
  Kennedy and, 111, 113–114
  Kissinger on, 174
  Nixon and, 174, 179
  noninterventionist principles and, 137–138
Viguerie, Richard, 201, 203
"virtuecrats," 309
Voegelin, Eric, 306, 318
Vogt, William, 73, 74
Voice of America, 158, 258, 299, 301
von Mises, Ludwig, 16, 44, 51, 136, 306
Voting Rights Act of 1965, 135

Wallace, George, 143, 159–160, 179–180, 208, 211, 216, 257
  coalition with Reagan, 215–216
Wallace, Henry, 67
Wall Street Journal, 83, 237, 247, 331
Walmart, 251
Warden, Chris, 237, 256
Warner, David, 59
Washington, George, 314
Washington Examiner, 349
Washington Monthly, 239
Washington Post, 154, 226, 280, 293, 302
Washington Times, 12, 229, 237, 261
waterbug journalism, 241
Watergate, 5, 178, 182–186, 190–194, 197–198, 202, 268
Wayne, John, 98
Weaver, Richard, 41, 84
Wechsler, James, 332
Wednesday Group, 14
Weiss, Paul, 38
Welch, Robert, 72, 73
welfare state, 135, 160–161
  conservative, 309
West, Diana, 336–338
West, Thomas G., 310
Western Political Quarterly, 101
Weyrich, Paul, 203, 284, 312
"What Conservatives Think of Ronald Reagan," 284
What Is Conservatism?, 307
Whitcomb, Edgar, 76, 149
White, Harry Dexter, 324, 336
White, Lynn, 74
"Why America Has Plenty of Oil," 226
"Why I Am an Anti-Intellectual," 29–30
"Why Not Real Health Care Reform?", 303

"Why Oil Companies Need Higher Profits,"
226
Why Orwell Matters, 22
"Why Reagan Won," 262–263
Whyte, William H., 86
"Why the GOP Must Move Right," 147–148
Why Trilling Matters, 22
Why X Matters Series, 22
Wicker, Tom, 198
Wiesner, Jerome, 141–142
Will, George, 4, 16–17, 195–196, 308–309, 321
Williams, Walter, 259
Willkie, Wendell, 119
Wills, Garry, 131, 317
"Will They Get Strauss?", 69
Wilson Quarterly, 99
Winter, Tom, 164, 167, 169, 217, 282
Wirthlin, Richard, 203
With Reagan, 299
Wood, Col. Robert E., 36
Wood, Gordon, 310
Wooster, Martin Morse, 3, 238
Wordsworth, William, 2–3

World Trade Organization, 304
Wright, Gridley, 40–41
"Wrong Way on Foreign Aid," 56–57

Yale Daily News, 39–40
Yale University
    conservative students at, 31–32, 38–40
    Lee Bass and, 247–248
    liberalism at, 30–32
    Party of the Right at, 39–41
    Stan Evans's legacy at, 41–42
Young Americans for Freedom (YAF), 13, 52,
    94–101, 211, 308
    endorsement of Reagan by, 176
    Kissinger and, 169–170
    Sharon Statement, 18, 20, 95–99, 307, 308
    views on Nixon, 167
Young America's Foundation, 13, 237, 256

Zakaria, Fareed, 6
Zambia, 232
Zimbabwe, 230–235
Zinn, Howard, 307